Poverty, inequality and health in Britain: 1800-2000

A reader

Edited with an Introduction
by George Davey Smith, Daniel Dorling
and Mary Shaw

The POLICY

First published in Great Britain in July 2001 by

The Policy Press
34 Tyndall's Park Road
Bristol BS8 1PY
UK

Tel +44 (0)117 954 6800
Fax +44 (0)117 973 7308
e-mail tpp@bristol.ac.uk
www.policypress.org.uk

© The Policy Press 2001

British Library Cataloguing in Publication Data

A catalogue record for this book is available from the British Library

ISBN 1 86134 211 X
A hardback version of this book is also available

George Davey Smith is Professor of Clinical Epidemiology, Department of Social Medicine, University of Bristol, **Daniel Dorling** is Professor of Quantitative Human Geography, University of Leeds, and **Mary Shaw** is Senior Research Fellow, School of Geographical Sciences, University of Bristol.

Cover design by Qube Design Associates, Bristol.

Front cover: Photographs supplied by kind permission of Mark Simmons Photography, Bristol and the City of York Library.

Printed and bound in Great Britain by Hobbs the Printers Ltd, Southampton.

Contents

[Note: first date given is the original date of publication; subsequent dates refer to reprints and the final date is the edition from which the extract is taken.]

Sources and acknowledgements

1. **Clarkson, T. (1788)** *An essay on the impolicy of the African slave trade* (2nd edn), printed and sold by J. Phillips, George-Yard, Lombard Street, London, pp 53-7
    Photograph of Thomas Clarkson from www.spartacus.schoolnet.co.uk/REclarkson.htm

    Clarkson, T. (1785, 1817) *An essay on the slavery and commerce of the human species, particularly the African* (translated from a Latin dissertation, which was honoured with the first prize in the University of Cambridge for the year 1785, with additions), printed by J. Phillips, George-Yard, Lombard Street, London, pp 138-55

2. **Malthus, T. (1798, 1985)** *An essay on the principle of population and summary view of the principles of population*, Penguin, London, pp 93-103
    Photograph of Thomas Malthus from www.twist.lib.uiowa.edu/wproblems/rights/malthus.html

3. ***Factory Inquiry Commission Report (1833)*** Parliamentary Papers, vol XX, microfiche, pp 25-32
    Photograph of factory from www.spartacus.schoolnet.co.uk/IRinspectors.htm, taken from E. Baines (1835) *History of cotton manufacture*

4. **Farr, W. (1837, 1885, 1975)** *Vital statistics: A memorial volume of selections from the reports and writings of William Farr* (with an introduction by Mervyn Susser and Abraham Adelstein), The Scarecrow Press Inc, Metuchen, NJ, pp 147-55
    Photograph of William Farr from *Vital statistics*

5. **Chadwick, E. (1842, 1965)** *Report on the sanitary conditions of the labouring population of Gt Britain* (with an introduction by M.W. Flinn), Edinburgh University Press, Edinburgh, pp 396-403
    Photograph of Edwin Chadwick reproduced by kind permission of The Wellcome Trust

6. **Engels, F. (1845, 1987)** *The condition of the working class in England* (edited with a foreword by Victor Kiernan), Penguin Books, Harmondsworth, pp 100-9, 127-38
    Photograph of Friedrich Engels from www.newyouth.com/archives/imagegallery/engels/fredrick_engels_at_age_20/

7. **Mayhew, H. (1851-52)** *London labour and the London poor* (selections made and introduced by Victor Neuberg), Penguin, London, pp 173-6
   Drawings of Henry Mayhew and the mud-lark from *London labour and the London poor*

8. **Marx, K. (1864, 1992)** 'Inaugural address of the International Working Men's Association' in K. Marx (1992) *The First International and after, Political Writings: Volume 3*, Penguin Classics, London, pp 73-81
   Photograph of Karl Marx from www.appstate.edu/~stanovskydj/marxfiles.html

9. **Rowntree, B.S. (1901, 1971)** *Poverty: A study of town life*, Howard Fertig, New York, NY, pp 235-47
   Text reproduced by kind permisison of the Joseph Rowntree Charitable Trust

10. **Booth, C. (1902-3, 1967)** *On the city: Physical pattern and social structure* (selected writings, edited with an introduction by Harold W. Pfautz), University of Chicago Press, Chicago, IL and London, pp 173-84 and 243-9
    Charles Booth's Map from London Topographical Society (1889)
    Permission to reproduce photograph of Charles Booth and his family by kind permission of Belinda Norman Butler

11. **Pember Reeves, M.S. (1913, 1988)** *Round about a pound a week*, reprinted by Virago Press, London (originally G. Bell & Sons Ltd), pp 176-94
    Text reproduced by kind permission of HarperCollins Publishers Ltd
    Photograph of Maud Pember Reeves from www.spartacus.schoolnet.co.uk/PHpember.htm

12. **Tressell, R. (1914, 1955)** *The ragged trousered philanthropists*, Lawrence & Wishart, London, pp 53-8
    Text reproduced by kind permission of Lawrence & Wishart
    Photograph of Robert Tressell from www.1066.net/tressell/index.htm

13. **Collis, E.L. and Greenwood, M. (1921)** *The health of the industrial worker*, J. and A. Churchill, 7 Great Marlborough Street, London, pp 126-42
    Permission to reproduce the text sought
    Photograph of protective clothing from *The health of the industrial worker*

14. **White, F.W. (1928)** 'Natural and social selection: a 'Blue-Book' analysis', *Eugenics Review*, vol 20, pp 98-104
Illustration of poster from www.xenith.com/articles.htm

15. **M'Gonigle, G.C.M. and Kirby, J. (1936)** *Poverty and public health*, Victor Gollancz, London, pp 108-29
Text reproduced by kind permission of The Orion Publishing Group
Section from diagram from *Poverty and public health*

16. **Boyd Orr, J. (1936, 1937)** *Food, health and income*, Report on a survey of adequacy of diet in relation to income, Macmillan, London, pp 44-56
Text reproduced by kind permission of Palgrave Publishers Ltd for Macmillan Ltd
Photograph of family meal from J. Boyd Orr (1943) *Food and the people*

17. **Hannington, W. (1937)** *The problem of distressed areas*, Victor Gollancz, London, pp 56-76
Text reproduced by kind permission of the Orion Publishing Group
Photograph of 'Search for employment' from *The problem of distressed areas*

18. **Spring Rice, M. (1939)** *Working-class wives: Their health and conditions*, Pelican Books, Harmondsworth, pp 94-106
Permission to reproduce text sought
Photograph of children by Edith Tudor Hart from *Working-class wives*

19. **Beveridge, W. (1942)** *Social Insurance and Allied Services*, Cmnd 6404, HMSO, London, Part 1
Photograph of William Beveridge reproduced by kind permission of The Wellcome Trust

20. **Titmuss, R. (1943)** *Birth, poverty and wealth*, Hamish Hamilton Medical Books, London, pp 11-21
Text and photograph of Richard Titmuss reproduced by kind permission of Ann Oakley

21. **Morris, J.N. (1944)** *Health*, no 6, Handbooks for Discussion groups, Association for Education in Citizenship, London, pp 1-21
Permission to reproduce text sought.
Permission to reproduce photograph of J.N. Morris from www.jech.bmjjournals.com/cgi/content/hill/54/12/88/a sought

22. **Hewetson, J. (1946)** *Ill-health, poverty and the state*, Freedom Press, London, pp 62-79
    Text and photograph of John Hewetson reproduced by kind permission of the Freedom Press

23. **Bevan, A. (1947)** *In place of fear*, William Heinemann, London, pp 73-80
    Text reproduced by kind permission of David Higham Associates Limited
    Photograph of Aneurin Bevan from www.oheschools.org/check4pg1.html

24. **Abel-Smith, B. and Townsend, P. (1965)** *The poor and the poorest*, G. Bell & Sons, London, pp 58-64
    Permission to reproduce the text sought
    Photograph of children kindly provided by Peter Townsend

25. **Roberts, R. (1971)** *The classic slum: Salford life in the first quarter of the century*, Penguin, London, pp 75-81, 102-9
    Permission to reproduce the text sought
    Photograph of corner shop from *The classic slum* © Samuel Coulthurst, Worsley

26. **Tudor Hart, J. (1971)** 'The inverse care law', *The Lancet*, 27 February, pp 406-12
    Text reproduced by kind permission of The Lancet
    Drawing kindly provided by Julian Tudor Hart

27. **Inequalities in health: Report of a Research Working Group chaired by Sir Douglas Black (The Black Report) (1980)**
    Inequalities in health: The Black Report and the health divide, Penguin, London, pp 198-208
    Permission to reproduce text sought

28. ***Independent Inquiry into Inequalities in Health* (1998)** The Stationery Office, London, pp 10-25, 29-31
    Crown copyright material is reproduced with the permission of the Controller of Her Majesty's Stationery Office

Acknowledgements

Mary Shaw is funded by ESRC Fellowship R000271045. Thanks to Elaine Osborne and Maureen Rosindale for their diligent copytyping, and to Marie-Claire Hamilton and Clare Snadden for their assistance in preparing the typescript. Thanks to the Special Collections staff of the Brotherton Library, University of Leeds and the staff at the libraries of the University of Bristol. Thanks to Jonathan Tooby for invaluable assistance with the illustrations. Thanks to Julian Tudor Hart for his fine pen-and-ink drawing and to Peter Townsend for the photograph accompanying Chapter 24. Thanks to Freedom Press for information on, and the photograph, of John Hewetson; to the Labour History Archive and Study Centre, John Rylands University Library of Manchester for information on Wal Hannington; and to Susan McLaurin for information on G.M.C. M'Gonigle. Finally, many thanks to Dawn Rushen, Karen Bowler and Dave Worth and the rest of the editorial and production team at The Policy Press for their enduring patience.

For our parents and grandparents

Introduction

Poverty, politics and progress

Two hundred years is both a very long and a very short period of history. For those not familiar with this period we have provided a timeline of events (see pages lix-lxxxvii). Some of the ideas, theories and beliefs expressed through this timeline can be recognised in current debates. Other views appear abhorrent to us now, while they were accepted usually without much thought in the past. In the future many views seen as reasonable or fair today will be viewed with derision and amazement. We begin our timeline just over two centuries ago, when Thomas Clarkson wrote a treatise against slavery in a world which accepted slavery and its effects on the health and welfare of human beings as palatable, if not essential and blessed by god. Much less than a century ago Frank White, influenced by the eugenics movement, argued that human beings are fundamentally unequal and so should experience unequal life chances:

> **Child mortality ...**
>
> Under tolerably hard general conditions, in fact, a comparatively low death-rate in any group of persons can be relied upon always to point to a sound endowment. But under much softened conditions (when food and State reliefs are broadcast, and institutional care and nurture easily obtained), a precisely similar (or even reduced) death-rate might well be compatible with a considerably lower average of inherited gifts....
>
> **The invisible costs ...**
>
> The labours of a great number of highly efficient persons needed for their [eugenically 'unfit' individuals] care, are withdrawn from other purposes in consequence. This is true alike of paid State-officials, voluntary philanthropic workers, and relatives of 'unfits' in the home circle. Were it not for the existence of so many 'unproductives,' more fit individuals would unquestionably be born every year.
>
> How long can any nation continue to bear the growing strain?

Today slavery is still prevalent despite the widespread adoption of the findings of Clarkson's PhD thesis (see timeline, 1788, 1817, 1833 and 2000). Many still adhere to some of the principles of eugenics, although they often label it genetics (see also 2000 in timeline). In some areas there appears to have been great progress, in others the arguments of centuries ago are being constantly reiterated. Often what is now seen as progressive was viewed as dangerously radical in its time. What was then mainstream now appears hopelessly conservative and ignorant. Some of what may have appeared radical in its day, for instance White's work and that of his predecessors (see the extract from Malthus' essay on pages 13 to 22) appears extremely conservative with hindsight. And hindsight is a wonderful thing. We begin this introduction by taking one particular route through the past. A route showing where and when we think progress was made in our understanding of the core theme of this book: the links between poverty, inequality and health.

As an unequivocal example of progress, slavery was abolished in England in 1833. Clarkson's writing subsequently had more influence on Africa and the Americas than it did on England, but most of the writers we have selected lived in England and so we concentrate on the social, political, medical and economic history of this one small country. We include slavery partly because arguments over poverty and health were used to promote the abolition of slavery and partly because slavery clearly had (and still has) the most dire of consequences for poverty and health. Figure 1 shows how the lives of the writers we have chosen often overlapped in time as well as space. Many of them knew each other personally. More were influenced by others' writing and therefore many of our later extracts refer back to the work of authors who precede them in the Reader.

We used many criteria in order to choose which writers to draw extracts from. Our only limiting criteria was space. We wanted to show where changes have been made and so we begin at what can be seen as the cusp between an old and a new world, around 1800. We wanted to show how scholarly as well as popular writing can influence society in a very short amount of time (and how scholarly writing can become popular, and popular writing can be scholarly). We wanted to show how often the same arguments are re-run again and again. In the rest of this introduction we touch on some of those arguments that this book deliberately exposes as being perennial. All too often an argument about poverty, inequality and health is made today which was dismissed in the past for reasons which are still valid now. But for the ignorance of our past it is doubtful that so many poor arguments would continue to be made, often ones which legitimise so many people suffering from poverty, inequality and ill-health world-wide today.

Today, for instance, many who claim that poverty or sickness are

Figure 1: The overlapping chronologies of writers on poverty, inequality and health

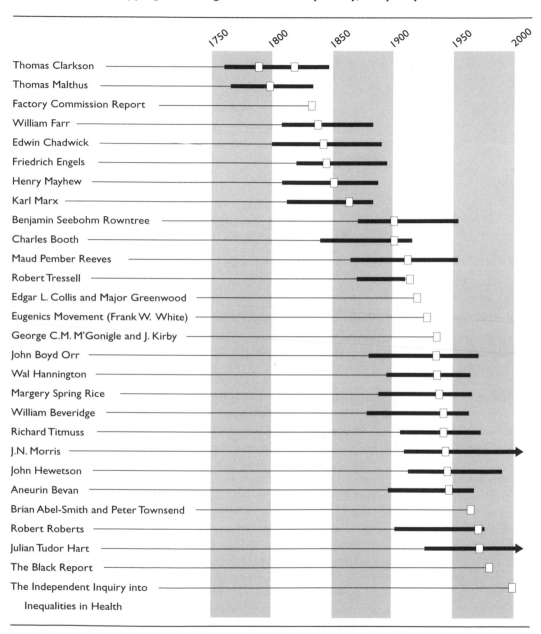

Note: The black lines mark birth and death dates (arrows indicate that an author is still living); the boxes indicate publication dates.

outcomes of the inherent characteristics of people are not aware that such arguments have their origins in the ideas of eugenicists in the early decades of the 20th century (Kevles, 1985) which were only briefly dismissed world-wide following the Nazi holocaust, which began in Germany only a few years after Frank White's views were published. His views themselves relied on and reflected many other academic papers claiming the existence of inalienable racial or social weaknesses that were reflected in poverty and poor health. This approach of 'blame the victim' quickly turned to advocating 'imprison, sterilise, or kill the victim'. For those who argue that particular groups in society suffer poverty, inequality, or ill-health due to their own inability to 'seize opportunities', some reading from the past could be salutary.

The extracts we have chosen for this Reader help to illustrate how social trends and arguments are often woven together. In the same year that slavery was abolished in England and the British Empire, within England the rights of workers were improved. Children and young people were allowed to have a holiday from work on both Christmas Day and Good Friday (see timeline 1833 and the *Factory Inquiry Commission Report* in this volume page 23). The changing of the law on slavery and the slight improvement in some of the slavery-like working practises of England cannot be unrelated. It was during the establishment of this new way of behaving that William Farr published his seminal work, exposing inequalities in health across England in 1837. Five years later Edwin Chadwick's report on sanitary conditions, summarised here, was published and some of its findings were implemented two years later (see timeline 1844).

While progressive social change can be seen to have begun 150 years ago in England, many disagreed with both the pace of such change and with the underlying motives for such change. We provide extracts from the writings of Friedrich Engels (1845) and Karl Marx (1864) which arguably had the greatest long-term impacts world-wide. These two writers were as influenced by what they saw in the world around them as by academic arguments. While Marx was writing about the world, in London others were writing on the conditions seen just in that one city. Henry Mayhew documented the lives of the London poor in 1851/52 and Charles Booth's analysis of poverty in London was finally published in 1902/3. Both are presented here along with an extract from Seebohm Rowntree's study of poverty in York (published 1901, a year after the Labour Representation Committee, the forerunner of the Labour Party, was established in 1900).

In 1906 a progressive Liberal government was elected in Britain. The social reforms which followed are detailed in the timeline. The election of this government both reflected and influenced the social circumstances of the time. Robert Tressell was writing on the conditions of workers and early arguments for socialism (his work was published posthumously in 1914, see page 135), while Maud Pember Reeves wrote about the struggles of existing on 'around about a pound a week' in 1913 (see page 125). Following the First World War the Ministry of Health was established (see timeline 1919). Collis and Greenwood published work on the health of the industrial worker in 1921. For a brief period in 1924 a Labour Prime Minister held office. Progressive legislation was introduced in 1925, and in response to mass unemployment the General Strike of 1926 was called. Unemployment peaked in 1932. The works of M'Gonigle and Kirby and John Boyd Orr – on life, health and poverty through those years – were published in 1936 and the inability of government policy to deal with the inequalities which arose were exposed by Wal Hannington in 1937. Margery Spring Rice revealed the lives of working-class wives to middle-class readers in 1939. We provide extracts from all these works here.

In 1906 the Labour Party was officially formed from the Labour Representation Committee of the Unions; Welsh miners went on strike for almost a year in 1911; the Easter uprising in Dublin in 1916 was followed by the Government of Ireland Act of 1920 and the Irish Free State Agreement of 1922. In 1927 general strikes were outlawed, but the franchise was extended to allow women aged 21 to 30 to vote in 1928; a year later Ramsay MacDonald became Labour Prime Minister for a second time; this was the year the New York stock exchange crashed. A year later slum clearance provision was extended (see the excerpt from *The classic slum* by Robert Roberts, page 301) and a further year later Ramsay MacDonald split the Labour Party by agreeing to lead a largely Conservative national government. The atom was split in the following year; Adolf Hitler elected the year after; free school milk introduced a year after that; and 10 years after the general strike a Conservative was again elected to form a government that would remain in power for a further decade.

The outbreak of war in 1939 spurred on progressive writing on poverty, inequality and health ranging from Beveridge's report of 1942, to Titmuss' writing on birth, poverty and wealth in 1943 and the work of Morris a year later on health. Labour was elected to office in 1945; John Hewetson published *Ill-health, poverty and the state* as the National Health Service Act was passed in 1946; Nye Bevan published on the purpose of the National Health Service – *In place of fear* – in 1947; and the NHS began to provide care free at the point of delivery in the year the World Health Organization was established in 1948. We include these writings from this decade in this Reader. Who in 1939 could have foreseen that so much could have changed in a mere 10 years? To change so rapidly, however, required much that had to have been established before. The Beveridge Report was not written out of thin air; Nye Bevan could only become

Minister for Health because a health ministry was already in place; the war also profoundly changed how people were valued – and thought they deserved to be valued – in society.

After the Second World War and the progressive Labour administration of 1945-50 there was a lull in writing and policy developments on poverty, inequality and health. Rowntree's survey of 1899 (see page 97) was repeated again in the 1930s and 1940s with reports published as *Progress and poverty* in 1941 and *Poverty and the welfare state* in 1951. The later results were interpreted as showing that poverty had almost been abolished in England by the 1950s, from a dire situation in the 1930s. Certainly inequalities in health were at an all-time low between areas in this period, whereas they had been at an all-time high in the 1930s (see Table 1).

Table 1: Inequality ratios of SMRs for deaths under 65 in Britain and % of households below half average income (HBAI) (1950-95)

Decile	1950-53	1959-63	1969-73	1981-85	1986-89	1990-92	1993-95	1996-98	1999
Ratio 10:1	1.60	1.75	1.58	1.70	1.78	1.87	1.98	2.01	2.08
HBAI (%)	–	11	9	11	17	24	23	25	25

Note: No HBAI figures are available for 1950-53; the minimum estimate has been taken for each period; SMR data are only available for certain years before 1981 from the Decennial Reviews
Sources: Shaw et al (1991, 2001); DSS (2000)

Thirteen years of Conservative rule followed the Labour government of 1945-50, but that brief period of Labour rule had changed the agenda. It was not until 1965, when a new Labour administration had been in power for a year, that Brian Abel-Smith and Peter Townsend's report on *The poor and the poorest* was published, revealing that poverty continued to be a persistent feature of life in England with disastrous consequences for health (see page 289). Fifteen years later, in 1980, the *Black Report* (see page 331) was published providing unassailable evidence of the continued link between poverty, inequality and ill-health. From the 1970s we have reprinted Julian Tudor Hart's classic paper on the inverse care law (where the wealthy benefit most from the supposedly national health service in Britain). The Labour Party, in opposition for 18 years from 1979, supported the recommendations of the *Black Report* and included some of them in election manifestos.

To bring this collection of extracts up to date we end with the publication, in 1998, of the report of the 'Independent' Inquiry into Inequalities in Health which was established by the newly elected Labour government of 1997. In power New Labour did not implement the recommendations of the Black Report which it had accepted while in opposition. However, New Labour did announce plans to eradicate child poverty in 1999. We still wait to see to what extent it will address any of the important recommendations of its own Inquiry. One hundred years after the establishment of the Labour Representation Committee the newly re-elected Labour Prime Minister, Tony Blair, announced that he was not concerned with rising inequality (see timeline 2001). There is clearly still much to be learnt from the past. We do not believe that the year 2001 marks any great resolution, as far as poverty, inequality and health are concerned. The last five years of the timeline, therefore, elaborate on what still needs to be achieved, and we return to the current situation at the end of this introduction.

The remainder of this introduction examines some particular themes in detail and includes reference to other sources from those which we have been able to reprint in this collection. We begin by illustrating how the overall debate concerning the ways in which poverty, inequality and health are connected has changed or remained the same over the last two centuries. We show how the argument about whether poverty should be measured in relative or absolute terms has re-surfaced repeatedly. We demonstrate how the still-current opinion that poverty and ill-health arises from fecklessness or ignorance has been made many times in the past. With hindsight it is easy to see how offensive and erroneous such arguments are. Hindsight could help us avoid such mistakes again. We then look at opinions regarding whether charity, self-help or welfare should be the weapons with which to attack poverty. The recurring debate as to whether ill-health causes poverty is highlighted and the casual link between poverty, inequality and ill-health is reaffirmed. We end by considering how improvements in poverty and ill-health within England were often brought at the expense of worsening conditions of life elsewhere in the world. Following this introduction we invite you to read the collected extracts of a selection of the most influential writers of the past two hundred or so years.

Poverty, inequality and health 1800-2000

Around 1805 a commentator on the relationship between social position and health could assert that when considering the health of the population, people only needed to be "divided into two classes, viz the rich and the poor" (Hall, 1805). Dr Hall went on:

> When the Equitable Insurance Office at Blackfriars Bridge was first established, the premiums taken were according to the ratio proposed by Dr Price, who formed it from the accounts of the annual deaths taken from the bills of mortality

kept in different cities of Europe. These deaths were about 1 in 22, annually, of all the people, taken indiscriminately. Proceeding thus, the profits of the Society were so great, that in a few years they realised their enormous capital, upon which, their premiums were lowered…. The Society, notwithstanding, continued to increase in riches. The cause of the phenomenon, therefore, was a matter of inquiry, on which it was found that they had adapted their premiums to the deaths of the rich and poor taken together; and it soon occurred that none but the rich were insured. Their extraordinary profit, therefore, must arise from the circumstances of there being fewer deaths annually among the rich than among the poor, in proportion to the numbers of both … it seems probable, that the deaths of the poor are to those of the rich as two to one, in proportion to the numbers of each.

Blackfriars Bridge, circa 1905

Blackfriars Bridge, circa 2000

Over 200 years ago the apparatus for calculating differences in death rates by social position was much improved. The basic rough arithmetic of a two-fold ratio in mortality between the poor and the rich remained, however (Drever and Whitehead, 1997). The main classificatory system for relating social position and health in the 20th century was the Registrar General's occupational social class categorisation outlined in Box 1.

Differences in death rates by social classes at different ages can be converted into life expectancies at birth (on the assumption that the social class specific rates at any one time apply across the lifetime of individuals). Table 2 presents such life expectancy differences at the end of the 20th century (Hattersley, 1999). For men there is nearly a 10-year difference between professionals and unskilled manual workers; for women the equivalent difference is around 6.5 years.

Box 1: Registrar General's social class (based on occupation)

Social class occupation type

I Professional (eg accountants, electronic engineers)

II Managerial and technical/intermediate (eg proprietors and managers – sales, production, works and maintenance managers)

IIIN Skilled non-manual (eg clerks and cashiers – not retail)

IIIM Skilled manual (eg drivers of road goods vehicles, metal working production fitters)

IV Partly skilled (eg storekeepers and warehouse people, machine tool operators)

V Unskilled (eg building and civil engineering labourers, cleaners etc)

Source: Bunting (1997)

Over 200 years Britain has been transformed (refer to the timeline presented at the end of this chapter which highlights some key changes), yet the association between wealth and health remains. In 1801 the population of England, Wales and Scotland was 10.5 million; by the end of the 20th century it was 57.8 million (Figure 2). Britain was one of the most urbanised places in the world, yet only a fifth of the population lived in towns of over 10,000 people. London was the only western city to have a population of over a million. By the mid-19th century over half the population were urban dwellers and at the end of the 20th century this figure was 80% with the population of London standing at 7.3 million.

Agricultural work was the main employment early in the 19th century, but has declined dramatically in importance since then (Figure 3). Mining became an increasingly major employer in the second half of the 19th century and for the first three decades of the 20th

Table 2: Total expectation of life by social class (ONS LS) for men and women, England and Wales (1992-96)

Social class	Men	Women
I	77.7	83.4
II	75.8	81.1
IIIN	75.0	80.4
IIIM	73.5	78.8
IV	72.6	77.7
V	68.2	77.0
All	73.9	79.2

Source: Hattersley (1999)

Figure 2: Total population (1801-1999) (millions)

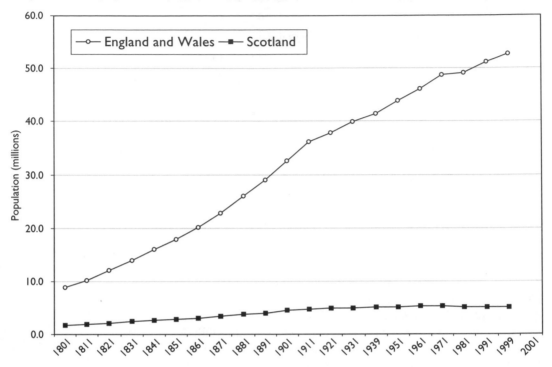

Note: There was no Census in 1941 and so 1939 mid-year estimates are used.
Sources: 1801-1971: Mitchell (1988) and 1981-91: ONS (2000) for 1999

century, but subsequently declined in importance to be almost non-existent today (see timeline 1984 and Figure 4). Clerical work rose dramatically from a low level at the beginning of the 20th century, to reach a peak at the end of the century (Figure 5). By contrast, professional occupations have constantly expanded, from a low level in the 19th and early 20th century (Figure 6). However, over time, more and more people are encouraged to describe their employment as 'professional'.

Overall, health levels improved dramatically over the last 200 years (Figures 7 and 8). Life expectancy at birth was well under 40 in 1800; it had doubled by the end of the 20th century, to around 75 for men and 80 for women. The improvements have been particularly great for death in early life. Around 1 in 5 babies born in 1800 would not survive to celebrate their 1st birthday, meaning that losing a child in infancy was a common experience for families at that time. Now it is a rare tragedy; considerably less than 1% of newborn babies fail to survive for a year.

Members of the very best-off families in 1800 – and especially the youngest members of these families – would have experienced

Figure 3: Agricultural workers, England and Wales (1841-2000) (000s)

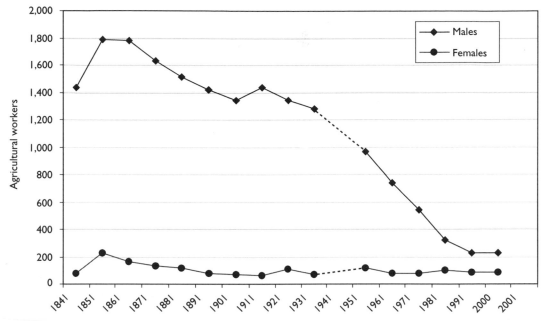

Sources: for 1841-1971: Mitchell (1988). Category = agricultural, horticulture and forestry. 1841-1911 based on 1911 Census categories. 1921-51 based on 1951 Census categories. 1961 and 1971 based on 1961/71 Census categories. For 1981, 1991, Censuses of Population. For 2000: ONS agricultural Census statistics

Figure 4: Mining workers (males) in England and Wales (1841-1994) (000s)

Sources: 1841-1971: Mitchell (1988). 1841-1911 based on 1911 Census categories (Mining and quarrying and workers in the products of mines). 1921-51 based on 1951 Census categories (Mining and quarrying). 1961 and 1971 based on 1961/71 Census categories (Mining and quarrying). 1981, 1991 and 1994 refer to numbers employed by British Coal: Fieldhouse and Hollywood (1998)

Figure 5: Clerical workers (males and females) England and Wales (1911-91) (000s)

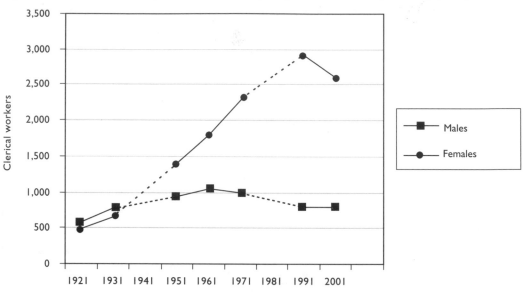

Sources: Mitchell (1988). 1991 and 1999 ONS statbase. Data for 1981 are not comparable

Figure 6: Professional occupations (males and females), England and Wales (1841-1999) (000s)

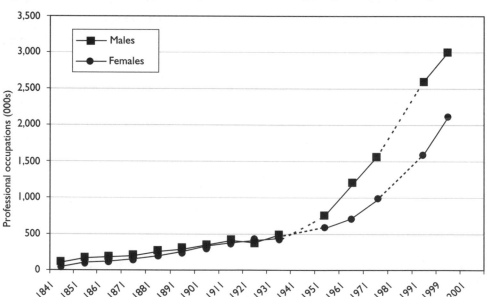

Sources: 1841-1971: Mitchell (1988). 1841-1911 based on 1911 Census categories (Professional occupations and their subordinate services). 1921-51 based on 1951 Census categories (Professional and technical services). 1961 and 1971 based on 1961/71 Census categories (Professional and technical services, and artists). No comparable data available for 1981. 1991 and 1999 ONS statbase

Figure 7: Crude death rate per 1,000, England and Wales (1841-1999) and Scotland (1861-1999)

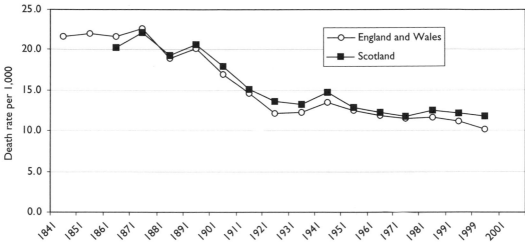

Sources: For all figures: Mitchell (1988) except for Scotland 1981 and 1991: Dorling (1997), 1999: ONS (2001) UK in figures and GRO(S) website

Figure 8: Infant mortality per 1,000 live births (1841-1998)

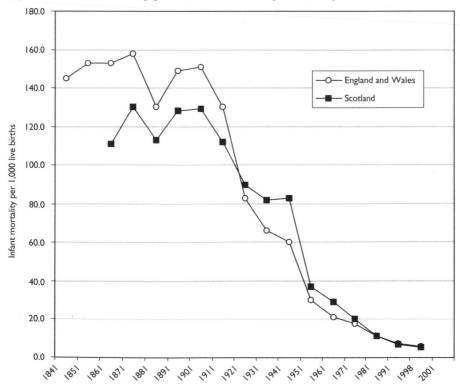

Sources: 1841-1971: Mitchell (1988); 1981, 1991 and 1998: Macfarlane et al (2000)

probabilities of death higher than members of the worst-off families at the end of the 20th century. The situation with respect to life expectancy has been almost entirely transformed: within England only the homeless had life expectancies of around 40 as the 20th century drew to a close (Shaw et al, 1999b). This transformation of mortality experience is reflected in equally dramatic changes in other parameters. Despite the sense of continuity provided by seeing present day actors playing people from 200 years ago in television historical dramas, we would, if confronted with each other, notice

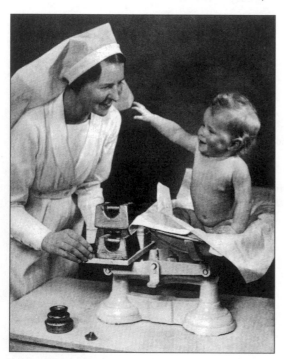

obvious physical differences. Men are almost 6 inches taller on average in 2000 than 200 years before, with a somewhat smaller (and less well defined) increase in the height of women (Floud et al, 1990). Many of us would tower over our ancestors from 1800 if we were to meet them.

Of course many aspects of life in 1800 would be mysterious to us today. Children were working unrestricted hours in factories and mines, there had been no Census of the population, the first public railway service was still 25 years away and it took at least 2½ days to travel from London to Edinburgh by road. Steam power was just beginning to be widely utilised and the major towns other than London had populations of under 100,000 (Table 3), meaning that outside of London the urban experience would now be considered the small-town experience. Our timeline (see below) documents some of the events and changes in the way of life which occurred over the subsequent 200 years. We have seen that

A baby being weighed in the 1930s

one of the concerns of this Reader – health – is dramatically better by the end of the 20th century than the beginning of the 19th century: the same is true of overall standards of living, with both improving substantially after 1850. Certainly reading the excerpts from the *Factory Inquiry Commission Report*, Edwin Chadwick's *Sanitary conditions of the labouring population*, Friedrich Engels' *Conditions of the working class in England* and Henry Mayhew's *London labour and the London poor* should leave little doubt that for the vast majority of the population conditions are considerably better today than in the first half of the 19th century. When a recent book celebrating 150 years since the publication of Engels' *The condition of the working class in England* says on its back cover that the "material conditions of life in Britain for growing numbers of people – the young, the homeless and women in particular – are moving progressively closer to those described by Engels" (Lea and Pilling, 1996), this statement cannot be taken literally.

Table 3: Population of five major towns (000s)

	1801	1831	1861	1891	1911	1931	1961	1991	1999
London	1,117	1,907	3,227	5,638	7,256	8,216	8,183	6,890	7,285
Manchester	90	187	358	505	714	766	661	439	431
Liverpool	80	165	444	518	747	856	748	481	456
Leeds	53	123	207	367	446	483	510	717	727
Glasgow	77	202	420	658	784	1,088	1,055	663	611

Sources: 1801-1961: Bartley et al (1997); 1991: ONS mid-year estimates; 1999: ONS and GRO(S) mid-year estimates for the contemporary boundaries for the cities (1961 and earlier data use pre-1964/74 boundaries)

The issue of how to define poverty, when time and technological change transforms what are the expected norms of life, is a constant theme of discussions and disputes in this area. This is one of several themes which run through discussions of poverty and health over the 19th and 20th centuries which we will briefly discuss in this introduction.

Homelessness in London, 2000

Poverty – relative or absolute?

The United Nations has defined absolute poverty as "a condition characterised by severe deprivation of basic human needs, including food, safe drinking water, sanitation facilities, health, shelter, education and information" (UN, 1995). This definition is largely physiological, and would appear not to be contestable. However, a constant refrain over 200 years is that the presence of absolute poverty has been overstated and has been disappearing. Engels, for example, quotes the philosopher of industrialisation, Andrew Ure, as suggesting that rather than being starved, the working class pampered themselves into nervous ailments "by a diet too rich and exciting for their indoor employments" (Engels, 1845). Earlier in the century Thomas Malthus had contributed to the debate regarding diet, food supply and growth of population by stating that it was inevitable that "part of the society must necessarily feel a difficulty of living" (see page 13). Two other contributors to this Reader – Edwin Chadwick and William Farr – engaged in a controversy in 1839 regarding whether anyone starved to death in England. Chadwick claimed that the deaths which Farr attributed to starvation actually reflected ignorance of infant feeding, drunkenness or were disguised homicides (Hamlin, 1995). In many places the capitalist and middle classes painted a rosy picture of the life of the working class. Engels quoted Andrew Ure on how he saw the work of children in factories:

> I have visited many factories, both in Manchester and in the surrounding districts, during a period of several months, entering the spinning-rooms unexpectedly, and often alone, at different times of the day, and I never saw a single instance of corporal chastisement inflicted on a child; nor, indeed, did I ever see children in ill-humour. They seemed to be always cheerful and alert; taking pleasure in the light play of their muscles, enjoying the mobility natural to their age. The scene of industry, so far from exciting sad emotions, in my mind, was always exhilarating. It was delightful to observe the nimbleness with which they pieced broken ends, as the mule carriage began to recede from the fixed roller beam, and to see them at leisure, after a few seconds' exercise of their tiny fingers, to amuse themselves in any attitude they chose, till the stretch and winding on were once more completed. The work of these lively elves seemed to resemble a sport, in which habit gave them a pleasing dexterity. Conscious of their skill, they were delighted to show it off to any stranger. As to exhaustion by the day's work, they evinced no trace of it on emerging from the mill in the evening; for they immediately began to skip about any neighbouring play-ground, and to commence their little games with the same alacrity as boys issuing from a school. (Engels, 1845)

London street scene

The experience sounds an enviable one, and indeed factory owners claimed that working-class children aged 5 to 10 had lower death rates than middle-class children, and that therefore factory labour was good for the under-10s (Bennett, 1995).

Despite the rosy view of propagandists for unfettered capitalism, the grim mortality statistics and the impressionistic accounts of Engels, Mayhew and some of Chadwick's informants clearly point to serious levels of poverty. However, attempts at the detailed quantification of the prevalence of poverty awaited the work undertaken by Booth (see Box 2) and Rowntree.

Box 2: Charles Booth's survey of London

Charles Booth was the son of a corn merchant and became a successful businessman with international interests in the leather industry and a steam shipping line. His interests, however, extended far beyond business. Booth's extended family debated issues of the day, such as the extension of the franchise, the works of Charles Darwin and the doctrine of positivism. In 1871 Booth married the well-educated and intelligent Mary Macaulay, who influenced his subsequent work. The Booth's circle included such notable figures as Mary's cousin Beatrice Potter (later Beatrice Webb), Octavia Hill of the Charity Organisation Society, and social reformer Canon Samuel Barnett. In this milieu the social problems of the day were readily discussed. One of the key issues of debate was the unprecedented scale of poverty in the rapidly growing Victorian cities. This was reported by the press, but rarely witnessed at first hand by the privileged, many of whom were sceptical as to the actual prevalence of poverty. In the autumn of 1885 Henry Hyndman published the results of an inquiry into poverty which claimed to show that up to 25% of the population of London lived in extreme poverty. In early 1886 Booth visited Hyndman, who records in his autobiography that Booth told him that "in his opinion we had grossly overstated the case". Booth set about his own social investigation to disprove Hyndman.

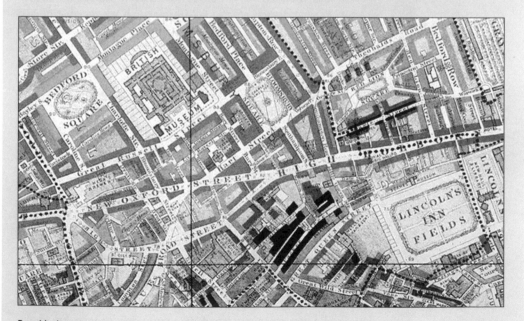

Booth's descriptive map of London poverty; the poorest areas are shaded black

Booth went on to design, organise and fund one of the most comprehensive and scientific social surveys of London life ever to be undertaken. This work started in 1886 and ran until 1903, comprising of three editions of his survey of poverty and seventeen volumes of *Life and labour of the people in London*. The inquiry was organised into three broad sections: poverty, industry and religious influences. The poverty series gathered information from the School Board Visitors about the levels of poverty and types of occupation among the families for which they were responsible. Special studies into subjects such as the trades associated with poverty, housing and population movements were also included. In excess of 120,000 households were included in the survey, covering an area bounded by Pentonville prison to the North, Millwall docks to the East, Stockwell smallpox hospital to the South and Kensington Palace to the West. Booth's inquiry also produced a remarkable series of maps of London – coloured house-by-house and street-by-street to indicate levels of poverty and wealth.

Booth's results indicated that contrary to his expectations some 30% of Londoners were living in poverty at the end of the 19th century. From his research he developed a profound sense of obligation and responsibility towards the poor and to the improvement of social conditions. Although he remained a Conservative, Booth added his voice to the cause of state old-age pensions as a practical instrument of social policy to alleviate destitution in old age, arguing for a universal rather than means-tested pension system.

Source: Adapted from the LSE Charles Booth online archive at www.booth.lse.ac.uk

Rowntree employed investigators who identified households in poverty, based on behavioural and visible features, and sometimes information collected from elsewhere. Within this group identified as being in poverty, he distinguished between those in primary poverty, because their income was below that at which physical efficiency could be maintained, and households in secondary poverty, which were those identified as being in poverty, but with an income level above the threshold Rowntree identified (Veit-Wilson, 1986). In his book *Poverty: A study of town life*, from which we reprint an extract, Rowntree pointed out how life at the poverty line was one of severe constraint:

> Let us clearly understand what 'merely physical efficiency' means. A family living upon the scale allowed for in this estimate must never spend a penny on railway fare or omnibus. They must never go into the country unless they walk. They must never purchase a halfpenny newspaper or spend a penny to buy a ticket for a popular concert. They must write no letters to absent children, for they cannot afford to pay the postage. They must never contribute to their church or chapel, or give any help to a neighbour which costs them money. They cannot save, nor can they join a sick club or Trade Union, because they cannot pay the necessary subscriptions. The children must have no pocket money for dolls, marbles, or sweets. The father must smoke no tobacco, and must drink no beer. The mother must never buy any pretty clothes for herself or for her children, the character of the family wardrobe as for the family diet, being governed by the regulation, 'nothing must

be bought but that which is absolutely necessary for the maintenance of physical health, and what is bought must be of the plainest and most economical description.' Should a child fall ill, it must be attended by the parish doctor; should it die, it must be buried by the parish. Finally the wage-earner must never be absent from his work for a single day.

Rowntree was aware that he would be criticised for attempting to exaggerate the problem of poverty, therefore he set his primary poverty line at a low level:

> My primary poverty line represented the minimum sum on which physical efficiency could be maintained. It was a standard of bare *subsistence* rather than *living*. The diet I selected was more economical and less attractive than was given to paupers in work houses. I purposely selected such a diet so that no one could possibly accuse me of placing my subsistence level too high. (Rowntree, 1941)

The level of income at which physiological efficiency could be maintained has been disputed for centuries. Karl Marx quoted Benjamin Thompson, who in his *Essays* (published around 1800), printed recipes which would reduce the cost of the food workers were eating (Marx, 1976). We have already seen Andrew Ure's view of the diet of the working class, and Edwin Chadwick thought that less food was healthier than more food (Hamlin, 1998). The notion that the working class were simply not shopping for food appropriately, or preparing the cheapest and most nutritious meals, has been frequently argued throughout the 20th century (Smith and Nicolson, 1995), from Noël Patton's advocacy of a return to porridge and milk for the Glasgow poor in the early 20th century, through to the British Ministry of Health's Advisory Committee on Nutrition recommendations for a cheap and wholesome diet, to the Conservative MP and then Junior Minister Ann Widdecombe's response to a report in 1991 on the poor nutritional status of low-income families, which was for charities "to educate those on low incomes how to buy healthy, nutritional food", and her fellow MP Olga Maitland's suggestion that single mothers should avoid processed foods, buy in bulk from cheap shops and learn to make stews from inexpensive cuts of meat, vegetables and pulses (Smith and Nicolson, 1995). These attempts to put the blame for poor nutrition and health on working-class ignorance have been challenged by many of those excerpted in this volume, including Maud Pember Reeves, Margery Spring Rice, M'Gonigle and Kirby, Wal Hannington and Lord John Boyd Orr. The gist of the work of these commentators was that income and benefit levels were simply inadequate for many to meet minimal nutritional standards. In 2000 another contributor to this Reader, Professor Jerry Morris, calculated the minimum income required for a healthy life – adequate housing, food, exercise, medical care, transport and social engagement – and demonstrated that this was below the level provided by social security or work paid at the minimum wage (Morris et al, 2000).

The fact that the costs of meeting the 'physical efficiency' poverty definition of Rowntree have been widely debated indicates that poverty lines and definitions of poverty can be disputed. Perhaps the best known example of this is the uncertain distinction between absolute poverty and relative poverty. Amartya Sen has suggested that there is:

> ... an irreducible absolutist core in the idea of poverty. If there is starvation and hunger then, no matter what the relative picture looks like there clearly is poverty. (Sen, 1983)

This absolutist core involves the ability to:

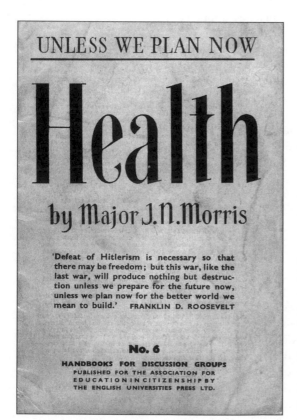

The cover of *Health* by J.N. Morris (1944)

> ... meet nutritional requirements, to escape avoidable disease, to be sheltered, to be clothed, to be able to travel, to be educated ... to live without shame. (Sen, 1983)

While starvation seems an unproblematic – if extreme – indicator of poverty, there has been widespread recognition that what is generally taken to be poverty is evaluated in relation to social norms. As the late 18th century economist Adam Smith wrote, poverty was the absence of:

> ... not only the commodities which are indispensably necessary for the support of life, but whatever the custom of the country renders it indecent for creditable people, even of the lowest order, to be without. (Smith, 1804)

Karl Marx – in a report delivered to the General Council of the International Working Men's Association nine months after his inaugural address, and reprinted in this Reader – made a clear distinction between the merely physical costs of maintaining labour power and the historical or socially relative costs. The physical element was limited simply by the ability of the working class to maintain and reproduce itself, and thus to perpetuate its physical existence (Marx, 1968). Besides this basic physical element, the cost of labour was determined by the traditional standards of life: satisfaction of needs arising from the social conditions in which people live. These historical, social and moral costs of labour differ over time and between countries, and reflect the power at any one time or place of the working class to resist the attempts of the capitalist class to reduce wages to a minimum.

Being able to maintain a standard of life at a socially accepted level is seen as key by another contributor to this volume, Professor Peter Townsend. He provided an influential definition of relative poverty in his 1979 book, *Poverty in the United Kingdom*:

> Individuals, families and groups in the population can be said to be in poverty when they lack the resources to obtain the type of diet, participate in the activities and have the living conditions and amenities which are customary, or are at least widely encouraged or approved in the societies to which they belong. Their resources are so seriously below those commanded by the average individual or family that they are, in effect, excluded from ordinary living patterns, customs and activities. (Townsend, 1979)

Rowntree has been viewed by some as the instigator of a definition of absolute poverty; however, others have pointed out that in practice Rowntree's definition of poverty recognised the degree to which social norms can influence what are seen as necessities (Veit-Wilson, 1986; Harris, 2000). Peter Townsend and his colleague David Gordon have argued that even apparently 'absolute' thresholds of poverty, such as advanced by Amartya Sen, can be seen as relative to some potentially changeable conditions. For example the amount that people need to eat to avoid starvation will depend on the amount of work people have to do or are expected to do; that what counts as adequate shelter will depend on the socially appropriate uses for such shelter – which may just be to protect people from adverse climate, but may also involve such functions as providing privacy, places to sleep, cook, work or socialise (Townsend and Gordon, 1991). In this sense, where even the definitions of absolute poverty may not be constant over time and place, the distinction between absolute and relative poverty can become blurred.

This, perhaps necessary, blurring has not led to the distinction becoming any less controversial, however. It is often suggested that the high level of consumer durable ownership even among the low-income groups (see Table 4) indicates that poverty no longer exists in

Britain. Politicians from the Conservative Party have been particularly keen on this argument, with Peter Lilley (Social Security Minister in 1996) citing the high level of video ownership as the definitive refutation of the existence of poverty (Brindle, 1996). However, if video ownership is taken as the cut-off line for poverty then we are forced to consider that 100% of the population was in poverty in the 1930s. As overall communication methods and personal transport facilities improve, then the need to have access to them for social participation, for being able to compete in the labour market, and for fulfilling domestic obligations, has increased. The notion that an inability to meet the needs, material and social, which are recognised as essential within a society is a meaningful definition of poverty and provides an approach which sees poverty and inequality as being extinct, without insisting on a purely physiological definition of poverty. The European Economic Community has produced a definition of poverty (see Box 3) which is broadly in line with this reasoning.

Table 4: Access to consumer durables of the bottom decile income group (%)

Percentage of individuals in household with access to a:	1962-63	1972-73	1982-83	1992-93	1999-2000
Telephone	8	20	58	78	95
Washing machine	-	54	79	89	91
Fridge or fridge-freezer	-	52	95	99	99
Car	-	26	44	56	71
Video cassette recorder	-	-	-	68	86
Central heating	-	20	46	73	90

Sources: Goodman et al (1997) for 1962-63 to 1992-93, and ONS (2000) for 1999-2000

Box 3: EEC definition of poverty

... the poor shall be taken to mean persons, families and groups of persons whose resources (material, cultural and social) are so limited as to exclude them from the minimum acceptable way of life in the Member State in which they live. (EEC, 1995)

When reading the excerpts in this Reader it is interesting to consider how contemporary social norms would have influenced the perception of what counted as poverty at any particular time period. Certainly the very nature of what could legitimately be considered as poverty was strongly contested across the entire time period with which we are concerned.

Poverty, fecklessness or ignorance?

Considerations of poverty have never been far from considerations of morality. Were the miserable lives of the poor created by externally imposed poverty, or did this misery reflect fecklessness – in particular an inability to stay sober and practice thrift – or ignorance, indicated by an inability to manage on a budget which, with care, would have proved adequate? The codification of the distinction between the deserving and the undeserving poor can be seen in a policy statement by George Goschen, the President of the Poor Law Board, in 1869 (Jones, 1991). Goschen considered that the 1834 Poor Law Amendment Act – which was aimed at reducing the amount of support given to the poor in the community (known as outdoor relief), replacing this with a system of workhouses – was failing. The workhouse system, set up on the famous principle of 'less eligibility', meaning that the conditions there should be such that the poor should want to avoid them if possible, was failing, in that very few Poor Law unions (as the amalgamated groups of parishes which were the administrative units of the law were called) were still providing outdoor relief. Goschen thus proposed the distinction between the deserving poor – who could aspire to be aided towards independence through the help of charity – and the undeserving, destined for the workhouse. The deserving poor were sober, potentially hardworking, tidy and knew their place and how to behave in the presence of their betters; the undeserving poor were drunk, rude, lazy, immoral and filthy.

The notion that poverty was the outcome of fecklessness or ignorance – and thus that the poor health of those in poverty was due to their fecklessness and ignorance – was one which Engels had already addressed. Rather than view behavioural factors which would worsen the health of those in poverty as being the outcome of their ignorance, he saw them as being determined by the economic circumstances of the poor. Thus to Engels it was obvious that deficiencies in nutrition contributed to the poor health of the labouring classes; however, the dependence of dietary adequacy on financial wherewithal was also clear.

> The better paid workers, especially those in whose families every member is able to earn something, have good food as long as this state of things lasts; meat daily and bacon and cheese for supper. Where wages are less, meat is used only two or three times a week, and the proportion of bread and potatoes increases. Descending gradually, we find the animal food reduced to a small piece of bacon cut up with the potatoes; lower still, even this disappears, and there remain only bread, cheese, porridge, and potatoes, until on the lowest

rung of the ladder, among the Irish, potatoes form the sole food.

Engels recognised that the financial disadvantages of the poor were compounded by other social factors in determining their poor diet. The payment of wages on Saturday evening meant that workers could only buy their food after the middle classes had had first choice during Saturday morning. When the workers reached the market:

> The best has vanished, and, if it was still there, they would probably not be able to buy it. The potatoes which the workers buy are usually poor, the vegetables wilted, the cheese old and of poor quality, the bacon rancid, the meat lean, tough, taken from old, often diseased, cattle, or such as have died a natural death, and not fresh even then, often half decayed.

The working classes were also more liable to be sold adulterated food, because while the rich developed sensitive palates through habitual good eating and could detect adulteration, the poor had little opportunity to cultivate their taste and were unable to detect adulteration. They also had to deal with small retailers who could not sell:

> … even the same quality of goods so cheaply as the largest retailers, because of their small capital and the large proportional expenses of their business, must knowingly or unknowingly buy adulterated goods in order to sell at the lower prices required, and to meet the competition of the others.

Engels did not deny that the working class engaged in behaviours which would damage their health. However, he saw the health-damaging behaviours as an outcome of the intolerable conditions of life experienced by the poor. Thus in the excerpt from *The conditions of the working class in England* we reprint, Engels recognised the detrimental effect of excessive alcohol consumption, but saw such alcohol use as the only source of pleasure available to the poor, who must do something to make "the prospect of the next day endurable".

Polarisation of viewpoints on the degree to which poverty (and the consequences of poverty) were self-inflicted can be seen in the two competing reports from the Royal Commission on the Poor Laws published in 1909. The Majority Report considered "the causes of distress are not only economic and industrial; in their origin and character they are largely moral", while the Minority Report (signed by the socialists on the Commission, including George Lansbury and Beatrice Webb) stressed that the roots of poverty lay in the economic system. Many of the excerpts in this Reader discuss the association of poverty and moral judgements regarding behaviour. This remains an issue at the end of the 20th century. In 1992 the Conservative Social Security Secretary Peter Lilley told the Conservative Party Conference that he had "a little list for the young ladies who get pregnant just to jump the housing list", while the Social Security Select Committee Member, Conservative MP Alan Duncan, referred explicitly to "the deserving poor". While the language with which the distinction is made between those seen as poor through no fault of their own and those thought to be culpable has generally become more subtle over two centuries this remains an underlying – although often disguised – component of discourses about poverty and health. In a 1990 editorial in the *British Medical Journal*, for example, the poor health of construction workers was explained by stating that "the industry attracts feckless men who enjoy an irregular, physical outdoor life and danger" (Snashall, 1990). This claim was made with regard to the behaviour of roofers. However, occupational mortality statistics from Britain show that the main reason for increased premature deaths among roofers are falls from high places – for which there is a ten-fold excess. This is not unexpected, and probably reflects the risks of the job, rather than particular individual behaviours of the workers concerned (Davey Smith et al, 1990).

Charity, welfare or self-reform?

We have seen that different commentators perceived poverty as either arising from the failings of individuals or from the failings of society. The appropriate responses to poverty envisaged by these commentators reflected their perception of where the origins of poverty lay. For those concerned with individual moral failure, self-reform (perhaps helped by the goodness of others, who provided charitable support) was viewed as the appropriate solution. On the other hand, those who saw social and economic structures as underlying poverty envisaged a central role for the state in alleviating the situation.

In Britain the roots of the debate can be seen in the pressures to reform the Elizabethan Poor Law, originally instituted in 1601. The old Poor Law located responsibility for maintaining the sick, the orphaned, the elderly and the poor with the parishes, who provided relief, funded through local taxation (known as 'rates', the level of which reflected the value of property). The system survived, with local variation in its generosity, for 200 years with relatively little reform. Towards the end of the 18th century there was a perception that the problems of poverty were increasing and also a fear developed of radicalisation of the poor, generated by news of the French

Revolution and its aftermath. How to improve the lot of those who were poor even though they were working became an issue of concern, dealt with at different times and in varying ways by different parishes. Famously in the parish of Speenhamland, in Berkshire, low wages were supplemented by financial help from the local Poor Law authorities – based on the size of the family an agricultural labourer was supporting and the price of bread at the time. This approach, introduced in 1795, became known as the 'Speenhamland system', and was an early example of income support.

The increase in costs of meeting Poor Law support became a contentious issue. One of the contributors to this volume – Thomas Malthus (see pages 13-22) – considered that subsidising the wages of the poor was a disastrous policy. It encouraged larger families, since subsidy depended on the number of children a labourer had. Malthus saw population growth as inevitably leading to pauperisation of an increasing segment of the population, since the growth of population would outrun the growth of food supply. The poor, however, were unconcerned with the future in Malthus' view, and were unlikely to plan either their family size or financial affairs in a responsible manner. Malthus thought that even when the poor "have an opportunity for saving they seldom exercise it, that all that is beyond their present necessities goes, generally speaking, to the ale-house".

The Poor Law Amendment Act of 1834 followed on from the report of the Poor Law Commission, of which Edwin Chadwick was a member. This Act introduced the principle of 'less eligibility', whereby being supported by the Poor Law was intended to be less desirable than other ways out of pauperism. The workhouse, to which the Act ruled the poor would have to move to receive relief, was intended to be a discouraging prospect. Subsidies to wages – known as 'outdoor relief', because it was given to those who were not in the workhouses – was scheduled to be abolished.

Implementation of the Poor Law was patchy and outdoor relief remained a reality in many parishes. However, the spectre of the workhouse certainly hung over the poor. In 1838 a series of essays by an anonymous author known as Marcus appeared, entitled 'On the possibility of limiting populousness' (Hamlin, 1998). These essays proposed state-instituted infanticide to limit population size to two children per pauper couple. The workhouses were viewed as potential extermination centres, and rumours abounded about the horrors that occurred inside them. The work which inmates were assigned was certainly unpleasant, with bone crushing being the least favoured job. The foul smell was apparently sufficient to allow location of where this work was taking place to be easily determined from some distance away. Scandals followed, such as that in 1845 involving a workhouse in Andover, where sexual and physical abuse of residents was said to be commonplace.

The alternative to the workhouse was self-help, perhaps supported by charity. Charity and self-help were the approved means of dealing with poverty after the new Poor Law came into effect. The best known symbols of this movement were Samuel Smile's book *Self-help* published in 1882 and the formation of the Charity Organisation Society (COS) in 1869. Smiles discussed how individuals fallen on hard times could raise themselves from this unfortunate situation through hard work and restraint, while the COS considered how charity could be used to encourage moral improvement. The COS was firmly in the business of using its supposed philanthropy for promulgating the view that the values of its members were the appropriate values for society in general. Its largely middle-class membership were active in propagandising for the view that financial relief could lead to greater poverty, through inculcating behaviours which would deepen social distress. These principles were similar to those of the new Poor Law, and COS members were active in local Poor Law commissions, although their influence in this regard was patchy, and they were actively opposed by some other organisations. The COS engaged 'visitors' – largely female volunteers – to take social work approaches to the poor, although financial relief was based on a strict application of whether the poor were deserving or undeserving. Relief also tended to be supplied in terms of goods such as food, fuel or clothing rather than money, which these charitable organisations thought could be misspent. The COS remained influential well into the 20th century and the Majority Report of the Royal Commission on the Poor Laws was strongly influenced by leading COS member Helen Bosanquet.

There was considerable working-class resistance to the 'strings-attached' form of charity offered by the COS, its 'visitors' and similar organisations. Robert Robert's *The classic slum* (see pages 301-10) and Robert Tressell's *The ragged trousered philanthropist* (see pages 135-42) both excerpted in this Reader, contain examples of this. Tressell's book also indicates that there was another side to self-help, which was working-class organisations offering mutual support. These ranged from burial societies providing funds for a 'respectable' burial in return for small regular subscriptions; friendly societies offering money for medical care and sometimes sickness benefit, in return for a higher rate of subscription; trade unions which were involved in welfare as well as in organising resistance to attempts by the owners and managers to reduce wages; and cooperative associations which bought goods in bulk and sold them without profit. In addition to these there were strong informal networks providing practical and moral support.

State-supported welfare, beyond the Poor Law and workhouses, was little developed until the 1906 Liberal government came to office after a landslide general election victory (see timeline). The

Parliamentary Reform Acts gradually extended the proportion of the population who could vote, with the 1884 Act leading to 6 out of 10 men being able to do so (Box 4).

Box 4: Widening of the franchise in the 19th century

The change in the franchise is reflected in the table below.

The successive Parliamentary Reform Acts increased the percentage of men in the population who could vote, although no women could vote until well into the 20th century. The increasing percentage of men who could vote basically reflected some working-class men obtaining the vote, with the proportion of such working-class men increasing over time. The manner by which the franchise was expanded meant that the more 'respectable' working class – that is, the better-off, and those with stable residences – could vote, these being the working class who would be least likely to agitate for revolutionary change. Also the table demonstrates how a large proportion of parliamentary seats used to be simply given to the candidate of one of the main two parties. In 1847, for example, in more than half of the seats there was only one candidate. This proportion decreased over time.

Table 5: Expansion of the electorate, England and Wales (1832-92) (selected years) (population and electorate in 000s)

Year	Adult male population (20+)	Electorate Number	%	Contested seats	Unopposed returns
1832	3,673	652	17.8	361	135
1847	4,511	883	19.6	226	268
1865	5,510	1,032	18.7	287	209
1868	5,676	2,007	35.4	374	114
1880	6,584	2,489	37.8	408	76
1885	6,955	4,377	62.9	481	9
1892	7,625	4,794	62.9	454	36

Source: Justman and Gradstein (1999)

The wider franchise, involving more of the working class, worried the established political order into thinking that revolutionary forces could be developing. Social reform and welfare were seen as one way to stem this tide. In the words of the future Conservative Prime Minister A.J. Balfour in 1895, such action was "the most effective antidote" to socialism. By 1906 Labour MPs were being elected on an ostensibly socialist programme. In the Colne Valley in 1907 the even more radical Victor Grayson was elected, with his election address making the intentions of socialists clear (see Box 5).

Box 5: To the electors in the Colne Valley

I am appealing to you as one of your own class. I want emancipation from the wage-slavery of Capitalism.

I do not believe that we are divinely destined to be drudges.

Through the centuries we have been the serfs of an arrogant aristocracy.

We have toiled in the factories and workshops to grind profits with which to glut the greedy maw of the Capitalist class.

Their children have been fed upon the fat of the land. Our children have been neglected and handicapped in the struggle for existence.

We have served the classes and we have remained a mob.

The time for our emancipation has come.

We must break the rule of the rich and take our destinies into our own hands.

Let charity begin with our children.

Workers, who respect their wives, who love their children, and who long for a fuller life for all:

A VOTE FOR THE LANDOWNER OR THE CAPITALIST IS TREACHERY TO YOUR CLASS.

To give your child a better chance than you have had, think carefully where you make your cross.

The other classes have had their day. It is our turn now.

ALBERT VICTOR GRAYSON

Source: Groves (1975, p 31)

In its final lines – "The other classes have had their day. It is our turn now" – Grayson's message was an unambiguous threat. As well as fear of socialism, the Liberal government of 1906 was dealing with the aftermath of the 'great depression' at the end of the 19th century, high unemployment and in full knowledge of the social investigations of Booth, Rowntree and others, which made clear the state of the poorest sections of society. Furthermore, the Inter-Departmental Committee on Physical Deterioration had confirmed the evidence of high levels of infirmity among young men of military age, noted during recruitment for the Boer War of 1899-1902. A series of Parliamentary Acts legislated for school meals for children in need; medical inspections in schools; the prevention of children from drinking alcohol or buying cigarettes; non-contributory pensions for those aged over 70 and on a low income; the protection of children through removing those being abused or neglected; inspection of institutions for children; establishment of minimum wages in certain trades, including mining; a national health insurance plan for those in work, and national insurance unemployment benefit in the event of job loss. The origins of the 'welfare state' that emerged during the

Second World War can clearly be seen in the Liberal reforms, although the latter remained strongly influenced by the moral stance of COS and its fellow thinkers.

Does poverty cause ill-health or does ill-health cause poverty?

To all but the most myopic commentator the association between poverty and ill-health has been apparent across the two centuries with which we are concerned. The direction of cause and effect in this association has, however, been viewed in disparate ways. To Thomas Malthus disease was nature's "terrible corrective" to increasing population, with disease emerging from the miserable conditions of life which over-population insured would be experienced by an increasing section of the population. While causes of disease were various and mysterious, Malthus thought, it was certain that "among these causes, we ought certainly to rank crowded houses, and insufficient or unwholesome food, which are the natural consequences of an increase of populations faster than the accommodations of a country with respect to habitations and food will allow" (Hamlin, 1998).

The clearly complex links between poverty and ill-health are evident in many of the excerpts in this Reader. For example, Engels considered that poverty produced poor health as a direct consequence, but also that poor health could lead to increasing destitution by reducing a person's capacity to work. Indeed, Engels thought that the Capitalist class was acting against its own best interests by impoverishing the working class, since the poor health and poor physiques generated by the low standards of living meant that the workers had a lower work output than they would have if healthier and better nourished.

Edwin Chadwick, on the other hand was concerned with ill-health and sickness leading to destitution and poverty. In this scheme the insanitary conditions of the population would, through generating poor health among the working class, lead to an increasing proportion of them being unable to work and to earn their own living. In this way they would become a burden on the middle-class ratepayers, and sanitary reform, while also costing money, was in the long run a worthwhile investment. Chadwick supported his contention by reference to illness among the relatively well-to-do, which demonstrated that poverty was not necessary for disease. For example, he addressed a meeting to raise funds for the widow of a London medical officer, Jordan Lynch, who died of a fever contracted while working with the poor. The death of Lynch meant that "we could place even well-conditioned persons under such circumstances ...

[and] produce typhus. Low and insufficient diet amidst filth, spread and aggravate it, by depressing the system ... cleanliness and ventilation will diminish it, even against mental depression and ... low diet" (Hamlin, 1998). The major concern then was not with the direct consequences of poverty – such as inadequate diet – but poor ventilation and sanitation, and given poor ventilation and sanitation even the wealthy would suffer. The physical and economic health of the middle class in this way became a problem intimately linked with the physical and sanitary conditions of the towns and cities.

The debate regarding the direction of causation between poverty and ill-health in the 19th century took a new turn in the 20th century with the rise of eugenics. Francis Galton is widely considered to be the founder of eugenics as an influential movement (Kevles, 1985). Influenced by the publication of Darwin's *Origin of species* in 1859, Galton applied statistics to the characteristics of individuals within populations and assumed that heredity and natural selection determined the make-up of successive generations. He thought that physical and intellectual capacity went together (citing the fact that Queen Elizabeth inspected the calves of those she selected to be bishops) and therefore thought that breeding for the highest order of intellect would also produce a more physically robust population (Kevles, 1985). Galton's books *Hereditary genius*, published in 1869, and *Natural inheritance*, published in 1889, were influential and much-cited as demonstrating that intelligence and many other characteristics were heritable. His disciple, Karl Pearson, simultaneously advanced the science of statistics and the cause of eugenics. Pearson argued that heredity had a greater influence on health than did the environment: "health is a real hereditary characteristic and the health of the parents is far more important than the question of back-to-back houses, one-apartment tenements, the employment of mothers or breast-feeding ..." (Pearson, 1912). In this formulation, hereditary characteristics determined health and also determined ability, which would be related to occupation, income and social circumstances. Pearson therefore thought that the decrease in infant mortality in the early years of the 20th century was "nothing short of calamitous, since death was a method to check Nature's effective and roughshod methods of race betterment" (Semmel, 1958). He supported his assertions by demonstrating that infant mortality rates correlated negatively with mortality rates for children aged one to five years between 1838 and 1900, suggesting that higher levels of early infant mortality meant lower levels of later childhood mortality. Pearson's assumption here was that the higher infant mortality eliminated more of those who would have been destined to be sick if they had survived.

Eugenics clearly attracted a wide spectrum of support, with differing views within the eugenics movement regarding the balance between heredity and environment in determining population characteristics and also with differing views as to the practical implications of eugenics and how improvement of the population could be brought about. Frank White, whom we reprint in this Reader, was clearly at the harder edge of the eugenics movement. He considered that occupational and social class differences in health were largely determined by inheritance. White followed Pearson in considering that the decline in infant mortality rates was a national disaster: "The number of infants and young children ... who are being saved today – at any rate for a while – is evident. But what is the *nature* of many of these children saved? In the majority of cases are they of the best stocks, or of the worst? The answer in view of the existing differential death and birth rates is unfortunately only too obvious. They are, for the most part, physical and mental defectives who, under a sterner regime, would unquestionably have been eliminated soon after birth by natural selection. And, unhappily, the more of such we save the worse becomes the outlook for the State" (see White, pages 161-72). He linked this to apparent increases in the burden of cancer, mental disability and poverty.

The birth rate declined in Britain during the first part of the 20th century (Figure 9), and such a decrease may have contributed to the views of the eugenicists becoming increasingly influential in the early decades of the 20th century. These views were not confined to conservatives or crypto-fascists: Pearson, for example, was an influential

Figure 9: Births per 1,000 women (England and Wales and Scotland) (1841-1998)

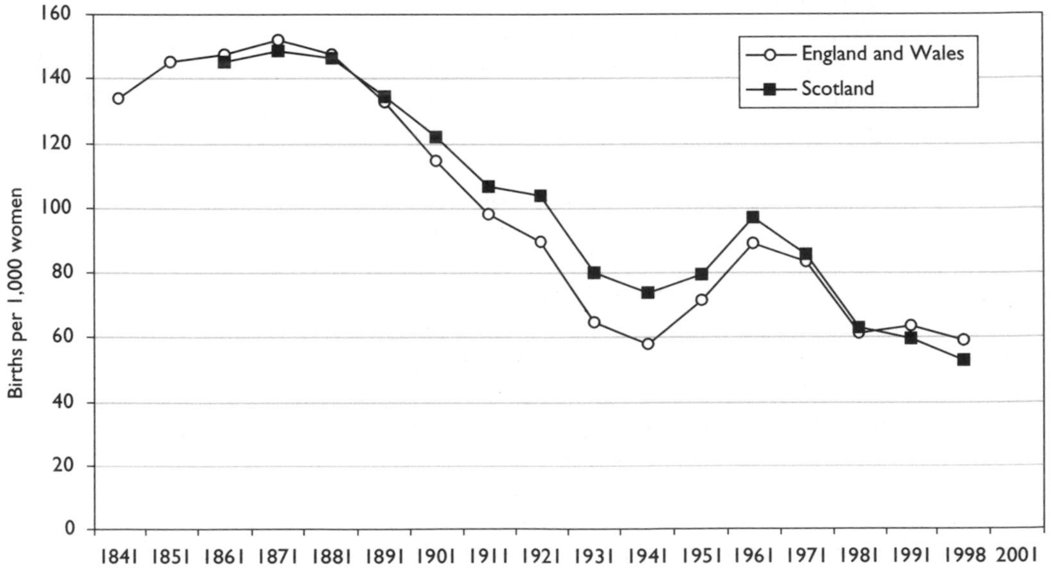

Source: Mitchell (1988); Macfarlane et al (2000)

member of the Fabians, an important middle-class socialist grouping. Richard Titmuss – initially a Liberal but later a member of the Labour Party and one of the founders of the post-war welfare state – was a member of the Eugenics Society until shortly before his death in 1973 (Oakley, 1996); indeed the Eugenics Society provided a grant towards the publication of *Birth, poverty and wealth,* which we excerpt in this Reader (see pages 237-44).

The empirical basis of the eugenicists' case, that decreasing early-life mortality, by weakening the power of natural selection to improve the population and thus leading to health deterioration, was spectacularly refuted by improving trends of mortality at most ages during the 20th century (Davey Smith and Kuh, 2001). A considerable body of statistical research was carried out to demonstrate the fallacy of Pearson's analyses, for example, and the role of the environment – in particular nutrition in childhood – as opposed to heredity in determining population health levels was demonstrated (Kuh and Davey Smith, 1993).

Eugenics was discredited by its association with the racial hygiene movement in Nazi Germany, and simplistic notions of co-determinacy of poverty and ill-health by hereditary characteristics have largely disappeared from the literature. However, an influential older statesman of British medical research, Professor Harold Himsworth, published a scientific paper arguing for this point of view with respect to infant mortality in 1984 (Himsworth, 1984), and such thinking is often implicit – although usually disguised – in discussions of ethnic differences in health. For several decades after the Second World War a strong consensus opposed such arguments – perhaps reflected in the responses to Himsworth's article (for example, Humphrey and Elford, 1988; Chalmers, 1985). The increasing distance from examples of the consequences of deterministic thinking with respect to heredity (and the related category of 'race'), together with the much-trumpeted move into a post-genome world, is likely to result in a resurgence of interest in the genetic determinants of human health, and perhaps of human social characteristics. The central problem for such theorising is one that confronted Galton – that hereditary characteristics should remain similar from generation to generation, given the slow effect that differential fertility and mortality patterns could have. For many health and social outcomes, however, the greater importance of the environment is demonstrated by time-trends. Thus the rapid declines in mortality rates that have been seen at most ages over the past 30 years in Britain, or the equally rapid increases in obesity levels, cannot be explained by any change in the genetic make-up of the population. The same applies to factors such as intelligence, where levels have increased relatively rapidly over quite a recent period – a phenomenon known as the Flynn effect (Flynn, 1994).

The notion that common hereditary characteristics determined both health and poverty is one example of theorising in which poverty is not to blame for poor health. This thinking is also reflected in some current discussions which suggest that people who get sick (or who have characteristics during youth which will make them sick) are downwardly socially mobile – either during their own occupational careers or during the intergenerational movement from their parents to their own social class. Despite much recent research having shown that as an explanation of current day inequalities in health such 'social selection' explanations are only a minor contributor (Shaw et al, 1999a), they reflect an old tradition of such theorising, which served different purposes at different times.

Exporting misery?

This Reader has been concerned with debates regarding poverty, inequality and health within Britain. We start the Reader, however, with a piece by Thomas Clarkson regarding the effects of the African slave trade. The consequences of this inhuman trade were obviously dire for the enslaved population, and also, to an extent, for the crews of slave ships. The influence of the slave trade on British economic development has been an issue of considerable dispute. In 1944 Eric Williams – who was later to become Prime Minister of Trinidad and Tobago – advanced the influential argument that the slave trade provided the economic basis for the development of industrial capitalism in Britain (Williams, 1944), although many have argued that the profits from the slave trade were simply too low to provide the major stimulus for industrialisation (Engerman, 1994). The slave trade and the associated importation of sugar and other basic commodities into Britain from plantations in the Americas and Caribbean can, however, be viewed as a way of exporting the ecological consequences of population growth, since a considerable amount of land which would be required for the production of such agricultural goods was saved for other purposes as a consequence (Pomeranz et al, 1999).

British imperialism also had some positive consequences for the internal British economy, although they were probably not as large as have often been assumed (Edelstein, 1994). The slave trade and British imperialism are unlikely to have had a crucial or determining role in stimulating the industrial growth of Britain. They did, however, certainly impose misery on populations living outside of Britain. The economic growth of these countries may also have been adversely affected, leading to poverty which has stretched long beyond the time when the slave trade and imperialism ended in their formal sense.

The interrelationships between economic development in one country, the effects on the working class in that country, and the influence on other populations is made clear in Engels' *The condition of the working class in England* (see pages 57-78). He discusses how the poor economic circumstances in Ireland are exacerbated by English exploitation, although this cannot be held to be *the* cause of poverty in Ireland, since exploitation within the country was also rife. The condition of the Irish workers within England was also shown to be miserable, with the Irish workers usually living in the worst conditions and in the worst parts of the towns in which they resided. Engels also considered that the low wages which it was possible to pay Irish labourers depressed the wages of the rest of the working class within England. The only people to gain by this cycle were the bourgeoisie in England and the big landowners in Ireland. The common interests of the working class in different countries was clear to Engels, and divisions between them on the grounds of ethnic origin further helped those who exploited them, either in Britain or elsewhere. Engels, however, remained a "man of his time", and some of his formulations regarding the Irish would strike readers today as verging on being racist (Fryer, 1996). In Britain today ethnicity remains an important indicator of both probability of being in poverty and of experiencing poor health (Davey Smith et al, 2000), reflecting the effects of national, institutional and personal discrimination.

Poverty, inequality and health at the end of the 20th century

During the 19th century industrialisation led to widespread changes in British society and to a considerable increase in income inequality. Towards the end of the century and into the 20th century this inequality decreased. It has been argued that the growing working class and their potential radicalisation led to forms of containment, through extending the political franchise and, partly as a consequence of this, to reforms which benefited the working class (Acemoglu and Robinson, 2000; Justman and Gradstein, 1999). Income inequality appears to have decreased in the last two decades of the 19th century and through the 20th century up until the mid-century, from when it was relatively stable until the mid-1970s, since when it has increased dramatically (Atkinson, 1999). As we show in Table 1 income and mortality inequality have tracked each other fairly closely across the second half of the 20th century. In Figure 10 the recent trend in income inequality up until 1999 is presented. The dramatic increase started during the 1974-79 Labour government, when the chancellor, Denis Healey, reneged on election promises to help the poor at the expense of the rich, and invited the International Monetary Fund to

Figure 10: Percentage of the population with below half average incomes after housing costs (1961-99)

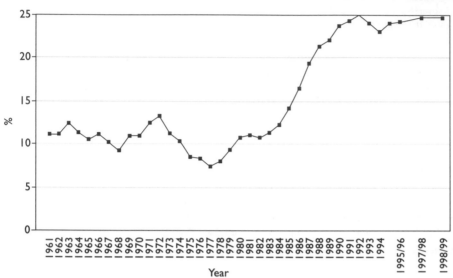

Source: HBAI volumes (DSS, 1998, 2000); Goodman and Webb (1995)

guide economic policy in the interests of international capital rather than the (largely) working-class voters who had elected his government. A Labour government that was failing to deliver was replaced by Margaret Thatcher's first Conservative administration in 1979 and the policies introduced by this and subsequent administrations continued to increase the incomes of the already well-paid, at the expense of the poor. The economic recession of the early 1990s led to a stabilisation of income inequality during the Major years, but an upward tendency re-emerged after the election of the Tony Blair Labour government in 1997, partly in response to the economic recession ending, and partly due to labour failing to introduce re-distributive fiscal policies (Lakin, 2001). Health inequalities clearly reflect the accumulation of disadvantage across the life-course – and the origins of current-day poor health can be traced to deprivation which was acting long in the past (see Box 6). However, changes in social inequality will influence health currently, in addition to feeding into potential adverse trends in the future. As Table 5 shows, recent increases in income inequality have been accompanied by increases in inequality in premature mortality. The resonance of many of the debates which are covered in this Reader can be seen in the difference between current official recommendations – from the Chief Medical Officer – for how to improve health, in comparison to alternative recommendations, formulated in the recognition of the structured nature of exposure to many factors which make people sick (see Box 7).

Box 6: Charles Booth's maps revisited a century on

New technology allows us to revisit Booth's map of poverty in London and to compare it to the contemporary distribution of poverty and mortality. A recent analysis digitised Booth's map using a Geographical Information System and related this to the 1991 and digitised mortality records (Dorling et al, 2000). This allows investigation of the extent to which late 20th century patterns of premature mortality in London are predicted by contemporary patterns of poverty and by late 19th century patterns of poverty.

This analysis shows that the pattern on poverty in late 20th century London is remarkably similar to that of late 19th century London, despite the many social and economic changes that have transpired. Looking at which of the measures best predicted premature mortality, in the 1990s for many causes of death the measure of poverty made by Booth and the measure of social class in 1991 both contributed strongly to the prediction of the current spatial distribution of life chances. Contemporary mortality from diseases which are known to be related to deprivation in early life (stomach cancer and stroke) is predicted *more strongly* by the distribution of poverty in 1896 than that in 1991. In addition, all cause mortality among those over the age of 65 is slightly more strongly related to the geography of poverty in the late 19th century than the contemporary distribution.

This study indicates that the patterns of some diseases that we see today have their roots in the past. The life chances of people dying in the current period are affected not only by current conditions but also by the legacy of the inequalities of the past.

Source: Dorling et al (2000)

Table 5: Age and sex standardised SMRs (0-74) according to decile of poverty, and the relative index of inequality (RII)

SMR 0-74	1990-91	1992-93	1994-95	1996-97	1998-99
Decile 1	129	132	134	136	138
Decile 2	117	119	118	120	122
Decile 3	110	112	111	113	114
Decile 4	109	109	109	110	111
Decile 5	101	100	100	101	103
Decile 6	96	95	96	95	97
Decile 7	92	91	91	92	92
Decile 8	87	88	87	87	87
Decile 9	85	83	84	84	83
Decile 10	81	81	81	80	80
RII	1.68	1.74	1.75	1.80	1.85

Source: authors' own analysis

Box 7: Ten official and alternative tips for improving health

The Chief Medical Officer's ten tips for better health	Alternative ten tips
1. Don't smoke. If you can, stop. If you can't, cut down.	1. Don't be poor. If you are poor, try not to be poor for too long.
2. Follow a balanced diet with plenty of fruit and vegetables.	2. Don't live in a deprived area. If you do, move.
3. Keep physically active.	3. Don't be disabled or have a disabled child.
4. Manage stress by, for example, talking things through and making time to relax.	4. Don't work in a stressful low-paid manual job.
5. If you drink alcohol, do so in moderation.	5. Don't live in damp, low quality housing or be homeless.
6. Cover up in the sun, and protect children from sunburn.	6. Be able to afford to pay for social activities and annual holidays.
7. Practise safer sex.	7. Don't be a lone parent.
8. Take up cancer screening opportunities.	8. Claim all benefits to which you are entitled.
9. Be safe on the roads: follow the Highway Code.	9. Be able to afford to own a car.
10. Learn the First Aid ABC – airways, breathing and circulation.	10. Use education as an opportunity to improve your socio-economic position.
Source: DoH (1999)	*Source:* Shaw (2001: forthcoming)

The collection of work we have presented here – spanning more than two centuries – illustrates many things. It shows how the writings of influential authors are affected by their daily lives and the conditions they see around them. Our collection also shows many instances where the influence of one writer and policy maker has had an impact on another. By contrast, our current Prime Minister is and has been cosseted from the harder side of life. We have also tried to show how different kinds of evidence can be brought to bear in understanding the links between everyday conditions of poverty and inequality, and ill-health. From individual anecdote, to structured investigation, to reams of statistics – all have had a part to play in developing our understanding over time.

Finally, we should point out that in no way are we approaching any end point in our need to understand the links between poverty, inequality and health, as a brief survey of the final years of the timeline reveals. The degree of acceptance of their responsibility for poverty in the poorer countries by the richer parts of the world in 2001 is often less than it has been in the past. Policies remain unfair and misguided. What has been learnt over the last two centuries is usually ignored by those with an interest in making a profit in the short term, being re-elected in the short term, and being personally rewarded in the short term. A long-term perspective reveals what is missing in such a strategy.

We look back at what we now dismiss as misguided ideas, or only remember to hold them in contempt. Health, inequality and poverty are as intricately linked as they have ever been, and perhaps some ideas strongly held today will similarly be seen as outrageous in the future. Those who defend increasing social inequality, and preserve poverty, sanction the concentration of poor health and premature death on those who are already most disadvantaged.

References

Acemoglu, D. and Robinson, J.A. (2000) 'Why did the west extend the franchise? Democracy, inequality, and growth in historical perspective', *Quarterly Journal of Economics*, vol 115, pp 1167-99.

Atkinson, A.B. (1999) 'The distribution of income in the UK and OECD countries in the twentieth century', *Oxford Review of Economic Policy*, pp 1556-75.

Bartley, M., Blane, D. and Charlton, J. (1997) 'Socioeconomic and demographic trends, 1841-1994', in J. Charlton and M. Murphy (eds) *The health of adult Britain 1841-1994*, London: The Stationery Office.

Bennett, A. (1995) *A working life: Child labour through the nineteenth century* (2nd edn), Launceston: Waterfront Publications.

Brindle, D. (1996) ' "Poverty, what poverty?" says Lilley', *The Guardian*, 17 April.

Bunting, J. (1997) 'Appendix A: sources and methods', in F. Drever and M. Whitehead (eds) *Health inequalities*, No DS15, London: The Stationery Office.

Chalmers, I. (1985) 'Short, Black, Baird, Himsworth, and social class differences in foetal and neo-natal mortality rates', *BMJ*, vol 291, pp 231-2.

Davey Smith, G., Egger, M. and and Blane, D. (1990) 'Safety and health in the construction industry' (letter), *BMJ*, vol 301, p 932.

Davey Smith, G., Chaturvedi, N., Harding, S., Nazroo, J. and Williams, R. (2000) 'Ethnic inequalities in health: a review of UK epidemiological evidence', *Critical Public Health*, vol 10, pp 375-408.

DoH (Department of Health) (1999) *Saving lives: Our healthier nation*, London: The Stationery Office.

Dorling, D. (1997) *Death in Britain: How local mortality rates have changed: 1950s-1990s: Technical report*, York: Joseph Rowntree Foundation.

Dorling, D., Mitchell, R., Shaw, M., Orford, S. and Davey Smith, G. (2000) 'The ghost of Christmas past: the health effects of poverty in London in 1896 and 1991', *BMJ*, vol 321, pp 1547-51.

Drever, F. and Whitehead, M. (eds) (1997) *Health inequalities*, No DS15, London: The Stationery Office.

DSS (Department of Social Security) (1998) *Households below average income 1979-1996/7*, London: The Stationery Office.

DSS (2000) *Households below average income 1994/5 to 1998/9*, London: The Stationery Office.

Edelstein, M. (1994) 'Imperialism; cost and benefit', in R. Floud and D.M. McCloskey (eds) *The economic history of Britain since 1700* (2nd edn), Cambridge: Cambridge University Press.

EEC (European Economic Community) (1995) 'On specific community action to combat poverty', *Official Journal of the EEC* 85/8/EEC, pp 2-24.

Engels, F. (1845) *The condition of the working class in England*, Harmondsworth: Penguin.

Fieldhouse, E. and Hollywood, E. (1998) 'Life after mining: hidden unemployment and changing patterns of economic activity among miners in England and Wales, 1981-1991', *UPDATE*, News from the LS user group, Issue 19, London: Centre for Longitudinal Studies, University of London.

Floud, R., Wachter, K. and Gregory, A. (1990) *Height, health and history*, Cambridge: Cambridge University Press.

Flynn, J.R. (1994) 'IQ gains over time', in R.J. Sternberg (ed) *Encyclopedia of human intelligence*, New York, NY: Macmillan, pp 617-23.

Gallie, D. (2000) 'The labour force', in A.H. Halsey and J. Webb (eds) *Twentieth-century British social trends*, Basingstoke: Palgrave.

Goodman, A., Johnson, P. and Webb, S. (eds) *Inequality in the UK*, Oxford: Oxford University Press.

Groves, R. (1975) *The strange case of Victor Grayson*, London: Pluto Press.

Hall, C. (1805) *The effects of civilisation on the people in European states*, London, printed for the author, 1805; as quoted by G. Miller (2000) *On fairness and efficiency: The privatisation of the public income over the past millennium*, Bristol: The Policy Press.

Hamlin, C. (1995) 'Could you starve to death in England in 1839? The Chadwick-Farr controversy and the loss of the "social" in public health', *American Journal of Public Health*, vol 85, pp 856-66.

Hamlin, C. (1998) *Public health and social justice in the age of Chadwick: Britain 1800-1854*, Cambridge: Cambridge University Press.

Harris, B. (2000) 'Seebohm Rowntree and the measurement of poverty, 1899-1951', in J. Bradshaw and R. Sainsbury (eds) *Getting the measure of poverty: The early legacy of Seebohm Rowntree*, Aldershot: Ashgate, pp 60-84.

Hattersley, L. (1999) 'Trends in life expectancy by social class – an update', *Health Statistics Quarterly*, vol 2, pp 16-24.

Himsworth, H. (1984) 'Epidemiology, genetics and sociology', *Journal of Biosocial Science*, vol 16, pp 159-76.

Humphrey, C. and Elford, J. (1988) 'Social class differences in infant mortality: the problem of competing hypotheses', *Journal of Biosocial Science*, vol 20, no 4, pp 497-504.

Jones, K. (1991) *The making of social policy in Britain 1830-1990*, London: Athlone Press.

Justman, M. and Gradstein, M. (1999) 'The industrial revolution, political transition, and the subsequent decline in inequality in 19th-century Britain', *Explorations in Economic History*, vol 36, pp 109-27.

Kevles, V.J. (1985) *In the name of eugenics: Genetics and the uses of human heredity*, Harvard, MA: Harvard University Press.

Kuh, D. and Davey Smith, G. (1993) 'When is mortality risk determined? Historical insights into a current debate', *Social History of Medicine*, vol 6, pp 101-23.

Lakin, C. (2001) 'The effects of taxes and benefits on household incomes on 1999-2000', *Economic Trends*, vol 569, pp 35-74.

Lea, J. and Pilling, G. (1996) *The condition of Britain: Essays on Frederick Engels*, London: Pluto Press.

Macfarlane, A., Mugford, M., Henderson, J., Furtado, A. and Dunn, A. (2000) *Birth counts: Statistics of childbirth and pregnancy. Volume 2 – Tables*, London: The Stationery Office.

Marx, K. (1968) 'Wages, price and profit', in K. Marx and F. Engels, *Selected works in one volume*, USSR: Progress Publishers.

Marx, K. (1976) *Capital. Volume 1* (original edn 1867), Harmondsworth: Penguin.

Mitchell, B.R. (1988) *British historical statistics*, Cambridge: Cambridge University Press.

Morris, J.N., Donkin, A.J.M., Wonderling, D., Wilkinson, P. and Dowler, E.A. (2000) 'A minimum income for healthy living', *Journal of Epidemiology and Community Health*, vol 54, pp 885-9.

Oakley, A. (1996) *Man and wife*, London: HarperCollins Publishers.

ONS (Office for National Statistics) (2000) *UK 2000 in figures*, London: Government Statistical Service.

Pearson, K. (1912) 'Eugenics and public health', *Questions of the Day and of the Fray No VI*, London.

Pomeranz, K., Topik, S. and Reilly, K. (1999) *The world that trade created: Society, culture and the world economy, 1400 – the present*, M.E. Sharpe.

Rowntree, B.S. (1941) *Poverty and progress*, London: Longmans Green.

Rowntree, B.S. (1951) *Poverty and the welfare state*, London: Longmans Green.

Semmel, B. (1958) 'Karl Pearson: socialist and Darwinist', *British Journal of Sociology*, vol 9, pp 111-25.

Sen, A.K. (1983) 'Poor, relatively speaking', *Oxford Economic Papers*, vol 35, pp 135-69.

Shaw, M. (2001: forthcoming) *Health Service Journal*.

Shaw, M., Dorling, D. and Brimblecombe, N. (1999b) 'Life chances in Britain by housing wealth and for the homeless and vulnerably housed', *Environment and Planning A*, vol 31, pp 2239-48.

Shaw, M., Dorling, D, and Davey Smith, G. (2001) Did things get better for Labour voters?: Premature death rates and voting in the 1997 election, Bristol: Townsend Centre for International Poverty Research.

Shaw, M., Dorling, D., Gordon, D. and Davey Smith, G. (1999a) *The widening gap: Health inequalities and policy in Britain*, Bristol: The Policy Press.

Smiles, S. (1882) *Self-help*, London: John Murray.

Smith, A. (1804) *An inquiry into the nature and causes of the wealth of nations, in two volumes*, Hartford: Oliver D. Cooke.

Smith, D.F. and Nicolson, M. (1995) 'Nutrition, education, ignorance and income: a 20th century debate', in H. Kamminga and A. Cunningham (eds) *The science and culture of nutrition 1840-1940*, Amsterdam: Clio Medica.

Snashall, D. (1990) 'Safety and health in the construction industry', *BMJ*, vol 301, pp 563-4.

Townsend, P. (1979) *Poverty in the United Kingdom*, Harmondsworth: Penguin.

Townsend, P. and Gordon, D. (1991) 'What is enough? New evidence on poverty allowing the definition of a minimum benefit', in M. Adler, C. Bell, J. Clasen and A. Sinfield (eds) *The sociology of social security*, Edinburgh: Edinburgh University Press, pp 35-9.

UN (United Nations) (1995) *The Copenhagen declaration and programme of action: World Summit for social development*, 6-12 March, New York, NY: UN Department of Publications.

White, F. (1928) 'Natural and social selection, a "blue book analysis"', *Eugenics Review*, vol 20, pp 98-104.

Veit-Wilson, J.H. (1986) 'Paradigms of poverty: a rehabilitation of BS Rowntree', *Journal of Social Policy*, vol 15, pp 69–99.

Williams, E. (1944) *Capitalism and slavery*, Chapel Hill: University of North Carolina Press.

Further reading

We hope that we may have ignited some interest in at least some of our readers to read further on the topic of poverty, inequality and health. Most of the texts we reproduce in this reader are excerpted from books and we would encourage readers to read these in full. However, many of these may not be readily available. Here we provide a few pointers to some recent books which relate to many of the themes covered in this Reader; these books in turn provide references to a wide range of primary material.

Statistics

Mitchell, B.R. (1988) *British historical statistics*, Cambridge: Cambridge University Press.

Surveys of economic and social conditions

Flood, R. and McCloskey, D.N. (1994) *The economic history of Britain since 1700* (2nd edn), Volume 1: 1700–1860; Volume 2: 1860–1939; Volume 3: the period since 1939, Oxford: Oxford University Press.

More, C. (1997) *The industrial age: Economic and society in Britain 1750–1990* (2nd edn), London: Longman.

Health

Porter, R. (1997) *The greatest benefit to mankind: A medical history of humanity from antiquity to the present*, London: HarperCollins.

Doyal, L. with Pennell, I. (1979) *The political economy of health*, London: Pluto Press.

Charlton, J. and Murphy, M. (eds) (1997) *The health of adult Britain 1841–1994* (2 volumes), London: The Stationery Office.

Health and economic change

McKeown, T. (1979) *The role of medicine: Dream, mirage or nemesis?*, Oxford: Basil Blackwell.

Flood, R., Wachter, K. and Gregory, A. (1990) *Height, health and history*, Cambridge: Cambridge University Press.

Sheard, S. and Power, H. (2000) *Body and city: Histories of urban public health*, Aldershot: Ashgate.

McMichael, T. (2001) *Human frontiers, environments of disease*, Cambridge: Cambridge University Press.

Woods, R. (2000) *The demography of Victorian England and Wales*, Cambridge: Cambridge University Press.

Brief background surveys

Flood, R. (1997) *The people and the British economy 1830-1914*, Oxford: Oxford University Press.

Harvie, C. and Matthew, H.C.G. (2000) *19th century Britain: A very short introduction*, Oxford: Oxford University Press.

Morgan, K. (2000) *20th century Britain: A very short introduction*, Oxford: Oxford University Press.

Poverty and welfare

Townsend, P. (1979) *Poverty in the United Kingdom: A survey of household resources and standards of living*, Harmondsworth: Penguin Books.

Mokyr, J. (ed) (1999) *The British industrial revolution* (2nd edn), Oxford: Westview Press.

Murray, P. (1999) *Poverty and welfare 1830-1914*, London: Hodder & Stoughton.

More, C. (2000) *Understanding the industrial revolution*, London: Routledge.

Social policy and social investigation

Jones, K. (1991) *The making of social policy in Britain 1830-1990*, London: Athlone Press.

Englander, D. and O'Day, R. (eds) (1995) *Retrieved riches: Social investigation in Britain 1840-1914*, Aldershot: Scholar Press.

Social inequality at the end of the 20th century

Dorling, D. (1995) *A new social atlas of Britain*, Chichester: John Wiley and Sons.

Shaw, M., Dorling, D., Gordon, D. and Davey Smith, G. (1999) *The widening gap: Health inequalities and policy in Britain*, Bristol: The Policy Press.

Gordon, D. and Townsend, P. (2001) *Breadline Europe: The measurement of poverty*, Bristol: The Policy Press.

The history of public health

Hamlin, C. (1998) *Public health and social justice in the age of Chadwick: Britain, 1800-1834*, Cambridge: Cambridge University Press.

Porter, D. (1999) *Health, civilization and the state: A history of public health from ancient to modern times*, London: Routledge.

Health inequalities

Wilkinson, R. and Marmot, M. (eds) (1999) *Social determinants of health*, Oxford: Oxford University Press.

Leon, D., and Walt, G. (2001) *Poverty, Inequality and Health: an international perspective* Oxford: Oxford University Press.

Timeline

This timeline, which has been adapted from www.chronology.org.uk, indicates some key events in the past two centuries which are pertinent to understanding changes in poverty, inequality and health in Britain. Although the timeline largely concentrates on England and Wales up to 1846, it begins with events in France and reports a selection of noteworthy events world-wide. We concentrate on events in England and Wales as this is the context within which the writers we have selected were writing.

1788	Thomas Clarkson publishes *An essay on the impolicy of the African slave trade.*
1789	Crowds stormed the Bastille in Paris, which symbolised the political oppression of the Ancient Regime, starting the French Revolution. This sowed the seeds of democracy that was later to be adopted throughout Europe and America.
1798	Thomas Malthus publishes *An essay on the principle of population and summary view of the principle of population.*
1801	The first Census of the population of England and Wales counted 8.9 million people. Henry Addington became Prime Minister (Tory).
1802	*Health and Morals of Apprentices Act* limited the work of children in textile mills to 12 hours per day, prohibited night work, required minimum standards of accommodation, some elementary education to be provided, factories to be periodically lime-washed and infectious diseases to be reported and attended to.
1804	The steam railway locomotive was developed. William Pitt became Prime Minister (Tory).
1805	Battle of Trafalgar. A Central Board of Health was established by Royal proclamation to advise the government on how to ward off yellow fever, which around this time was ravaging the southern shores of Spain.
1806	Installation of first steam operated loom. Lord Grenville became Prime Minister (Whig).
1807	Duke of Portland became Prime Minister (Tory).
1808	The National Vaccination Board was established under the auspices of the Royal College of Physicians of London to encourage vaccination.
1809	Spencer Perceval became Prime Minister (Tory).
1811	The Census estimated the population of England and Wales at 10.2 million.
1812	The Earl of Liverpool became Prime Minister (Tory).

1815	Battle of Waterloo. The *Apothecaries Act* introduced compulsory apprenticeship and formal qualification. The *Poor Law Act* extended the power to give outdoor relief. Corn Law prohibited the importation of corn into Britain until the home price reached 80 shillings per quarter; the cost of a four pound loaf of bread in London averaged over one shilling between 1816 and 1818.
1817	**Thomas Clarkson publishes *An essay on the slavery and commerce of the human species, particularly the African, translated from a Latin dissertation, which was honoured with the first prize in the University of Cambridge for the year 1785, with additions.***
1817	Typhus epidemic in Edinburgh.
1819	Peterloo Massacre – thousands of workers from Manchester and the surrounding cotton mills gathered peacefully at St Peter's Field, to be addressed by their leaders. They were savagely dispersed by the local yeomanry and regular cavalry acting on orders from the magistrates. Eleven civilians were killed and over 400 wounded. The *Cotton Mills and Factories Act* prohibited children under the age of nine years from working in cotton mills, and restricted those aged nine to a 12-hour day.
1820	Street lighting installed in Pall Mall, London.
1821	Census of England and Wales estimated the population to be 12 million.
1823	Capital punishment for minor offences was abolished.
1825	*Cotton Mills and Factories Act* limited the hours of work of children under the age of 16 years to 12 per day between 5am and 8pm with half an hour off for breakfast and one hour off for lunch. The first passenger steam railway opened, going from Stockton to Darlington.
1827	George Canning became Prime Minister (Tory) followed by Viscount Goderich (Tory).
1828	Edwin Chadwick published 'The means of assurance against the casualties of sickness, decrepitude, and morality' in the *Westminster Review*, in which he urged that it was the duty of government to collect accurate statistics about sickness and death. The Duke of Wellington became Prime Minister (Tory).
1830	Creation of the Metropolitan Police by Sir Robert Peel. Discontent and fear exploded throughout south and east England as agricultural labourers and others destroyed threshing machines and burned barns and ricks. Earl Grey became Prime Minister (Whig).
1831	Census of England and Wales estimated the population at 13.9 million.

1832 Cholera arrived in Britain for the first time and by June there had been 22,000 deaths. The *Cholera Act* and *Cholera (Scotland) Act* enabled the Privy Council to make orders for the prevention of cholera provided that any expense incurred should be taken out of money raised for the relief of the poor by the parishes and townships. Report of the Select Committee on the Bill for the Regulation of Factories described appalling conditions, excessive hours of work and cruelty to children in factories. The *Reform Act* was introduced, which was the first reform of Parliamentary elections; it enfranchised the urban middle class and abolished the 'rotten boroughs'.

1833 *Factory Inquiry Commission Report* is published.

1833 Abolition of slavery. The *Mills and Factories Act* repealed and extended the Act of 1831: younger children were to attend school for at least two hours, six days a week, and holidays for children and young persons were to be all day on Christmas Day and Good Friday, and eight half days. A Select Committee of the House of Commons recommended state registration of births, marriages and deaths. The first government grant to education was made towards building Church of England schools (£20,000).

1834 *Poor Law Amendment Act* limited outdoor relief to the aged and infirm who were 'wholly unable to work'; encouraged the building of workhouses introducing a spartan regime and the 'Workhouse Test'; any relief given was considered to be a loan. The Act required wards to be set aside for the impoverished sick and empowered Justices of the Peace to give an order for medical relief to any poor person with 'sudden and dangerous illness'. The Act set up the Poor Law Commission to consist of three commissioners to supervise the implementation of the Act, the first secretary of the Commission was Edwin Chadwick. Disraeli proclaimed that the new law was "announcing to the world that in England poverty was a crime". The *Chimney Sweeps Act* forbade the apprenticing of any boy under the age of 10 years, and the employment of children under 14 in chimney sweeping unless they were apprenticed or on trial. The Act was largely ineffective as there were no means of enforcement. The Tolpuddle martyrs, six agricultural workers in Dorset, were transported for taking oaths when forming a local branch of the Friendly Society of Agricultural Workers. There were three new Prime Ministers in this year: Viscount Melbourne (Whig), the Duke of Wellington (Tory) and Sir Robert Peel (Tory).

1835 Viscount Melbourne became Prime Minister (Whig).

1836 Influenza pandemic. The *Births, Deaths and Marriages Registration Act* introduced registration and established the General Register Office, dividing the country into registration districts. Registration became effective from 1 July 1837.

1837 William Farr's article *Vital statistics* is published.

1837 Queen Victoria's reign began. Start of a smallpox epidemic which continued until 1840, causing an estimated 42,000 deaths. There was also an outbreak of typhus in London.

1838	Capital punishment retained only for murder and treason.
1839	William Farr appointed compiler of abstracts at the General Register Office. He introduced the first classification of causes of death.
1840	*Vaccination Act* made free vaccination the first free health service provided through legislation on a national scale and available to all. The *Chimney Sweeps Act* prohibited any child under the age of 16 years being apprenticed. Start of the publication of the Registrar General's *Weekly Returns* of deaths in London. Report of the Select Committee on the Health of the Towns exposed squalid conditions in many industrial areas and recommended the institution of district boards of health: "The principal duty and object of these boards of health would be precautionary and preventive, to turn the public attention to the causes of illness, and to suggest means by which the sources of contagion might be removed." Universal penny post introduced for letters throughout the UK.
1841	The Census was the first to be conducted by the Registrar General and counted the population of England and Wales to be 15.9 million. Sir Robert Peel became Prime Minister (Tory).
1842	Edwin Chadwick's Report on *The sanitary conditions of the labouring population of Gt Britain* is published.
1842	*Mines and Collieries Act* was introduced after a Royal Commission had revealed the terrible conditions in which women and children worked underground. It prohibited the employment underground of women, and children aged under 10 in mines and collieries, and provided for the appointment of inspectors of mines. Ether vapour was used for the first time by C.W. Long as an anaesthetic.
1843	Influenza pandemic. In the annual report of the Registrar General, William Farr pointed out the number of deaths caused by puerperal fever (a type of infection affecting women after childbirth) that was spread by doctors and attendants.
1844	*Labour in Factories Act* amended the regulations concerning factory inspectors and certifying surgeons. For the first time machinery was required to be guarded; the age at which children could be employed was reduced from 9 to 8 years; and the maximum hours of work for children and women was prescribed. The Health of the Towns Association established to "substitute health for disease, cleanliness for filth, order for disorder, economy for waste, prevention for palliation, justice for charity, enlightened self-interest for ignorant selfishness and to bring to the poorest and meanest – Air, Water, Light". Ragged School Union and London School Mission formed to provide schooling for those unable to pay the 'school pence' demanded by voluntary schools.
1845	Friedrich Engels publishes *The condition of the working class in England*.

| 1845 | Final Report of the Health of the Towns Commission (see 1844) was published. The Report covered arrangements for drainage, paving, cleansing and water supply and deplored the extent of overcrowding; called for a central inspectorate of housing; and recommended that local authorities should be able to demand that landlords clean and repair properties dangerous to public health. Potato blight in Ireland caused widespread famine; this recurred until 1849 resulting in high mortality and emigration. Scotland was also affected with similar results. |

| 1846 | *Improvement of the Sewerage and Drainage of Liverpool Act* was the first comprehensive sanitary Act in Great Britain. The *Public Baths and Washhouses Act* enabled local authorities to provide washing amenities. Abolition of the Corn Laws. Lord John Russell became Prime Minister (Whig). |

| 1847 | Cholera epidemics in London and elsewhere; typhus epidemic in Scotland. The *Hours of Labour of Young Persons and Females in Factories Act*, the 'Ten Hours' Act, reduced the permitted maximum hours of work for women and children to 10 hours per day and 58 hours in any one week. The Corn Laws were repealed. Sir James Simpson introduced chloroform as an anaesthetic. |

| 1848 | Major cholera epidemic with about 60,000 deaths, about 14,000 of which were in London. Influenza pandemic with about 50,000 deaths in London alone. The *Public Health Act* created a new central department, the General Board of Health, under a nominated president, and provided for local boards of health to be set up. The Act contained numerous sanitary clauses including the cleansing of sewers, sanitation of houses, supervision of lodging houses and slaughter-houses, and maintenance of pavements. Karl Marx and Friedrich Engels published *The Communist Manifesto*. |

| 1849 | Cholera epidemic reached its peak in the week ending 15 September, when 3,183 deaths were reported in London. *On the mode of communication of cholera* was published by Dr John Snow suggesting that water was a major mode of transmitting the causative agent of cholera. Elizabeth Blackwell of Bristol qualified in medicine at Geneva College, New York State; in 1859 she returned to England and became the first woman to be placed on the British medical register. |

| 1850 | *Factories Act* amended the Act of 1847 by stating the times between which young people and women could be employed in factories and increased the total hours which could be worked by them to 60 per week. The *Coal Mines Inspection Act* introduced the appointment of inspectors of coal mines and set out their powers and duties. |

1851 Census carried out under Farr's supervision and collected more details than former censuses; the population in England and Wales was given as 17.9 million. During the 1850s one death in every three was attributed to an infectious disease, among which tuberculosis dominated. The *Common Lodging Houses Act* and the *Labouring Classes Lodging Houses Act* checked the worst abuses of housing standards. The General Board of Health issued a statement of the duties of 'officers of health'. These included "giving instructions and directions for the removal or prevention of causes of disease common to several persons, and also for the prevention or removal of causes of disease to individuals, where those causes come within the province of local administration under the Public Health Act". The Great Exhibition was held in Crystal Palace.

1851-2 Henry Mayhew publishes *London labour and the London poor.*

1852 Completion of the connection of major cities by telegraph wires. Manchester City opened the first free library. Earl of Derby (Conservative) and then Earl of Aberdeen (Conservative) became Prime Minister.

1853 Start of the Crimean War which finished in 1856. 1,933 soldiers were killed in action, 2,314 died later of wounds and injuries and 15,398 died of diseases. The *Vaccination Act* introduced compulsory vaccination for all infants within four months of birth, but contained no powers of enforcement.

1854 Report of a Select Committee on Medical Poor Relief. Much of the evidence given to the Committee favoured extending the medical services of the Poor Law to a much larger section of the population through such schemes as free dispensaries. Cholera outbreak around Broad Street, Golden Square, London, led to John Snow's famous investigations set out in the second and much enlarged edition of *On the communication of cholera* in 1855.

1855 Influenza pandemic. The first report on occupational mortality was published by the Registrar General. The *Nuisances Removal Act* dealt with control of epidemics and the inspection of common lodging houses and the removal of nuisances (most notably sewage). Pasteur published his 'germ theory' of fermentation and putrefaction. Viscount Palmerston became Prime Minister (Liberal).

1857 *Matrimonial Causes Act* allowed civil divorce without the need for a private Act of Parliament. The Ladies National Association for the Diffusion of Sanitary Knowledge (Ladies Sanitary Association) was founded, and distributed tracts on pregnancy and child rearing.

1858 *Medical Act* established the General Medical Council requiring all medical practitioners to register with the Council and for the Council to supervise the training of doctors. 'The Great Stink' of the Thames necessitated the closure of the windows of Parliament. The London Omnibus Company was founded with about 600 buses and 6,000 horses. Earl of Derby (Conservative) and then Viscount Palmerston (Liberal) became Prime Minister.

1859   Florence Nightingale's *Notes on hospitals* suggested that the high rate of mortality in large hospitals was preventable. Charles Darwin published *Origin of the species*.

1860   *Adulteration of Food Act* empowered local authorities to control adulteration of food and drink.

1861   Start of the American Civil War. The Census estimated the population of England and Wales at 20.1 million. For the first time a separate Census was held in Scotland conducted by the Registrar General for Scotland. The *Local Government Act* required local authorities to purify sewerage before discharging it into natural waterways.

1862   Manchester and Salford Ladies Health Society appointed the first 'health visitors', being women of the working class, to visit the poorer people and teach them the rules of health and child care. The rapid growth in railways since 1840 had linked all the main cities and revolutionised passenger and freight transport; London to Edinburgh by rail now took 10½ hours which was reduced to 8½ hours in 1888 (in 2001 it is supposed to take less than 5 hours).

1863   International Red Cross founded by Swiss Jean-Henri Dunant. First underground railway, the Metropolitan Railway (Paddington to the City of London), opened; it later became known as 'the Sewer'.

1864   **Karl Marx gives his *Inaugural address of the International Working Men's Association*.**

1864   *Factory Acts (Extension) Act* incorporated previous factory Acts and extended their coverage of industries. The *Contagious Diseases Act* attempted to control venereal diseases by the compulsory medical examination of 'common prostitutes' in garrison towns and 10 miles around them. The *Chimney Sweeps (Regulation) Act* amended the 1840 Act and permitted chimney sweeps to employ children under 10 years on their own premises. A Select Committee reported that there were not sufficient grounds for materially interfering with the existing system of medical relief for the poor, despite the evidence presented to it of abuse and deprivation. Louis Pasteur demonstrated that infections were caused by micro-organisms.

1865   *Sewerage Utilisation Act* created sewer authorities; gave town councils and other health authorities powers to dispose of sewerage for agricultural purposes; and to take proceedings against persons polluting rivers. The *Locomotives on Turnpike and Other Roads Act*, the '*Red Flag' Act*, introduced a 4 miles per hour limit on highways; mechanical vehicles had to be preceded by a man carrying a red flag. Start of the main drainage scheme for London. Earl Russell (Liberal) became Prime Minister.

| 1866 | *Sanitary Act* required local authorities to undertake sanitary regulation; set out general powers for the provision of sewage disposal and supply of water, and the abatement of nuisances; made overcrowding of residences illegal; introduced penalties for persons suffering from dangerous infectious diseases who endangered others in public places; and gave powers to authorities to provide hospitals or contract for the use of hospitals or parts thereof. Last great cholera epidemic in London ended. Earl of Derby (Conservative) became Prime Minister. |

| 1867 | *Representation of the People Act* enfranchised urban working-class householders adding about one million eligible voters. The *Metropolitan Poor Act* provided for the establishment of hospitals (with nursing staff) for the sick, infirm, insane and other classes of the poor; for the setting up of dispensaries; and for the distribution over the metropolis of the charge for poor relief. The *Public Health (Scotland) Act* consolidated previous legislation relating to nuisances, sewers, water supplies, common lodging houses and prevention of diseases; and permitted the appointment of medical officers of health and the levy of a general rate for public health purposes, but only a few authorities appointed medical officers of health. The *Factory Acts Extension Act* brought all factories employing more than 50 people under the terms of all existing factory Acts; forbade the employment of children, young people and women on Sundays; and amended some regulations of previous Acts. The London National Society for Women's Suffrage was formed. |

| 1868 | Trades Union Congress founded. The *Artisans and Labourers Dwelling Act* empowered local authorities to compel owners to demolish or repair insanitary dwellings, and to keep their properties in a habitable state – this was the first national legislation to tackle slum dwellings, although action was limited by legal procedures and the high compensation involved. The *Capital Punishment within Prisons Act* prohibited public executions. The first annual meeting of the Trades Union Council was held in Manchester. Benjamin Disraeli (Conservative) and then William Ewart Gladstone (Liberal) each became Prime Minister. |

| 1869 | Suez canal opened. Income tax was 6d in the pound. The Charity Organisation Society was founded, aimed at encouraging self-reliance among the poor. |

| 1870 | *Education Act* attempted to provide elementary education for all children; permitted school boards to be set up where voluntary school places were insufficient; the boards could build schools and compel attendance, but many boards did not use this power; fees of a few pennies per week were charged, with exemption for poorer parents. The *Married Women's Property Act* gave wives possession of any money they earned. The Poor Law Board raised in its annual report the possibility of establishing a system of free medical advice for all wage-earners; in the words of the report, to consider "how far it may be advisable, in a sanitary or social point of view, to extend gratuitous medical relief beyond the actual pauper classes generally". From 1870 to 1873 there were widespread outbreaks of smallpox. About 44,000 people in England, 10,000 of them in London, died from the disease. There was also an influenza pandemic during this year. |

| 1871 | Census found the population of England and Wales to be 22.7 million. The *Trade Union Act* legalised trade unions. The *Criminal Law Amendment Act* made intimidation, violence, obstruction and picketing against an employer or other employees illegal. The *Vaccination Act* improved the organisation of vaccination against smallpox and introduced compulsory appointments of vaccination officers. The *Bank Holidays Act* laid down that Easter Monday, Whit Monday, the first Monday in August and 26 December (if a weekday) should be official holidays. |

| 1872 | *Public Health Act* established urban and rural sanitary authorities and set out their duties which included the appointment of a medical officer of health (being a legally qualified medical practitioner) and an inspector of nuisances. The *Scottish Education Act* created the Scottish Board of Education and local school boards; and made school attendance compulsory for children aged between 5 and 13 years. The *Metalliferous Mines Regulation Act* prohibited the employment in the mines of all those under the age of 12 years. The *Bastardy Laws Amendment Act* gave the right to the mother of an illegitimate child to apply to a court for a maintenance order against the father of the child. The *Licensing Act* introduced licensing of premises selling beer and spirits; limited the number of such places; limited their opening hours to between 6am and 11pm; limited the sale of intoxicating liquor to any person 'apparently under the age of 16 years'; and prohibited gambling on licensed premises. |

| 1873 | Return of Owners of Land (The New Doomsday Survey) found that less than 7,000 men owned more than four fifths of all land. The *Agricultural Children's Act* stated that children between the ages of 8 and 10 years could be employed in agriculture only if the parent signed a certificate stating that the child had completed 250 school attendances, and if the child was over 10 150 attendances in the preceding 12 months, but the Act lacked any means of enforcement. |

| 1874 | *Births and Deaths Registration Act* consolidated and amended previous Acts; introduced a penalty for failure to notify; and required medical certification of the cause of death. The *Factory Act* raised the minimum working age to nine; limited the working day for women and young people to 10 hours in the textile industry; to be between 6am and 6pm; and reduced the working week to 56½ hours. Benjamin Disraeli (Conservative) became Prime Minister. |

1875	*Public Health Act* consolidated and amended previous Acts (national and local) relating to public health. The Act was divided into 11 parts and contained 343 sections dealing with the responsible authorities, sanitary provisions, local government districts and their procedures and the Local Government Board. The Act provided a code of sanitary law concerned with the supply of wholesome water; prevention of pollution of water; removal of sewerage; housing standards; regulation of streets; inspection of food; control of nuisances; prevention and control of epidemic diseases; and burial. The Act empowered local authorities to provide hospitals and charge patients (except paupers), and to provide medicines and medical assistance to their poorer inhabitants. The *Artisans and Labourers' Dwellings Improvement Act* gave local authorities powers of compulsory purchase of 'areas unfit for human habitation', so that they could be rebuilt and the houses let by the authorities, but little was actually achieved because of the compensation that had to be paid. The *Conspiracy and Protection of Property Act* amended the law in regard to conspiracy in trade disputes; made peaceful picketing lawful; and stated that anything that could be legally done by an individual could be legally done by a union. Income tax was 2*d* in the pound.
1876	*Elementary Education Act* placed a duty on parents to ensure that their children received elementary instruction in reading, writing and arithmetic; created school attendance committees, which could compel attendance; and the Poor Law guardians were given permission to help with the payment of school fees.
1877	*Married Women's Property (Scotland) Act* made wages, earnings and property acquired by a wife her own and not her husband's property.
1880	*Elementary Education Act* extended the provisions of the 1876 Act regarding compulsory school attendance for children aged 5 to 10 years. The *Statutes (Definition of Time) Act* defined Greenwich Mean Time as the 'legal' time in all Acts and legal documents and agreements unless otherwise stated. In a single week in February 3,376 deaths were recorded in London, the highest number for any week during the previous 40 years since civil registration was introduced, except for two weeks during cholera epidemics in 1849 and 1854; the excess was attributed to the recent fog. Income tax was 5*d* in the pound. William Ewart Gladstone (Liberal) became Prime Minister.
1881	In the Census the population of England and Wales was estimated at 26 million. Changes were introduced in the classification of causes of death. The *Married Women's Property Act* gave married women the right to separate ownership of property of all kinds; and made married women having separate property liable to the parish for the maintenance of her husband and children. The Democratic Federation (later the Social Democratic Federation), a socialist political organisation, was launched.

| 1883 | *Diseases Prevention (Metropolis) Act* improved the provisions for the isolation and treatment of persons suffering from infectious diseases in the metropolis; and legalised admission to Poor Law hospitals without any criteria of poor relief. The *Cheap Trains Act* required all railway companies to offer cheap workmen's fares, and to provide proper third class accommodation. The Association of Public Sanitary Inspectors was formed with Sir Edwin Chadwick as president. |

| 1884 | National Society for the Prevention of Cruelty to Children was founded. Robert Koch published his identification of the cholera vibrio, and its transmission by drinking water, food and clothing. The Fabian Society was formed. |

| 1885 | Report of the Royal Commission on the Housing of the Working Classes drew attention to the shortage of suitable housing for working-class people and the resulting overcrowding. This was followed by the *Housing of the Working Classes Act* which laid down that every local authority entrusted with the execution of laws relating to public health must enforce them so as to secure the proper sanitary condition of all premises within their district; and empowered local authorities to make bylaws in respect of houses let in lodgings. The *Criminal Law Amendment Act* raised the age of illegal sexual intercourse with girls from 12 to 16 years. Outbreak of milk-borne scarlet fever in Hendon, London. German engineer K.F. Benz built the first car using an internal combustion engine. Marquess of Salisbury (Conservative) became Prime Minister. |

| 1886 | *Shop Hours Regulation Act* attempted to regulate the hours of work of children and young persons in shops; the hours of work were not to exceed 74 per week, including meal times. The *Contagious Diseases Act* was repealed. William Ewart Gladstone (Liberal) and then Marquess of Salisbury (Conservative) became Prime Minister. |

| 1887 | Select Committee on Smoke Nuisances considered that fog in London had increased significantly during the preceding years, and that fog was as lethal as any epidemic. |

| 1888 | *Local Government Act* created county and county borough councils, elected by ratepayers, to take over from the justices of the peace in rural areas the duties of rating, licensing, asylums, police, highways and weights and measures. It gave women, if unmarried and otherwise eligible, the right to vote for county and county borough councillors; permitted county councils to appoint medical officers of health (see 1909), and made the holding of a registrable diploma of public health (or equivalent) compulsory for medical officers of health in districts with populations of 50,000 or more. |

| 1889 | *Infectious Diseases (Notification) Act* permitted any local authority to require general practitioners to notify the medical officer of health of cases of specified infectious diseases; cholera, diphtheria, relapsing fever, scarlet fever, smallpox, typhoid, paratyphoid, and typhus became notifiable. The *Prevention of Cruelty to, and Protection of, Children Act* made ill-treatment, neglect of or causing suffering to children punishable; and prohibited begging by boys under 14 and girls under 16 years of age. Influenza pandemic between 1889 and 1892. |

| 1890 | *Housing of the Working Classes Act* simplified procedures; empowered local authorities to build council houses using money from the rates; and made it a duty of medical officers of health to report unfit houses and slum areas. The *Infectious Disease (Prevention) Act* empowered medical officers of health to inspect dairies and to prohibit the supply of milk among other measures. |

| 1891 | Census estimated the population at 29 million. The *Public Health (London) Act* consolidated and revised the laws in London referring to general sanitary measures, nuisances, infectious diseases and the prevention of epidemic diseases, hospitals and ambulances; permitted any sanitary authority, with the sanction of the Local Government Board, to provide medicine and medical assistance to the poorer inhabitants of their district; and required each authority to appoint a medical officer of health who had to have a recognised diploma in sanitary science, public health or state medicine or have had adequate previous experience in public health practice. The *Factory and Workshop Act* consolidated and extended safety and sanitary regulations; including raising the minimum age for employment in factories to 11 years and prohibited the owner of a factory from knowingly employing a woman within four weeks of giving birth. The *Elementary Education Act* made grants available to all schools to enable them to cease charging for basic elementary education. Dense fog in London from 20 to 25 December. |

| 1892 | William Ewart Gladstone (Liberal) became Prime Minister. |

| 1893 | Elementary Education raised the school leaving age to 11 years. The *Married Women's Property Act* assimilated the rights of married women to ownership of property to that of unmarried women. Outbreaks of cholera were widespread in Europe, but only small outbreaks occurred in the eastern counties of England involving 287 persons, of whom 135 died. |

| 1894 | Death duties introduced by Sir William Harcourt (Chancellor of the Exchequer) with a graduated tax. Manchester Ship Canal was opened allowing ocean-going ships to reach Manchester. Earl of Rosebery (Liberal) became Prime Minister. |

| 1895 | The Royal Commission on the Aged Poor considered that "pauperism is becoming a constantly diminishing evil, ultimately to disappear before the continuous progress of thrift and social well-being". X-rays were discovered by German physicist W.K. Rontgen. Italian physicist G. Marconi made the first radio transmission over one mile. Manufacture of cars (Wolseley) began in Birmingham. Marquess of Salisbury (Conservative) became Prime Minister. |

| 1896 | *Locomotives on Highways Act* repealed the *'Red Flag' Act* of 1865 and introduced a speed limit of 14 miles per hour, which was lowered by the Local Government Board to 12 miles per hour. |

1897	In the year of Queen Victoria's Diamond Jubilee, an editorial in *Public Health* stated "of all the achievements of the Victorian Era ... history will find none worthier of record than the efforts made to ameliorate the lives of the poor, to curb the ravages of disease, and to secure for all pure air, food, and water, all of which are connotated by the term 'sanitation'" (*Public Health*, IX, 10, January, 1897, p 286). The *Workmen's Compensation Act* established the principle that persons injured at work should be compensated.
1898	*Vaccination Act* introduced a 'conscientious objection' clause, enabling parents to be excused the compulsory vaccination of their children. The First Infant Welfare Centre opened in St Helens providing the first supply of free milk to nursing mothers.
1899	Start of the Boer War (1899-1902) in which 9.5 soldiers per 1,000 were killed in action, 3.3 died from wounds and 20.4 died from diseases. The *Infectious Disease (Notification) Act* made notification of the prescribed diseases (see 1889) compulsory throughout England and Wales. A similar measure was passed for Scotland. The *Elementary Education (School Attendance) Act* (1893) raised school leaving age to 12 years. Aspirin, discovered by chemist Felix Hoffmann, was introduced by Bayer.
1900	Labour Representation Committee – forerunner of the Labour Party – was formed by Trades Unions and socialist groups, including the Social Democratic Federation.

1901   B.S. Rowntree publishes *Poverty: A study of town life.*

| 1901 | Queen Victoria died. In the Census the population of England and Wales was estimated to be 32.5 million with over 80% of the population living in urban areas. The *Factory and Workshop Act* dealt with health and safety, employment and education of children, dangerous and unhealthy industries, fire escapes, fencing of machinery, meal times, overtime, night work, homework, wages and administration and legal proceedings. The minimum working age was raised to 12. There were outbreaks of smallpox, which continued into 1903. |
| 1902 | *Midwives Act* created the Central Midwives Board with responsibility for the registration of midwives, rules for their training and examination, and the regulation of their practice. Arthur Balfour (Conservative) became Prime Minister. |

1902-3   Charles Booth publishes his *Poverty Series.*

| 1903 | *Motor Car Act* raised the speed limit to 20 miles per hour; required numbering, registering and lighting of all cars; and introduced an offence of reckless driving. The Wright brothers made the first powered, sustained and controlled flight in an aeroplane. Income tax was one shilling and three pence in the pound. |

1904 Report of the Interdepartmental Committee on Physical Deterioration made recommendations on a wide spectrum of health matters, many of which were gradually implemented during the next 50 years. These included: standards of purity for all food and drinks; registration of stillbirths; health visitors to be appointed in every authority; periodic medical examination of all school children; defining standards of overcrowding; enforcement of the laws against smoke pollution; health education classes in schools, including instruction about the effects of alcohol; and the provision by local authorities of meals for schoolchildren.

1905 *Unemployed Workmen Act* permitted local authorities to set up labour bureaux to help unemployed people to find work, and to finance the voluntary emigration of those out of work. The Act removed the disqualification from franchise of unemployed men. Albert Einstein proposed the theory of relativity. Henry Campbell-Bannerman (Liberal) became Prime Minister after the resignation of Balfour.

1906 *Education (Provision of Meals) Act* allowed local education authorities to contribute to the provision of school meals. The *Trades Disputes Act* laid down that no cases could be brought against unions for damages done by a strike, made peaceful picketing lawful and removed some liabilities of legal actions against trade unions. The Labour Party emerges from the Labour Representation Committee. The Liberal Party was elected to power in a landslide general election victory.

1907 *Notification of Births Act* introduced, on a permissive basis, notification of births to the medical officer of health, thus enabling the mother and baby to be visited. Vitamin C was identified, and its deficiency shown to be the cause of scurvy.

1908 *Old Age Pensions Act* provided for a pension of five shillings a week for people over 70 years old with incomes of less than £31-10s a year. The *Coal Mines Regulation Act* for the first time limited the hours of work of adult males; the limit was eight hours per day. During his speech on the Bill, Winston Churchill, President of the Board of Trade, said "the general march of industrial democracy is not towards inadequate hours of work, but towards sufficient hours of leisure ... [working people] demand time to look about them, time to see their homes by daylight, to see their children, time to think and read and cultivate their gardens – time, in short, to live." Herbert H. Asquith (Liberal) became Prime Minister. Ford began to mass produce the Model T Ford in Detroit.

1909   *Labour Exchanges Act* led to the setting up of labour exchanges to provide information about available work. The *Trades Boards Act* established the principle of minimum wages in defined occupations; established new trade boards; and powers to prosecute any employer exploiting his employees. The Royal Commission on the Poor Laws and Relief of Distress reported. There was unanimous agreement on the need to reshape the Poor Law and to change public attitudes; that the boards of guardians should be replaced; more help was needed for older people, children and the unemployed; school leaving age should be raised to 15 years; and that unemployment and invalidity insurance should be encouraged. An influential Minority Report, stressing the economic causes of poverty, is also released by a group of commissioners unhappy with the tone of the Majority Report (which included the claim that "the causes of distress are not only economic and industrial; in their origin and character they are largely moral"). The first closed top double-decker buses began service in Widnes, Cheshire.

1910   *Mines Accident (Rescue and Aid) Act* provided for fire precautions, rescue work and first aid treatment to be available at mines. American biologist T.H. Morgan refines the concept of genes.

1911   The Census estimated the population at 36.1 million. The *National Insurance Act* established health and unemployment insurance to be paid for by contributions from the state, employers and employees. The health insurance, which came into operation on 15 July 1912, provided sickness, disablement and maternity benefits, a medical practitioner service and free treatment for tuberculosis, for all insured people but not for their dependants. The *Coal Mines Act* legislated for the management and inspection of mines, the health and safety of miners and prohibited the employment of boys, girls and women below ground. Between 1910 and 1914 there were many strikes. In 1911 the miners in South Wales returned to work after a nine-month strike; dockers in various ports were on strike; and there was a strike of railway workers. Norwegian Roald Amundsen reached the South Pole.

1912   *Coal (Minimum Wage) Act* set up district boards to fix minimum wages for workers employed underground. The *Trades Union Act* allowed unions to use special, but not general, funds for political purposes under certain conditions. The Titanic sank with the loss of approximately 1,500 lives.

1913   Maud Pember Reeves publishes *Round about a pound a week*.

1913   Report of the Departmental Committee on Tuberculosis recommended that dispensaries for the diagnosis, treatment and after-care of tuberculous patients and sanatorium facilities should be available to the whole population and should be provided by county and county borough councils. At this time it has been estimated that nearly eight million people were living on incomes of less than 25 shillings per week, underhoused, underfed, and insufficiently clothed.

1914   Robert Tressell's *The ragged trousered philanthropists* is published.

1914	Outbreak of the First World War (1914-18) on 4 August. This was the first major war, as distinct from battles, in which deaths from enemy action outnumbered those from disease. The *Government of Ireland Act* (Irish Home Rule) provided for the establishment of an Irish Parliament to consist of an Irish House of Commons and Irish Senate. The *Milk and Dairies Act* introduced regulations about dairies and prohibited the sale of milk likely to cause tuberculosis.
1915	*National Registration Act* provided for the registration of all males aged 15 to 65. The *Increase of Rent and Mortgage Interest (War Restrictions) Act* restricted such increases for the duration of the war. The Act marked the beginning of rent control and the protection of the interests of tenants.
1916	Conscription of all men of military age was introduced. The *Police, Factories (Miscellaneous Provisions) Act* was an important stage in the statutory encouragement of industrial welfare. The Act provided for securing the welfare of workers in factories including the heating of workplaces; taking of meals; provision of protective clothing; seating; washing; accommodation; and the availability of first aid and ambulances. David Lloyd George (Liberal) became Prime Minister. Easter uprising in Dublin.
1917	*Corn Production Act* encouraged the production of corn; set a minimum wage for farm workers; and introduced rent restriction on farm cottages. The Royal Commission on the Housing of the Industrial Population of Scotland described the squalid state of much of Scotland's housing stock and emphasised the correlation between bad housing and poor health; it also recommended that the state should accept some direct responsibility for the housing of the working classes. The Russian revolution started.
1918	Rationing of certain foods was introduced on 1 January. Armistice was declared on 11 November. Start of a world-wide pandemic (1918-19) of influenza during which about 500 million people were infected and 25 million died from the disease. The *Representation of the People Act* established a common franchise for parliamentary and local government elections and introduced enfranchisement of women aged over 30 years if they were ratepayers or wives of ratepayers. The *Education Act* included: raising the school leaving age to 14 (although action was postponed), abolishing all fees for elementary education and restricting the employment of school children. The *Trade Board Act* extended the 1909 Act by stating that minimum wages could be applied to any seriously underpaid trades. The Building Construction of Dwellings for the Working Classes Committee of the Local Government Board recommended higher minimum standards, and stated that it was "essential that each house should contain as a minimum three rooms on the ground floor (living room, parlour and scullery), three bedrooms above, two of which being capable of containing two beds, and a larder and bathroom".
1919	*Ministry of Health Act* established the Ministry "to take all such steps as may be desirable to secure the preparation, effective carrying out and co-ordination of measures conducive to the health of the people". In addition to its health functions the new ministry became responsible for the Poor Law, national insurance, local government, planning, housing, environmental health and roads.

1920	*Government of Ireland Act* established separate parliaments for Southern and Northern Ireland, and a council for all Ireland. The *Dangerous Drugs Act* regulated the importation, exportation, manufacture, sale and use of opium, cocaine and morphine. The *Unemployed Insurance Act* extended the scope of the 1911 Act to include more than 12 million workers. The *Employment of Women, Young Persons and Children Act* brought into effect conventions agreed by the International Labour Organisation of the League of Nations; amended previous Acts; and raised the age of employment of children to 14 years. British Communist Party founded.

1921   *The health of the industrial worker* by Collis and Greenwood is published.

1921	The Census estimated the population of England and Wales to be 37.9 million. Marie Stopes established the first birth control clinic in north London.
1922	*Irish Free State Agreement Act* and the *Irish Free State Constitution Act* followed the 1920 Act. Andrew Bonar Law (Conservative) became Prime Minister.
1923	*Matrimonial Causes Act* allowed wives to petition for divorce on the grounds of their husbands' adultery. Stanley Baldwin (Conservative) became Prime Minister.
1924	James Ramsay MacDonald (Labour) and then Stanley Baldwin (Conservative) became Prime Minister. In India, Gandhi fasts for peace.
1925	*Housing Act* consolidated earlier legislation relating to housing of the working classes including their sanitary conditions; maintenance of buildings; closure of houses unfit for human habitation; and improvement and reconstruction schemes. Similar provisions were enacted for Scotland. The *Public Health Act* contained miscellaneous clauses concerning streets; noise; drains; offensive trades; vermin; recreation grounds; infectious disease in common lodging houses; rag and bone dealers; and baths and wash houses. The *Widows, Orphans and Old Age Contributory Pensions Act* introduced contributory pensions for widows, orphans and men aged 65 and women aged 60 as from 1926.
1926	Electrical engineer J.L. Baird first demonstrated television. In May there was a general strike (4-12).
1927	*Trade Disputes and Trade Union Act* followed the general strike in 1926 outlawing general and sympathy strikes. The *Unemployment Insurance Act* reduced benefits. BCG vaccine against tuberculosis was first used in the UK.

1928   'Natural and social selection' by Frank White is published.

1928	*Representation of the People Act* lowered the voting age of women from 30 to 21 years. Alexander Fleming observed the antibacterial effects of penicillin. The people of the UK became the largest consumers of tobacco at 3.4lbs per head annually, mainly smoked as cigarettes. Mickey Mouse is 'born'.

| 1929 | *Age of Marriage Act* raised the minimum age for marriage to 16 years. Financial crash on Wall Street, New York, in October led to a general industrial and trade depression. James Ramsay MacDonald became Prime Minister (Labour). |

| 1930 | *Housing Act and Housing (Scotland) Act* made further provisions for slum clearance by local authorities, although implementation was delayed by the financial crisis of 1931. The *Unemployment Insurance Act* removed some restrictions on claiming benefit. The Archbishop of Canterbury cautiously approved the use of birth control methods; Ministry of Health Memorandum empowered local authorities to provide birth control advice to limited categories of women when necessary for medical reasons. Two-and-a-half million people were unemployed. |

| 1931 | The Census enumerated the population of England and Wales at 40 million. The Committee on National Expenditure recommended cuts in public service salaries, reduction in public works programmes and a 20% reduction in unemployment benefits. James Ramsay MacDonald is re-elected as Prime Minister, but as the nominal leader of a largely Conservative national government, having split the Labour Party. |

| 1932 | Unemployment reached a peak figure of 2,745,000, dropping to 1,755,000 in 1936 and to 1,514,000 in 1939. John Cockcroft and Ernest Walton split the atom for the first time. |

| 1933 | *Housing (Financial Provisions) Acts* for England and Wales and for Scotland removed the power of the Minister of Health to grant subsidies under the Acts of 1923 and 1924; emphasised that the government's policy was to concentrate public effort and money on the clearance and improvement of slum conditions; and that private enterprise would be mainly relied on to provide ordinary working-class houses. The *Children and Young Persons' Act* consolidated and extended legislation concerning employment of children; cruelty to children; exposure to moral and physical danger; juvenile courts; and remand homes and approved schools. Adolf Hitler became Chancellor of Germany. |

| 1934 | *Unemployment Act* improved and tightened up the national insurance scheme – eligibility for relief was widened but means testing on a family basis was continued, although with some alleviations. Cheap or free milk was introduced on a national basis for all children at school. |

| 1935 | *Housing Act* defined 'overcrowding' and made it an offence; it placed an obligation on local authorities to rehouse persons from clearance areas and unfit houses scheduled for demolition. Similar provisions made for Scotland. Stanley Baldwin became Prime Minister (Conservative). |

| 1936 | *Poverty and public health* by M'Gonigle and Kirby and *Food, health and income* by Boyd Orr are published. |

1936	*Public Health Act* consolidated the law relating to sanitation; drainage; nuisances; offensive trades; common lodging houses; water supplies; control of infectious diseases including tuberculosis; maternity and child welfare; child protection; registration of nursing homes; and the provision of hospitals. The *Housing Act* consolidated the law relating to housing and slum clearance; obliged housing authorities to inspect their districts and to order unfit houses to be repaired, closed or demolished; and provided powers for the authorities to declare clearance areas and redevelopment areas and to compulsorily purchase unfit property. The *National Health Insurance Act* amended and consolidated the law relating to insured persons, their contributions, benefits, the approved societies, insurance committees, and central finance and administration. The *Education Act* raised the school leaving age to 15 years (not enforced until 1947). Jesse Owens, a black American athlete, won four gold medals at the Olympic Games in Berlin.

1937   Wal Hannington's *The problem of distressed areas* is published.

1937	*Factories Act* consolidated and extended previous legislation; limited the hours of work of young persons under the age of 16 to 44 per week, and of those aged 16 to 18 and all women to 48; and introduced new regulations regarding lighting, heating and cleaning. The *Maternity Services (Scotland) Act* entitled every expectant mother to have the services of a midwife and a doctor; and, if the need arose, of a consultant obstetrician. Fees were to be charged to patients according to means, with the poorest receiving services free of charge. The *Matrimonial Causes Act* extended the grounds for divorce to include desertion, cruelty, and incurable insanity. Neville Chamberlain became Prime Minister (Conservative).

1938	*Eire (Confirmation of Agreements) Act* confirmed that the provisions of the 1922 Act relating to the Irish Free State should be construed as referring to 'Eire'. The *Increase of Rent and Mortgage Interest (Restrictions) Act* removed rent control except for houses worth £35 or less in London and £20 or less elsewhere. The *Holidays with Pay Act* enabled wage regulating authorities to provide for holidays and holiday pay for workers whose wages they regulated.

1939   Margery Spring Rice publishes *Working-class wives*.

1939	Outbreak of the Second World War on 3 September. The *Civil Defence Act* was passed in July setting out extensive regulations about air-raid shelters, utilities, black-out of buildings, evacuation of children and pregnant women, and the treatment of casualties and control of diseases. The *Emergency Powers (Defence) Act* empowered the government to make such regulations as appeared necessary to secure public safety; the defence of the realm; maintenance of public order; the efficient prosecution of the war; and the maintenance of supplies and services essential to the life of the community. The *National Registration Act* required every civilian in Great Britain to register and be given an 'Identity Card' bearing his or her personal registration number, name, address and date of birth. The *National Service (Armed Forces) Act* made all men between the ages of 18 and 41 years liable for conscription. All infants and nursing mothers were to be provided with fresh milk, either free or at not more than 2d per pint.

| 1940 | Food rationing (bacon, butter and cheese) introduced in January, followed by meat rationing two months later. Winston Churchill became Prime Minister (Conservative). |

| 1941 | Owing to the war there was no Census in 1941, but the population had been registered in 1939. The Minister of Health announced the government's intention to ensure the provision of a comprehensive hospital service. Introduction of purchase tax. |

1942   *The Beveridge Report* is published.

| 1942 | The Beveridge Report laid the foundations of the post-war welfare state. |

1943   Richard Titmuss publishes *Birth, poverty and wealth*.

| 1943 | The Medical Planning Committee of the Society of Medical Officers of Health recommended the creation of a new Ministry of Health which brought together the health functions of all ministries. |

1944   J.N. Morris publishes *Health*, with the Association for Education in Citizenship.

| 1944 | *Education Act* included the following: elementary schools to be replaced by infant and junior schools for primary education; secondary education to be provided free for all children in grammar, technical or secondary modern schools, selection for which was to be by an examination taken at age 11 (the 'eleven-plus exam'); school leaving age to be raised to 15 years (implemented in 1947) and later to 16 (implemented in 1973); and free school milk, subsidised meals and free medical and dental inspections to be provided for all children in state schools. |

| 1945 | End of the war in Europe, 5 May and in Japan, 15 August. On 6 August an atomic bomb was exploded over Hiroshima, and another over Nagasaki on 9 August. The *Family Allowances Act* provided an allowance for second and subsequent children to be paid to the mother. Clement Attlee became Prime Minister (Labour). The Cold War began. |

1946   John Hewetson publishes *Ill-health, poverty and the state*.

| 1946 | *National Health Service (NHS) Act* established a comprehensive health service to "secure improvement in the physical and mental health of the people of England and Wales and the prevention, diagnosis and treatment of illness" by providing services free of charge, except where the Act expressly provided for charges; the NHS began in 1948. The *National Insurance Act* established the welfare state on lines set out in the Beveridge Report (1942) with compulsory contributions to cover unemployment (except for the self-employed), sickness, maternity, widows and old age benefits, and funeral grants. Free school milk introduced nationally. |

1947   Nye Bevan publishes *In place of fear*.

1947   *NHS (Scotland) Act* made provisions similar to those of the 1946 Act for England and Wales. The *National Service Act* continued conscription; men aged 18 to 25 years were liable to be called up for full-time service with the armed forces for a period of 18 months (later reduced to 12 months) and a further period of part-time service. School leaving age raised from 14 years to 15. The coal industry was nationalised.

1948   The World Health Organization was created. The National Health Service began in the UK from July. The *Criminal Justice Act* introduced more leniency towards criminals and virtually abolished flogging. Compulsory vaccination of infants ended. The first three comprehensive schools opened. Railways and the electricity industry were nationalised.

1949   *Housing Act* extended the 1936 Act to enable account to be taken of the housing conditions and needs of all members of the community and not only of the 'working classes'. BCG vaccination introduced for the protection of nurses, midwives, medical students and contacts of tuberculous patients; extended to school leavers in 1952. Clothing rationing ended. The gas industry was nationalised.

1950   Korean war started, ended in 1953.

1951   The Census estimated the population of England and Wales at 43.8 million. The *NHS Act* authorised charges for dental and optical appliances. The government increased housing subsidies and pledged to build 300,000 houses per year. The Minister of Health ceased to be a member of the Cabinet. Winston Churchill became Prime Minister (Conservative).

1952   National Registration abolished. The *NHS Act* provided for charges for drugs, medicines, appliances and dental treatment provided by the NHS. The *Housing Act* raised the subsidies on house building; encouraged council tenants to buy their houses; and allowed improvement grants to be available to private landlords. Outbreak of smallpox (135 cases) in south east Lancashire. The Great Smog of London, 5-9 December, caused about 4,000 deaths; led to a committee of enquiry and new legislation on smoke pollution.

1953   J.D. Watson and F.H.C. Crick published *The structure of DNA* (see also 1960).

1954   *Mines and Quarries Act* consolidated legislation dealing with health, safety and welfare, and the employment of women and young persons in mines and quarries. The *Housing Repairs and Rent Act* extended previous Acts; and set out details to be considered in defining houses as 'unfit for human habitation'. In July food rationing, introduced in 1940, came to an end.

1955   *Food and Drugs Act* consolidated legislation relating to the sale of food to the public, prevention of food poisoning, milk, dairies, markets, and slaughter houses.

1956	Suez crisis during October and November. The *Clean Air Act* introduced smokeless zones. The Minister of Health refused to mount a campaign against smoking as he was not convinced that smoking was harmful. The first kidney transplant operation was carried out in England. The first atomic power station in the UK, at Calder Hall, Cumbria, became operational.
1957	*Housing Act* consolidated previous Acts dealing with inspection; sanitation; repair and demolition; clearance and redevelopment of areas; overcrowding; the provision and management of houses; and set standards of overcrowding. The *Rent Act* abolished rent control on some houses, and allowed modest increases in rent on houses below certain rateable value. Sir Anthony Eden and then Harold Macmillan (both Conservative) became Prime Minister.
1959	*National Insurance Act* introduced retirement pensions and contributions related to earnings, which was a major departure from the Beveridge principle of flat rate contributions and pensions; the scheme became effective in 1961.
1960	*Offices Act* was concerned with the health, safety and welfare of office workers. The *Noise Abatement Act* made noise a statutory nuisance. The 1948 *National Service Act* requiring compulsory military training was repealed. First issue of a behind-the-ear hearing aid through the NHS. F. Crick, J. Watson and M. Wilkins deciphered the genetic code of DNA.
1961	The Census was the first to be processed by computer and enumerated 46.1 million people in England and Wales. The *Factories Act* replaced the Acts of 1937, 1948 and 1959; it dealt with cleanliness; overcrowding; lighting; sanitary conveniences; safety; welfare; accidents; industrial diseases; employment of women and young persons; home work; and the duties of factory inspectors and public health inspectors in factories not using mechanical power. There was an outbreak of smallpox in England and Wales following its introduction by travellers from Pakistan; there were 46 cases in Wales and 16 in England, with 24 deaths. Thalidomide was withdrawn following the birth of babies with limb deformities since its introduction in 1958. The contraceptive pill was approved for use in family planning clinics.
1962	*Education Act* imposed a duty on local authorities to make grants to students who obtained places on certain courses at universities and establishments of further education. The *Commonwealth Immigrants Act* narrowed the qualifications required for Commonwealth citizens to obtain British citizenship. For the first time over 100,000 deaths were registered as due to cancer. Severe fog in London caused about 700 deaths. Technical improvements in artificial hip joints led to widespread adoption of hip replacement operations in older people.

| 1963 | Committee on Higher Education recommended radical changes in the structure of higher education with the doubling of student places available and believed that "courses in higher education should be available for all those who are qualified by ability and attainment to pursue them and who wish to do so". Subsequently 10 new universities in England and four in Scotland were established, including the conversion of colleges of advanced technology into universities. Sir Alec Douglas-Home (Conservative) became Prime Minister. President John F. Kennedy was shot dead. |

| 1964 | Start of the war in Vietnam; ceased in 1975, after the withdrawal of US troops in 1973. An outbreak of typhoid in Aberdeen infected more than 400 persons and was traced to contaminated tins of corned beef. Helen Brook set up Brook Clinics in London, Bristol and Birmingham to give contraceptive and other advice to unmarried women and young girls. A free vote in the House of Commons abolished the death penalty for murder, becoming effective in 1965. Harold Wilson (Labour) became Prime Minister. |

1965 — Brian Abel-Smith and Peter Townsend publish *The poor and the poorest.*

| 1965 | *Redundancy Payments Act* provided redundancy payments graduated according to the length of service of the employees. The *Rent Act* reintroduced rent control for the majority of privately owned unfurnished accommodation; gave tenants security of tenure; and introduced a scheme for the assessment of fair rents. The *Race Relations Act* prohibited discrimination on racial grounds in places of public resort and in regard to tenancies; made incitement to racial hatred an offence; and constituted the Race Relations Board. Cigarette advertising was banned on TV. |

| 1966 | Outbreaks of smallpox (variola minor) in the West Midlands and Monmouthshire with 71 cases in all and no deaths. One hundred and sixteen children were killed in school by the slippage of a rain-soaked colliery tip in Aberfan, Wales. Increasing financial crisis caused a freeze on wages, dividends and prices, operated through the National Board for Prices and Incomes. The Vietnam Solidarity Campaign was launched by philosopher Bertrand Russell and others. England wins the football World Cup. |

| 1967 | *Abortion Act* permitted pregnancies to be terminated where two doctors agreed that termination was necessary on medical or social grounds. The *NHS (Family Planning) Act* enabled local health authorities to provide a family planning service for all persons, without regard to marital status or medical need, either directly or through a voluntary body. The *Sexual Offences Act* legalised homosexual practices in private between consenting adults in England and Wales. The World Health Organization began a programme for the eradication of smallpox. |

1968	January: Tet Offensive in Vietnam begins a change of mood in America (later in the year resonating in mass demonstrations against the Vietnam war in Britain). February: Richard Nixon stands for president; in March Robert Kennedy enters the race for president. April: Martin Luther King Jr assassinated. May: Students and workers revolt in Paris. June: Andy Warhol is shot by Valerie Solanas in New York (struggling actress, and writer of the SCUM Manifesto); Robert Kennedy shot by Sirhan Sirhan. August: the Soviet Union invades Czechoslovakia quashing the liberalising forces of the Prague Spring and restoring hard-line communism. October: President Johnson announces a total halt to US bombing in North Vietnam. November: Nixon wins the US election. December: Apollo 8 was launched to orbit the moon. In Britain the *Clean Air Act* prohibited the emission of dark smoke from industrial and trade premises.
1969	*Representation of the People Act* lowered the age of voting to 18 years. The *Divorce Reform Act* introduced the criterion of irretrievable breakdown of the marriage. Widespread epidemic of influenza. The abolition of capital punishment was made permanent. Neil Armstrong was the first man to set foot on the moon.
1970	*National Insurance (Old Persons' and Widows' Pensions and Attendance Allowance) Act* extended the eligibility for widows' pensions; introduced non-contributory pensions, as of right, to all people aged 80 years or more; and an 'Attendance Allowance' for a disabled person needing frequent or continuous attention. The *Family Income Supplements Act* provided for a new benefit, administered by the Supplementary Benefits Commission, for families with small incomes. Such families were exempted from health service charges and the children were eligible for free school meals. The *Equal Pay Act* disallowed discrimination between men and women in terms and conditions of pay; and obliged firms to pay men and women doing the same job the same wage by the end of 1975. The *Matrimonial Proceedings and Property Act* established that a wife's work, as either a housewife or wage earner, should be considered as an equal contribution towards the creation of the family home. Rubella vaccine was introduced. Edward Heath (Conservative) became Prime Minister. The Beatles split up.
1971	**Robert Roberts *The classic slum: Salford life in the first quarter of the century* is published, as well as Julian Tudor Hart's *The Inverse Care Law*.**
1971	In the Census the population of England and Wales was estimated at 48.7 million. The *Immigration Act* drew a distinction between those persons who had a right of abode in the UK and all other persons who are subject to immigration control whatever their citizenship or ethnic origin. The *Education (Milk) Act* restricted the duty of education authorities to provide milk for pupils. The Office of Population Censuses and Surveys began an ongoing General Household Survey based on a sample of 15,000 households, which included questions on health and social and economic conditions. The first shelter for battered wives was opened. Routine smallpox vaccination ceased to be recommended in Great Britain. Decimal currency was introduced in the UK. Micro-processor chips were incorporated into micro-computers.

1972	*Housing Finance Act* required local councils to charge 'fair rents' for subsidised council accommodation, and introduced rent rebates and allowances. The *Children's Act* prohibited the employment of children below the age of 13 years, and prescribed the hours of employment for children who were eligible for employment. School leaving age was raised to 16 years. Unemployment rose to above one million, and a compulsory freeze on prices and wages was introduced as a severe financial crisis developed.
1973	Britain joined the European Community. International oil crisis. Four cases of smallpox (with two deaths) occurred in connection with a laboratory infection at the London School of Hygiene and Tropical Medicine; one other case was reported in a person who had returned recently from Calcutta. Six cases of imported cholera were notified. The Longitudinal Study, linking a sample of individuals from Census to Census and to records in the registration system, was started by the Office of Population Censuses and Surveys.
1974	Family planning services were made available, without charge, from all NHS family planning clinics to men and women irrespective of age and marital status. The government agreed a 'social contract' whereby the trade unions would moderate wage demands in return for promises of increased government spending on pensions, the NHS, and child benefit, price control and restricted increases in council house rents. Harold Wilson (Labour) became Prime Minister.
1975	The country was coming to grips with a recession caused by the oil crisis. The *Social Security Pensions Act* introduced earnings-related retirement pensions. The *Sex Discrimination Act* made discrimination on the grounds of sex in employment, training and related matters an offence; and established the Equal Opportunities Commission. General practitioners started providing free contraceptive advice and supplies after negotiating an extra 'item for service' payment. Unemployment rose to over one million and the inflation rate reached 25%.
1976	*Education Act* required local education authorities to submit proposals for introducing comprehensive schooling (see 1948); direct-grant grammar schools were to be gradually phased out. The Commission for Racial Equality was set up with a remit to promote the elimination of discrimination and the equality of opportunity for all racial groups; to support local community relations councils; and to undertake advisory and educational work. The Resource Allocation Working Party recommended in its report 'Sharing resources for health in England' the use of a formula reflecting relative need rather than supply or demand to secure equal opportunity of access to health care for people at equal risk. James Callaghan became Prime Minister (Labour).
1977	*Housing (Homeless Persons) Act* extended the duties of local authorities to house homeless people. The *Inner Urban Areas Act* designated districts of deprivation for special treatment. The *Protection of Children Act* made the taking, distributing or showing of indecent photographs and films of children an offence. The World Health Organization in the Declaration of Alma Ata challenged the countries of the world to attain 'Health for All by the Year 2000'; and to reduce the gross inequality in the health status of people in developed and developing countries. Elvis Presley died.

1978	The 'winter of discontent' began – a period of sustained and widespread industrial action.
1979	Widespread industrial action in the NHS, mainly by ancillary workers and ambulancemen. Margaret Thatcher (Conservative) became Prime Minister.
1980	***The Black Report* is published.**
1980	*Education Act* relaxed the obligation to provide milk and meals; limited free school meals to children receiving supplementary benefits or family income supplement; removed the obligation to provide nursery education; and supported parental preference for schools and assisted places at independent schools. The *Housing Act* introduced the 'Tenants' Charter' giving council tenants, with some exceptions, the right to buy the houses they occupied. The *Social Security Act* removed the link between benefits and earnings. The *Employment Act* introduced trade union ballots and codes of practice; banned secondary picketing; and limited the number of people on picket lines to six. In November the number of people unemployed passed 2 million. The World Health Organization formally announced the eradication of smallpox. John Lennon was shot dead in New York.
1981	The Census counted the population of England and Wales at 49.1 million. The *British Nationality Act* replaced citizenship of the UK and colonies with three categories of citizenship: British citizenship, British dependent territories citizenship, and British overseas citizenship. Seat belts became compulsory for drivers and front seat passengers in cars. The first case of Acquired Immune Deficiency Syndrome (AIDS) was reported in the UK. The registered number of unemployed people rose above 3 million.
1982	'Falklands War' lasted from 2 April to 14 June. The *Employment Act* prohibited the requirement of union membership as a criterion for employment. Surveillance of the incidence of cases of AIDS started at the Communicable Disease Surveillance Centre.
1983	The Board of Science and Education of the British Medical Association published *The medical effects of nuclear war* reviewing the data concerning the expected consequences of a nuclear attack on Great Britain and concluding that the NHS could not deal with the casualties expected. Over 3 million people were registered as unemployed in Great Britain.
1984	*Data Protection Act* regulated the use of automatically processed information relating to individuals; required the registration of data users; and established new legal rights for individuals with regard to personal data processed by computing equipment. Miners' Strike begins, and lasts into 1985.
1985	Pasteurisation of all milk for retail sale through shops and dairies became compulsory in England and Wales. Small businesses were given exemption from some health and safety regulations.

1986	*Sex Discrimination Act* strengthened the powers of the 1975 Act, and brought the law into line with European Community law. The *Protection of Children (Tobacco) Act* made it illegal to sell any tobacco product to children aged under 16 years. The *Animals (Scientific Procedures) Act* made new provisions for the protection of animals used for scientific purposes. The Department of Health and Social Security started a campaign to prevent the spread of AIDS. Government scientists made the first official diagnosis of bovine spongiform encephalopathy (BSE). In April an explosion and fire occurred at the nuclear reactor at Chernobyl in Ukraine. During the following weeks radioactive material was dispersed over large areas of the Western hemisphere.
1987	*Channel Tunnel Act* provided for the construction and operation of a railway tunnel under the English Channel to France. During the year increasing cash crises in the NHS led to closure of wards.
1988	*Local Government Finance Act* made provision for the replacement of the local rates by the community charge (the 'Poll Tax'). Protests against the tax escalated. The *Immigration Act* made further provisions to regulate immigration. Charges for eye tests and dental check-ups were introduced. The combined measles, mumps and rubella (MMR) vaccine was introduced. Public attention was drawn to the prevalence of salmonella in eggs and poultry.
1989	*Employment Act* removed restrictions on the employment of women in heavy industries, including potteries, mining and lead manufacture; extended the permitted hours of work of young people and allowed them to do night work. The *Electricity Act* provided for the privatisation of the electricity industry. The Berlin Wall fell.
1990	Poll Tax was introduced in England and Wales in April, having been introduced the previous year in Scotland. The *Education (Student Loans) Act* provided for students in higher education to be granted loans towards their maintenance while at university, as grants were cut. Digital networking was introduced. John Major (Conservative) became Prime Minister.
1991	Gulf War, January and February. The Census counted the population of England and Wales as 49.8 in England and Wales (and missed a million due to the Poll Tax). The Department of Health published *The health of the nation*, a consultative document, outlining a health strategy focused on the main health problems, with the intention of, among other matters, reducing deaths due to heart disease, strokes and cancer, and of improving rehabilitation services.
1992	Under Neil Kinnock, Labour lose their fourth general election in a row.
1993	Council Tax replaced the Poll Tax. The *British Coal and British Rail (Transfer Proposals) Act* made possible the transfer of the functions, property, rights and liabilities of British Coal and British Rail to private companies. The *National Lottery Act* enabled a national lottery to be set up and regulated.

| 1994 | *Criminal Justice and Public Order Act* made new provisions concerning public order, bail, right of silence; obscenity; measures against terrorism; trespassers; squatters; and illegal camping; and provided for the contracting out of prisons and prison escorts to private companies. |

| 1995 | *Disability Discrimination Act* made it illegal to discriminate against disabled people. |

| 1996 | There was widespread concern about the link between bovine spongiform encephalopathy (BSE) and Creutzfeldt-Jakob disease (CJD). |

| 1997 | In a landslide election victory Tony Blair became Prime Minister (Labour). The first Minister of Public Health (Tessa Jowell) was appointed, and a health strategy was developed to break the cycle of ill-health due to poverty and deprivation (see 1840, 1980, and 1995). Princess Diana died. |

1998   The Report of the Independent Inquiry into Inequalities in Health is published.

| 1998 | *Human Rights Act* enshrined the European Human Rights Convention into British law; it was to come into force in 2000. The *Scotland Act* established the Scottish Parliament and set out its procedures and administration. The *Government of Wales Act* established the National Assembly for Wales. The *National Minimum Wage Act* introduced a national minimum wage; to start on 1 April 1999. Separate health strategy documents were published for England, Scotland and Wales. They discussed the influence of adverse social, economic and environmental factors as causes of ill-health and promised action across government departments to tackle poor housing, low wages, unemployment, crime and air pollution. |

| 1999 | The Scottish Parliament officially opened; the Welsh Assembly took over the functions of the Welsh Office. The *House of Lords Act* removed the right of all but 92 of the hereditary peers to continue to sit as legislators in the House of Lords. The *Immigration and Asylum Act* introduced powers to disperse asylum-seekers around the country; to issue food vouchers in place of social security benefits; to speed up the appeals system; to regulate immigration advisers; and to investigate alleged bogus marriages. In *Opportunity for all, tackling poverty and social exclusion* the government announced plans to eradicate child poverty. |

| 2000 | The millennium bug didn't happen; the Millennium Dome did but failed to entice the predicted number of visitors. The Human Genome sequence was published. Ken Livingstone was elected Mayor of London. The *Human Rights Act* came into force. According to the United Nations more than 5 million people die from diarrhoeal diseases caused by water contamination every year; 840 million people world-wide are malnourished; the income of the richest fifth of the world's population is 74 times that of the poorest fifth; more than 880 million people lack access to health services; and more than 250 million children are working as child labourers. The American Anti-Slavery group estimates that there are 27 million slaves in the world, more than at any other time in history. |

| 2001 | Government figures show that income inequality increased under the Labour administration. The 2001 Census was taken, the results of which are likely to show that there were 52.7 million people in England and Wales in 2001. Tony Blair is re-elected as Prime Minister (Labour), but with a record low turnout of the electorate and widespread apathy. On 11 June Mr Blair awarded himself a 40% pay increase raising his salary to £163,000 a year. In an interview a week earlier in response to the question 'Is it acceptable for the gap between rich and poor to get bigger?' he would only answer by saying 'It is acceptable for those people on lower incomes to have their incomes raised'. He was not concerned about the gap between 'the person who earns the most in the country and the person that earns the least'. Research conducted on behalf of the Joseph Rowntree Foundation finds that 2 million children in Britain – more than one in six – are experiencing multiple deprivation and poverty. |

Thomas Clarkson, 1760–1846

Born into a wealthy Quaker family, Thomas Clarkson dedicated his life to the abolition of slavery and the slave trade. His work started after he won a prize in 1785 for an essay while he was studying at Cambridge, entitled *An essay on the slavery and commerce of the human species*. It was this that provoked him to pursue the goal of the abolition of slavery, and he worked towards this aim in conjunction with other prominent Abolitionists – including Granville Sharp and William Wilberforce. Clarkson's efforts included petitioning political allies as well as collecting and disseminating information on the barbaric conditions of the slave ships, to which end he claimed to have interviewed over 20,000 sailors. On board these ships the captured slaves were chained by their hands and feet and had little room to move. Many died from diseases such as smallpox and dysentery; others thought death more preferable than the life that faced them and committed suicide by refusing food and water. Death rates on the ships often reached 50%. Clarkson was also motivated by the immorality and inhumanity of the concept of human slavery. Legislation was first put to Parliament in 1788, but it was not until 1807 that a Bill to end the British organised slave trade was successfully passed.

Here we present two extracts from Clarkson's work. The first is taken from *An essay on the impolicy of the slave trade* and highlights the high mortality rates of sailors. The second extract refers to the conditions of the slaves and is taken from his *History of the abolition of the African slave trade* which was first published in 1817, a book that he had been persuaded to write to chronicle the struggle against slavery in which he played a such vital role.

Clarkson, T. (1788) *An essay on the impolicy of the African slave trade*

Chapter V
Section I

I come now to the argument, upon which so great a stress has been laid, that *the slave trade is a nursery for our seamen*.

The truth of this argument I deny in the most explicit and unequivocal manner. I assert, on the other hand, that it is a *grave* for our seamen, and that it destroys more in *one* year, than *all the other* trades of Great Britain, when put together, destroy in *two*.

To show this in the clearest manner, I shall divide the loss, which the state experiences in her seamen by the prosecution of the slave trade, into *three* parts. The first will contain such as are actually on the dead list, while on pay, and in the service of their respective ships. This shall be immediately explained. The other two shall be each of them canvassed in a distinct section.

I am aware, that in attempting to ascertain the first to the satisfaction of the reader, I must avoid all general assertion, and produce many of those *particular facts*, which have induced me to speak with so much confidence on the subject. I shall therefore submit to this inspection an account of the loss sustained by the last eighty-eight vessels in this trade, that had returned to Liverpool from their respective voyages in the September of the year 1787. I give him so great a number for three reasons, first, because it includes all vessels both great and small; secondly, because it includes destinations to all parts of the coast; and thirdly, because it is from a number only, that any inference can be justly drawn.

The reader will see, by casting his eye on the [following] list, *that the slave trade cannot possibly be a nursery for our seamen*, for it clearly appears from thence, that if we refer the estimate to the *number of ships*, every vessel, that sails from the port of Liverpool in this trade loses more than *seven* of her crew, and that if we refer it to the *number of seamen* employed, more than a *fifth* perish.

This has been the invariable proportion for the port of Liverpool for many years; – and I should have stated it to the reader without the [following] list, but that I thought it would be far more satisfactory for him to see at least a part of the foundation, on which it has been raised.

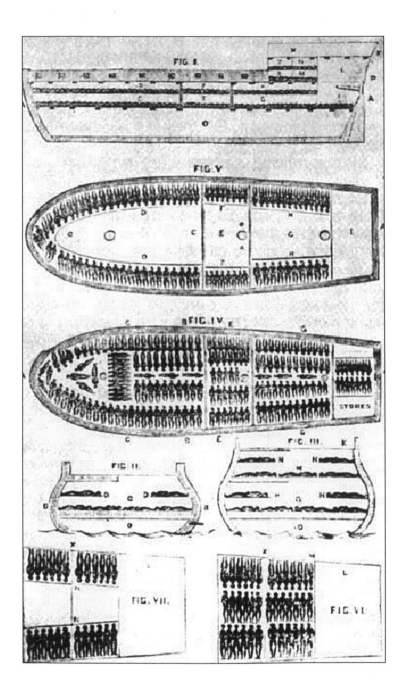

Diagram showing cross-section of a typical slave ship in the 18th century

Ship names	Number of seamen lost* in each	Ship names	Number of seamen lost* in each
Sisters	3	Tarleton	5
Hornet	15	Africa	19
Molly	14	Quixote	4
Fair American	10	Hero	8
Lyon	15	Rose	12
Will	17	James	8
Telemachus	8	Oronooko	6
Peggy	9	Blaydes	17
Pedros Valle	3	Kitty	5
Doe	3	Tartar	15
Matty and Betty	3	Golden Age	11
Gregson	12	Fancy	7
Bloom	5	Ally	11
William	8	Mungo	2
Brooks	9	Jane	7
Vulture	5	George	5
Enterprize	3	Hornet	13
Venus	1	Sarah	0
Mermaid	6	Venus	2
Christopher	8	Mary	0
Thomas	2	Mary	5
Africa	2	Jemmy	2
Little Joe	1	Lord Stanley	5
President	8	Madam Pookata	3
Mary Ann	13	Mercer	6
Madam Pookata	3	Hannah	3
Hinde	2	Fanny	3
Mary	6	Mary Ann	6
Brothers	4	Mossley Hill	5
Chambers	7	Chambers	0
Vale	1	Will	5
John	17	Vulture	16
Benson	3	Crescent	0
Mary	3	Colonel	7
Gascoyne	13	Gregson	6
Bud	5	Little Joe	4
Essex	8	Favourite	15
Elliott	7	Peggy	3
King Pepple	5	Maria	24
Juba	9	Enterprize	5
Garland	13	Heart of Oak	1
Mossley Hill	8	Bloom	9
Mary	9	Ingam	15
Cato	10		
Darnal	10	Total lost	631
		Employed	3,082

*Under the term lost is included those that died, or were killed, or were drowned. Neither the captains, nor any of those seamen that were taken in at the West Indies, are included in this account.

The other ports also have had, in consequence of the same kind of investigation, their different proportions of loss assigned them, which are so accurate, that if applied to any number of ships taken promiscuously, and exceeding twenty, they will be found to answer on almost every occasion. These, with the former, I shall now state with one reserve,

First: Every vessel that sails from the port of Liverpool to the coast of Africa, loses on an average more than seven of her crew, or a fifth of the whole number employed.

Secondly: Every vessel from the port of Bristol loses on an average nearly nine, or almost a fourth of the whole crew.

Thirdly: Every vessel from the port of London loses more than eight, and between a fourth and fifth of the whole complement of her men.

By these statements it will appear, that if we compound the loss at the different ports of this kingdom, which are used for the prosecution of the slave trade, every vessel may be said to lose more than *eight* of her crew; and if we refer the loss to the number employed, *between a fourth and a fifth* may be said to perish. To these observations I shall only add, that in the year 1786, *eleven hundred and twenty-five* seamen will be found upon the dead list, in consequence of this execrable trade.

AN

E S S A Y

ON THE

SLAVERY AND COMMERCE

OF THE

HUMAN SPECIES,

PARTICULARLY

THE AFRICAN,

TRANSLATED FROM A

LATIN DISSERTATION,

WHICH WAS HONOURED WITH

THE FIRST PRIZE

IN THE

UNIVERSITY OF CAMBRIDGE,

FOR THE YEAR 1785,

WITH ADDITIONS.

Neque premendo alium me extuliffe velim. –LIVY.

─────────────◆─────────────

L O N D O N

PRINTED BY J.PHILLIPS, GEORGE YARD, LOMBARD
STREET, AND SOLD BY T.CADELL, IN THE STRAND
AND J.PHILLIPS.

────────────

M.DCC.LXXXVI.

Clarkson, T. (1785)
An essay on the slavery and commerce of the human species, particularly the African

Chapter IV

But to return to the narration. When the wretched Africans are conveyed to the plantations, they are considered as *beasts of labour*, and are put to their respective work. Having led, in their own country, a life of indolence and ease, where the earth brings forth spontaneously the comforts of life, and spares frequently the toil and trouble of cultivation, they can hardly be expected to endure the drudgeries of servitude. Calculations are accordingly made upon their lives. It is conjectured, that if three in four survive what is called the *seasoning*, the bargain is highly favourable. This seasoning is said to expire, when the two first years of their servitude are completed. It is the time which an African must take to be so accustomed to the colony, as to be able to endure the common labour of a plantation, and to be put into the *gang*. At the end of this period the calculations become verified,[1] twenty thousand of those, who are annually imported, dying before the seasoning is over. This is surely an horrid and awful consideration: and thus does it appear, (and let it be remembered, that it is the lowest calculation that has been ever made upon the subject) that out of every annual supply that is shipped from the coast of Africa,[2] *forty thousand lives* are regularly expended, even before it can be said, that there is really any additional stock for the colonies.

When the seasoning is over, and the survivors are thus enabled to endure the usual task of slaves, they are considered as real and substantial supplies.[3] From this period therefore we shall describe their situation. They are summoned at five in the morning to begin their work. This work may be divided into two kinds, the culture of the fields, and the collection of grass for cattle. The last is the most laborious and intolerable employment; as the grass can only be collected blade by blade, and is to be fetched frequently twice a day at a considerable distance from the plantation. In these two occupations they are jointly taken up, with no other intermission than that of taking their subsistence twice, till nine at night. They then separate for their respective huts, when they gather sticks, prepare

[1] One third of the whole number imported, is often computed to be lost in the seasoning, which, in round numbers, will be 27,000. The loss in the seasoning depends, in a great measure, on two circumstances, *viz* on the number of what are called refuse slaves that are imported, and on the quantity of new land in the colony. In the French windward islands of Martinico, and Guadaloupe, which are cleared and highly cultivated, and in our old small islands, one fourth, including refuse slaves, is considered as a general proportion. But in St Domingo, where there is a great deal of new land annually taken into culture, and in other colonies in the same situation, the general proportion, including refuse slaves, is found to be one third. This therefore is a lower estimate than the former, and reduces the number to about 23,000. We may observe, that this is the common estimate, but we have reduced it to 20,000 to make it free from all objection.

[2] Including the number that perish on the voyage, and in the seasoning. It is generally thought that not half the number purchased can be considered as an additional stock, and of course that 50,000 are consumed within the first two years from their embarkation.

[3] That part of the account, that has been hitherto given, extends to all the Europeans and their colonists, who are concerned in this horrid practice. But we are sorry that we must now make a distinction, and confine the remaining part of it to the colonists of the British West India islands, and to those of the southern provinces of North America. As the employment of slaves is different in the two parts of the world last mentioned, we shall content ourselves with describing it, as it exists in one of them, and we shall afterwards annex such treatment and such consequences as are applicable to both. We have only to add, that the reader must not consider our account, as universally, but only generally true.

[4] This computation is made on a supposition, that the gang is divided into three bodies; we call it therefore moderate, because the gang is frequently divided into two bodies, which must therefore set up alternatively every other night.

[5] An hand or arm being frequently ground off.

[6] The reader will scarcely believe it, but it is a fact that a slave's annual allowance from his master, for provisions, clothing, medicines when sick, etc, is limited, upon average, to thirty shillings.

their supper, and attend their families. This employs them till midnight, when they go to rest. Such is their daily way of life for rather more than half the year. They are *sixteen* hours, including two intervals at meals, in the service of their masters: they are employed *three* afterwards in their own necessary concerns; *five* only remain for sleep, and their day is finished.

During the remaining portion of the year, or the time of crop, the nature, as well as the time of their employment, is considerable changed. The whole gang is generally divided into two or three bodies. One of the these, besides the ordinary labour of the day, is kept in turn at the mills, that are constantly going, during the whole of the night. This is a dreadful encroachment upon their time of rest, which was before too short to permit them perfectly to refresh their wearied limbs, and actually reduces their sleep, as long as this season lasts, to about three hours and an half a night, upon a moderate[4] computation. Those who can keep their eyes open during their nightly labour, and are willing to resist the drowsiness that is continually coming upon them, are presently worn out; while some of those, who are overcome, and who feed the mill between asleep and awake, suffer, for thus obeying the calls of nature, by the[5] loss of a limb. In this manner they go on, with little or no respite from their work, till the crop season is over, when the year (from the time of our first description) is completed.

To [6]support a life of such unparalleled drudgery, we should at least expect to find, that they were comfortably clothed, and plentifully fed. But sad reverse! they have scarcely a covering to defend themselves against the inclemency of the night. Their provisions are frequently bad, and are always dealt out to them with such a sparing hand, that the means of a bare livelihood are not placed within the reach of four out of five of these unhappy people. It is a fact, that many of the disorders of slaves are contracted from eating vegetables, which their little spots produce, before they are sufficiently ripe; a clear indication, that the calls of hunger are frequently so pressing, as not to suffer them to wait, till they can really enjoy them.

This situation, of a want of the common necessaries of life, added to that of hard and continual labour, must be sufficiently painful of itself. How then must the pain be sharpened, if it be accompanied with severity! If an unfortunate slave does not come into the field exactly at the appointed time, if, drooping with sickness or fatigue, he appears to work unwillingly, or if the bundle of grass that he has been collecting, appears too small in the eye of the overseer, he is equally sure of experiencing the whip. This instrument erases the skin, and cuts out small portions of the flesh at almost every stroke; and is so frequently applied, that the smack of it is all day long in the ears of those who are in the vicinity of the plantations. This severity of masters, or managers, to their slaves, which is considered only as common discipline, is attended with bad effects. It enables them to behold instances of cruelty without commiseration, and to be guilty of them without remorse. Hence those many acts of deliberate mutilation, that have taken place on the slightest occasions: hence those many acts of inferior, though shocking, barbarity, that have taken place without any occasion at all:[7] the very slitting of ears has been considered as an operation, so perfectly devoid of pain, as to have been performed for no other reason than that for which a brand is set upon cattle, as a *mark of property*.

But this is not the only effect, which this severity produces: for while it hardens their hearts, and makes them insensible of the misery of their fellow-creatures, it begets a turn for wanton cruelty. As a proof of this, we shall mention one, among the many instances that occur, where ingenuity has been exerted in contriving modes of torture.

"An iron coffin, with holes in it, was kept by a certain colonist, as an auxiliary to the lash. In this the poor victim of the master's resentment was inclosed, and placed sufficiently near a fire, to occasion extreme pain, and consequently shrieks and groans, until the revenge of the master was satiated, without any other inconvenience on his part, than a temporary suspension of the slave's labour. Had he been flogged to death, or his limbs mutilated, the interest of the brutal tyrant would have suffered a more irreparable loss.

In mentioning this instance, we do not mean to insinuate, that it is common. We know that it was reprobated by many. All that we would infer from it is, that where men are habituated to a system of severity, they become *wantonly cruel*, and that the mere toleration of such an instrument of torture, in any country, is a clear indication, *that this wretched class of men do not there enjoy the protection of any laws, that may be pretended to have been enacted in their favour*."

Such then is the general situation of the unfortunate Africans. They are beaten and tortured at discretion. They are badly clothed. They are miserably fed. Their drudgery is intense and incessant, and their rest short. For scarcely are their heads reclined, scarcely have their bodies a respite from the labour of the day, or the cruel hand of the overseer, but they are summoned to renew their sorrows. In this manner they go on from year to year, in a state of the lowest degradation, without a single law to protect them, without the possibility of redress, without a hope that their situation will be changed, unless death should terminate the scene.

Having described the general situation of these unfortunate people, we shall now take notice of the common consequences that are found to attend it, and relate them separately, as they result either from long and painful *labour*, a *want* of the common necessaries of life, or continual severity.

Oppressed by a daily task of such immoderate labour as human

[7] "A boy having received six slaves as a present from his father, immediately slit their ears, and for the following reason, that as his father was a whimsical man, he might claim them again, unless they were marked."

We do not mention this instance as a confirmation of the passage to which it is annexed, but only to show how cautious we ought to be in giving credit to what may be advanced in any work written in defence of slavery, by any native of the colonies: for being trained up to scenes of cruelty from his cradle, he may, consistently with his own feelings, represent that treatment as mild, at which we, who have never been used to see them, should absolutely shudder.

nature is **utterly** unable to perform, many of them run away from their masters. They fly to the recesses of the mountains, where they choose rather to live upon anything that the soil affords them, nay, the very soil itself, than return to that *happy situation*, which is represented by the *receivers*, as the conditions of a slave.

It sometimes happens, that the manager of a mountain plantation, falls in with one of these; he immediately seizes him, and threatens to carry him to his former master, unless he will consent to live on the mountain and cultivate his ground. When his plantation is put in order, he carries the delinquent home, abandons him to all the suggestions of despotic rage, and accepts a reward for his *honesty*. The unhappy wretch is chained, scourged, tortured; and all this, because he obeyed the dictates of nature, and wanted to be free. And who is there, that would not have done the same thing, in the same situation? Who is there, that has once known the charms of liberty, that would not fly from despotism? And yet, by the impious laws of the *receivers*, the[8] absence of six months from the lash of tyranny is – death.

[8] In this case he is considered as a criminal against the state. The *marshal*, an officer answering to our sheriff, superintends his execution, and the master receives the value of the slave from the public treasury. We may observe here, that in all cases where the delinquent is a criminal of the state, he is executed, and his value is received in the same manner. He is tried and condemned by two or three justices of the peace, and without any intervention of a *jury*.

But this law is even mild, when compared with another against the same offence, which was in force sometime ago, and which we fear is even now in force, in some of those colonies which this account of the treatment comprehends. "Advertisements have frequently appeared there, offering a reward for the apprehending of fugitive slaves either alive or *dead*. The following instance was given us by a person of unquestionable veracity, under whose own observation it fell. As he was travelling in one of the colonies alluded to, he observed some people in pursuit of a poor wretch, who was seeking in the wilderness an asylum from his labours. He heard the discharge of a gun, and soon afterwards stopping at a house for refreshment, the head of the fugitive, still reeking with blood, was brought in and laid upon a table with exultation. The production of such a trophy was the proof *required by law* to entitle the heroes to their reward." Now reader determine if you can, who were the most execrable; the rulers of the state in authorising murder, or the people in being bribed to commit it.

This is one of the common consequences of that immoderate share of labour, which is imposed upon them; nor is that, which is the result of a scanty allowance of food, less to be lamented. The wretched African is often so deeply pierced by the excruciating fangs [sic] of hunger, as almost to be driven to despair. What is he to do in such a trying situation? Let him apply to the *receivers*. Alas! The majesty of *receivership* is too sacred for the appeal, and the intrusion would be fatal. Thus attacked on the one hand, and shut out from every possibility of relief on the other, he has only the choice of being starved, or of relieving his necessities by taking a small portion of the fruits of his own labour. Horrid crime! to be found eating the cane, which probably his own hands have planted, and to be eating it, because his necessities were pressing! This crime however is of such a magnitude, as always to be accompanied with the whip; and so unmercifully has it been applied on such an occasion, as to have been the cause, in wet weather, of the delinquent's death. But the smart of the whip has not been the only pain that the wretched Africans have experienced. Any thing that passion could seize, and convert into an instrument of punishment, has been used; and, horrid to relate! The very knife has not been overlooked in the fit of frenzy. Ears have been slit, eyes have been beaten out, and bones have been broken; and so frequently has this been the case, that it has been a matter of constant lamentation with disinterested people, who out of curiosity have attended the[9] markets to which these unhappy people weekly resort, that they have not been able to turn their eyes on any group of them whatever, but they have beheld these inhuman marks of passion, despotism, and caprice.

[9] Particularly in Jamaica. These observations were made by disinterested people, who were there for three or four years during the late war.

But these instances of barbarity have not been able to deter them from similar proceedings. And indeed, how can it be expected that they should? They have still the same appetite to be satisfied as before, and to drive them to desperation. They creep out clandestinely by night, and go in search of food into their master's, or some neighbouring plantation. But here they are almost equally sure of suffering. The watchman, who will be punished himself, if he neglects his duty, frequently seizes them in the fact. No excuse or entreaty will avail; he must punish them for an example, and he must punish them, not with a stick, nor with a whip, but with a cutlass. Thus it happens, that these unhappy slaves, if they are taken, are either sent mangled in a barbarous manner, or are killed upon the spot.

We may now mention the consequences of the severity. The wretched Africans, daily subjected to the lash, and unmercifully whipped and beaten on every trifling occasion, have been found to resist their opposers. Unpardonable crime! That they should have the feelings of nature! That their breasts should glow with resentment on an injury! That they should be so far overcome, as to resist those, whom *they are under no obligations to obey*, and whose only title to their services consists in *a violation of the rights of men!* What has been the consequence! – But here let us spare the feelings of the reader, (we wish we could spare our own) and let us only say, without a recital of the cruelty, *that they have been murdered at the discretion of their masters.* For let the reader observe, that the life of an African is only valued at a price, that would scarcely purchase an horse; that the master has a power of murdering his slave, if he pays but a trifling fine, and that the murder must be attended with uncommon circumstances of horror, if it even produces an inquiry.

Immortal Alfred! father of our invaluable constitution! parent of the civil blessings we enjoy! how ought thy laws to excite our love and veneration, who hast forbidden us, thy posterity, to tremble at the frown of tyrants! How ought they to perpetuate thy name, as venerable, to the remotest ages, who has secured, even to the meanest servant, a fair and impartial trial! How much does nature approve thy laws, as consistent with her own feelings, while she absolutely turns pale, trembles, and recoils, at the institutions of these *receivers!* Execrable men! You do not murder the horse, on which you only ride; you do not mutilate the cow which only affords you her milk; you do not torture the dog, which is but a partial servant of your pleasures; but these unfortunate men, from whom you derive your very pleasures and your fortunes, you torture, mutilate, murder at discretion! Sleep then you *receivers*, if you can, while you scarcely allow these unfortunate people to rest at all! feast if you can, and indulge your genius, while you daily apply to these unfortunate people the stings of severity and hunger! Exult in riches, at which even avarice ought to shudder, and which humanity must detest!

Thomas Malthus, 1766-1834 2

Thomas Robert Malthus was born into a wealthy family who lived near Dorking in Surrey. He studied mathematics at Jesus College, Cambridge, but was also widely read in English, French, Greek and Latin literature and had a good knowledge of physics and history. He was ordained in 1797 and later became a professor of political economy. In 1798 he published, anonymously, the first edition of his *Essay on the principle of population*, which argued that the population has a natural tendency to increase faster than the means of subsistence, and that efforts should be made to cut the birth rate, either by self-restraint or birth control. Malthus concluded that unless family size was regulated, the misery of famine would become globally epidemic and eventually consume humanity. It was his view that poverty and famine were natural outcomes of population growth and limited food supply, a theory that was not popular among social reformers who believed that with appropriate social structures the problems of society could be alleviated and even eradicated.

In his essay Malthus proposes two principle checks to population growth. The first, which appears to operate at all ranks of society, is that men defer marrying and having a family due to the costs that this incurs and the pleasures that it terminates. In this extract he refers to the second 'preventive check' to population growth which is generally confined to the 'lowest orders' of society – that due to the limited availability of resources 'a part of the society must necessarily feel a difficulty of living'.

Malthus, T. (1798)
An essay on the principle of population

Chapter V

The second, or positive check to population examined, in England – The true cause why the immense sum collected in England for the poor does not better their condition – The powerful tendency of the poor laws to defeat their own purpose – Palliative of the distresses of the poor proposed – The absolute impossibility, from the fixed laws of our nature, that the pressure of want can ever be completely removed from the lower classes of society – All the checks to population may be resolved into misery or vice.

The positive check to population, by which I mean the check that represses an increase which is already begun, is confined chiefly, though not perhaps solely, to the lowest orders of society. This check is not so obvious to common view as the other I have mentioned, and, to prove distinctly the force and extent of its operation would require, perhaps, more data than we are in possession of. But I believe it has been very generally remarked by those who have attended to bills of mortality that of the number of children who die annually, much too great a proportion belongs to those who may be supposed unable to give their offspring proper food and attention, exposed as they are occasionally to severe distress and confined, perhaps, to unwholesome habitations and hard labour. This mortality among the children of the poor has been constantly taken notice of in all towns. It certainly does not prevail in an equal degree in the country, but the subject has not hitherto received sufficient attention to enable anyone to say that there are not more deaths in proportion among the children of the poor, even in the country, than among those of the middling and higher classes. Indeed, it seems difficult to suppose that a labourer's wife who has six children, and who is sometimes in absolute want of bread, should be able always to give them the food and attention necessary to support life. The sons and daughters of peasants will not be found such rosy cherubs in real life as they are described to be in romances. It cannot fail to be remarked by those who live much in the country that the sons of labourers are very apt to be stunted in their growth, and are a long while arriving at maturity. Boys that you would guess to be fourteen or fifteen are, upon inquiry, frequently found to be eighteen or nineteen. And the lads who drive plough, which must certainly be a healthy exercise, are very rarely seen with any appearance of calves to their legs: a circumstance which can only be attributed to a want either of proper or of sufficient nourishment.

To remedy the frequent distresses of the common people, the poor laws of England have been instituted; but it is to be feared, that though they may have alleviated a little the intensity of individual misfortune, they have spread the general evil over a much larger surface. It is a subject often started in conversation and mentioned always as a matter of great surprise that, notwithstanding the immense sum that is annually collected for the poor in England, there is still so much distress among them. Some think that the money must be embezzled, others that the church-wardens and overseers consume the greater part of it in dinners. All agree that somehow or other it must be very ill-managed. In short the fact that nearly three millions are collected annually for the poor and yet that their distresses are not removed is the subject of continual astonishment. But a man who sees a little below the surface of things would be very much more astonished if the fact were otherwise than it is observed to be, or even if a collection universally of eighteen shillings in the pound, instead of four, were materially to alter it. I will state a case which I hope will elucidate my meaning.

Suppose that by a subscription of the rich the eighteen pence a day which men earn now was made up five shillings, it might be imagined, perhaps, that they would then be able to live comfortably and have a piece of meat every day for their dinners. But this would be a very false conclusion. The transfer of three shillings and sixpence a day to every labourer would not increase the quantity of meat in the country. There is not at present enough for all to have a decent share. What would then be the consequence? The competition among the buyers in the market of meat would rapidly raise the price from sixpence or sevenpence, to two or three shillings in the pound, and the commodity would not be divided among many more than it is at present. When an article is scarce, and cannot be distributed to all, he that can shew the most valid patent, that is, he that offers most money, becomes the possessor. If we can suppose the competition among the buyers of meat to continue long enough for a greater number of cattle to be reared annually, this could only be done at the expense of the corn, which would be a very disadvantagous exchange, for it is well known that the country could not then support the same population, and when subsistence is scarce in proportion to the number of people, it is of little consequence whether the lowest members of the society possess eighteen pence or five shillings. They must at all events be reduced to live upon the hardest fare and in the smallest quantity.

It will be said, perhaps, that the increased number of purchasers in every article would give a spur to productive industry and that the whole produce of the island would be increased. This might in some degree be the case. But the spur that these fancied riches would give to population would more than counterbalance it, and the increased produce would be to be divided among a more than proportionably increased number of people. All this time I am supposing that the same quantity of work would be done as before. But this would not really take place. The receipt of five shillings a day, instead of eighteen pence, would make every man fancy himself comparatively rich and able to indulge himself in many hours or days of leisure. This would give a strong and immediate check to productive industry, and, in a short time, not only the nation would be poorer, but the lower classes themselves would be much more distressed than when they received only eighteen pence a day.

A collection from the rich of eighteen shillings in the pound, even if distributed in the most judicious manner, would have a little the same effect as that resulting from the supposition I have just made, and no possible contributions or sacrifices of the rich, particularly in money, could for any time prevent the recurrence of distress among the lower members of society, whoever they were. Great changes might, indeed, be made. The rich might become poor, and some of the poor rich, but a part of the society must necessarily feel a difficulty of living, and this difficulty will naturally fall on the least fortunate members.

It may at first appear strange, but I believe it is true, that I cannot by means of money raise a poor man and enable him to live much better than he did before, without proportionably depressing others in the same class. If I retrench the quantity of food consumed in my house, and give him what I have cut off, I then benefit him, without depressing any but myself and family, who, perhaps, may be well able to bear it. If I turn up a piece of uncultivated land, and give him the produce, I then benefit both him and all the members of the society, because what he before consumed is thrown into the common stock, and probably some of the new produce with it. But if I only give him money, supposing the produce of the country to remain the same, I give him a title to a larger share of that produce than formerly, which share he cannot receive without diminishing the shares of others. It is evident that this effect, in individual instances, must be so small as to be totally imperceptible; but still it must exist, as many other effects do, which, like some of the insects that people the air, elude our grosser perceptions.

Supposing the quantity of food in any country to remain the same for many years together, it is evident that this food must be divided according to the value of each man's patent, or the sum of money that he can afford to spend on this commodity so universally in request. It is a demonstrative truth, therefore, that the patents of one set of men could not be increased in value without diminishing the value of the patents of some other set of men. If the rich were to subscribe and give five shillings a day to five hundred thousand men without retrenching their own tables, no doubt can exist, that as these men would naturally live more at their ease and consume a greater quantity of provisions, there would be less food remaining to divide among the rest, and consequently each man's patent would be diminished in value or the same number of pieces of silver would purchase a smaller quantity of subsistence. (Mr Godwin calls the wealth that a man receives from his ancestors a mouldy patent. It may, I think, very properly be termed a patent, but I hardly see the propriety of calling it a mouldy one, as it is an article in such constant use.)

An increase of population without a proportional increase of food will evidently have the same effect in lowering the value of each man's patent. The food must necessarily be distributed in smaller quantities, and consequently a day's labour will purchase a smaller quantity of provisions. An increase in the price of provisions would arise either from an increase of population faster than the means of subsistence, or from a different distribution of the money of the society. The food of a country that has been long occupied, if it be increasing, increases slowly and regularly and cannot be made to answer any sudden demands, but variations in the distribution of the money of a society are not infrequently occurring, and are undoubtedly among the causes that occasion the continual variations which we observe in the price of provisions.

The poor laws of England tend to depress the general condition of the poor in these two ways. Their first obvious tendency is to increase population without increasing the food for its support. A poor man may marry with little or no prospect of being able to support a family in independence. They may be said therefore in some measure to create the poor which they maintain, and as the provisions of the country must, in consequence of the increased population, be distributed to every man in smaller proportions, it is evident that the labour of those who are not supported by parish assistance will purchase a smaller quantity of provisions than before and consequently more of them must be driven to ask for support.

Secondly, the quantity of provisions consumed in workhouses upon a part of the society that cannot in general be considered as the most valuable part diminishes the shares that would otherwise belong to more industrious and more worthy members, and thus in the same manner forces more to become dependent. If the poor in the workhouses were to live better than they now do, this new distribution of the money of the society would tend more conspicuously to depress the condition of those out of the workhouses by occasioning a rise in the price of provisions.

Fortunately for England, a spirit of independence still remains among the peasantry. The poor laws are strongly calculated to eradicate this spirit. They have succeeded in part, but had they succeeded as completely as might have been expected their pernicious tendency would not have been so long concealed.

Hard as it may appear in individual instances, dependent poverty ought to be held disgraceful. Such a stimulus seems to be absolutely necessary to promote the happiness of the great mass of mankind, and every general attempt to weaken this stimulus, however benevolent its apparent intention, will always defeat its own purpose. If men are induced to marry from a prospect of parish provision, with little or no chance of maintaining their families in independence, they are not only unjustly tempted to bring unhappiness and dependence upon themselves and children, but they are tempted, without knowing it, to injure all in the same class with themselves. A labourer who marries without being able to support a family may in some respects be considered as an enemy to all his fellow-labourers.

I feel no doubt whatever that the parish laws of England have contributed to raise the price of provisions and to lower the real price of labour. They have therefore contributed to impoverish that class of people whose only possession is their labour. It is also difficult to suppose that they have not powerfully contributed to generate that carelessness and want of frugality observable among the poor, so contrary to the disposition frequently to be remarked among petty tradesmen and small farmers. The labouring poor, to use a vulgar expression, seem always to live from hand to mouth. Their present wants employ their whole attention, and they seldom think of the future. Even when they have an opportunity of saving they seldom exercise it, but all that is beyond their present necessities goes, generally speaking, to the ale-house. The poor laws of England may therefore be said to diminish both the power and the will to save among the common people, and thus to weaken one of the strongest incentives to sobriety and industry, and consequently to happiness.

It is a general complaint among master manufacturers that high wages ruin all their workmen, but it is difficult to conceive that these men would not save a part of their high wages for the future support of their families, instead of spending it in drunkenness and dissipation, if they did not rely on parish assistance for support in case of accidents. And that the poor employed in manufactures consider this assistance as a reason why they may spend all the wages they earn and enjoy themselves while they can appears to be evident from the number of families that, upon the failure of any great manufactory, immediately fall upon the parish, when perhaps the wages earned in this manufactory while it flourished were sufficiently above the price of common country labour to have allowed them to save enough for their support till they could find some other channel for their industry.

A man who might not be deterred from going to the ale-house from the consideration that on his death, or sickness, he should leave his wife and family upon the parish might yet hesitate in thus dissipating his earnings if he were assured that, in either of these cases, his family must starve or be left to the support of casual bounty. In China, where the real as well as nominal price of labour is very low, sons are yet obliged by law to support their aged and helpless parents. Whether such a law would be advisable in this country I will not pretend to determine. But it seems at any rate highly improper, by positive institutions, which render dependent poverty so general, to weaken that disgrace, which for the best and most humane reasons ought to attach to it.

The mass of happiness among the common people cannot but be diminished when one of the strongest checks to idleness and dissipation is thus removed, and when men are thus allured to marry with little or no prospect of being able to maintain a family in independence. Every obstacle in the way of marriage must undoubtedly be considered as a species of unhappiness. But as from the laws of our nature some check to population must exist, it is better that it should be checked from a foresight of the difficulties attending a family and the fear of dependent poverty than that it should be encouraged, only to be repressed afterwards by want and sickness.

It should be remembered always that there is an essential difference between food and those wrought commodities, the raw materials of which are in great plenty. A demand for these last will not fail to create them in as great a quantity as they are wanted. The demand for food has by no means the same creative power. In a country where all the fertile spots have been seized, high offers are necessary to encourage the farmer to lay his dressing on land from which he cannot expect a profitable return for some years. And before the prospect of advantage is sufficiently great to encourage this sort of agricultural enterprise, and while the new produce is rising, great distresses may be suffered from the want of it. The demand for an increased quantity of subsistence is, with few exceptions, constant everywhere, yet we see how slowly it is answered in all those countries that have been long occupied.

The poor laws of England were undoubtedly instituted for the most benevolent purpose, but there is great reason to think that they have not succeeded in their intention. They certainly mitigate some cases of very severe distress which might otherwise occur, yet the state of the poor who are supported by parishes, considered in all its circumstances, is very far from being free from misery. But one of the principal objections to them is that for this assistance which some of the poor receive, in itself almost a doubtful blessing, the whole class of the common people of England is subjected to a set of grating, inconvenient, and tyrannical laws, totally inconsistent with the genuine spirit of the constitution. The whole business of settlements, even in its present amended state, is utterly contradictory to all ideas of freedom. The parish persecution of men whose families are likely to become chargeable, and of poor women who are near lying-in, is a most disgraceful and disgusting tyranny. And the obstructions continually occasioned in the market of labour by these laws have a constant tendency to add to the difficulties of those who are struggling to support themselves without assistance.

These evils attendant on the poor laws are in some degree irremediable. If assistance be to be distributed to a certain class of people, a power must be given somewhere of discriminating the proper objects and of managing the concerns of the institutions that are necessary, but any great interference with the affairs of other people is a species of tyranny, and in the common course of things the exercise of this power may be expected to become grating to those who are driven to ask for support. The tyranny of Justices, Churchwardens, and Overseers, is a common complaint among the poor, but the fault does not lie so much in these persons, who probably, before they were in power, were not worse than other people, but in the nature of all such institutions.

The evil is perhaps gone too far to be remedied, but I feel little doubt in my own mind that if the poor laws had never existed, though there might have been a few more instances of very severe distress, yet that the aggregate mass of happiness among the common people would have been much greater than it is at present.

Mr Pitt's Poor Bill has the appearance of being framed with benevolent intentions, and the clamour raised against it was in many respects ill directed, and unreasonable. But it must be confessed that it possesses in a high degree the great and radical defect of all systems of the kind, that of tending to increase population without increasing the means for its support, and thus to depress the condition of those that are not supported by parishes, and, consequently, to create more poor.

To remove the wants of the lower classes of society is indeed an arduous task. The truth is that the pressure of distress on this part of a community is an evil so deeply seated that no human ingenuity can reach it. Were I to propose a palliative, and palliatives are all that the nature of the case will admit, it should be, in the first place, the total abolition of all the present parish-laws. This would at any rate give liberty and freedom of action to the peasantry of England, which they can hardly be said to possess at present. They would then be able to settle without interruption, wherever there was a prospect of a greater plenty of work and a higher price for labour. The market of labour would then be free, and those obstacles removed which, as things are now, often for a considerable time prevent the price from rising according to the demand.

Secondly, premiums might be given for turning up fresh land, and all possible encouragements held out to agriculture above manufactures, and to tillage above grazing. Every endeavour should be used to weaken and destroy all those institutions relating to corporations, apprenticeships, etc., which cause the labours of agriculture to be worse paid than the labours of trade and manufactures. For a country can never produce its proper quantity of food while these distinctions remain in favour of artisans. Such encouragements to agriculture would tend to furnish the market with an increasing quantity of healthy work, and at the same time, by augmenting the produce of the country, would raise the comparative price of labour and ameliorate the condition of the labourer. Being now in better circumstances, and seeing no prospect of parish assistance, he would be more able, as well as more inclined, to enter into associations for providing against the sickness of himself or family.

Lastly, for cases of extreme distress, county workhouses might be established, supported by rates upon the whole kingdom, and free for persons of all counties, and indeed of all nations. The fare should be hard, and those that were able obliged to work. It would be desirable that they should not be considered as comfortable asylums in all difficulties, but merely as places where severe distress might find some alleviation. A part of these houses might be separated, or others built for a most beneficial purpose, which has not been infrequently taken notice of, that of providing a place where any person, whether native or foreigner, might do a day's work at all times and receive the market price for it. Many cases would undoubtedly be left for the exertion of individual benevolence.

A plan of this kind, the preliminary of which should be an abolition of all the present parish laws, seems to be the best calculated to increase the mass of happiness among the common people of England. To prevent the recurrence of misery, is alas! beyond the power of man. In the vain endeavour to attain what in the nature of things is impossible, we now sacrifice not only possible but certain benefits. We tell the common people that if they will submit to a code of tyrannical regulations, they shall never be in want. They do submit to these regulations. They perform their part of the contract, but we do not, nay cannot, perform ours, and thus the poor sacrifice the valuable blessing of liberty and receive nothing that can be called an equivalent in return.

Notwithstanding, then, the institution of the poor laws in England, I think it will be allowed that considering the state of the lower classes altogether, both in the towns and in the country, the distresses which they suffer from the want of proper and sufficient food, from hard labour and unwholesome habitations, must operate as a constant check to incipient population.

To these two great checks to population, in all long occupied countries, which I have called the preventive and the positive checks, may be added vicious customs with respect to women, great cities, unwholesome manufactures, luxury, pestilence, and war.

All these checks may be fairly resolved into misery and vice. And that these are the true causes of the slow increase of population in all the states of modern Europe, will appear sufficiently evident from the comparatively rapid increase that has invariably taken place whenever these causes have been in any considerable degree removed.

Factory Inquiry Commission, 1833   3

Much of Britain's force as the leading industrial nation in the 19th century was built on the success of the factories comprising the textile industry, which in turn was built on the exploitation of labour, including the work of children. In the early years of industrial development the working conditions of factories went unregulated. Factory legislation was first passed by parliament in 1802 (the Health and Morals of Apprentices Act) seeking to ameliorate the conditions of the 'apprentices' (children from the age of seven) who had been placed into the hands of cotton mill owners from pauper institutions; however, the legislation did not cover those working in woollen mills.

Here we present an extract from the report of the Factory Inquiry Commissioners, the full title of which is: *First Report of the Central Board of His Majesty's Commissioners appointed to collect Information in the Manufacturing Districts, as to the Employment of children in factories, and as to the Propriety and means of curtailing the hours of their labour: with Minutes of Evidence, and Reports by the District Commissioners.* Information about the conditions of the workers presented in this report was used as a basis for subsequent legislation regarding working conditions in factories, particularly relating to the employment of children and the effects on their moral and physical health. Despite there being many proponents of the continued use of child labour, legislation in 1833 prohibited the employment in mills of children under the age of nine and those under 18 could not work more than 12 hours a day. It was not until 1847 that the general workday for women and children in textile factories was set at 10 hours, and it was another 30 years before this applied to all factories.

Factory Inquiry Commission Report (1833)

Children in factories

... Having thus considered the general treatment of children in factories, and the collateral circumstances under which their employment is carried on, and which influence in no inconsiderable degree the effects of that employment, we come now to consider what those effects really are, as far as they are ascertained by the evidence collected under the present investigation.

The effects of factory labour on children are immediate and remote: the immediate effects are fatigue, sleepiness, and pain; the remote effects, such at least as are usually conceived to result from it, are, deterioration of the physical constitution, deformity, disease, and deficient mental instruction and moral culture.

1. The degree of fatigue produced on children by ordinary factory labour may be gathered from their own account of their feelings, and from the statements of parents, adult operatives, overlookers, and proprietors.

The statements of the children, and more especially of the younger children, as to their own feeling of fatigue, may be said to be uniform. The intensity of the feeling is influenced, without doubt, by the age of the child, and the constitutional robustness or feebleness of the individual; but the feeling itself is always the same, and differs only in degree. The expressions of fatigue are the strongest and the most constant on the part of the young children employed in the factories in Scotland, because there the ordinary hours of work are in general longer by an hour or an hour and a quarter than in the factories of England. We have been struck with the perfect uniformity of the answers returned to the Commissioners by the young workers in this country, in the largest and best regulated factories as well as in the smaller and less advantageously conducted. In fact, whether the factory be in the pure air of the country, or in the large town; under the best or the worst management; and whatever be the nature of the work, whether light or laborious; or the kind of treatment, whether considerate and gentle or strict and harsh; the account of the child, when questioned as to its feeling of fatigue, is the same. The answer always being "Sick-tired, especially in the winter nights." "So tired when she leaves the mill that she can do nothing." "Feels so tired, she throws herself down when she gangs hame, no caring what she does." "Often much tired, and feels sore, standing so long on her legs." "Often so tired she could not eat her supper." "Night and morning very tired; has two sisters in the mill; has heard them complain to her mother, and she says they must work." "When the tow is coarse, we are so tired we are not able to set one "foot by the other." "Whiles I do not know what to do with myself, as tired every morning as I can be."

Young persons of more advanced age, speaking of their own feelings when younger, give to the Commissioners such representations as the following: "Many a time has been so fatigued that she could hardly take off her clothes at night, or put them on in the morning; her mother would be raging at her, because when she sat down she could not get up again through the house." "Looks on the long hours as a great bondage." "Thinks they are no much better than the Israelites in Egypt, and their life is no pleasure to them." "When a child, was so tired that she could seldom eat her supper, and never awoke of herself." "Are the hours to be shortened?" earnestly demanded one of these girls of the Commissioner who was examining her, "for they are too long."

The truth of the account given by the children of the fatigue they experience by the ordinary labour of the factory is confirmed by the testimony of their parents. In general the representation made by parents is like the following: "Her children come home, so tired and worn out they can hardly eat their supper." "Has often seen his daughter come home in the evening so fatigued that she would go to bed supperless." "Has seen the young workers absolutely oppressed, and unable to sit down or rise up; this has happened to his own children."

These statements are confirmed by the evidence of the adult operatives. The depositions of the witnesses of this class are to the effect that "the younger workers are greatly fatigued;" that "children are often very swere (unwilling) in the mornings;" that "children are quite tired out;" that "the long hours exhaust the workers, especially the young ones, to such a degree that they can hardly walk home;" that "young workers are absolutely oppressed, and so tired as to be unable to sit down or rise up;" that "younger workers are so tired they often cannot raise their hands to their head;" that "all the children are very keen for shorter hours thinking them now such bondage that they might as well be in a prison;" that "the children, when engaged in their regular work, are often exhausted beyond what can be expressed;" that "the sufferings of the children absolutely require that the hours should be shortened."

The depositions of the overlookers are to the same effect; namely, that though the children may not complain, yet that they seem tired and sleepy, and happy to get out of doors to play themselves. That "the work overtires workers in general." "Often sees the children very tired and very stiff–like." "Is entirely of the opinion, after real experience, that the hours of labour are far too long for the children, for their health and education; has from twenty-two to twenty-four boys under his charge, from nine to about fourteen years old; and they are generally much tired at night, always anxious, asking if it be near the mill stopping." "Never knew a single worker among the children that did not complain of the long hours which prevent them from getting education, and from getting health in the open air."

The managers in like manner state that "the labour exhausts the children;" that "workers are tired in the evening;" that "children inquire anxiously for the hour of stopping;" and admissions to the same effect on the part of managers and proprietors will be found in every part of the Scotch depositions.

In the north-eastern district the evidence is equally complete that the fatigue of the young workers is great. "I have known the children" says one witness, "hide themselves in the stove 'mong, the wool, so that they should not go home when the work was over, when we have worked till ten or eleven. I have seen six or eight fetched out of the stove and beat home; beat out of the mill however. I do not know why they should hide themselves, unless it was that they were too tired to go home."

"Many a one I have had to rouse in the last hour when the work is very slack, from fatigue." "The children were very much jaded, especially when we worked late at night." "The children bore the long hours very ill indeed." "Exhausted in body and depressed in mind by the length of the hours and the height of the temperature." "I found when I was an overlooker", that "after the children from eight to twelve years had worked eight or nine or ten hours they were nearly ready to faint; some were asleep; some were only kept to work by being spoken to, or by a little chastisement, to make them jump up. I was sometimes obliged to chastise them when they were almost fainting, and it hurt my feelings; then they would sprint up and work pretty well for another hour; but the last two or three hours were my hardest work, for they then got so exhausted." "I have never seen fathers carrying their children backwards nor forwards to the factories, but I have seen children apparently under nine, and from nine to twelve years of age, going to the factories at five in the morning, almost asleep in the streets."

"Some children do appear fatigued and some do not." "I have noticed the drawers exhausted beyond what I could express." "Many times the drawers are worked beyond their strength." There is however a striking contrast in the statements of all the witnesses relative to the fatigue of the children in the factories of the western district, in which the hours of labour for children are so much shorter than in the other factories of the kingdom.

2. Children complain as much of sleepiness as of fatigue. "Often feels so sleepy that he cannot keep his eyes open." "Longs for the mill's stopping, is so sleepy." "Often falls asleep while sitting, sometimes while standing." "Her little sister falls asleep, and they wake her by a cry." "Has two younger sisters in the mill; they fall asleep directly they get home." "Was up before four this morning, which made her fall asleep when the mill was inspected at one today by the Factory Commissioners; often so tired at night she falls asleep before leaving the mill."

"I always found it more difficult to keep my piecers awake the last hours of a winter's evening. I have told the master and I have been told by him that I did not half hide them. This was when they worked from six to eight." "I have seen them fall asleep, and they have been performing their work with their hands while they were asleep, after the billey had stopped, when their work was over. I have stopped and looked at them for two minutes, going through the motions of piecening fast asleep, when there was really no work to do, and they were really doing nothing. I believe when we have been working long hours, that they have never been washed, but on a Saturday night, for weeks together." "Children at night are so fatigued that they are asleep often as soon as they sit down, so that it is impossible to waken them to sense enough to wash themselves, or scarcely to eat a bit of supper, being so stupid in sleep. I experience it by my own child, and I did myself when a child for once I fell asleep, even on my knees to pray on my bedside, and slept a length of time till the family came to bed." Overlookers and managers in innumerable instances depose to the same effect.

3. Pains in the limbs, back, loins, and side are frequent, but not as frequent as fatigue and drowsiness. The frequency and severity of the pain uniformly bears a strict relation to the tender age of the child and the severity of the labour. Pain is seldom complained of when the labour did not commence until the age of nine, and was not immoderate. Girls suffer from pain more commonly than boys, and up to a more advanced age; though occasionally men, and not infrequently young women, and women beyond the meridian of life, complain of pain, yet there is evidence that the youngest children are so distressed by pain of their feet, in consequence of the long standing, that they sometimes throw off their shoes, and so take cold. "Feet feel so sair that they make him greet." "Was quite well when she went to the mill, but the confinement brought on a complaint in her head, and her left side is now pained." "Many nights I do not get a wink of sleep for the pain." "At first suffered so much from the pain

that he could hardly sleep, but it went off." "Knee failed from excessive labour; severe pains and aches would come on, particularly in the morning; it was better in the evening; felt no pains in any other parts. There were two or three complaining at the same time of their knees aching." "I have seen children under eighteen years of age before six at night, their legs has hurt them to that degree that they have many a time been crying."

4. Swelling of the feet is a still more frequent source of suffering. "Obliged to bathe her feet to subdue the swelling." "The long standing gives her swelled feet and ancles, and fatigues her so much that sometimes does nae ken how to get to her bed." "Night and morning her legs swell and are often very painful." That this affection is common is confirmed by the concurrent statements of parents, operatives, overlookers, and managers.

5. That this excessive fatigue, privation of sleep, pain in various parts of the body, and swelling of the feet experienced by the young workers, coupled with the constant standing, the peculiar attitudes of the body, and the peculiar motions of the limbs required in the labour of the factory, together with the elevated temperature, and the impure atmosphere in which that labour is often carried on, do sometimes ultimately terminate in the production of serious, permanent, and incurable disease, appears to us to be established. From cases detailed in the evidence, and the accuracy of which has been strictly investigated, we do not conceive it to be possible to arrive at any other conclusion. The evidence, especially from Dundee and Glasgow, from Leicester, Nottingham, Leeds, and Bradford, from Manchester and Stockport, in a word, from all the great manufacturing towns, with the exception, perhaps, of those in the western district, in which there is little indication of disease produced by early and excessive labour, shows that grievous and incurable maladies do result in young persons from labour commenced in the factory at the age at which it is at present not uncommon to begin it, and continued for the number of hours during which it is not unusual to protract it.

6. From the same evidence it appears, that the physical evil inflicted on children by factory labour, when commenced as early and continued as long as it now is, is not the only evil sustained by them. From the statements and depositions of witnesses of all classes it appears, that even when the employment of children at so early an age, and for so many hours as is customary at present, produces no manifest bodily disease, yet in the great majority of cases it incapacitates them from receiving instruction. On this head the statements of the children themselves must be admitted to be of some importance; and it will be found that the young children very generally declare that

they are too much fatigued to attend school, even when a school is provided for them. This is more uniformly the declaration of the children in the factories of Scotland than in those of England. The evidence of other witnesses, both as to the capacity of the children for receiving instruction, and as to their actual state in regard to education, is conflicting. Few will be prepared to expect the statements that will be found on this head in regard to Scotland, where the education of the children is neglected to a far greater extent than is commonly believed; where only a very small number can write; where, though perhaps the majority can read, many cannot; and where, with some honourable exceptions, it seems certain that the care once bestowed on the instruction of the young has ceased to be exemplary. The reports of the Commissioners for Scotland, who will be found to have kept this subject continually before their view, are decisive on this head. "Many of the persons sworn could not write nor sign their depositions. The reports mark the signatures in every case where the parties could write. I suspect the want of education so general on the part of these people, which has surprised me, is to be attributed to their being for so long a period of the day confined to the factories." "The overseers of the small mills, when the proprietors are absent, almost uniformly, as the Central Board will notice, declare their aversion to the present long hours of working, as injurious to the health of the workers, and as rendering their education impossible." "Still the employment of workers in factories cannot, where proper regulations are attended to, be in most cases with propriety termed an unhealthy one; and it would therefore seem that the long confinement of labour is more injurious to them, in preventing them from being sufficiently educated, and of course sufficiently instructed in their moral duties, than in other respects. Here too, although there is abundance of evidence from clergymen, as well as from teachers, of a conflicting description, I think it upon the whole impossible to doubt, that the young workers must be so much fatigued with the very long hours of labour, that they cannot be so fit to receive instruction as other young people, and that they have too little time for being at school, even to enable them to learn to read, write, and to understand accounts tolerably. Want of education cannot fail to have an unfavourable influence on their morals."

"The number that can write is very small; many here, as elsewhere, asserting while under examination they could, and afterwards being unable to write their own signatures."

"Thinks as a class they are very deficient in learning. Knows many twenty years old that are incapable of reading a chapter of the New Testament. Many cannot write at all. In some cases evening schools have been established, but from the long hours the girls are too exhausted to derive much advantage. On some occasions when he has requested parents to send their children, they have answered, that they were too tired, and were more fit for their bed than for the Bible. Has often heard the working people say that they are prepared to forego some of their wages for the sake of obtaining the time of educating their children." "Not changed in the opinion given by him (No 214 of the Report of Evidence) that the great length of labour during the day in a great measure precludes all adequate instruction in the evening, and that there are a great many children who would willingly go to school if they were earlier dismissed. Believes that there is not a single school carried on by a manufacturer in Aberdeen; that the only opportunities afforded to the children were set up within these seven years by two clergymen; that in these two schools the girls who attend regularly are generally superior in character to those who do not so attend; that therefore the circumstance of a number of those being able to read and write ought not to be taken as a specimen of the advancement of the whole; at the same time a considerable portion or those who do attend are unable to read, and a still larger are unable to write." "Has been for the last sixteen years well acquainted with the working population of Glasgow, and has perceived a great change effected for the worse in the moral habits and education of the children. About twelve or fourteen years ago it was a very rare occurrence to meet with a child that could not read; whilst very much the contrary is the case now. About three years ago a number of girls from Messrs Muir, Brown, & Co's, of the ages of sixteen or seventeen, attended for the first time his school, when, to his surprise, he found, that they could scarcely read at all. He found that each of these had formerly learnt to read, but had forgotten their knowledge. After a short attendance, shame at not being equally instructed with much younger children drove them away again. The present body of master manufacturers, with few exceptions, seem to entertain a very different idea of the necessity of having schools attached to their establishments than that which influenced them a few years back. Knows of only one evening school attached to a factory in Glasgow; and the result of that disregard of education is, that the children, with some exceptions, employed in public works, drink, smoke, curse and swear, and are generally very profligate."

Dr Stevenson Macgill, professor of divinity in the university of Glasgow, states "that the time for education is in general too short; that were it longer, fatigue renders the scholars capable of learning but little; that these observations apply principally to the manufactories in populous cities and their neighbourhood. That in several large manufactories and cotton mills carried on in healthy situations, where the people form small villages, have their houses and small gardens, are all known and superintended, and have their chaplains and teachers, a very different order of things takes place; at the same time he must express his opinion even respecting these, that the children in general are obliged to work at too early an age; that the health of body and mind requires a longer period to be allotted for a good education, and for those relaxations which are necessary to the well-being of early youth."

One of the great evils to which people employed in factories are exposed is, the danger of receiving serious and even fatal injury from the machinery. It does not seem possible, by any precautions that are practicable, to remove this danger altogether. There are factories in which everything is done that it seems practicable to do to reduce this danger to the least possible amount, and with such success that no serious accident happens for years together. By the returns which we have received, however, it appears that there are other factories, and that these are by no means few in number, not confined to the smaller mills, in which serious accidents are continually occurring, and in which, notwithstanding, dangerous parts of the machinery are allowed to remain unfenced. The greater the carelessness of the proprietors in neglecting sufficiently to fence the machinery, and the greater the number of accidents, the less their sympathy with the sufferers. In factories in which precaution is taken to prevent accidents care is taken of the workpeople when they do occur, and a desire is shown to make what compensation may be possible. But it appears in evidence that cases frequently occur in which the workpeople are abandoned from the moment that an accident occurs; their wages are stopped, no medical attendance is provided, and whatever the extent of the injury no compensation is afforded.

From the whole of the evidence laid before us of which we have thus endeavoured to exhibit the material points we find

1st That the children employed in all the principal branches of manufacture throughout the kingdom work during the same number of hours as the adults.

2nd That the effects of labour during such hours are, in a great number of cases,

Permanent deterioration of the physical constitution:

The production of disease often wholly irremediable: and

The partial or entire exclusion (by reason of excessive fatigue) from the means of obtaining adequate education and acquiring useful habits, or of profiting by those means when afforded.

3rd That at the age when children suffer these injuries from the labour they undergo, they are not free agents, but are let out to hire, the wages they earn being received and appropriated by their parents and guardians.

William Farr, 1807-83 **4**

U nlike many of his now well-known contemporaries, William Farr did not have an affluent upbringing. He was, however, at an early age adopted from his poor family and was able to receive schooling and study medicine in Paris. He taught himself mathematics and regularly published in the newly established journal, *The Lancet*. In 1839 he was appointed to the government's General Register Office as superintendent for England. Before his appointment the Registrar's Office had mainly concerned itself with simply collecting birth, marriages and death registrations. Farr combined this information with the decennial censuses of population to attempt to both describe more fully and to begin to explain the patterns that these registrations revealed. In doing this he has been credited as being one of the founders of epidemiology.

William Farr produced an enormous volume of work and developed many of the analytical methods himself. For instance he wrote and worked in detail on the cholera epidemics of his time, and corresponded greatly with Florence Nightingale and John Snow. His work was later used by Edwin Chadwick and Friedrich Engels. He developed the precursor for the International Classification of Diseases used today and introduced the standardised mortality ratio.

Farr is best known for his work on vital statistics. Here we have taken one short extract from his work on mortality which was reproduced in a memorial volume. In this piece Farr argues that the health of the best-off in society should be used to measure the numbers of people who are dying unnecessarily.

Farr, W. (1837, 1885[*]) *Vital statistics: A memorial volume of selections from the reports and writings of William Farr*

* Editors' note: *Vital statistics* was originally published in 1837. It was reprinted in a memorial volume in 1885.

Healthy District Mortality. – The proportion of the deaths in a given time to a given population is not an exact measure of its vitality; the mortality being very different at different ages, and the proportional numbers of young and old being disturbed by excesses of births over deaths, and by emigration, the deaths in two equal populations may vary from differences in their composition as to age, without implying any real differences in the vitality. A disturbance may also be produced from disproportions in the sexes. Under ordinary circumstances the annual rate of mortality, however, at all ages, serves as a sufficiently accurate measure of the relative sanitary condition of the population; and where this is insufficient, the mortality at quinquennial or decennial periods of life may be separately determined.

The mortality of England and Wales in 1857 has been compared with the mortality of England and Wales in the ten previous years, and it may be compared with the mortality (22.36 per 1,000) in the 19 years 1838-56. It is below that average. But is that average itself, it may be asked, the true standard? What is the natural rate of mortality among Englishmen, under favourable sanitary conditions? Under such conditions how long do they live? How many of them die annually? No direct answer can be given to these questions. No large body of Englishmen is breathing pure air, living on a perfectly sound diet, free from all defilement, and free from vice, exercising duly the mind and body generation after generation. We can point to no model city – to no model caste; we can discover no model parish in the country. In the matter of health we are all very ignorant or desperately negligent. What courses then remain open to the inquirer? One only. The mortality of the districts of England in which the sanitary conditions are the least unfavourable, can be employed as the standard measure until happier times supply the real standard of vitality. Sixty-four districts in various parts of the country are found where the mortality of the people ranged on an average extending over ten years from *fifteen to seventeen* deaths in 1,000 living. This is not an accidental event; the mortality only fluctuates in such places slightly from year to year, and the death rate under the same circumstances will not be exceeded. The people dwell in sixty-four districts extending over 4,797,315 acres, and their number at the last

Census was 973,070. Undoubtedly the sanitary conditions in which they live are in many respects favourable. They generally follow agricultural pursuits; and they are scattered thinly over an open country, often on high ground, so that the impurities which they produce are dispersed and diluted in the air and water. They do not breathe each other's exhalations in theatres and churches. They do not drink water sullied by impurities. They do not drink poison in gin palaces. Their minds are not overwrought by dissipation, passion, intellectual effort. But visit their dwellings, and amidst much that is most commendable you will discover many sources of insalubrity. The bed-rooms are often small, close, crowded; personal cleanliness is not much studied; the dirty pig and the filth of various kinds lie here in close proximity to the house; the land there is imperfectly drained; in the winter, clothing, fuel, and food are scantily enjoyed in all large or improvident families; ignorance yields its baneful fruits; medical advice is ill supplied or unskilful. Yet the annual mortality per 1,000 of this million men, women, and children, year after year, does not exceed 17. Is it not evident that under more favourable auspices the death rate would be still lighter? Under such sanitary conditions as are known, and with all the mechanical appliances existing, can we not imagine a community living a healthier life than these isolated people?

Without affirming on physiological grounds that man was created to live a destined number of years, or go through a series of changes which are only completed in eighty, ninety, or a hundred years, experience furnishes us with a standard which can only be said to be too high. 17 in 1,000 is supplied as a standard by experience. Here we stand upon the actual. Any deaths in a people exceeding 17 in 1,000 annually are unnatural deaths. If the people were shot, drowned, burnt, poisoned by strychnine, their deaths would not be more unnatural than the deaths wrought clandestinely by disease in excess of the quota of natural death; that is, in excess of *seventeen* deaths in 1,000 living.

But it may be said that this standard cannot fairly be applied to determine the excessive mortality of large towns, which can never become so healthy as the country. How healthy towns may become we do not know. It is only proved that the population of parts of many towns experiences a mortality little above the natural standard; and that the prevalent diseases are referable to causes which evidently from their nature admit of removal. The question, however, is not, Does the excessive mortality admit of removal? but, does it exist? – and these two questions have no logical connection. The existence of the excess is established by comparing the actual mortality with the standard. Then the chief causes of the excessive mortality are now ascertained; and if the people have done all they can to remove them, the residual excess may be held to be inevitable. But what is inevitable at one time and in one place is not inevitable at other times and in other places. It is therefore of the utmost importance to keep steadily in view all the excessive mortality over and above that which is implied in the great decree: "It is appointed unto man once to die." In London during the sixteenth century the population lived about twenty years on an average, and 50 died out of 1,000 living; consequently the excess over 17 was 33. That this excess was not inevitable is now demonstrated; for, with a great increase in number, the population now lives about 37 years, and the mortality has fallen to 25 in 1,000. Is the excess of 8 deaths a year among every 1,000 living inevitable? This cannot be admitted for a moment, if we regard only the imperfect state of those sanitary arrangements which the public authorities of London have within their power. Nor can it be admitted that the excess of 5 deaths – or 22 deaths instead of 17 – a year in every 1,000 living is inevitable in England and Wales, with evidence before our eyes of the same violations of the laws of nature in every district.

Whether the causes admit or do not admit of removal, the fact, then, is incontestable, and must not be lost sight of, that the excess of deaths in England and Wales over those from causes which exist in sixty-four districts was 91,652 in the year 1857; for 419,815 persons died in that year, and only about 328,163 persons would have died had the mortality not exceeded the standard of 17 deaths in 1,000 living. – (20th Annual Report, pp xxxv-xl.)

Exceptionally Healthy Districts, 1841-70. – There are two districts in England exceptionally healthy; Glendale and Rothbury.[1] Their annual mortality during the 30 years 1841-70 was at the low average rate of 15 per 1,000.

In Rothbury, a third of the population is employed in healthy occupations connected with agriculture. The remarkable low death-rates, ruling at the different ages, are shown in the subjoined table, where they are compared with the rates in the healthiest parts of England [see table on p 37].

The District of Rothbury contains several very large ancient parishes. That of Alwinton on the southern slopes of the Cheviots extends over 46,681 acres, and comprises 16 townships. The population of this parish decreased from 1,325 in 1861 to 1,205 in 1871, when 39 births and only 9 deaths were registered, so the birth-rate of the parish in 1871 was 32.4 per 1,000 of population, whereas the death-rate was but 7.5 per 1,000.

The nine deaths registered during that year included two of infants under one of age, one of a person 25 years, three aged 50 and under 60, one aged 68 years, and another aged 92 years.

[1] In the Rothbury district the village of Harbottle has 120 inhabitants, and Dr Frank Richardson states that among them are 37 children under 14 years of age. During the last 20 years no child has died. He gives another instance of the vitality of children in the parish.

"A farmer and his three shepherds, who have occupied their present situations nearly 30 years, have among them 47 children, and not a single death has occurred in these families. The inhabitants have abundance of plain substantial food, excellent water, good residences as a rule, and regular but not severe work in a pure bracing atmosphere; they are highly intelligent and generally abstemious. I am indebted to the Rev A. Proctor, who has been upwards of 40 years the esteemed vicar, for the corroboration of the statistics of this parish which I have now given you."

Such exceptional cases are well worthy of study; and our young health officers may learn a useful lesson of hygiene from these farmers and shepherds living on the southern slopes of the Cheviot Hills. Dr Benjamin Richardson can scarcely hope that the mothers of his Hygiea will be more successful in rearing children – their lambs – than these shepherds' wives.

In the year 1874 only six deaths were registered, and assuming the population to have been stationary since 1871, the mortality was at the rate of only 5 per 1,000 (37th Annual Report, pp. xxi-xxii).

Healthy and Unhealthy Districts of England, 1838-44. – Although no regular Registers of Deaths were kept before the Reformation, the chronicles show clearly enough that England has been periodically devastated by famines and plagues from the earliest times. A large proportion of the population of the island has been more than once swept away by these visitations. The great plagues of the sixth and seventh centuries – which destroyed, according to some estimates, half the inhabitants of the Eastern empire – extended to Britain. Besides the Black Death in the fourteenth century, the sweating sickness of the sixteenth century, and the plagues of the seventeenth century, terminating in the plague of 1665, described in detail by the historians – a long catalogue of famines and epidemics may be given, which, though briefly and imperfectly noticed in the chronicles, were perhaps not much less fatal.

After the Revolution the great plagues ceased; but the mortality was kept up by typhus, small-pox, influenza, and other zymotic diseases. The writings of Mead, Pringle, Lind, Blane, Jackson, Price, and Priestley, – the sanitary improvements in the navy, the army, and the prisons, – as well as the discovery of vaccination by Jenner, – all conduced to the diffusion of the sound doctrines of public health, and had a practical effect, which, with the improved condition of the poorer

Ages	Mean population 1861-71	Rothbury District Deaths in the 10 years, 1861-70	Annual mortality Deaths to 1,000 living	Healthy districts of England Annual mortality Deaths to 1,000 living 1849-53	Division II South Eastern counties Annual mortality Deaths to 1,000 living 1861-70
All ages	7,114	1,105	15.5	17.5	19.1
0-	931	270	29.0	40.4	51.1
5-	834	56	6.7	6.9	6.5
10-	751	34	4.5	4.3	3.9
15-	1,316	60	4.6	7.3	6.6
25-	956	69	7.2	8.6	9.3
35-	768	74	9.6	9.6	11.9
45-	627	65	10.4	12.3	15.1
55-	486	101	20.8	22.3	25.7
65-	293	150	51.2	52.3	56.1
75 and upwards	152	226	148.7	145.3	151.5

classes, led to a greatly reduced mortality in the present century. Since 1816 the returns indicate a retrograde movement. The mortality has apparently increased. Influenza has been several times epidemic, and the Asiatic cholera reached England, and cut off several thousands of the inhabitants in 1832. It reappeared and prevailed again, as we have seen, with no mitigated violence, in 1849.

The health of all parts of the kingdom is not equally bad. Some districts are infested by epidemics constantly recurring; the people are immersed in an atmosphere that weakens their powers, troubles their functions, and shortens their lives. Other localities are so favourably circumstanced that great numbers attain old age in the enjoyment of all their faculties, and suffer rarely from epidemics. The variations in the mortality are seen in the tables of the Ninth Annual Report. The rate of mortality is calculated on 2,436,648 deaths in the 7 years 1838-44; and on the population taken at the census of 1841, in the middle of the period. On tracing over 324 sub-divisions of the country, the force of death in males and females of different ages, the most remarkable differences are discovered. Here of 1,000 young children under 5 years of age *forty* die, there a *hundred and twenty* die annually; here, of 1,000 men of mature age (35-45) *nine* die, there *nineteen* die yearly; of 1,000 men of 45-55 years of age *twelve* die in one district, *thirty* in another; at the more advanced ages of the next decennium (55-65) *twenty-four* die annually in one, *fifty* in another district: of 1,000 females of all ages without distinction, 14 die annually in three districts, 15 die in eighteen districts, 17 (or less) in forty-eight districts. And in strong contrast, 23 in 1,000 females die in twenty districts, 26 in 1,000 in three districts, 27 in seven districts, 31 in two districts.

The mortality at all ages, without distinction, differs much less than the mortality of children, and less even than the mortality of men and women of the age of 35 and upwards in the several parts of the country. The population from the age of 15 to 35 is unsettled; at that age the emigration of servants and artizans from the country to the towns takes place; and as consumption, the disease then most fatal, is slow in its course, its victims in many cases retreat from the towns to their parents' homes in the villages to die. And the death is registered where it happens, not where the fatal disease began, so that, on comparison, it is told twice in favour of the towns; once in being withdrawn from the town register, and a second time in being added to the country register, to which it does not properly belong.

Independently of external causes, and by the force of a natural law, the mortality varies at different periods of life; so that the rate of dying in two mixed populations may differ according to the varying proportions of children, young persons, or old people. The series of tables shows the rate of mortality at six periods of life, under five years, at 10-15, 35-45, 45-55, 55-65, and 65-75. It is shown in the extreme cases, that when the general mortality is either high or low, the mortality at nearly all these ages is high or low; and a collation of the whole leaves little doubt on the question of the relative insalubrity of the various parts of the country.

Upon looking generally at the health of the population, it will be found that people suffer most in the great town districts. Liverpool and Manchester are the places of highest mortality, then follow some of the districts of London, Merthyr Tydfil, Bristol, South Shields, Macclesfield, Hull, several districts of Lancashire, Sheffield, Nottingham, Leicester, Stoke-upon-Trent, Wolstanton and Burslem, Leeds, Newcastle-on-Tyne, Birmingham, Coventry, Wolverhampton, Newcastle-under-Lyme, Derby, Salisbury, Northampton, Bradford, Gateshead, Shrewsbury, Walsall, Norwich, Colchester, Sunderland, Exeter, Worcester, Bedford, Dudley, Bath, Ipswich, Carlisle, Lancaster, Cambridge, Aylesbury, Maidstone, Canterbury, Wycombe, Gloucester, Wakefield, and Reading.

The mortality is not increased equally at every age in these districts. And it varies considerably in the two sexes; the returns for childhood, manhood, and old age, males and females, conspire in proving the prevalence of general causes of insalubrity operating with different degrees of intensity, but with much greater force than in other parts of the country.

It is probable that under any circumstances a certain number of children born will never reach maturity; that in a numerous population there will every year be deaths at all ages, from internal or external causes. In the present state of mankind it is impossible to say how small the inevitable loss by death is, as in every place, and among all classes of people, certain known sources of insalubrity exist, which unquestionably account for a part of the prevalent mortality. The annual mortality of males and females of all ages in England is at the rate of 22 in 1,000; in Glendale, Bellingham, and Haltwhistle, three districts of Northumberland, the mortality in the same seven years was 14 in 1,000. Not to take an extreme case, a group of 21 statistical districts has been formed, and a table of the mean mortality has been deduced from the whole; which, as it represents the lowest rates of mortality hitherto observed, over a period of seven years in a considerable population, may for the present be called the mortality of man from natural causes. The excess of mortality over this standard may be unhesitatingly referred to artificial, unnecessary causes, in such tables as the following, showing the waste of life and health in 40 town and city districts. An equal population (100,000) is taken at six ages; and it will be observed that the insalubrity tells with most effect against childhood: the mortality under 5 years of age is raised 124 per cent; in manhood it is raised 77, 83, 70 per cent at three ages, and in puberty and old age 45 per cent. Out of *a given number of men*, at different ages, the deaths by unnatural causes increase every year; for the table shows that to 100,000 living in each period, the deaths are 700 by unnatural causes at the age of 35-45; and 1,060 at 45-55; 1,682 at 55-65. The rate of mortality is raised in a less ratio, but to a much greater extent in old than in middle age, for the natural mortality in old age is high. The absolute number of deaths is greatest in infancy, as the number of old persons living is small compared with the number of children living in every population; so that whether the ratio of increase on the natural rate of mortality, the actual increase in the rate of mortality, or the number of deaths be regarded, children are the most cruelly treated by the destroyer. Yet of every 17 men who die in towns, 7 die by unnatural causes; and of 1,000 living at the age of 40, *seven* die; at the age of 50, *eleven* die; at the age of 60, *seventeen* die; at the age of 70, *twenty-six* die every year from causes evidently external and unnatural. Women escape with the least loss; yet five in every fifteen annual deaths would not happen in healthy places.

It often happens that unhealthy and healthy villages, streets, parishes, and towns are in immediate juxtaposition; and constitute parts of the same district. The effect of this admixture on the results is, that the unhealthy districts are *less unhealthy*, and experience a lower rate of mortality than they would if all the healthy parts were eliminated. Upon the other hand, the healthy districts are made to appear less healthy than they would if they consisted only of healthy places, inhabited by people in good circumstances, under a proper course of diet, discipline, and exercise. The difference in the mortality of the two classes of districts is therefore understated. (Cholera Report, 1849; pp v-vi.)

Annual rate of mortality per cent [or per 100,000] in healthy and unhealthy districts, also the excess of mortality due to unhealthiness

Age	Males			Females		
	Low	High	Excess	Low	High	Excess
0-5	4.323	9.678	5.355	3.660	8.405	4.745
10-15	0.393	0.572	0.179	0.460	0.603	0.143
35-45	0.913	1.613	0.700	0.992	1.411	0.419
45-55	1.276	2.336	1.060	1.172	1.895	0.723
55-65	2.396	4.078	1.682	2.131	3.323	1.192
65-75	5.657	8.224	2.567	4.799	6.964	2.165

The table may be read thus without reference to decimal points. Of 100,000 boys living, 4,323 die in comparatively healthy places, and 9,678 in unhealthy places, the excess of deaths chargeable on the latter is 5,355.

Excessive Mortality in Towns. – The influence of air, water, food, and temperature on health and of the other conditions with which the Health of Towns Bill deals, was emphatically stated 60 years ago by Dr Price, no mere theorist in this matter, but the scientific founder of the Equitable Insurance Society. After showing, from a comparison of the duration of life in London and Holy Cross, Stockholm and Sweden, Manchester and the parts around, that human life is shorter by almost one half in cities than in the country, he adds:

> "From this comparison it appears with how much truth great cities have been called the graves of mankind. It must also convince all who consider it, that, according to the observation at the end of the Second Essay, it is by no means strictly proper to consider our diseases as the original intention of nature. They are, without doubt, in general, our own creation. Were there a country where the inhabitants led lives entirely natural and virtuous, few of them would die without measuring out the whole period of the present existence allotted them; and death would come upon them like a sleep, in consequence of no other cause than gradual and unavoidable decay. Let us, then, instead of charging our Maker with our miseries, learn more to accuse and reproach ourselves.

> "The reasons of the baneful influence of great towns, as it has been now exhibited, are plainly – First, the irregular modes of life, the luxuries, debaucheries, and pernicious customs, which prevail more in towns than in the country. Secondly, the foulness of the air in towns, occasioned by uncleanliness, smoke, the perspiration and breath of the inhabitants, and putrid streams from drains, churchyards, kennels, and common sewers."

This induction, drawn with great sagacity from a limited number of facts, gradually acquired strength; the experiments in prisons and the navy confirmed it; Mr Milne, after Dr Price, demonstrated the high mortality of towns, and of marsh lands; and Mr Edmonds in the *Lancet*, proved from the Census and the returns, imperfect as they were, of the parish registers for six towns of England, for London, and the several counties, as well as from correct returns for Glasgow, that the mortality at all ages was from about 2.8 to 3.0 per cent in towns – nearly 2.1 per cent in all England, and as low as 1.7 or 1.8 in some counties. Mr Edmonds also showed that the mortality bears a certain relation to sickness at each age. For every annual death, two persons are constantly suffering from sickness, of a severity that disables labouring men from work. According to Mr Neison's recent observations, there are 2.5 constantly sick in Friendly Societies to one death under 60; the recorded sickness after 60 is greater; the sickness in infancy is unknown. But if we assume that 2.5 are sick to one death – and this proportion certainly does not include slight illness, or all for which people take physic – the numbers constantly sick in London were 122,000, and the annual attacks of sickness more than 1,220,000, during the seven years 1838-44; the number of annual attacks would have been at least 350,000 less, and the number constantly sick would have been 35,000 less, if the health of London had been as good even as that of Lewisham, one of the districts within its own limits. This view, and all the principal facts known in connexion with the public health of England are discussed in the article Vital Statistics, of McCulloch's Statistical Account of the British Empire, which appeared in 1837. The cholera epidemic, followed by an influenza in 1837, more fatal than cholera, and an epidemic of typhus, had drawn attention to the state of public health; the Registration Bill was brought into operation; Dr Arnott, Dr Kay (now Kay Shuttleworth), and Dr Southwood Smith, were appointed by the Poor Law Commissioners to inquire into the causes of fever in parts of London in 1838; Mr Chadwick conducted an inquiry into the health of many towns of the kingdom in 1839; subsequently, a Committee of the House of Commons, of which Mr Slaney was chairman, collected evidence and drew up a report in 1840; and in 1843, a Royal Commission was appointed to inquire into the whole subject. The reports of the Commission appeared in 1844 and 1845 (10th Annual Report, pp xiii-xiv).

Excessive Urban Mortality, London, 1838-44. – The English system of registration, however imperfect it may still be, has realised the expectation held out in the opening speech of the minister who introduced the measure to parliament, in so far as "it enables the Government to acquire a general knowledge of the state of the population of the country".[2] In successive Reports the births, deaths, and marriages have been compared with the population of different districts; the prevalence of diseases has been traced in various parts; and the irrefragable proofs of the high mortality in towns induced the late Government to appoint a commission of inquiry, which resulted in a Bill submitted to Parliament by Lord Lincoln and Sir James Graham. A new bill for improving the health of towns has been prepared and brought in by the Viscount Morpeth, Lord John Russell, and Sir George Grey. As this Bill is likely to occupy the attention of Parliament in the present session, it may be useful to introduce here some extracts from a series of calculations, based on the Census returns of 1841, and the deaths registered during the seven years 1838-44. The facts and methods of calculation are given

[2] See speech of Lord John Russell on bringing forward the Bill for the Registration of Births, Deaths, and Marriages (*Mirror of Parliament*, 1836, p 131).

at length in the Ninth Annual Report, 8vo in the mean time it will be sufficient to observe that the object of the investigation is to exhibit the mortality at different periods of life in the divisions, counties, towns, and groups of country districts into which England and Wales have been divided. From these results the duration of life can be deduced. Corrections have been made for the increase of population, deaths in hospitals, and other disturbing causes.

The mortality in Liverpool, Manchester, and some other places has been before adverted to. The tables show the mortality of all the districts now included in the London tables of mortality. They afford ample materials for reasoning; but I shall here only direct attention to a few of the points bearing more immediately on the great question of the health of towns. London contained 1,950,000 inhabitants in the middle of the year 1841; and 342,565 deaths were registered within its limits in the septennial period of which 1841 was the middle year. The deaths on an average were 48,938 annually. To 1,000 females living at all ages 23 died, while to 1,000 males living at all ages 27 died yearly. The mortality of females in the neighbouring counties during the same seven years, was from 18 to 20; of males 19 to 21 in the 1,000; the mortality of females in London was 5, of males 8 in the 1,000 more than in the healthiest county. Out of an equal number of males living, there were 3 deaths in London for every 2 in the healthy counties. Out of 1,000 boys under 5 years of age in Surrey, and 1,000 in Sussex, 48 and 50 died annually; out of 1,000 in London, 93 died annually. The mortality of children under 5 years of age is twice as great in London as in the adjacent counties, including several towns.

The excess of deaths in London is not the result of climate, for the climate differs little from that of surrounding counties; and some of the London districts are not more unhealthy than many country districts. Take Lewisham, for instance, comprising Blackheath, Sydenham, Eltham, and Lewisham itself. The annual mortality of females was 16; of males, 18 in 1,000.

	Annual deaths at all ages to		Annual deaths under 5 years of age to	
	1,000 females living	1,000 males living	1,000 girls living	1,000 boys living
Surrey	18	19	41	48
Sussex	18	19	42	50
Hampshire	18	20	44	52
Kent	19	21	48	57
Berkshire	20	20	46	53
London	23	27	80	93

The deaths registered in London during the 7 years 1838-44 were	342,000
If the mortality during the period had not been greater than in Lewisham, the deaths of London would have been about	244,128
Excess of deaths in London	97,872

Here are 97,000 deaths in 7 years from causes peculiar to London. Other districts may be taken in the place of Lewisham, but the result would be the same.

A considerable part of the population of London is recruited from the country, immigrants entering chiefly at the ages 15 to 35, in a state of good health. The sick and weakly probably remain at home; many of the new comers, too, unmarried, when attacked in London by slow consumption – the most fatal disease at the ages 15 to 35 – return to their parents' houses to die; so that the mortality of the great city is made to appear in the returns lower at those ages than it is. If we take children under 5 years of age, where neither these disturbing causes nor occupation interferes, the deleterious influence on health of London in its present state will appear undisguised in all its magnitude.

The deaths registered in London (1838-44) under 5 years of age were	139,612
The deaths, if the mortality had not been higher than in Lewisham, would have been	80,632
Excess of deaths in London among children	58,980

Here are more than 58,000 children destroyed in London within 7 of the last 10 years.

Edwin Chadwick, 1800-90

E dwin Chadwick was the son of a wealthy Manchester businessman. He trained as a lawyer in
London and become influential in the London debating society. He wrote and talked widely
on many issues and, as a result of his interest in sanitary reform, was appointed
to the Royal Commission of Enquiry on the Poor Laws established by the Prime Minister, Earl Grey,
in 1832. His work for the commission enabled the Poor Law Amendment Act of 1834 to be drawn
up and passed as law. However, the Act was used to force people to enter workhouses and was
seen as responsible for the abolition of outdoor relief – for which Chadwick was held responsible.
Because of the weaknesses of this Act Chadwick devoted himself to further measures to improve
sanitation which would be more effective in alleviating the conditions of the poor, and the burden on
the middle class that he thought they constituted.

Chadwick became secretary to the Poor Law Commission and was largely responsible for the
establishment of a Board of Guardians for groups of parishes, each with a medical officer attached.
After the influenza and typhoid epidemics of 1837 and 1838 and the economic depression of 1837
he was asked to carry out a new enquiry into sanitation by the government. This led to his report,
The sanitary conditions of the labouring population, published in 1842, from which the following extract
is taken. The report was highly influential. However, its recommendations were not implemented
until after the Liberal Government of 1847 came into power and passed the Public Health Act in
1848. Chadwick became one of the directors of the newly established Board of Health.

Chadwick was never a popular civil servant and was pensioned off in 1854. He has been described
as single-minded, a fanatic and a bore. However, without such single-mindedness it is doubtful that
a survey as comprehensive as his would have been produced. He used as evidence the testimony of
medical officers working in the field as well as his own personal experiences.

Chadwick, E. (1842) *Report on the sanitary conditions of the labouring population of Gt Britain*

Boards of Health, or Public Officers for the Prevention of Disease

In reports and communications, the institution of district Boards of Health is frequently recommended, but in general terms, and they nowhere specify what shall be their powers, how they shall seek out information or receive it, and how act upon it. The recommendation is also sanctioned by the committee which sat to inquire into the health of large towns; and the committee state that "the principal duty and object of these boards of health would be precautionary and preventive, to turn the public attention to the causes of illness, and to suggest means by which the sources of contagion might be removed. Such boards would probably have a clerk, paid for his services, whose duty it would be to make minutes of the proceedings, and give such returns in a short tabular form as might be useful for reference, and important, as affording easy information on a subject of such vital interest to the people."[1]

I would submit that it is shown by the evidence collected in the present inquiry, that the great preventives – drainage, street and house cleansing by means of supplies of water and improved sewerage, and especially the introduction of cheaper and more efficient modes of removing all noxious refuse from the towns – are operations for which aid must be sought from the science of the civil engineer, not from the physician, who has done his work when he has pointed out the disease that results from the neglect of proper administrative measures, and has alleviated the sufferings of the victims. After the cholera had passed,[2] several of the local boards of health that were appointed on its appearance continued their meetings and made representations; but the alarm had passed, and although the evils represented were often much greater than the cholera, the representations produced no effect, and the boards broke up. In Paris a Board of Health has been in operation during several years, but if their operations, as displayed in their reports, be considered, it will be evident that, although they have examined many important questions and have made representations, recommending for practical application

[1] *Report of the Select Committee on the Health of Towns, Parliamentary Paper 1840, XI, p xix.*

[2] The cholera epidemic of 1831-2, when the local Boards of Health were established.

some of the principles developed in the course of the present inquiry; still as they had no executive power, their representations have produced no effect, and the labouring population of Paris is shown to be, with all the advantages of climate, in a sanitary condition even worse than the labouring population of London. In the Appendix I have submitted a translation of a report descriptive of the labours of the Conseil de Salubrité, in Paris.[3] From this report it will be seen that they have few or no initiative functions, and that they are chiefly called into action by references made to them by the public authorities to examine and give their opinion on medical questions that may arise in the course of public administration as to what manufacturing or other operations are or are not injurious to the public health.

The action of a board of health upon such evils as those in question must depend upon the arrangements for bringing under its notice the evils to be remedied. A body of gentlemen sitting in a room will soon find themselves with few means of action if there be no agency to bring the subject matters before them; and an inquiring agency to seek out the evils from house to house, wherever those evils may be found, to follow on the footsteps of the private practitioner would be apparently attended with much practical difficulty.

The statements of the condition of considerable proportions of the labouring population of the towns into which the present inquiries have been carried have been received with surprise by persons of the wealthier classes living in the immediate vicinity, to whom the facts were as strange as if they related to foreigners or the natives of an unknown country. When Dr Arnott with myself and others were examining the abodes of the poorest classes in Glasgow and Edinburgh, we were regarded with astonishment; and it was frequently declared by the inmates, that they had never for many years witnessed the approach or the presence of persons of that condition near them. We have found that the inhabitants of the front houses in many of the main streets of those towns and of the metropolis, have never entered the adjoining courts, or seen the interior of any of the tenements, situate at the backs of their own houses, in which their own workpeople or dependents reside.

The duty of visiting loathsome abodes, amidst close atmospheres compounded of smoke and offensive odours, and everything to revolt the senses, is a duty which can only be expected to be regularly performed under much stronger motives than can commonly be imposed on honorary officers, and cannot be depended upon even from paid officers where they are not subjected to strong checks. The examination of loathsome prisons has gained one individual a national and European celebrity. Yet we have seen that there are whole streets of houses, composing some of the wynds of Glasgow and Edinburgh, and great numbers of the courts in London, and the older towns in England, in which the condition of every inhabited

[3] *San. Rep.*, Appendix 14, pp 409-23.

room, and the physical condition of the inmates, is even more horrible than the worst of the dungeons that Howard ever visited. In Ireland provisions for the appointment of Boards of Health have been made, but they appear to have failed entirely. One of the medical practitioners examined before the Committee of the House of Commons was asked, in respect to the operation of these provisions:

> But in ordinary times, when the fever is not of very great intensity, and is confined to the dwellings of the humbler classes, there is no such provision put into force? No, but then there is another provision which may be put into force; this Act provides, that "whenever in any city, town, or district, any fever or contagious distemper shall prevail, or be known to exist, it shall and may be lawful for any one or more magistrates, upon the requisition of five respectable householders, to convene a meeting of the magistrates and householders of such city, town, or district, and of the medical practitioners within the same, in order to examine into the circumstances attending such fever or contagious distemper." There is another Act of 59 Geo. III., c.41, which enables the parishes to appoint officers of health; that is, a permanent power. Those officers have very considerable authority; they can assess a rate.
>
> Are they appointed? – They are appointed, I think, in all the parishes in Dublin except two; but they are inoperative: they are unpaid, and it is a very disgusting duty. They can be made to serve, but there is not control as to the amount of service they perform; so that the provision is quite inoperative, unless an alarm exists.
>
> Do you not think the appointment of some such officers, properly appointed, properly paid, and having reasonable power, for the purpose of suggesting and enforcing such measures as shall be beneficial, would be highly valuable? – I am sure it would, and it would save an amazing quantity of expenditure to the country.'[4]

[4] *Report of the Select Committee on the Health of Towns*, P.P. 1840, XI, evidence of Dr H. Maunsell, Qs 3297-9.

It has only been under the strong pressure of professional duties by the physicians and paid medical and relieving officers responsible for visiting the abodes of the persons reduced to destitution by disease that the condition of those abodes in the metropolis have of late been known; and I believe that it is only under continued pressure and strong responsibilities and interests in prevention that investigation will be carried into such places, and the extensive physical causes of disease be effectually eradicated.

Whilst experience gives little promise even of inquiries from such a body as Boards of Health without responsibilities, still less of any important results from the mere representations of such bodies separated from executive authority, I would submit for consideration what appears to me a more advantageous application of medical science, viz, by uniting it with boards having executive authority.

Now, the claim to relief on the ground of destitution created by sickness, which carries the medical officer of the union to the interior of the abode of the sufferer, appears to be the means of carrying investigation precisely to the place where the evil is the most rife, and where the public intervention is most called for. In the metropolis the number of cases of fever alone on which the medical officers were required to visit the applicants for relief, at their own residences, amounted during one year to nearly 14,000. The number of medical officers attached to the new unions throughout the country, and engaged in visiting the claimants to relief on account of sickness, is at this time about 2,300.

Were it practicable to attach as numerous a body of paid officers to any local Boards of Health that could be established, it would scarcely be practicable to insure as certain and well directed an examination of the residences of the labouring classes as I conceive may be ensured from the medical officers of the unions. In support of these anticipations of the efficiency of the agency of the medical officers when directed to the formation of sanitary measures, I beg leave to refer to the experience of a partial trial of them under a clause of the recent Metropolitan Police Act[5], by which it is provided, that if the guardians of the poor of an union or parish, or the churchwardens and overseers of the poor of any parish within the Metropolitan Police district, together with the medical officer of any such parish or union, shall be of opinion, and shall certify under the hands of two or more of such guardians, church-wardens, and overseers, and of such medical officer, that any house, or part of any house, is in such a filthy unwholesome condition that the health of the inmates is thereby endangered, then the magistrates may, after due notice to the occupier, cause the house to be cleansed at his expense.

[5] 1, 2 & 3 Vic, c 71, of 1839.

The defects of the provision are, that it only authorizes cleansing and not providing for the means of cleansing and personal cleanliness, by directing supplies of water to be laid on; that it does not extend to the alterations of the external condition of the dwelling; that the immediate expense falls upon the occupier, who is usually in so abject a state of destitution as to serve as a barrier to any proceeding apparently tending to any penal infliction. With all these disadvantages, its working may be submitted to show the general eligibility of the medical officers of unions as officers for the execution of sanitary measures. The following account is given by the clerk to the Board of Guardians of Bethnal Green of the working of the provision in that part of the metropolis:

> *Mr William Brutton* – We have taken prompt measures to execute the clause of the Metropolitan Police Act, and the Commissioners' recommendations upon it, in our parish, and the effect produced has already been beneficial. For example, the medical officer recently reported, through me, to the Board of Guardians, that fever had arisen in certain small tenements in a court called Nicholl's Court, and that it was likely to spread amongst the poorer classes in the district. He reported that others of the houses than those in which fever existed (and the inmates) were in a filthy condition, and that, unless measures were taken for cleansing them properly, fever must necessarily ensue. The Board, on receiving this communication, desired me to proceed instantly, and take such measures as appeared to me to be necessary for the abatement and prevention of the evil. I immediately obtained a summons from the magistrates for the attendance of the owner of the houses. He came directly, and stated that he was not aware that the premises were in the condition in which our medical officer had found them; and he promised that measures should be taken for proper cleansing. Those measures were taken: the furniture of the houses was taken out and washed; the houses were limewashed. Some of those who were ill died, but the progress of the fever was certainly arrested.
>
> The Board followed up these proceedings by circulating the Commissioners' instruction and form of notification in every part of the parish.
>
> But the proceeding had a very good effect in the immediate neighbourhood. The proceeding was observed by the neighbours, and there is every reason to believe that they have set to work to cleanse and prevent a similar visitation. We have also learned that the landlords of some of these smaller tenements have been rather more particular than before: they have said we must see to the cleansing of these places lest we should be had up for it before the magistrates.
>
> The guardians, considering the form of notifications useful, have directed that they should be issued periodically before the times when disease usually appears. In the course of a fortnight or three weeks hence, when the equinoctial gales

prevail, and when we have usually much sickness and claims to relief, we shall probably have another issue of the notifications.

We have also given instructions to the relieving officer, as well as the medical officer, to report on the existence of any filth or things likely to be productive of disease that he may observe in the course of his visits to the houses where he is called by the claims to relief. The services of the relieving officer are highly important, as he has an opportunity of observing the state of filth and the obvious predisposition, and perhaps of causes of disease, preventing it before the visits of the medical officer, who is of course only called upon to attend when disease has arisen. The relieving officers visit more frequently than the medical officer, and give the tickets or orders requiring his attendance.

You are Commissioner of the Sewers in the Tower Hamlets, are you not? – Yes, I am.

Are you are of course aware of their procedure? – Yes.

Do you think that body would be available for the execution of sanitary measures? – Certainly not as compared with the Board of Guardians: the Commissioners of Sewers meet only monthly, and have no medical officers and no relieving officers. The Board of Guardians meets weekly, and their officers are constantly at work, night and morning. We have not even waited for the landlords, where prompt measures appeared to be necessary for the removal of any active cause of disease. Where cesspools have overflowed, and where there has been a stoppage of water, we have directed the surveyor of the roads to ascertain the cause of the stoppage, and to remedy the mischief forthwith.

But what legal right have the guardians had to do that: they have no legal right to direct the road surveyor in the performance of his duties? – Strictly speaking, we have not, but we have forcibly suggested it as a matter of expediency.

Between the notification of the evil and the execution of the remedy, in the example you have cited by the Board of Guardians, what length of time elapsed? – From the Friday to the Monday following.

What time, so far as you have had experience, need ordinarily elapse if execution follow immediately on the report? – Execution would follow immediately on the order of the Board of Guardians. I think, however, that the union officers should, in case of emergency, have a summary acting power immediately for the preservation of life. The Guardians thought their examination of the spot unnecessary after the report of the medical officer.

The following is the examination of the clerk to the Strand union as to the practical working of the same measure in another district: *Mr James Corder*, clerk to the Strand union, examined:

What has been done in the Strand union in respect to the provisions of the Metropolitan Police Act, 2 and 3 Vict., c. 71, sec. 41, with respect to the powers conferred by that statute for the cleansing of houses which are in an unwholesome condition?

The attention of the medical officers was immediately drawn to the section of the Act, and the instructions of the Poor Law Commissioners relating thereto; and the result has been that proceedings have been had in several cases, in all of which the necessary cleansing has been performed by the owners, without the guardians being driven to the necessity of causing the requisite lime-whiting and cleansing to be done. The medical officer had frequently complained of the condition of the places into which the cleansing had been carried. Those places had for years been in the filthiest and most unwholesome condition: in some courts and alleys the pavements were covered with an accumulation of the most offensive matter, including the carcases of dead animals, such as dogs and cats, which the scavengers said formed no part of their contract to remove: their contract was only to cleanse the carriage ways. Some of these courts and alleys abound in the principal thoroughfares in the metropolis. The public, in passing through a thorough-fare like the Strand, would scarcely imagine that an evil of so much magnitude was close at hand.

The powers conferred by the clause in question appears to be restricted to the cleansing of the houses and the passages within the cartilage. What proceedings did the guardians take with relation to these external passages?

They directed the condition of the places to be represented to the Commissioners for paving and cleansing the district, who caused the filth complained of to be removed. The cleansing of the footways, however, forms no part of the duty of the Commissioners of Pavement, nor of their surveyor, nor of the scavenger appointed by them; and what was done was done extra-officially.

It cannot, therefore, be relied upon for the future?

No; and it is to be observed that the Metropolitan Paving Act evidently contemplates that the cleansing of the footways shall be done by the inmates of the houses. In the poorer districts, however, this is entirely omitted to be done; in addition to which these courts and alleys are frequently made, on account of their obscurity, a depository for most offensive matter. In the better neighbourhoods, the service of cleansing is performed by the servants; but the poor people, who rise before daylight, go to their work, and return at a late hour, have no time to cleanse their courts, and their earnings are too scanty to allow payment to others for the performance of the duty. In the better neighbourhoods, the cleansing does not always take place. The medical officers report, that there is a better average health in the streets that are well cleansed than in others where the people are otherwise in the same condition of life.

What are the main defects you have experienced in respect to the provision of the Metropolitan Police Act, empowering the guardians to take measures for cleansing houses?

First, the delay which must take place before the provisions of the Act can be put in operation. The medical officer has first to make his report to the Board of Guardians; several days elapse before the Board meets; then guardians have to inspect the premises in conjunction with the medical officer previously to certifying as to the state thereof: then application is made to the magistrate, who issues his summons, returnable in seven days; at the expiration of which, if the cleansing be not performed, the guardians are empowered to cause it to be done; but they must first obtain a magistrate's warrant for the purpose. All this engenders delay; in addition to which our guardians have, in the first instance, caused the landlord to be written to with a view to prevent further proceedings, which in some instances have been successful; but when it is not successful, it creates a further delay, during which disease may rapidly increase and spread. The second defect of the provision is, that the owners are not liable for the expenses incurred; and the occupiers are mostly of the poorest class, who have no effects on which a distraint could be made. With all these difficulties, however, this provision has been very beneficial in its operation; and it is very much to be desired that large facilities should be afforded for carrying its intention more fully into effect. It may be added, that the medical officer should have remuneration for the trouble he entails upon himself, by a report, in attending before magistrates, until the object is effected.

Mr John Smith, the clerk to the Whitechapel union:

Have you taken any proceedings under the 41st clause of the Metropolitan Police Act?

We have issued notifications to every house in the union of the necessity of cleansing the houses by whitewashing them inside and out, and that the owners and occupiers were amenable for any neglect. The relieving officers report to me, that these notifications have already been productive of very good effects, and that whitewashing has been actively practised. The relieving officers were instructed, wherever they found a case of neglect, to threaten the landlord that he would be proceeded against unless the tenement was duly cleansed. But as yet we have taken no legal proceedings, because we have advised with the magistrates, who do not consider that the owners can be proceeded against in the first instance, and the occupiers of the tenements, which are liable to be proceeded against, are most of them paupers and persons in extreme poverty.

With respect to the remedies. I find that the personal inconvenience to which the clause subjects the guardians of visiting the spot is a provision which will greatly obstruct its operations, and will at all events greatly delay proceedings from time to time. The guardians who, in our union, are men of business, consider that their time is full occupied at the Board, and they object to any attendance out of the Board, and would give it reluctantly. If the cases are taken before the magistrate, it appears desirable that the medical officer should not be compelled to attend unless it were absolutely requisite, and that the relieving officer should be allowed to prove the facts as to the state of the dwellings recited in the medical officer's certificate, which could rarely be disputed. If the point were disputed by the owner, then the medical officer or other witnesses might be forthcoming.

What is the number of houses in the union? – About 8,000.

How many cases on the average do your medical officers visit in the year? – About 4,000.

Those visits of course are sometimes to different rooms or the same tenement? – No doubt of that, and very frequently to the inmates of the same room.

Are the visits of the relieving officers to the dwellings of the labouring classes more extensive than the visits of the medical officers? – I should say more extensive.

Between the two, are any class of the poorer and otherwise neglected residences that would probably escape visitation? – I should say that they must visit every spot within the district.

Within such districts as that of Whitechapel, do you think the three present medical officers and the relieving officers would suffice to carry out sanitary measures actively and efficiently? – I think that for efficiency additional strength would be required; perhaps one officer, whose especial duty it should be to attend to the duties connected with sanitary measures, supposing them carried out by the agency of the existing establishments.

From the consideration of such practical evidence, it will be seen that the ordinary duties of the relieving officer in the first instance, and of the medical officer afterwards, ensure domiciliary inspection of large districts to an extent and with a degree of certainty that could scarcely be ensured or expected of any agents or members of a board of health unconnected with positive administrative duties. The inspection of these officers of the boards of guardians more than supplies the external inspection of inquests or of the leets; and it is submitted that in their position these boards may most beneficially exercise the functions of the leet in reclaiming the execution of the law, as against acts of omission and of commission, by which the poorest of the labouring classes are injured and the ratepayers burdened.

It may therefore be submitted as an eligible preliminary general arrangement, that it shall be required of the medical officer as an extra duty, for the due performance of which he should be fairly remunerated, that on visiting any person at that person's dwelling, on an order for medical relief, he shall, after having given such needful immediate relief as the case may require, examine or cause to be examined any such physical and removable causes as may have produced disease or acted as a predisposing cause of it; that he shall make out a particular statement of them, wherein he will specify any things that may be and are urgently required to be immediately removed. This statement should be given to the relieving officer, who should thereupon take measures for the removal of the nuisance at the expense of the owner of the tenement, unless he, upon notice which shall be given to him, forthwith proceed to direct their removal. Except in the way of appeal by the owner against the proceedings of either officer, or where a higher expense than 5*l* [£5] or a year's rent of the tenement, were involved by the alterations directed by the medical officer, it appears to be recommended that no application to the Board of Guardians or the magistrates should be required in the first instance, as it frequently happens that the delay of a day in the adoption of measures may occasion the loss of life and the wide spread of contagious disease; and an application to the Board of Guardians or to the petty sessions would usually incur delay of a week or a fortnight. To repeat the words of Blackstone, – "The security of the lives and property may sometimes require so speedy a remedy, as not to allow time to call on the person on whose property the mischief has arisen to remedy it". When any tenement is in a condition to endanger life from disease, as it comes within the principle of the law, so it should be included within its provisions, and should be placed in the same condition as a tenement condemned as being ruinous and endangering life from falling.

Friedrich Engels, 1820-95   6

Friedrich Engels was born in Wuppertal, Germany, where his father owned a factory manufacturing textiles. He travelled to England in1842 to be the Manchester agent for his father's business. Since his youth he had had a strong interest in philosophy, especially the work of Hegel, and while in England he became interested in the problems of the newly created urban working class produced by the industrial revolution. In 1845 he published *The condition of the working class in England* which was based not only in his own observations of working conditions but also on secondary sources and official documents.

Engels is better known for his collaboration with Marx, which began in 1844, soon after Engels had adopted communist beliefs. Engels' ideas contributed to the *Manifesto of the Communist Party* which was written by Marx in 1848. Engels also completed the second and third volumes of Marx's *Capital*, after Marx died. He was the sole author of *Principles of communism* (1847) – which was in some ways a first draft of the manifesto of the Communist Party – and *Socialism: Utopian and scientific* (1880). He died in London in 1895.

Here we present an extract *The condition of the working class in England* (1845), which was the major text in which Engels dealt with the health consequences of capitalist industrialisation and urbanisation.

Engels, F. (1845) *The condition of the working class in England*

The Great Towns

... Such are the various working people's quarters of Manchester as I had occasion to observe them personally during twenty months. If we briefly formulate the result of our wanderings, we must admit that 350,000 working people of Manchester and its environs live, almost all of them, in wretched, damp, filthy cottages, that the streets which surround them are usually in the most miserable and filthy condition, laid out without the slightest reference to ventilation, with reference solely to the profit secured by the contractor. In a word, we must confess that in the working men's dwellings of Manchester, no cleanliness, no convenience, and consequently no comfortable family life is possible; that in such dwellings only a physically degenerate race, robbed of all humanity, degraded, reduced morally and physically to bestiality, could feel comfortable and at home. And I am not alone in making this assertion. We have seen that Dr Kay gives precisely the same description; and, though it is superfluous, I quote further the words of a Liberal, recognized and highly valued as an authority by the manufacturers, and a fanatical opponent of all independent movements of the workers[1].

[1] Nassau W. Senior, *Letters on the Factory Act to the Rt Hon the President of the Board of Trade* (Chas Poulett Thomson, Esq), London, 1837, p 24.

As I passed through the dwellings of the mill-hands in Irish Town, Ancoats, and Little Ireland, I was only amazed that it is possible to maintain a reasonable state of health in such homes. These towns, for in extent and number of inhabitants they are towns, have been erected with the utmost disregard of everything except the immediate advantage of the speculating builder. A carpenter and builder unite to buy a series of building sites (ie, they lease them for a number of years), and cover them with so-called houses. In one place we found a whole street following the course of a ditch, because in this way deeper cellars could be secured without the cost of digging, cellars not for storing wares or rubbish, but for dwellings for human beings. *Not one house of this street escaped the cholera.* In general, the streets of these suburbs are unpaved, with a dung-heap or ditch in the middle; the houses are built back to back, without ventilation or drainage, and whole families are limited to a corner of a cellar or a garret.

I have already referred to the unusual activity which the sanitary police manifested during the cholera visitation. When the epidemic was approaching, a universal terror seized the bourgeoisie of the city. People remembered the unwholesome dwellings of the poor, and trembled before the certainty that each of these slums would become a centre for the plague, whence it would spread desolation in all directions through the houses of the propertied class. A Health Commission was appointed at once to investigate these districts, and report upon their condition to the Town Council. Dr Kay, himself a member of this Commission, who visited in person every separate police district except one, the eleventh, quotes extracts from their reports. There were inspected, in all, 6,951 houses — naturally in Manchester proper alone, Salford and the other suburbs being excluded. Of these, 6,565 urgently needed whitewashing within; 960 were out of repair; 939 had insufficient drains; 1,435 were damp; 452 were badly ventilated; 2,221 were without privies. Of the 687 streets inspected, 248 were unpaved, 53 but partially paved, 112 ill-ventilated, 352 containing standing pools, heaps of débris, refuse, etc. To cleanse such an Augean stable before the arrival of the cholera was, of course, out of the question. A few of the worst nooks were therefore cleansed, and everything else left as before. In the cleansed spots, as Little Ireland proves, the old filthy condition was naturally restored in a couple of months. As to the internal condition of these houses, the same Commission reports a state of things similar to that which we have already met with in London, Edinburgh, and other cities.[2]

It often happens that a whole Irish family is crowded into one bed; often a heap of filthy straw or quilts of old sacking cover all in an indiscriminate heap, where all alike are degraded by want, apathy, and wretchedness. Often the inspectors found, in a single house, two families in two rooms. All slept in one, and used the other as a kitchen and dining-room in common. Often more than one family lived in a single damp cellar, in whose pestilent atmosphere twelve to sixteen persons were crowded together. To these and other sources of disease must be added that pigs were kept, and other disgusting things of the most revolting kind were found.

We must add that many families, who had but one room for themselves, receive boarders and lodgers in it, that such lodgers of both sexes by no means rarely sleep in the same bed with the married couple; and that the single case of a man and his wife and his adult sister-in-law sleeping in one bed was found, according to the 'Report concerning the sanitary condition of the working class', six times repeated in Manchester. Common lodging-houses, too, are very numerous; Dr Kay gives their number in 1831 as 267 in Manchester proper, and they must have increased greatly since then. Each of these receives from twenty to thirty guests, so that they shelter all

[2] James Ph. Kay, MD, *The Moral and Physical Condition of the Working Class Employed in the Cotton Manufacture in Manchester*, 2nd edn, 1832. Dr Kay confuses the working class in general with the factory workers, otherwise an excellent pamphlet.

[3] P. Gaskell, *The Manufacturing Population of England: Its Moral, Social and Physical Condition, and the Changes which have arisen from the Use of Steam Machinery; with an Examination of Infant Labour. Fiat Justitia*, 1833. Depicting chiefly the state of the working class in Lancashire. The author is a Liberal, but wrote at a time when it was not a feature of Liberalism to chart the happiness of the workers. He is therefore unprejudiced and can afford to have eyes for the evils of the present state of things, and especially for the factory system. On the other hand, he wrote before the Factories Enquiry Commission, and adopts from untrustworthy sources many assertions afterwards refuted by the Report of the Commission. This work, although on the whole a valuable one, can therefore only be used with discretion, especially as the author, like Kay, confuses the whole working class with the mill-hands. The history of the development of the proletariat, contained in the introduction to the present work, is chiefly taken from this work of Gaskell's.

told, nightly, from five to seven thousand human beings. The character of the houses and their guests is the same as in other cities. Five to seven beds in each room lie on the floor – without bedsteads, and on these sleep, mixed indiscriminately, as many persons as apply. What physical and moral atmosphere reigns in these holes I need not state. Each of these houses is a focus of crime, the scene of deeds against which human nature revolts, which would perhaps never have been perpetrated but for this forced centralization of vice.[3] Gaskell gives the number of persons living in cellars in Manchester proper as 20,000. The *Weekly Dispatch* gives the number, 'according to official reports', as twelve per cent of the working class, which agrees with Gaskell's number; the workers being estimated at 175,000, 21,000 would form twelve per cent of it. The cellar dwellings in the suburbs are at least as numerous, so that the number of persons living in cellars in Manchester – using its name in the broader sense – is not less than 40-50,000. So much for the dwellings of the workers in the largest cities and towns. The manner in which the need of a shelter is satisfied furnishes a standard for the manner in which all other necessities are supplied. That in these filthy holes a ragged, ill-fed population alone can dwell is a safe conclusion, and such is the fact. The clothing of the working people, in the majority of cases, is in a very bad condition. The material used for it is not of the best adapted. Wool and linen have almost vanished from the wardrobe of both sexes, and cotton has taken their place. Shirts are made of bleached or coloured cotton goods; the dresses of the women are chiefly of cotton print goods, and woollen petticoats are rarely to be seen on the washline. The men wear chiefly trousers of fustian or other heavy cotton goods, and jackets or coats of the same. Fustian has become the proverbial costume of the working men, who are called 'fustian jackets', and call themselves so in contrast to the gentlemen who wear broad cloth, which latter words are used as characteristic for the middle class. When Feargus O'Connor, the Chartist leader, came to Manchester during the insurrection of 1842, he appeared, amidst the deafening applause of the working men, in a fustian suit of clothing. Hats are the universal head-covering in England, even for working men, hats of the most diverse forms, round, high, broad-brimmed, narrow-brimmed, or without brims – only the younger men in factory towns wearing caps. Anyone who does not own a hat folds himself a low, square paper cap.

The whole clothing of the working class, even assuming it to be in good condition, is little adapted to the climate. The damp air of England with its sudden changes of temperature, more calculated than any other to give rise to colds, obliges almost the whole middle class to wear flannel next the skin, about the body, and flannel scarfs and shirts are in almost universal use. Not only is the working class deprived of this precaution, it is scarcely ever in a position to use a thread of woollen clothing; and the heavy cotton goods, though thicker, stiffer, and heavier than woollen clothes, afford much less protection against cold and wet, remain damp much longer because of their thickness and the nature of the stuff, and have nothing of the compact density of fulled woollen cloths. And, if a working man once buys himself a woollen coat for Sunday, he must get it from one of the cheap shops where he finds bad, so-called 'Devil's-dust' cloth, manufactured for sale and not for use, and liable to tear or grow threadbare in a fortnight, or he must buy of an old-clothes'-dealer a half-worn coat which has seen its best days, and lasts but a few weeks. Moreover, the working man's clothing is, in most cases, in bad condition, and there is the oft-recurring necessity for placing the best pieces in the pawnbroker's shop. But among very large numbers, especially among the Irish, the prevailing clothing consists of perfect rags often beyond all mending, or so patched that the original colour can no longer be detected. Yet the English and Anglo-Irish go on patching, and have carried this art to a remarkable pitch, putting wool or bagging on fustian, or the reverse – it is all the same to them. But the true, transplanted Irish hardly ever patch except in the extremest necessity, when the garment would otherwise fall apart. Ordinarily the rags of the shirt protrude through the rents in the coat or trousers. They wear, as Thomas Carlyle says,[4] 'A suit of tatters, the getting on or off which is said to be a difficult operation, transacted only in festivals and the high tides of the calendar.' The Irish have introduced, too, the custom previously unknown in England, of going barefoot. In every manufacturing town there is now to be seen a multitude of people, especially women and children, going about barefoot, and their example is gradually being adopted by the poorer English.

As with clothing, so with food. The workers get what is too bad for the property-holding class. In the great towns of England everything may be had to the best, but it costs money; and the workman, who must keep house on a couple of pence, cannot afford much expense. Moreover, he usually receives his wages on Saturday evening, for, although a beginning has been made of the payment of wages on Friday, this excellent arrangement is by no means universal; and so he comes to market at five or even seven o'clock, while the buyers of the middle class have had the first choice during the morning, when the market teems with the best of everything. But when the workers reach it, the best has vanished, and, if it was still there, they would probably not be able to buy it. The potatoes which the workers buy are usually poor, the vegetables wilted, the cheese old and of poor quality, the bacon rancid, the meat lean, tough, taken from old, often diseased, cattle, or such as have died a natural death, and not fresh even then, often half decayed. The sellers are usually small hucksters who buy up inferior goods, and can sell them cheaply by reason of their badness. The poorest workers are forced to use still

[4] Thomas Carlyle, *Chartism* (London, 1840) p 28.

another device to get together the things they need with their few pence. As nothing can be sold on Sunday, and all shops must be closed at twelve o'clock on Saturday night, such things as would not keep until Monday are sold at any price between ten o'clock and midnight. But nine-tenths of what is sold at ten o'clock is past using by Sunday morning, yet these are precisely the provisions which made up the Sunday dinner of the poorest class. The meat which the workers buy is very often past using; but having bought it, they must eat it. On 6 January 1844 (if I am not greatly mistaken), a court leet was held in Manchester, when eleven meat-sellers were fined for having sold tainted meat. Each of them had a whole ox or pig, or several sheep, or from fifty to sixty pounds of meat, which were all confiscated in a tainted condition. In one case, sixty-four stuffed Christmas geese were seized which had proved unsaleable in Liverpool, and had been forwarded to Manchester, where they were brought to market foul and rotten. All the particulars, with names and fines, were published at the time in the *Manchester Guardian*. In the six weeks, from 1 July to 14 August, the same sheet reported three similar cases. According to the *Guardian* for 3 August, a pig, weighing 200 pounds, which had been found dead and decayed, was cut up and exposed for sale by a butcher at Heywood, and was then seized. According to the number for 31 July, two butchers at Wigan, of whom one had previously been convicted of the same offence, were fined £2 and £4 respectively, for exposing tainted meat for sale; and, according to the number for 10 August, twenty-six tainted hams, seized at a dealer's in Bolton, were publicly burnt, and the dealer fined twenty shillings. But these are by no means all the cases; they do not even form a fair average for a period of six weeks, according to which to form an average for the year. There are often seasons in which every number of the semi-weekly *Guardian* mentions a similar case found in Manchester or its vicinity. And when one reflects upon the many cases which must escape detection in the extensive markets that stretch along the front of every main street, under the slender supervision of the market inspectors – and how else can one explain the boldness with which whole animals are exposed for sale? – when one considers how great the temptation must be, in view of the incomprehensibly small fines mentioned in the foregoing cases; when one reflects what condition a piece of meat must have reached to be seized by the inspectors, it is impossible to believe that the workers obtain good and nourishing meat as a usual thing. But they are victimized in yet another way by the money-greed of the middle class. Dealers and manufacturers adulterate all kinds of provisions in an atrocious manner, and without the slightest regard to the health of the consumers. We have heard the *Manchester Guardian* upon this subject, let us hear another organ of the middle class – I delight in the testimony of my opponents – let us hear the *Liverpool Mercury:*

Salted butter is sold for fresh, the lumps being covered with a coating of fresh butter, or a pound of fresh being laid on top to taste, while the salted article is sold after this test, or the whole mass is washed and then sold as fresh. With sugar, pounded rice and other cheap adulterating materials are mixed, and the whole sold at full price. The refuse of soap-boiling establishments also is mixed with other things and sold as sugar. Chicory and other cheap stuff is mixed with ground coffee, and artificial coffee beans with the unground article. Cocoa is often adulterated with fine brown earth, treated with fat to render it more easily mistakable for real cocoa. Tea is mixed with the leaves of the sloe and with other refuse, or dry tea-leaves are roasted on hot copper plates, so returning to the proper colour and being sold as fresh. Pepper is mixed with pounded nut-shells; port-wine is manufactured outright (out of alcohol, dye-stuffs, etc), while it is notorious that more of it is consumed in England alone than is grown in Portugal; and tobacco is mixed with disgusting substances of all sorts and in all possible forms in which the article is produced.

I can add that several of the most respected tobacco dealers in Manchester announced publicly last summer, that, by reason of the universal adulteration of tobacco, no firm could carry on business without adulteration, and that no cigar costing less than threepence is made wholly from tobacco. These frauds are naturally not restricted to articles of food, though I could mention a dozen more, the villainy of mixing gypsum or chalk with flour among them. Fraud is practised in the sale of articles of every sort: flannel, stockings, etc, are stretched, and shrink after the first washing; narrow cloth is sold as being from one and a half to three inches broader than it actually is; stoneware is so thinly glazed that the glazing is good for nothing, and cracks at once, and a hundred other rascalities, *tout comme chez nous*. But the lion's share of the evil results of these frauds fall to the workers. The rich are less deceived, because they can pay the high prices of the large shops which have a reputation to lose, and would injure themselves more than their customers if they kept poor or adulterated wares; the rich are spoiled, too, by habitual good eating, and detect adulteration more easily with their sensitive palates. But the poor, the working people, to whom a couple of farthings are important, who must buy many things with little money, who cannot afford to inquire too closely into the quality of their purchases, and cannot do so in any case because they have had no opportunity of cultivating their taste – to their share fall all the adulterated, poisoned provisions. They must deal with the small retailers, must buy perhaps on credit, and these small retail dealers who cannot sell even the same quality of goods so cheaply as the largest retailers, because of their small capital and the large proportional expenses of their business, must knowingly or unknowingly buy adulterated goods in order to sell at the lower prices required, and to meet the competition of the others. Further, a large retail dealer who has extensive capital invested in his business is ruined with his ruined credit if detected in a fraudulent practice; but what harm does it do a small grocer, who has customers in a single street only, if frauds are proved against him? If no one trusts him in Ancoats, he moves to Chorton or Hulme, where no one knows him, and where he continues to defraud as before; while legal penalties attach to very few adulterations unless they involve revenue frauds. Not in the quality alone, but in the quantity of his goods as well, is the English working man defrauded. The small dealers usually have false weights and measures, and an incredible number of convictions for such offences may be read in the police reports. How universal this form of fraud is in the manufacturing districts, a couple of extracts from the *Manchester Guardian* may serve to show. They cover only a short period, and, even here, I have not all the numbers at hand:

> *Guardian*, 16 June 1844, Rochdale Sessions – Four dealers fined five to ten shillings for using light weights. Stockport Sessions. – Two dealers fined one shilling, one of them having seven light weights and a false scale, and both having been warned.

> *Guardian*, 19 June, Rochdale Sessions – One dealer fined five, and two farmers ten shillings.

> *Guardian*, 22 June, Manchester Justices of the Peace – Nineteen dealers fined two shillings and sixpence to two pounds.

> *Guardian*, 26 June, Ashton Sessions - Fourteen dealers and farmers fined two shillings and sixpence to one pound. Hyde Petty Sessions. – Nine farmers and dealers condemned to pay costs and five shillings fines.

> *Guardian*, 8 July, Manchester – Sixteen dealers condemned to pay costs and fines not exceeding ten shillings.

> *Guardian*, 13 July, Rochdale – Nine dealers fined from two shillings and sixpence to twenty shillings.

Guardian, 24 July, Rochdale – Four dealers fined ten to twenty shillings.

Guardian, 27 July, Bolton – Twelve dealers and innkeepers condemned to pay costs.

Guardian, 3 August, Bolton – Three dealers fined two shillings and sixpence, and five shillings.

Guardian, 10 August, Bolton – One dealer fined five shillings.

And the same causes which make the working class the chief sufferers from frauds in the quality of goods make them the usual victims of frauds in the question of quantity too.

The habitual food of the individual working man naturally varies according to his wages. The better paid workers, especially those in whose families every member is able to earn something, have good food as long as this state of things lasts; meat daily and bacon and cheese for supper. Where wages are less, meat is used only two or three times a week, and the proportion of bread and potatoes increases. Descending gradually, we find the animal food reduced to a small piece of bacon cut up with the potatoes; lower still, even this disappears, and there remain only bread, cheese, porridge, and potatoes, until on the lowest round of the ladder, among the Irish, potatoes form the sole food. As an accompaniment, weak tea, with perhaps a little sugar, milk, or spirits, is universally drunk. Tea is regarded in England, and even in Ireland, as quite as indispensable as coffee in Germany, and where no tea is used, the bitterest poverty reigns. But all this presupposes that the workman has work. When he has none, he is wholly at the mercy of accident, and eats what is given him, what he can beg or steal. And, if he gets nothing, he simply starves, as we have seen. The quantity of food varies, of course, like its quality, according to the rate of wages, so that among ill-paid workers, even if they have no large families, hunger prevails in spite of full and regular work; and the number of the ill-paid is very large. Especially in London, where the competition of the workers rises with the increase of population, this class is very numerous, but it is to be found in other towns as well. In these cases all sorts of devices are used; potato parings, vegetable refuse, and rotten vegetables[5] are eaten for want of other food, and everything greedily gathered up which may possibly contain an atom of nourishment. And, if the week's wages are used up before the end of the week, it often enough happens that in the closing days the family gets only as much food, if any, as is barely sufficient to keep off starvation. Of course such a way of living unavoidably engenders a multitude of diseases, and when these appear, when the father by whose work the family is chiefly supported, whose

[5] *Weekly Dispatch*, April or May 1844, according to a report by Dr Southwood Smith on the condition of the poor in London.

physical exertion most demands nourishment, and who therefore first succumbs – when the father is utterly disabled, then misery reaches its height, and then the brutality with which society abandons its members, just when their need is greatest, comes out fully into the light of day.

To sum up briefly the facts thus far cited. The great towns are chiefly inhabited by working people, since in the best case there is one of better class for two workers, often for three, here and there for four; these workers have no property whatsoever of their own, and live wholly upon wages, which usually go from hand to mouth. Society, composed wholly of atoms, does not trouble itself about them; leaves them to care for themselves and their families, yet supplies them no means of doing this in an efficient and permanent manner. Every working man, even the best, is therefore constantly exposed to loss of work and food, that is to death by starvation, and many perish in this way. The dwellings of the workers are everywhere badly planned, badly built, and kept in the worst condition, badly ventilated, damp, and unwholesome. The inhabitants are confined to the smallest possible space, and at least one family usually sleeps in each room. The interior arrangement of the dwellings is poverty-stricken in various degrees, down to the utter absence of even the most necessary furniture. The clothing of the workers, too, is generally scanty, and that of great multitudes is in rags. The food is, in general, bad; often almost unfit for use, and in many cases, at least at times, insufficient in quantity, so that, in extreme cases, death by starvation results. Thus the working class of the great cities offers a graduated scale of conditions in life, in the best cases a temporarily endurable existence for hard work and good wages, good and endurable, that is, from the worker's standpoint; in the worst cases, bitter want, reaching even homelessness and death by starvation. The average is much nearer the worst case than the best. And this series does not fall into fixed classes, so that one might say, this fraction of the working class is well off, has always been so, and remains so. If that is the case here and there, if single branches of work have in general an advantage over others, yet the condition of the workers in each branch is subject to such great fluctuations that a single working man may be so placed as to pass through the whole range from comparative comfort to the extremest need, even to death by starvation, while almost every English working man can tell a tale of marked changes of fortune. Let us examine the causes of this somewhat more closely.

Results

Having now investigated, somewhat in detail, the conditions under which the English working class lives, it is time to draw some further inferences from the facts presented, and then to compare our inferences with the actual state of things. Let us see what the workers themselves have become under the given circumstances, what sort of people they are, what their physical, mental, and moral status.

When one individual inflicts bodily injury upon another, such injury that death results, we call the deed manslaughter; when the assailant knew in advance that the injury would be fatal, we call his deed murder. But when society[6] places hundreds of proletarians in such a position that they inevitably meet a too early and an unnatural death, one which is quite as much a death by violence as that by the sword or bullet; when it deprives thousands of the necessaries of life, places them under conditions in which they *cannot* live – forces them, through the strong arm of the law, to remain in such conditions until that death ensues which is the inevitable consequence – knows that these thousands of victims must perish, and yet permits these conditions to remain, its deed is murder just as surely as the deed of the single individual; disguised, malicious murder, murder against which none can defend himself, which does not seem what it is, because no man sees the murderer, because the death of the victim seems a natural one, since the offence is more one of omission than of commission. But murder it remains. I have now to prove that society in England daily and hourly commits what the working men's organs, with perfect correctness, characterize as social murder, that it has placed the workers under conditions in which they can neither retain health nor live long; that it undermines the vital force of these workers gradually, little by little, and so hurries them to the grave before their time. I have further to prove that society knows how injurious such conditions are to the health and the life of the workers, and yet does nothing to improve these conditions. That it *knows* the consequences of its deeds; that its act is, therefore, not mere manslaughter, but murder, I shall have proved, when I cite official documents, reports of Parliament and of the Government, in substantiation of my charge.

That a class which lives under the conditions already sketched and is so ill–provided with the most necessary means of subsistence, cannot be healthy and can reach no advanced age, is self-evident. Let us review the circumstances once more with especial reference to the health of the workers. The centralization of population in great cities exercises of itself an unfavourable influence; the atmosphere of London can never be so pure, so rich in oxygen, as the air of the country; two and a half million pairs of lungs, 250,000 fires, crowded upon an area three to four miles square, consume an enormous amount of oxygen, which is replaced with difficulty, because the method of building cities in itself impedes ventilation. The carbonic acid gas, engendered by respiration and fire, remains in the streets by reason of its specific gravity, and the chief air current passes over the roofs of the city. The lungs of the inhabitants fail to receive the due supply of

[6] When as here and elsewhere I speak of society as a responsible whole, having rights and duties, I mean, of course, the ruling power of society, the class which at present holds social and political control, and bears, therefore, the responsibility for the condition of those to whom it grants no share in such control. This ruling class in England, as in all other civilized countries, is the bourgeoisie. But that this society, and especially the bourgeoisie, is charged with the duty of protecting every member of society, at least, in his life, to see to it, for example, that no one starves, I need not now prove to my *German* readers. If I were writing for the English bourgeoisie, the case would be different. (And so it is now in Germany. Our German capitalists are fully up to the English level, in this respect at least, in the year of grace, 1886.)

oxygen, and the consequence is mental and physical lassitude and low vitality. For this reason, the dwellers in cities are far less exposed to sudden, and especially to inflammatory, ailments than rural populations, who live in a free, normal atmosphere; but they suffer the more from chronic ailments. And if life in large cities is, in itself, injurious to health, how great must be the harmful influence of an abnormal atmosphere in the working people's quarters, where, as we have seen, everything combines to poison the air. In the country, it may, perhaps, be comparatively harmless to keep a dung-heap adjoining one's dwelling, because the air has free ingress from all sides; but in the midst of a large town, among closely built lanes and courts that shut out all movement of the atmosphere, the case is different. All putrefying vegetable and animal substances give off gases decidedly injurious to health, and if these gases have no free way of escape, they inevitably poison the atmosphere. The filth and stagnant pools of the working people's quarters in the great cities have, therefore, the worst effect upon the public heath, because they produce precisely those gases which engender disease; so too, the exhalations from contaminated streams. But this is by no means all. The manner in which the great multitude of the poor is treated by society today is revolting. They are drawn into the large cities where they breathe a poorer atmosphere than in the country; they are relegated to districts which, by reason of the method of construction, are worse ventilated than any others; they are deprived of all means of cleanliness, of water itself, since pipes are laid only when paid for, and the rivers so polluted that they are useless for such purposes; they are obliged to throw all offal and garbage, all dirty water, often all disgusting drainage and excrement into the streets, being without other means of disposing of them; they are thus compelled to infect the region of their own dwellings. Nor is this enough. All conceivable evils are heaped upon the heads of the poor. If the population of great cities is too dense in general, it is they in particular who are packed into the least space. As though the vitiated atmosphere of the streets were not enough, they are penned in dozens into single rooms, so that the air which they breathe at night is enough in itself to stifle them. They are given damp dwellings, cellar dens that are not waterproof from below, or garrets that leak from above. Their houses are so built that the clammy air cannot escape. They are supplied bad, tattered, or rotten clothing, adulterated and indigestible food. They are exposed to the most exciting changes of mental condition, the most violent vibrations between hope and fear; they are hunted like game, and not permitted to attain peace of mind and quiet enjoyment of life. They are deprived of all enjoyments except sexual indulgence and drunkenness, are worked every day to the point of complete exhaustion of their mental and physical energies, and are thus constantly spurred on to the maddest excess in the only two enjoyments at their command. And if they surmount all this, they fall victims to want of work in a crisis when all the little is taken from them that had hitherto been vouchsafed them.

How is it possible, under such conditions, for the lower class to be healthy and long lived? What else can be expected than an excessive mortality, an unbroken series of epidemics, a progressive deterioration in the physique of the working population? Let us see how the facts stand.

That the dwellings of the workers in the worst portions of the cities, together with the other conditions of life of this case, engender numerous diseases, is attested on all sides. The article already quoted from the *Artisan* asserts with perfect truth that lung diseases must be the inevitable consequences of such conditions, and that, indeed, cases of this kind are disproportionately frequent in this class. That the bad air of London, and especially of the working people's districts, is in the highest degree favourable to the development of consumption, the hectic appearance of great numbers of persons sufficiently indicates. If one roams the streets a little in the early morning, when the multitudes are on their way to their work, one is amazed at the number of persons who look wholly or half-consumptive. Even in Manchester the people have not the same appearance; these pale, lank, narrow-chested, hollow-eyed ghosts, whom one passes at every step, these languid, flabby faces, incapable of the slightest energetic expression, I have seen in such startling numbers only in London, though consumption carries off a horde of victims annually in the factory towns of the North. In competition with consumption stands typhus, to say nothing of scarlet fever, a disease which brings most frightful devastation into the ranks of the working class. Typhus, that universally diffused affliction, is attributed by the official report on the sanitary condition of the working class, directly to the bad state of the dwellings in the matters of ventilation, drainage, and cleanliness. This report, compiled, it must not be forgotten, by the leading physicians of England from the testimony of other physicians, asserts that a single ill-ventilated court, a single blind alley without drainage, is enough to engender fever, and usually does engender it, especially if the inhabitants are greatly crowded. This fever has the same character almost everywhere, and develops in nearly every case into specific typhus. It is to be found in the working people's quarters of all great towns and cities, and in single ill-built, ill-kept streets of smaller places, though it naturally seeks out single victims in better districts also. In London it has now prevailed for a considerable time; its extraordinary violence in the year 1837 gave rise to the report already referred to. According to the annual report of Dr Southward Smith on the London Fever Hospital, the number of patients in 1843 was 1,462, or 418 more than in any previous year. In the damp, dirty regions of the north, south, and east districts of London, this disease raged with extraordinary violence. Many of the patients were working people from the country, who had endured severest privation while migrating, and, after their arrival, had slept hungry and half-naked in the streets, and so fallen victims to the fever. These people were brought into the hospital in such a state of weakness, that unusual quantities of wine, cognac, and preparations of ammonia and other stimulants were required for their treatment; 16½ per cent of all patients died. This malignant fever is to be found in Manchester; in the worst quarters of the Old Town, Ancoats, Little Ireland, etc. it is rarely extinct; though here, as in the *English* towns generally, it prevails to a less extent than might be expected. In Scotland and Ireland, on the other hand, it rages with a violence that surpasses all conception. In Edinburgh and Glasgow it broke out in 1817, after the famine, and in 1826 and 1837 with especial violence, after the commercial crisis, subsiding somewhat each time after having raged about three years. In Edinburgh about 6,000 persons were attacked by the fever during the epidemic of 1817, and about 10,000 in that of 1837, and not only the number of persons attacked but the violence of the disease increased with each repetition.[7]

But the fury of the epidemic in all former periods seems to have been child's play in comparison with its ravages after the crisis of 1842. One-sixth of the whole indigent population of Scotland was seized by the fever, and the infection was carried by wandering beggars with fearful rapidity from one locality to another. It did not reach the middle and upper classes of the population, yet in two months there were more fever cases than in twelve years before. In Glasgow, twelve per cent of the population were seized in the year 1843; 32,000 persons, of whom thirty-two per cent perished, while this mortality in Manchester and Liverpool does not ordinarily exceed eight per cent. The illness reached a crisis on the seventh and fifteenth days; on the latter, the patient usually became yellow, which our authority[8] regards as an indication that the cause of the malady was to be sought in mental excitement and anxiety. In Ireland, too, these fever epidemics have become domesticated. During twenty-one months of the years 1817-18, 39,000 fever patients passed through the Dublin hospital; and in a more recent year, according to Sheriff Alison[9], 60,000. In Cork the fever hospital received one-seventh of the population in 1817-18, in Limerick in the same time one-fourth, and in the bad quarter of Waterford, nineteen-twentieths of the whole population were ill of the fever at one time[10].

When one remembers under what conditions the working people live, when one thinks how crowded their dwellings are, how every nook and corner swarms with human beings, how sick and well sleep in the same room, in the same bed, the only wonder is that a contagious disease like this fever does not spread yet farther. And when one reflects how little medical assistance the sick have at

[7] W.P. Alison, *Management of the Poor in Scotland.*

[8] A. Alison, *Principles of population*, vol ii.

[9] A. Alison in an article read before the British Association for the Advancement of Science, Oct 1844, in York.

[10] W.P. Alison, *Management of the Poor in Scotland.*

command, how many are without any medical advice whatsoever, and ignorant of the most ordinary precautionary measures, the mortality seems actually small. Dr Alison, who has made a careful study of this disease, attributes it directly to the want and the wretched condition of the poor, as in the report already quoted. He asserts that privations and the insufficient satisfaction of vital needs are what prepare the frame for contagion and make the epidemic widespread and terrible. He proves that a period of privation, a commercial crisis or a bad harvest, has each time produced the typhus epidemic in Ireland as in Scotland, and that the fury of the plague has fallen almost exclusively on the working class. It is a noteworthy fact, that according to his testimony, the majority of persons who perish by typhus are fathers of families, precisely the persons who can least be spared by those dependent upon them; and several Irish physicians whom he quotes bear the same testimony.

Another category of diseases arises directly from the food rather than the dwellings of the workers. The food of the labourer, indigestible enough in itself, is utterly unfit for young children, and he has neither means nor time to get his children more suitable food. Moreover, the custom of giving children spirits, and even opium, is very general; and these two influences, with the rest of the conditions of life prejudicial to bodily development, give rise to the most diverse affections of the digestive organs, leaving life-long traces behind them. Nearly all workers have stomachs more or less weak, and are yet forced to adhere to the diet which is the root of the evil. How should they know what is to blame for it? And if they knew, how could they obtain a more suitable regimen so long as they cannot adopt a different way of living and are not better educated? But new debility arises during childhood from impaired digestion. Scrofula is almost universal among the working class, and scrofulous parents have scrofulous children, especially when the original influences continue in full force to operate upon the inherited tendency of the children. A second consequence of this insufficient bodily nourishment, during the years of growth and development, is rickets, which is extremely common among the children of the working class. The hardening of the bones is delayed, the development of the skeleton in general is restricted, and deformities of the legs and spinal column are frequent, in addition to the usual rachitic affections. How greatly all these evils are increased by the changes to which the workers are subject in consequence of fluctuations in trade, want of work, and the scanty wages in time of crisis, it is not necessary to dwell upon. Temporary want of sufficient food, to which almost every working man is exposed at least once in the course of his life, only contributes to intensify the effect of his usually sufficient but bad diet. Children who are half-starved, just when they most need ample and nutritious food – and how many such there are during every crisis and even when trade is at its best — must inevitably become weak, scrofulous and rachitic in a high degree. And they do become so, their appearance amply shows. The neglect to which the great mass of working men's children are condemned leaves ineradicable traces and brings the enfeeblement of the whole race of workers with it. Add to this the unsuitable clothing of this class, the impossibility of precautions against colds, the necessity of toiling so long as health permits, want made more dire when sickness appears, and the only too common lack of all medical assistance; and we have a rough idea of the sanitary condition of the English working class. The injurious effects peculiar to single employments as now conducted, I shall not deal with here.

Besides these, there are other influences which enfeeble the health of a great number of workers, intemperance most of all. All possible temptations, all allurements combine to bring the workers to drunkenness. Liquor is almost their only source of pleasure, and all things conspire to make it accessible to them. The working man comes from his work tired, exhausted, finds his home comfortless, damp, dirty, repulsive; he has urgent need of recreation, he *must* have something to make work worth his trouble, to make the prospect of the next day endurable. His unnerved, uncomfortable, hypochondriac state of mind and body arising from his unhealthy condition, and especially from indigestion, is aggravated beyond endurance by the general conditions of his life, the uncertainty of his existence, his dependence upon all possible accidents and chances, and his inability to do anything towards gaining an assured position. His enfeebled frame, weakened by bad air and bad food, loudly demands some external stimulus; his social need can be gratified only in the public-house, he has absolutely no other place where he can meet his friends. How can he be expected to resist the temptation? It is morally and physically inevitable that, under such circumstances, a very large number of working men should fall into intemperance. And apart from the chiefly physical influences which drive the working man into drunkenness, there is the example of the great mass, the neglected education, the impossibility of protecting the young from temptation, in many cases the direct influence of intemperate parents, who give their own children liquor, the certainty of forgetting for an hour or two the wretchedness and burden of life, and a hundred other circumstances so mighty that the workers can, in truth, hardly be blamed for yielding to such overwhelming pressure. Drunkenness has here ceased to be a vice, for which the vicious can be held responsible; it becomes a phenomenon, the necessary, inevitable effect of certain conditions upon an object possessed of no volition in relation to those conditions. They who have degraded the working man to a mere object have the responsibility to bear. But as inevitably as a great number of working men fall a prey to drink, just so inevitably does it manifest its ruinous influence upon the body and mind of its victims. All the tendencies to disease arising from the conditions of life of the workers are promoted by it, it stimulates in the highest degree the development of lung and digestive troubles, the rise and spread of typhus epidemics.

Another source of physical mischief to the working class lies in the impossibility of employing skilled physicians in cases of illness. It is true that a number of charitable institutions strive to supply this want, that the infirmary in Manchester, for instance, receives or gives advice and medicine to 22,000 patients annually. But what is that in a city in which, according to Gaskell's calculation[11], three-fourths of the population need medical aid every year? English doctors charge high fees, and working men are not in a position to pay them. They can therefore do nothing, or are compelled to call in cheap charlatans, and use quack remedies, which do more harm than good. An immense number of such quacks thrive in every English town, securing their clientèle among the poor by means of advertisements, posters, and other such devices. Besides these, vast quantities of patent medicines are sold, for all conceivable ailments: Morrison's Pills, Parr's Life Pills, Dr Mainwaring's Pills, and a thousand other pills, essences, and balsams, all of which have the property of curing all the ills that flesh is heir to. These medicines rarely contain actually injurious substances, but, when taken freely and often, they affect the system prejudicially; and as the unwary purchasers are always recommended to take as much as possible, it is not to be wondered at that they swallow them wholesale whether wanted or not.

It is by no means unusual for the manufacture of Parr's Life Pills to sell 20-25,000 boxes of these salutary pills in a week, and they are taken for constipation by this one, for diarrhoea by that one, for fever, weakness, and all possible ailments. As our German peasants are cupped or bled at certain seasons, so do the English working people now consume patent medicines to their own injury and the great profit of the manufacturer. One of the most injurious of these patent medicines is a drink prepared with opiates, chiefly laudanum, under the name Godfrey's Cordial. Women who work at home, and have their own and other people's children to take care of, give them this drink to keep them quiet, and, as many believe, to strengthen them. They often begin to give this medicine to newly-born children, and continue, without knowing the effects of his 'heart's-ease', until the children die. The less susceptible the child's system to the action of the opium, the greater the quantities administered. When the cordial ceases to act, laudanum alone is given, often to the extent of fifteen to twenty drops at a dose. The Coroner of Nottingham testified before a Parliamentary Commission[12] that one apothecary had, according to his own statement, used thirteen hundred-weight of laudanum in one year in the preparation of Godfrey's Cordial. The

[11] *Manufacturing Population*, ch 8.

[12] Report of Commission of Inquiry into the Employment of Children and Young Persons in Mines and Collieries and in the Trades and Manufactures in which numbers of them work together, not being included under the terms of the Factories' Regulation Act. First and Second Reports, Grainger's Report. Second Report usually cited as 'Children's Employment Commission's Report'. [This is one of the best official reports, containing, as it does, a mass of the most valuable but also most frightful facts.] First Report, 1841; Second Report, 1843.

effects upon the children so treated may be readily imagined. They are pale, feeble, wilted, and usually die before completing the second year. The use of this cordial is very extensive in all great towns and industrial districts in the kingdom.

The result of all these influences is a general enfeeblement of the frame in the working class. There are few vigorous, well-built, healthy persons among the workers, i.e. among the factory operatives, who are employed in confined rooms, and we are here discussing these only. They are almost all weakly, of angular but not powerful build, lean, pale, and of relaxed fibre, with the exception of the muscles especially exercised in their work. Nearly all suffer from indigestion, and consequently from a more or less hypochondriac, melancholy, irritable, nervous condition. Their enfeebled constitutions are unable to resist disease, and are therefore seized by it on every occasion. Hence they age prematurely, and die early. On this point the mortality statistics supply unquestionable testimony.

According to the Report of Registrar-General Graham, the annual death-rate of all England and Wales is something less than 2¼ per cent. That is to say, out of forty-five persons, one dies every year[13]. This was the average for the year 1839-40. In 1840-41 the mortality diminished somewhat, and the death-rate was but one in forty-six. But in the great cities the proportion is wholly different. I have before me official tables of mortality (*Manchester Guardian*, 31 July 1844), according to which the death-rate of several large towns is as follows: – In Manchester, including Chorlton and Salford, one in 32.72; and excluding Chorlton and Salford, one in 30.75. In Liverpool, including West Derby (suburb), 31.90, and excluding West Derby, 29.90; while the average of all the districts of Cheshire, Lancashire, and Yorkshire cited, including a number of wholly or partially rural districts and many small towns, with a total population of 2,172,506 for the whole, is one death in 39.80 persons. How unfavourably the workers are placed in the great cities, the mortality for Prescott in Lancashire shows; a district inhabited by miners, and showing a lower sanitary condition than that of the agricultural districts, mining being by no means a healthful occupation. But these miners live in the country, and the death-rate among them is but one in 47.54, or nearly 2½ per cent better than that for all England. All these statements are based upon the mortality tables for 1843. Still higher is the death-rate in the Scotch cities; in Edinburgh, in 1838-9, one in 29; in 1831, in the Old Town alone, one in 22. In Glasgow, according to Dr Cowen[14], the average has been, since 1830, one in 30; and in single years, one in 22 to 24. That this enormous shortening of life falls chiefly upon the working class, that the general average is improved by the smaller mortality of the upper and middle classes, is attested upon all sides. One of the most recent depositions is that of a physician, Dr P.N. Holland, in Manchester, under official commission. He

[13] Fifth Annual Report of the Registrar-General of Births, Deaths, and Marriages.

[14] Dr Cowen, 'Vital Statistics of Glasgow', *Journal of the Statistical Society of London* (Oct 1840).

divided the houses and streets into three classes each, and ascertained the following variations in the death-rate:

First class of streets	Houses I class	Mortality one in	51
First class of streets	Houses II class	Mortality one in	45
First class of streets	Houses III class	Mortality one in	36
Second class of streets	Houses I class	Mortality one in	55
Second class of streets	Houses II class	Mortality one in	38
Second class of streets	Houses III class	Mortality one in	35
Third class of streets	Houses I class	Wanting	
Third class of streets	Houses II class	Mortality one in	35
Third class of streets	Houses III class	Mortality one in	25

It is clear from other tables given by Holland that the mortality in the *streets* of the second class is 18 per cent greater, and in the streets of the third class 68 per cent greater than in those of the first class; that the mortality in the *houses* of the second class is 31 per cent greater, and in the third class 78 per cent greater than in those of the first class; that the mortality in those bad streets which were improved, decreased 25 per cent. He closes with the remark, very frank for an English bourgeois[15]:

> When we find the rate of mortality four times as high in some streets as in others, and twice as high in whole classes of streets as in other classes, and further find that it is all but invariably high in those streets which are in bad condition, and almost invariably low in those whose condition is good, we cannot resist the conclusion that multitudes of our fellow-creatures, *hundreds of our immediate neighbours*, are annually destroyed for want of the most evident precautions.

[15] Report of Commission of Inquiry into the State of Large Towns and Populous Districts. First Report, 1844. Appendix.

The Report on the Sanitary Condition of the Working Class contains information which attests the same fact. In Liverpool, in 1840, the average life-span of the upper classes, gentry, professional men, etc, was thirty-five years; that of the business men and better-placed handicraftsmen, twenty-two years; and that of the operatives, day-labourers, and serviceable class in general, but fifteen years. The Parliamentary reports contain a mass of similar facts.

The death-rate is kept so high chiefly by the heavy mortality among young children in the working class. The tender frame of a child is least able to withstand the unfavourable influences of an inferior lot in life; the neglect to which they are often subject, when both parents work or one is dead, avenges itself promptly, and no one need wonder that in Manchester, according to the report last quoted, more than 57 per cent of the children of the working class perish before the fifth year, while but 20 per cent of the children of the higher classes, and not quite 32 per cent of the children of all classes in the country die under five years of age. The article of the *Artisan*, already several times referred to, furnishes exacter information on this point, by comparing the city death-rate in single diseases of children with the country death-rate, thus demonstrating that, in general, epidemics in Manchester and Liverpool are three times more fatal than in country districts; that affections of the nervous system are quintupled, and stomach troubles trebled, while deaths from affections of the lungs in cities are to those in the country as 2½ to 1. Fatal cases of smallpox, measles, scarlet fever, and whooping cough, among small children, are four times more frequent; those of water on the brain are three times, and convulsions ten times more frequent. To quote another acknowledged authority, I append the following table. Out of 10,000 persons, there die[16] – [see table on p 77]. Apart from the diverse diseases which are the necessary consequence of the present neglect and oppression of the poorer classes, there are other influences which contribute to increase the mortality among small children. In many families the wife, like the husband, has to work away from home, and the consequence is the total neglect of the children, who are either locked up or given out to be taken care of. It is, therefore, not to be wondered at if hundreds of them perish through all manner of accidents. Nowhere are so many children run over, nowhere are so many killed by falling, drowning, or burning, as in the great cities and towns of England. Deaths from burns and scalds are especially frequent, such a case occurring nearly every week during the winter months in Manchester, and very frequently in London, though little mention is made of them in the papers. I have at hand a copy of the *Weekly Dispatch* of 15 December 1844, according to which, in the week from 1 December to 7 December inclusive, *six* such cases occurred. These unhappy children, perishing in this terrible way, are victims of our social chaos, and of the property-holding classes interested in maintaining and prolonging this chaos. Yet one is left in doubt whether even this terribly torturing death is not a blessing for the children by rescuing them from a long life of toil and wretchedness, rich in suffering and poor in enjoyment. So far has it gone in England; and the bourgeoisie reads these things every day in the newspapers and takes no further notice of the matter. But it cannot complain if after the official and non-official testimony here cited which must be known to it, I broadly accuse it of social murder. Let the ruling class see to it that these frightful conditions are ameliorated, or let me surrender the administration of the common interests to the labouring class. To the latter course it is by no means inclined; for the former task, so long as it remains the bourgeoisie crippled by bourgeois prejudice, it has not the needed power. For if, at last, after hundreds of thousands of victims have perished, it manifests some little anxiety

[16] Factories' Inquiry Commission's Reports, 3rd vol Report of Dr Hawkins on Lancashire, in which Dr Robertson is cited – the 'Chief Authority for Statistics in Manchester'.

	Under 5 years	5-19	20-39	40-59	60-69	70-79	80-89	90-99	100+
In Rutlandshire, a healthy agricultural district	2,865	891	1,275	1,299	1,189	1,428	938	112	3
Essex, marshy agricultural district	3,159	1,110	1,526	1,413	963	1,019	630	177	3
Town of Carlisle, 1779-87, before introduction of mills	4,408	911	1,006	1,201	940	826	533	153	22
Town of Carlisle, after the introduction of mills	4,738	930	1,261	1,134	677	727	452	80	1
Preston, factory town	4,947	1,136	1,379	1,114	553	532	298	38	3
Leeds, factory town	5,286	927	1,228	1,198	593	512	225	29	2

for the future, passing a 'Metropolitan Buildings Act', under which the most unscrupulous overcrowding of dwellings is to be, at least in some slight degree, restricted; if it points with pride to measures which, far from attacking the root of the evil, do not by any means meet the demands of the commonest sanitary police, it cannot thus vindicate itself from the accusation. The English bourgeoisie has but one choice, either to continue its rule under the unanswerable charge of murder and in spite of this charge, or to abdicate in favour of the labouring class. Hitherto it has chosen the former course.

Henry Mayhew, 1812-87

HENRY MAYHEW.

Henry Mayhew was born in 1812 and was the son of a successful solicitor. He was sent to Westminster School where he proved to be a brilliant but indolent student. In 1827 he ran away and was subsequently sent to India as a mid-shipman. He went on to have a varied career which included law, journalism, various theatrical projects and writing novels. In 1842 he became editor of the newly founded magazine *Punch*.

Mayhew's most well-remembered work by far is *London labour and the London poor*, the first edition of which was published in 1851-52. This comprised a great study of the living and working conditions of London, a finely detailed chronicle of life on the streets. His focus was very much on people and he gives accounts of the worlds of costermongers, stall keepers, flower girls, coffee stall keepers, chimney sweeps, cabdrivers, vagrants, thieves and many many more. Here we present an extract about the 'mud-lark'.

Henry Mayhew continued to research and publish for the rest of his life. In 1856 he published the first of his series on *The great world of London* in the *Morning Chronicle*. In 1862 a collection of his articles was published on *The criminal prisoners of London* and in 1874 another collection entitled *London characters*. He died in London in 1887.

Mayhew, H. (1851–52) *London labour and the London poor*

Scavengers and cleaners
Of the mud-larks

There is another class who may be termed river-finders, although their occupation is connected only with the shore; they are commonly known by the name of 'mud-larks', from being compelled, in order to obtain the articles they seek, to wade sometimes up to their middle through the mud left on the shore by the retiring tide. These poor creatures are certainly about the most deplorable in their appearance of any I have met with in the course of my inquiries. They may be seen of all ages, from mere childhood to positive decrepitude, crawling among the barges at the various wharfs along the river; it cannot be said that they are clad in rags, for they are scarcely half covered by the tattered indescribable things that serve them for clothing; their bodies are grimed with the foul soil of the river, and their torn garments stiffened up like boards with dirt of every possible description.

Among the mud-larks may be seen many old women, and it is indeed pitiable to behold them, especially during the winter, bent nearly double with age and infirmity, paddling and groping among the wet mud for small pieces of coal, chips of wood, or any sort of refuse washed up by the tide. These women always have with them an old basket or an old tin kettle, in which they put whatever they chance to find. It usually takes them a whole tide to fill this receptacle, but when filled, it is as much as the feeble old creatures are able to carry home.

The mud-larks generally live in some court or alley in the neighbourhood of the river, and, as the tide recedes, crowds of boys and little girls, some old men, and many old women, may be observed loitering about the various stairs, watching eagerly for the opportunity to commence their labours. When the tide is sufficiently low they scatter themselves along the shore, separating from each other, and soon disappear among the craft lying about in every direction. This is the case on both sides of the river, as high up as there is anything to be found, extending as far as Vauxhall-bridge, and as low down as Woolwich. The mud-larks themselves, however, know only those who reside near them, and whom they are accustomed to meet in their daily pursuits; indeed, with but few exceptions, these people are dull, and apparently stupid; this is observable particularly among the boys and girls, who, when engaged in searching the mud, hold but little converse one with another. The men and women may be passed and repassed, but they notice no one; they never speak, but with a stolid look of wretchedness they plash [sic] their way through the mire, their bodies bent down while they peer anxiously about, and occasionally stoop to pick up some paltry treasure that falls in their way.

The mud-larks collect whatever they happen to find, such as coals, bits of old-iron, rope, bones, and copper nails that drop from ships while lying or repairing along shore. Copper nails are the most valuable of all the articles they find, but these they seldom obtain, as they are always driven from the neighbourhood of a ship while being new-sheathed. Sometimes the younger and bolder mud-larks venture on sweeping some empty coal-barge, and one little fellow with whom I spoke, having been lately caught in the act of so doing, had to undergo for the offence seven days' imprisonment in the House of Correction: this, he says, he liked much better than mud-larking, for while he staid there he wore a coat and shoes and stockings, and though he had not over much to eat, he certainly was never afraid of going to bed without anything at all – as he often had to do when at liberty. He thought he would try it on again in the winter, he told me, saying, it would be so comfortable to have clothes and shoes and stockings then, and not be obliged to go into the cold wet mud of a morning.

The coals that the mud-larks find, they sell to the poor people of the neighbourhood at 1*d* per pot, holding about 14 lbs. The iron and bones and rope and copper nails which they collect, they sell at the rag-shops. They dispose of the iron at 5 lbs for 1*d*, the bones at 3 lbs a 1*d*, rope at ½*d* per lb wet, and ¾ per lb dry, and copper nails at the rate of 4*d* per lb. They occasionally pick up tools, such as saws and hammers; these they dispose of to the seamen for biscuit and meat, and sometimes sell them at the rag-shops for a few halfpence. In this manner they earn from 2½*d* to 8*d* per day, but rarely the latter sum; their average gains may be estimated at about 3*d* per day. The boys, after leaving the river, sometimes scrape their trousers, and frequent the cab-stands, and try to earn a trifle by opening the cab-doors for those who enter them, or by holding gentlemen's horses. Some of them go, in the evening, to a ragged school, in the neighbourhood of which they live; more, as they say, because other boys go there, than from any desire to learn.

At one of the stairs in the neighbourhood of the pool, I collected about a dozen of these unfortunate children; there was not one of them over twelve years of age, and many of them were but six. It would be almost impossible to describe the wretched group, so motley was their appearance, so extraordinary their dress, and so stolid and inexpressive their countenances. Some carried baskets, filled with the produce of their morning's work, and others old tin kettles with iron handles. Some, for want of these articles, had old hats filled with the bones and coals they had picked up; and others, more needy still, had actually taken the caps from their own heads, and filled them with what they had happened to find. The muddy slush was dripping from their clothes and utensils, and forming a puddle in which they stood. There did not appear to be among the whole group as many filthy cotton rags to their backs as, when stitched together, would have been sufficient to form the material of one shirt. There were the remnants of one or two jackets among them, but so begrimed and tattered that it would have been difficult to have determined either the original material or make of the garment. On questioning one, he said his father was a coal-backer; he had been dead eight years; the boy was nine years old. His mother was alive; she went out charing and washing when she could get any such work to do. She had 1*s* a day when she could get employment, but that was not often; he remembered once to have had a pair of shoes, but it was a long time since. 'It is very cold in winter,' he said, 'to stand in the mud without shoes,' but he did not mind it in summer. He had been three years mud-larking, and supposed he should remain a mud-lark all his life. What else could be? for there was nothing else that he knew how to do. Some days he earned 1*d*, and some days 4*d*; he never earned 8*d* in one day, that would have been a 'jolly lot of money'. He never found a saw or a hammer, he 'only wished' he could, they would be glad to get hold of them at the dolly's. He had been one month at school before he went mud-larking. Some time ago he had gone to the ragged-school; but he no longer went there, for he forgot it. He could neither read nor write, and did not think he could learn if he tried 'ever so much'. He didn't know what religion his father and mother were, nor did know what religion meant. God was God, he said. He had heard he was good, but didn't know what good he was to him. He thought he was a Christian, but he didn't know what a Christian was. He had heard of Jesus Christ once, when he went to a Catholic chapel, but he never heard tell of who or what he was, and didn't 'particular care' about knowing. His father and mother were born in Aberdeen, but he didn't know where Aberdeen was. London was England, and England, he said, was in London, but he couldn't tell in what part. He could not tell where he could go to when he died, and didn't believe any one could tell *that*. Prayers, he told me, were what people said to themselves at night. *He* never said any, and didn't know any; his mother sometimes used to speak to him about them, but he could never learn any. His mother didn't go to church or to chapel, because she had no clothes. All the money he got he gave to his mother, and she bought bread with it, and when they had no money they lived the best way they could.

Such was the amount of intelligence manifested by this unfortunate child.

THE MUD-LARK.

Another was only seven years old. He stated that his father was a sailor who had been hurt on board ship, and been unable to go to sea for the last two years. He had two brothers and a sister, one of them older than himself; and his elder brother was a mud-lark like himself. The two had been mud-larking more than a year; they went because they saw other boys go, and knew that they got money for the things they found. They were often hungry, and glad to do anything to get something to eat. Their father was not able to earn anything, and their mother could get but little to do. They gave all the money they earned to their mother. They didn't gamble, and play at pitch and toss when they had got some money, but some of the big boys did on the Sunday, when they didn't go a mud-larking. He couldn't tell why they did nothing on a Sunday, 'only they didn't'; though sometimes they looked about to see where the best place would be on the next day. He didn't go to the ragged school; he should like to know how to read a book, though he couldn't tell what good it would do him. He didn't like mud larking, would be glad of some thing else, but didn't know anything else that he could do.

Another of the boys was the son of a dock labourer, – casually employed. He was between seven and eight years of age, and his sister, who was also a mud-lark, formed one of the group. The mother of these two was dead, and there were three children younger than themselves.

The rest of the histories may easily be imagined, for there was a painful uniformity in the stories of all the children: they were either the children of the very poor, who, by their own improvidence or some overwhelming calamity, had been reduced to the extremity of distress, or else they were orphans, and compelled from utter destitution to seek for the means of appeasing their hunger in the mud of the river. That the majority of this class are ignorant, and without even the rudiments of education, and that many of them from time to time are committed to prison for petty thefts, cannot be wondered at. Nor can it even excite our astonishment that, once within the walls of a prison, and finding how much more comfortable it is than their previous condition, they should return to it repeatedly. As for the females growing up under such circumstances, the worst may be anticipated of them; and in proof of this I have found, upon inquiry, that very many of the unfortunate creatures who swell the tide of prostitution in Ratcliff-highway, and other low neighbourhoods in the East of London, have originally been mud-larks; and only remained at that occupation till such time as they were capable of adopting the more easy and more lucrative life of the prostitute.

As to the numbers and earnings of the mud-larks, the following calculations fall short of, rather than exceed, the truth. From Execution Dock to the lower part of Limehouse Hole, there are 14 stairs or landing-places, by which the mud-larks descend to the shore in order to pursue their employment. There are about as many on the opposite side of the water similarly frequented.

At King James' Stairs, in Wapping Wall, which is nearly a central position, from 40 to 50 mud-larks go down daily to the river; the mud-larks 'using' the other stairs are not so numerous. If, therefore, we reckon the number of stairs on both sides of the river at 28, and the average number of mud-larks frequenting them at 10 each, we shall have a total of 280. Each mud-lark, it has been shown, earns on an average 3*d* a day, or 1*s* 6*d* per week; so that the annual earnings of each will be 3*l* [£3] 18*s*, or say 4*l*, a year, and hence the gross earnings of the 280 will amount to rather more than £1,000 per annum.

But there are, in addition to the mud-larks employed in the neighbourhood of what may be called the pool, many others who work down the river at various places as far as Blackwall, on the one side, and at Deptford, Greenwich, and Woolwich, on the other. These frequent the neighbourhoods of the various 'yards' along shore, where vessels are being built; and whence, at certain times, chips, small pieces of wood, bits of iron, and copper nails, are washed out into the river.

There is but little doubt that this portion of the class earn much more than the mud-larks of the pool, seeing that they are especially convenient to the places where the iron vessels are constructed; so that the presumption is, that the number of mud-larks 'at work' on the banks of the Thames (especially if we include those above bridge), and the value of the property extracted by them from the mud of the river, may be fairly estimated at double that which is stated above, or say 550 gaining £2,000 per annum.

As an illustration of the doctrines I have endeavoured to enforce throughout this publication, I cite the following history of one of the above class. It may serve to teach those who are still sceptical as to the degrading influence of circumstances upon the poor, that many of the humbler classes, if placed in the same easy position as ourselves, would become, perhaps, quite as 'respectable' members of society.

The lad of whom I speak was discovered by me now nearly two years ago 'mud-larking' on the banks of the river near the docks. He was a quick, intelligent little fellow, and had been at the business, he told me, about three years. He had taken to mud-larking, he said, because his clothes were too bad for him to look for anything better. He worked every day, with 20 or 30 boys, who might all be seen at day-break with their trowsers tucked up, groping about, and picking out the pieces of coal from the mud on the banks of the Thames. He went into the river up to his knees, and in searching the mud he often ran pieces of glass and long nails into his feet. When this was the case, he went home and dressed the wounds, but returned to the river-side directly, "for should the tide come up," he added, "without my having found something, why I must starve till next low tide." In the very cold weather he and his other shoe-less companions used to stand in the hot water than ran down the river side from some of the steam-factories, to warm their frozen feet.

At first he found it difficult to keep his footing in the mud, and he had known many beginners fall in. He came to my house, at my request, the morning after my first meeting with him. It was the depth of winter, and the poor little fellow was nearly destitute of clothing. His trousers were worn away up to his knees, he had no shirt, and his legs and feet (which were bare) were covered with chillblains. On being questioned by me he gave the following account of his life:—

He was fourteen years old. He had two sisters, one fifteen and the other twelve years of age. His father had been dead nine years. The man had been a coal-whipper, and, from getting his work from one of the publican employers in those days, had become a confirmed drunkard. When he married he held a situation in a ware-house, where his wife managed the first year to £4 10s out of her husband's earnings; but from the day he took to coal-whipping she had never saved one halfpenny, indeed she and her children were often left to starve. The man (whilst in a state of intoxication) had fallen between two barges, and the injuries he received had been so severe that he had lingered in a helpless state for three years before his death. After her husband's decease the poor woman's neighbours subscribed £1 5s for her; with this sum she opened a green-grocer's shop, and got on very well for five years.

When the boy was nine years old his mother sent him to the Red Lion school at Green-bank, near Old Gravel-lane, Ratcliffe-highway; she paid 1d a week for his learning. He remained there for a year; then the potato-rot came, and his mother lost upon all she bought. About the same time two of her customers died 30s in her debt; this loss, together with the potato-disease, completely ruined her, and the whole family had been in the greatest poverty from that period. Then she was obliged to take all her children from their school, that they might help to keep themselves as best they could. Her eldest girl sold fish in the streets, and the boy went to the river-side to 'pick up' his living. The change, however, was so great that shortly afterwards the little fellow lay ill eighteen weeks with the ague. As soon as the boy recovered his mother and his two sisters were 'taken bad' with a fever. The poor woman went into the 'Great House', and the children were taken to the Fever Hospital. When the mother returned home she was too weak to work, and all she had to depend on was what her boy brought from the river. They had nothing to eat and no money until the little fellow had been down to the shore and picked up some coals, selling them for a trifle. "And hard enough he had to work for what he got, poor boy," said his mother to me on a future occasion, sobbing; "still he never complained, but was quite proud when he brought home enough for us to get a bit of meat with; and when he has sometimes seen me down-hearted, he has clung round my neck, and assured me that one day God would see us cared for if I would put my trust in Him." As soon as his mother was well enough she sold fruit in the streets, or went out washing when she could get a day's work.

The lad suffered much from the pieces of broken glass in the mud. Some little time before I met with him he had run a copper nail into his foot. This lamed him for three months, and his mother was obliged to carry him on her back every morning to the doctor. As soon, however, as he could 'hobble' (to use his mother's own words) he went back to the river, and often returned (after many hours' hard work in the mud) with only a few pieces of coal, not enough to sell even to get them a bit of bread. One evening, as he was warming his feet in the water than ran from a steam factory, he heard some boys talking about the Ragged School in High-Street, Wapping.

"They was saying what they used to learn there," added the boy. "They asked me to come along with them for it was great fun. They told me that all the boys used to be laughing and making game of the master. They said they used to put out the gas and chuck the slates all about. They told me, too, that there was a good fire there, so I went to have a warm and see what it was like. When I got there the master was very kind to me. They used to give us tea-parties, and to keep us quiet they used to show us the magic lantern. I soon got to like going there, and went every night for six months. There was about 40 or 50 boys in the school. The most of them was thieves, and they used to go thieving the coals out of barges along shore, and cutting the ropes off ships, and going and selling it at the rag-shops. They used to get ¾*d* a lb, for the rope when dry, and ½*d* when wet. Some used to steal pudding out of shops and hand it to those outside, and the last boy it was handed to would go off with it. They used to steal bacon and bread sometimes as well. About half of the boys at the school was thieves. Some had work to do at ironmongers, lead-factories, engineers, soap-boilers, and so on, and some had no work to do and was good boys still. After we came out of school at nine o'clock at night, some of the bad boys would go a thieving, perhaps half-a-dozen and from that to eight would go out in a gang together. There was one big boy of the name of C–; he was 18 years old, and is in prison now for stealing bacon; I think he is in the House of Correction. This C– used to go out of school before any of us, and wait outside the door as the other boys came out. Then he would call the boys he wanted for his gangs on one side, and tell them where to go and steal. He used to look out in the daytime for shops where things could be "prigged", and at night he would tell the boys to go to them. He was called the captain of the gangs. He had about three gangs altogether with him, and there were from six to eight boys in each gang. The boys used to bring what they stole to C–, and he used to share it with them. I belonged to one of the gangs. There were six boys altogether in my gang; the biggest lad, that knowed all about the thieving, was the captain of the gang I was in, and C– was captain over him and over all of us.

There was two brothers of them; you seed them, sir, the night you first met me. The other boys, as was in my gang, was B–B–, and B–L–, and W–B–, and a boy we used to call "Tim"; these, with myself, used to make up one of the gangs, and we all of us used to go a thieving every night after school-hours. When the tide would be right up, and we had nothing to do along shore, we used to go thieving in the daytime as well. It was B–B–, and B–L–, as first put me up to go thieving; they took me with them, one night, up the lane [New Gravel-lane], and I see them take some bread out of a baker's, and they wasn't found out; and, after that, I used to go with them regular. Then I joined C–'s gang; and, after that, C– came and told us that his gang could do better than ourn, and he asked us to join our gang to his'n, and we did so. Sometimes we used to make 3s and 4s a day; or about 6d apiece. While waiting outside the school-doors, before they opened, we used to plan up where we would go thieving after school was over. I was taken up once for thieving coals myself, but I was let go again."

I was so much struck with the boy's truthfulness of manner, that I asked him, *would* he really lead a different life, if he saw a means of so doing? He assured me he would, and begged me earnestly to try him. Upon his leaving me, 2s were given him for his trouble. This small sum (I afterwards learned) kept the family for more than a fortnight. The girl laid it out in sprats (it being then winter-time); these she sold in the streets.

I mentioned the fact to a literary friend, who interested himself in the boy's welfare; and eventually succeeded in procuring him a situation at an eminent printer's. The subjoined letter will show how the lad conducted himself while there.

Whitefriars, April 22, 1850

Messrs Bradbury and Evans beg to say that the boy J.C. has conducted himself in a very satisfactory manner since he has been in their employment.

The same literary friend took the girl into his service. She is in a situation still, though not in the same family.

The boy now holds a good situation at one of the daily newspaper offices. So well has he behaved himself, that, a few weeks since, his wages were increased from 6s to 9s per week. His mother (owing to the boy's exertions) has now a little shop, and is doing well.

This simple story requires no comments, and is narrated here in the hope that it may teach many to know how often the poor boys reared in the gutter are thieves, merely because society forbids them being honest lads.

Karl Marx, 1818-83 **8**

Karl Marx was born in Trier, Germany, in 1818 into a middle-class German-Jewish family who converted to Protestantism when Marx was a young child. Marx's father was a lawyer and the young Marx attended university in Bonn and Berlin, where he studied law, history and philosophy. Early in his intellectual career he was influenced by the dialectical thinking of the idealist philosopher, Hegel, which he transformed into his own historical materialism which gave priority to social, economic and political forces in history, rather than to Hegel's ideas. Marx saw the condition of society as a product of its economic foundations and the organisation of the means of production. He saw revolution as the sole solution to the plight of the proletariat.

In 1844 Karl Marx started collaborating with Friedrich Engels, with whom he worked on the *Manifesto of the Communist Party*. The ideas put forward there were the basis of state socialism and communism. For a substantial part of the 20th century Marxist ideas (in various forms, derivations and distortions) were the organising principle for societies which together contained almost a third of the world's total population. As well as having great political influence, Marxist ideas have also have a profound influence on social theory and Marx is regarded as one of, if not the greatest, social scientists of modern times.

Marx spent many years in the British Museum researching for his great work, *Capital*, which analysed the capitalist mode of production. He also played a leading role in the International Working Men's Association, and here we present an extract from his inaugural address to this organisation in 1864.

Marx, K. (1864) *Inaugural address of the International Working Men's Association*

Documents of The First International:
1864–70 Inaugural Address of
The International Working
Men's Association[1]

[1] Marx drafted the Inaugural Address and the Provisional Rules of the International during the last week of October 1864. They were adopted by the General Council on 1 November, and published as a pamphlet: *Address and Provisional Rules of the Working Men's International Association*, London, 1864. In this and other texts originally published in English, printers' errors and archaic orthography have been corrected where necessary.

[2] The day of Gladstone's budget speech for 1864.

[3] The garotte panic was over a series of violent street robberies, some involving murder, which led to a parliamentary inquiry. The resulting blue book was the *Report of the Commissioners ... relating to Transportation and Penal Servitude*, vol 1, London, 1863.

Fellow working men,

It is a great fact that the misery of the working masses has not diminished from 1848 to 1864, and yet this period is unrivalled for the development of its industry and the growth of its commerce. In 1850, a moderate organ of the British middle class, of more than average information, predicted that if the exports and imports of England were to rise fifty per cent, English pauperism would sink to zero. Alas! On 7 April 1864[2] the Chancellor of the Exchequer delighted his parliamentary audience by the statement that the total import and export trade of England had grown in 1863 'to £443,955,000, that astonishing sum about three times the trade of the comparatively recent epoch of 1843'. With all that, he was eloquent upon 'poverty'. 'Think,' he exclaimed, 'of those who are on the border of that region,' upon 'wages ... not increased'; upon 'human life ... in nine cases out of ten but a struggle of existence'. He did not speak of the people of Ireland, gradually replaced by machinery in the north, and by sheep-walks in the south, though even the sheep in that unhappy country are decreasing, it is true, not at so rapid a rate as the men. He did not repeat what then had been just betrayed by the highest representatives of the upper ten thousand in a sudden fit of terror. When the garotte[3] panic had reached a certain height, the House of Lords caused an inquiry to be made into, and a report to be published upon, transportation and penal servitude. Out came the murder in the bulky blue book of 1863, and proved it was, by official facts and figures, that the worst of the convicted criminals, the penal serfs of England and Scotland, toiled much less and fared far better than the agricultural labourers of England and Scotland. But this was not all. When, consequent upon the civil war in America, the operatives of Lancashire and Cheshire were thrown upon the streets, the same House of Lords sent to the manufacturing districts a physician commissioned to investigate into the smallest possible amount of carbon and nitrogen, to be administered in the cheapest and plainest form, which on an average might just suffice to 'avert starvation diseases'. Dr Smith, the medical deputy, ascertained that 28,000 grains of carbon and 1,330 grains of nitrogen were the weekly allowance that would keep an average adult just over the level of starvation diseases, and he found furthermore that quantity pretty nearly to agree with the scanty nourishment to which the pressure of extreme distress had actually reduced the cotton operatives.[4] But now mark! The same learned doctor was later on again deputed by the Medical Officer of the Privy Council to inquire into the nourishment of the poorer labouring classes. The results of his researches are embodied in the *Sixth Report on Public Health*, published by order of Parliament in the course of the present year. What did the doctor discover? That the silk weavers, the needle women, the kid glovers, the stocking weavers, and so forth, received, on an average, not even the distress pittance of the cotton operatives, not even the amount of carbon and nitrogen 'just sufficient to avert starvation diseases'. Moreover, we quote from the report,

> as regards the examined families of the agricultural population, it appeared that more than a fifth were with less than the estimated sufficiency of carbonaceous food, that more than one-third were with less than the estimated sufficiency of nitrogenous food, and that in three counties (Berkshire, Oxfordshire, and Somersetshire) insufficiency of nitrogenous food was the average local diet.

'It must be remembered,' adds the official report,

> That privation of food is very reluctantly borne, and that, as a rule, great poorness of diet will only come when other privations have preceded it.... Even cleanliness will have been found costly or difficult, and if there still be self-respectful endeavours to maintain it, every such endeavour will represent additional pangs of hunger.... These are painful reflections, especially when it is remembered that the poverty to which they advert is not the deserved poverty of idleness; in all cases it is the poverty of working populations. Indeed, the work which obtains the scanty pittance of food is for the most part excessively prolonged.

The report brings out the strange, and rather unexpected fact, 'that of the divisions of the United Kingdom', England, Wales, Scotland, and Ireland, 'The agricultural population of England', the richest division, 'is considerably the worst fed'; but that even the agricultural

[4] We need hardly remind the reader that, apart from the elements of water and certain inorganic substances, carbon and nitrogen form the raw materials of human food. However, to nourish the human system, those simple chemical constituents must be supplied in the form of vegetable or animal substances. Potatoes, for instance, contain mainly carbon, while wheaten bread contains carbonaceous and nitrogenous substances in a due proportion [Marx].

labourers of Berkshire, Oxfordshire, and Somersetshire, fare better than great numbers of skilled indoor operatives of the east of London.

Such are the official statements published by order of Parliament in 1864, during the millennium of free trade, at a time when the Chancellor of the Exchequer[5] told the House of Commons that: 'The average condition of the British labourer has improved in a degree we know to be extraordinary and unexampled in the history of any country or any age.'

[5] Gladstone, in his 1864 budget speech.

Upon these official congratulations jars the dry remark of the official *Public Health Report:* 'The public health of a country means the health of its masses, and the masses will scarcely be healthy unless, to their very base, they be at least moderately prosperous.'

Dazzled by the 'Progress of the Nation' statistics dancing before his eyes, the Chancellor of the Exchequer exclaims in wild ecstasy: 'From 1842 to 1852 the taxable income of the country increased by 6 per cent; in the eight years from 1853 to 1861, it has increased from the basis taken in 1853 20 per cent. The fact is so astonishing to be almost incredible ... This intoxicating augmentation of wealth and power,' adds Mr Gladstone, 'is entirely confined to classes of property'.[6]

[6] This quotation is from Gladstone's budget speech of 16 April 1863. Marx was at one time accused of having invented the last sentence of this quotation, which he also cites in *Capital*. But although the sentence in question is not to be found in *Hansard*, whether by accident, or, as Marx believed, by Gladstone's censorship, it appears in the parliamentary reports of both *The Times* and the *Morning Star*, and Marx was thus able to vindicate himself. See Engels' Preface to the fourth German edition of *Capital*, vol I, Moscow, 1961, pp 27-9.

If you want to know under what conditions of broken health, tainted morals, and mental ruin, that 'intoxicating augmentation of wealth and power entirely confined to classes of property' was, and is being, produced by the classes of labour, look to the picture hung up in the last *Public Health Report* of the workshops of tailors, printers, and dressmakers! Compare the *Report of the Children's Employment Commission* of 1863, where it is stated, for instance, that:

> The potters as a class, both men and women, represent a much degenerated population, both physically and mentally.... The unhealthy child is an unhealthy parent in his turn.... A progressive deterioration of the race must go on.... The degenerescence of the population of Staffordshire would be even greater were it not for the constant recruiting from the adjacent country, and the intermarriages with more healthy races.

Glance at Mr Tremenheere's blue book on *The Grievances complained of by the Journeymen Bakers!*[7] And who has not shuddered at the paradoxical statement made by the inspectors of factories, and illustrated by the Registrar General, that the Lancashire operatives, while put upon the distress pittance of food, were actually improving in health because of their temporary exclusion by the cotton famine from the cotton factory, and that the mortality of the children was decreasing, because their mothers were now at last allowed to give them, instead of Godfrey's cordial, their own breasts.[8]

[7] London, 1862.

[8] *Report of the Inspectors of Factories ... for the half-year ending October 1863*, London, 1864.

Again reverse the medal! The Income and Property Tax Returns laid before the House of Commons on 20 July 1864 teach us that the persons with yearly incomes valued by the tax-gatherer at £50,000 and upwards, had, from 5 April 1862 to 5 April 1863, been joined by a dozen and one, their number having increased in that single year from 67 to 80. The same returns disclose the fact that about 3,000 persons divide amongst themselves a yearly income of about £25,000,000 sterling, rather more than the total revenue doled out annually to the whole mass of the agricultural labourers of England and Wales. Open the Census of 1861, and you will find that the number of the male landed proprietors of England and Wales had decreased from 16,934 in 1851, to 15,066 in 1861, so that the concentration of land had grown in 10 years 11 per cent. If the concentration of the soil of the country in a few hands proceeds at the same rate, the land question will become singularly simplified, as it had become in the Roman empire, when Nero grinned at the discovery that half the province of Africa was owned by six gentlemen.

We have dwelt so long upon these 'facts so astonishing to be almost incredible', because England heads the Europe of commerce and industry.[9] It will be remembered that some months ago one of the refugee sons of Louis Philippe publicly congratulated the English agricultural labourer on the superiority of his lot over that of his less florid comrade on the other side of the Channel. Indeed, with local colours changed, and on a scale somewhat contracted, the English facts reproduce themselves in all the industrious and progressive countries of the Continent. In all of them there has taken place, since 1848, an unheard-of development of industry, and an undreamed-of expansion of imports and exports. In all of them 'the augmentation of wealth and power entirely confined to classes of property' was truly 'intoxicating'. In all of them, as in England, a minority of the working classes got their real wages somewhat advanced; while in most cases the monetary rise of wages denoted no more a real access of comforts than the inmate of the metropolitan poor-house or orphan asylum, for instance, was in the least benefited by his first necessaries costing £9 15s 8d in 1861 against £7 7s 4d in 1852. Everywhere the great mass of the working classes were sinking down to a lower depth, at the same rate, at least, that those above them were rising in the social scale. In all countries of Europe it has now become a truth demonstrable to every unprejudiced mind, and only denied by those whose interest it is to hedge other people in a fool's paradise, that no improvement of machinery, no appliance of science to production, no contrivances of communication, no new colonies, no emigration, no opening of markets, no free trade, nor all these things put together, will do away with the miseries of the industrious masses; but that, on the present false base, every fresh development of the productive powers of labour must tend to deepen social contrasts and point social antagonisms. Death of starvation

[9] Marx's own German translation adds here: '... and in fact represents it on the world market'.

rose almost to the rank of an institution, during this intoxicating epoch of economical progress, in the metropolis of the British empire. That epoch is marked in the annals of the world by the quickened return, the widening compass, and the deadlier effects of the social pest called a commercial and industrial crisis.

After the failure of the revolutions of 1848, all party organizations and party journals of the working classes were, on the Continent, crushed by the iron hand of force, the most advanced sons of labour fled in despair to the transatlantic republic, and the short-lived dreams of emancipation vanished before an epoch of industrial fever, moral marasmus, and political reaction. The defeat of the continental working classes, partly owed to the diplomacy of the English government, acting then as now in fraternal solidarity with the cabinet of St Petersburg, soon spread its contagious effects on this side of the Channel. While the rout of their continental brethren unmanned the English working classes, and broke their faith in their own cause, it restored to the landlord and the money-lord their somewhat shaken confidence. They insolently withdrew concessions already advertised. The discoveries of new goldlands led to an immense exodus, leaving an irreparable void in the ranks of the British proletariat. Others of its formerly active members were caught by the temporary bribe of greater work and wages, and turned into 'political blacks'. All the efforts made at keeping up, or remodelling, the Chartist movement, failed signally; the press organs of the working class died one by one of the apathy of the masses, and, in point of fact, never before seemed the English working class so thoroughly reconciled to a state of political nullity. If, then, there had been no solidarity of action between the British and the continental working classes, there was, at all events, a solidarity of defeat.

And yet the period passed since the revolutions of 1848 has not been without its compensating features. We shall here only point to two great facts.

After a thirty years' struggle, fought with most admirable perseverance, the English working classes, improving a momentaneous split between the landlords and money-lords, succeeded in carrying the Ten Hours Bill.[10] The immense physical, moral, and intellectual benefits hence accruing to the factory operatives, half-yearly chronicled in the reports of the inspectors of factories, are now acknowledged on all sides. Most of the continental governments had to accept the English Factory Act in more or less modified forms, and the English Parliament itself is every year compelled to enlarge its sphere of action. But besides its practical import, there was something else to exalt the marvellous success of this working men's measure. Through their most notorious organs of science, such as Dr Ure, Professor Senior,[11] and other sages of that stamp, the middle class had predicted, and to their heart's content proved, that any legal restriction of the hours of

[10] Lord Shaftesbury's Act instituting the ten-hours limitation for women and children in textile factories was passed in June 1847.

[11] Dr Andrew Ure and Professor Nassau Senior were characteristic representatives of what Marx termed 'vulgar economy', the degenerate form of bourgeois political economy that, after 1830, abandoned the attempt of scientific explanation for mere apologetics, as a result of the development of the class struggle between capital and labour. See *Capital*, vol I, pp 15-16.

labour must sound the death knell of British industry, which vampire-like, could but live by sucking blood, and children's blood, too. In olden times, child murder was a mysterious rite of the religion of Moloch, but it was practised on some very solemn occasions only, once a year perhaps, and then Moloch had no exclusive bias for the children of the poor. This struggle about the legal restriction of the hours of labour raged the more fiercely since, apart from frightened avarice, it told indeed upon the great contest between the blind rule of the supply and demand laws which form the political economy of the middle class, and social production controlled by social foresight, which forms the political economy of the working class. Hence the Ten Hours Bill was not only a great practical success; it was the victory of a principle; it was the first time that in broad daylight the political economy of the middle class succumbed to the political economy of the working class.

But there was in store a still greater victory of the political economy of labour over the political economy of property. We speak of the cooperative movement, especially the cooperative factories raised by the unassisted efforts of a few bold 'hands'. The value of these great social experiments cannot be overrated. By deed, instead of by argument, they have shown that production on a large scale, and in accord with the behests of modern science, may be carried on without the existence of a class of masters employing a class of hands; that to bear fruit, the means of labour need not be monopolized as a means of dominion over, and of extortion against, the labouring man himself; and that, like slave labour, like serf labour, hired labour is but a transitory and inferior form, destined to disappear before associated labour plying its toil with a willing hand, a ready mind, and a joyous heart. In England, the seeds of the cooperative system were sown by Robert Owen; the working men's experiments, tried on the Continent, were, in fact, the practical upshot of the theories, not invented, but loudly proclaimed, in 1848.

At the same time, the experience of the period from 1848 to 1864 has proved beyond doubt[12] that, however excellent in principle, and however useful in practice, cooperative labour, if kept within the narrow circle of the casual efforts of private work-men, will never be able to arrest the growth in geometrical progression of monopoly, to free the masses, nor even to perceptibly lighten the burden of their miseries. It is perhaps for this very reason that plausible noblemen, philanthropic middle-class spouters, and even keen political economists, have all at once turned nauseously complimentary to the very cooperative labour system they had vainly tried to nip in the bud by deriding it as the utopia of the dreamer, or stigmatizing it as the sacrilege of the socialist. To save the industrious masses, cooperative labour ought to be developed to national dimensions, and, consequently, to be fostered by national means. Yet the lords of

[12] Marx's German translation adds: '– what the most intelligent leaders of the English working class already maintained in 1851-2, regarding the cooperative movement –.

[13] This refers to Palmerston's speech of 23 June 1863, in which he described the moderate reforms in the land tenure system proposed by Maguire and the Irish MPs, designed to guarantee an outgoing tenant compensation for the value of improvements made, as 'communist doctrines'.

[14] In January 1863 a new national uprising broke out in Poland. It was crushed within two months by Russian forces, in alliance with Prussia. See 'Proclamation on Poland', SE, pp 354-6.

land and the lords of capital will always use their political privileges for the defence and perpetuation of their economical monopolies. So far from promoting, they will continue to lay every possible impediment in the way of the emancipation of labour. Remember the sneer with which, last session, Lord Palmerston put down the advocates of the Irish Tenants' Right Bill. The House of Commons, cried he, is a house of landed proprietors.[13]

To conquer political power has therefore become the great duty of the working classes. They seem to have comprehended this, for in England, Germany, Italy and France there have taken place simultaneous revivals, and simultaneous efforts are being made at the political reorganization of the working men's party.

One element of success they possess – numbers; but numbers weigh only in the balance, if united by combination and led by knowledge. Past experience has shown how disregard of that bond of brotherhood which ought to exist between the workmen of different countries, and incite them to stand firmly by each other in all their struggles for emancipation, will be chastised by the common discomfiture of their incoherent efforts. This thought prompted the working men of different countries assembled on 28 September 1864, in public meeting at St Martin's Hall, to found the International Association.

Another conviction swayed that meeting.

If the emancipation of the working classes requires their fraternal concurrence, how are they to fulfil that great mission with a foreign policy in pursuit of criminal designs, playing upon national prejudices, and squandering in piratical wars the people's blood and treasure? It was not the wisdom of the ruling classes, but the heroic resistance to their criminal folly by the working classes of England, that saved the west of Europe from plunging headlong into an infamous crusade for the perpetuation and propagation of slavery on the other side of the Atlantic. The shameless approval, mock sympathy, or idiotic indifference, with which the upper classes of Europe have witnessed the mountain fortress of the Caucasus falling a prey to, and heroic Poland being assassinated by, Russia;[14] the immense and unresisted encroachments of that barbarous power, whose head is at St Petersburg, and whose hands are in every cabinet of Europe, have taught the working classes the duty to master themselves the mysteries of international politics; to watch the diplomatic acts of their respective governments; to counteract them, if necessary, by all means in their power; when unable to prevent, to combine in simultaneous denunciations, and to vindicate the simple laws of morals and justice, which ought to govern the relations of private individuals, as the rules paramount of the intercourse of nations.

The fight for such a foreign policy forms part of the general struggle for the emancipation of the working classes.

Proletarians of all countries, unite!

Benjamin Seebohm Rowntree, 1871-1954　9

B.S. Rowntree was brought up as a Quaker, strongly influenced by the beliefs and work of his father, Joseph Rowntree. He followed in his father's footsteps both in becoming a director of his chocolate factory in 1897 and in continuing and extending his father's studies of poverty. In 1899 he carried out an extensive survey of poverty in York, the town in which he was born and where the chocolate factory was based. Due to this wealth he was able to employ many people to carry out much of the survey work for him.

From the wealth of data his survey collected, Rowntree constructed a 'poverty line' and defined families as living in either primary or secondary poverty. The former were referred to as lacking the resources to live the most basic of lives. The latter were referred to as having these, but little else. From his first survey Rowntree found that poverty was worse for children, couples who had just had children and older people. His findings were influential to the introduction of the Old Age Pension Act of 1908 and the National Insurance Act of 1911.

Rowntree repeated his survey of York twice more in the 1930s and it was repeated again in the 1950s, finding a reduction in the extent of poverty on both occasions. By the 1930s unemployment was a more important cause of poverty than low wages. By the 1950s the introduction of the Welfare State was – he thought – helping to eliminate poverty. However, poverty was not eliminated but the name of Rowntree continues to be associated with research to that end. In 1959, two years after Seebohm's death an Act of Parliament was passed turning a Trust set up in his father's name into the Joseph Rowntree Memorial Trust "to seek out the underlying causes of weakness or evil" and "change the face of England". In 1990 the Trust was renamed the Joseph Rowntree Foundation and continues to sponsor research on poverty to this day.

Rowntree, B.S (1901)
Poverty: A study of town life

Vital statistics of typical sections
of the York population

Confining myself to the working-class districts, I have tried to measure the influence which poverty and its accompanying conditions have upon the health of the community. With this object in view certain typical areas of the city were selected, inhabited respectively by three sections of the working-class population:–

1. The poorest section.
2. The middle section.
3. The highest section.

The area representing No 1 consists of one district only, but was not found possible to select single districts inhabited by Sections 2 and 3 large enough for the purposes of the present inquiry.

The areas representing 2 and 3 are therefore made up of small districts not necessarily adjacent to each other, but each inhabited by the particular section of the population which it was wished to examine.

Let me briefly describe the three areas before considering their respective standards of health.

Area No 1 – *The poorest section – Walmgate inside the Bar, with Hungate*

This is the poorest large district in the city. It contains 1642 families, comprising 6803 persons. The average size of family is therefore 4.14. Of this population no less than 4737 or 69.3 per cent of the whole are living in poverty ("primary" or "secondary"). The birth-rate in this district is 39.83 per 1000 living, which is about 9 per 1000 above the average for the whole city. All classes of workers are represented in this area; there are many casual and unskilled workers, and, on the other hand, a number of artisans, many of whom would be living in better districts but for their unsteady habits. The population also includes a large contingent of Irish. A few of the women work in the fields during the summer time, whilst many of the young persons, both girls and boys, are employed in factories. The district is situated in the old part of the city, and lies entirely within the walls. It comprises some typical slum areas. A broad thoroughfare (Walmgate) runs through one portion of it. Some of the houses and shops in this, and in a few of the other streets, are of considerable size, and are inhabited by comparatively well-to-do people; but a number of narrow and often sunless courts and alleys branch from these larger streets, and it is here that the poverty is chiefly found.

There are thirty-nine public-houses in the district, or one for every 174 of the population. Thirty-four of these are fully licensed, five are beer-houses, and in addition there are four houses with "off" licenses.

The river Foss, which runs through the district, often becomes more or less stagnant and unsavoury in the summer time, although its condition is not such as to poison the fish.

Many of the yards and courts are unpaved, and brick ashpits and midden privies, cleared only at rare intervals, abound.

1613 persons, or about one-fourth of the whole population of the district, are living under over-crowded conditions − *ie* more than two persons to each room. Of these 1613 persons 200 are living under conditions of extreme overcrowding, *ie* more than four persons to each room. This fact alone would suffice seriously to affect the health standard, but the mere statement of over-crowding does not represent the full extent of the evil − not only are many of the houses over-crowded, but a large proportion of them are insanitary.

It has not been possible to ascertain the exact number of insanitary houses. A rough measure of the extent of insanitation is, however, afforded by the following facts. There are 584 back-to-back houses in the district,[1] equal to about one third of the whole number. Of the 1642 inhabited houses, only 742 have private sanitary accommodation. In the case of the remaining 900 the closets are used by two or more houses in common.

[1] Included in these 584 back-to-back houses there are 178 which are not actually back-to-back with other dwelling-houses, but which have no through ventilation. Some of them are back-to-back with stables, warehouses, and even water-closets.

In the case of 334 houses in the district 1 closet is shared by 2 houses.

"	381	"	"	"	3 "
"	104	"	"	"	4 "
"	35	"	"	"	5 "
"	30	"	"	"	6 "
"	7	"	"	"	7 "
"	9	"	"	"	9 "

It need hardly be said that very many of the closets are in a most filthy condition. There is likewise an inadequate water supply; less than half of the houses (only 809 out of 1642) can boast a private water-tap. In some cases one water-tap is shared by over twenty houses.

In the case of 56 houses in this district, I water-tap is shared by 2 houses.

"	52	"	"	"	3	"
"	112	"	"	"	4	"
"	80	"	"	"	5	"
"	150	"	"	"	6	"
"	56	"	"	"	7	"
"	72	"	"	"	8	"
"	36	"	"	"	9	"
"	70	"	"	"	10	"
"	11	"	"	"	11	"
"	68	"	"	"	12	"
"	22	"	"	"	22	"
"	23	"	"	"	23	"
"	25	"	"	"	25	"

Areas grouped as No 2 – *Representing the middle section*

The three districts which have been selected as most typically representing the middle class of labour are:

1. Parts of the Groves district
2. Parts of Nunnery Lane district
3. Leeman Road district

Altogether, these districts contain 2159 families, comprising 9945 people. The average size of family is therefore 4.65. 3699 persons, or 37 per cent of the whole population, are living in poverty either "primary" or "secondary". Although there are a number of public-houses just outside the area, there are only nine situated *actually within it;* This is equal to 1 per 1105 inhabitants, as compared with 1 per 174 inhabitants in Area No 1. Seven of these are fully licensed and two are beer-houses; there is also one "off" license in the area. The birth-rate in these districts is 40.32 per 1000 living.[2]

The population resident in these areas is engaged upon all kinds of labour, though there are few instances either of casual and very low class, or of the highest class of workers found here. These are typical working-class districts, containing row after row of small uninteresting-looking two-storeyed houses, built of the dingy York bricks, and roofed with slates, with here and there a small shop. The

[2] This high birth-rate is probably due to the facts that the districts under consideration are situated near to the chief workshops and factories, and the population comprises a large proportion of young married people.

streets are, with few exceptions, of moderate width, and the houses fairly sanitary. There are, however, about 32 back-to-back houses in the area, and some others have no back entrance, so that ashes, nightsoil, etc. have to be removed through the living-rooms. Most of the houses have midden privies, though some have water-closets. In the case of 360 houses, or 16.67 per cent of the whole, one closet is used by 2 or more houses.

In the case of 278 houses in this district, I closet is shared by 2 houses.

"	69	"	"	"	3	"
"	8	"	"	"	4	"
"	5	"	"	"	5	"

The water supply is upon the whole adequate. 248 houses are, however, without a separate supply.

In the case of 60 houses, I water-tap is shared by 2 houses.

"	21	"	"	3	"
"	108	"	"	4	"
"	5	"	"	5	"
"	18	"	"	6	"
"	24	"	"	8	"
"	12	"	"	12	"

The houses in the Leeman Road districts have been built somewhat recently, and a large proportion of them have been run up in the cheapest possible way.

Areas grouped as No 3 – *Highest section*

As stated on p 103, the houses of the best paid section of the working classes are not confined to any one part of the city; it was therefore necessary, for the purposes of the present investigation, to select small districts situated in different parts. These selected districts comprise 1348 families and 5336 persons, the average number of persons per family being therefore 3.96. None of these persons are living in poverty either "primary" or "secondary."

The birth-rate in these districts is 29 per 1000 living. It will be noted that this is about one-fourth less than in the case of the other two areas.

The population is employed in all classes of labour. Where the householder is an unskilled worker the wages are augmented by the earnings of the children. Many families are in the habit of taking a few days' holiday out of York during the summer. The houses contain as a rule 6 to 8 rooms; only a few have bathrooms.

In these districts there is no overcrowding, there are no back-to-back houses, the streets are wider than in Areas 1 and 2, and many of the houses have small gardens in front. There are no public-houses actually *in* the districts, though there are many immediately adjacent to them.

Generally speaking, it may be said that this section consists of people who are comfortably off, and are living under sanitary conditions.

Let us now examine the relation between the health of the people and the conditions which we have noted in these three areas. The statistics given are based upon a census specially taken for this inquiry by my investigators, and not upon the Medical Officer of Health's intercensal estimate.

General death-rate[3]

The death-rate is the best instrument for measuring the variations in the physical well-being of the people. Applying this test, we find the death-rate in the various areas to be as under[4]:–

Area No 1 (poorest), 27.78[5] deaths per annum per 1000 of the population.

Area No 2 (middle), 20.71[5] deaths per annum per 1000 of the population.

Area No 3 (highest), 13.49 deaths per annum per 1000 of the population.

Whole of York, 18.5[6] deaths per annum per 1000 of the population

It will thus be seen that the mortality amongst the very poor is more than twice as high as amongst the best paid section of the working-classes.

In considering these figures, it must be remembered that a high death-rate implies a low standard of general health, and much sickness and suffering which is not registered. As the late Lord Playfair said: "The record of deaths only registers, as it were, the wrecks which strew the shore, but it gives no account of the vessels which are tossed in the billows of sickness, stranded and maimed, as they often are, by the effects of recurrent storms."

Mortality of children under five years of age

If now we confine ourselves to the mortality of children below five years of age, we obtain the following results in the three areas:–

[3] In order to make a really accurate comparison between the death-rates in these three areas it would have been necessary to know the exact age distribution of the population living in each area, and in particular, the numbers under and over five years of age respectively. Although it has not been possible to obtain this information, there is no reason to suppose that such knowledge would have modified the figures given in this and subsequent tables so as to materially affect the broad conclusions which have been drawn from the statistics available.

[4] These figures, and the whole of the subsequent vital statistics given in this chapter, refer to the year 1898.

[5] Deaths of persons coming from these districts, but occurring in public institutions (eg workhouse, hospital, etc), have not been included in these figures.

[6] This figure of the death-rate for the whole of York in 1898 is based upon the estimated population for that year, corrected in accordance with the 1901 census return.

Area No 1 (poorest), 13.96 per annum per 1000 population of all ages living.

Area No 2 (middle), 10.50 per annum per 1000 population of all ages living.

Area No 3 (highest), 6.00 per annum per 1000 population of all ages living.

Whole of York, 7.37 per annum per 1000 population of all ages living.

In comparing these figures from the point of view of the present inquiry, it should be borne in mind that, whilst the birth-rate in Areas No 1 and No 2 is 40 per 1000 living, that of Area No 3 is only 29. This fact undoubtedly affects the statistics of mortality for the children under 5 years. Had the birth-rate in Area No 3 been 40 per 1000 instead of 29, it is probable that the death-rate of children under 5 years of age would have been somewhat higher.

Mortality of children under twelve months

When we examine the mortality of children under twelve months of age, we find the same terrible waste of human life proceeding in the poorer areas. In addition to the three areas previously considered, particulars have been ascertained regarding the infant mortality amongst the servant-keeping class. The results are as follows:-

Area No 1 (poorest), out of every 1000 children born			247	die
Area No 2 (middle),	"	"	"	184	before they
Area No 3 (highest),	"	"	"	173	are twelve
Servant-keeping class,	"	"	"	94	months old
Whole of York,	"	"	"	176	

We thus see that in the poorest area one child out of very four born dies before it is twelve months old. In one parish in this area one out of every three children born dies in its first year. Such facts as these bring out in strong relief the adverse conditions under which the poor are living.

It is sometimes urged that although the individual suffering indicated by a high infant mortality is considerable, it is not without some counterbalancing advantages, as the sickly children are thus weeded out. Even if this Spartan view be accepted, it must be remembered that of those who survive, a large proportion do so only with seriously enfeebled constitutions.

The high mortality in Area No 3 (highest class labour) in

[7] This view is strongly held by the Medical Officer of Health for the city.

comparison with that among the servant-keeping class calls for comment. As the housing conditions in this area are comparatively satisfactory, it is believed that the high mortality is largely due to ignorance regarding the feeding and management of infants, and to the close and stuffy rooms in which the children spend so large a proportion of their time.[7] This fact indicates the need which exists for further instruction upon health subjects, even amongst the highest section of the working-classes.

In view of the high infant mortality in Area No 1 (poorest class), it may perhaps be urged that the high general death-rate observed in that area is chiefly due to ignorance in the feeding and management of infants rather than to other causes arising out of the poverty of the people. The high rate of mortality is, however, not confined to the infants, for if we eliminate all deaths of children under five years, and consider only the mortality of those above that age, we obtain the following figures:–

Death-rate of persons above five years of age per 1000 living

Area No 1 (poorest), 13.8 deaths per annum per 1000 living

Area No 2 (middle), 10.2   "   "   "

Area No 3 (highest),   7.5   "   "   "

Whole of York,   11.1   "   "   "

It is thus seen that even after eliminating the children under five years of age, the death-rate in the poorest area is almost twice as high as in Area No 3.

The facts given above regarding the comparative mortality in the three areas are graphically shown in the diagram.

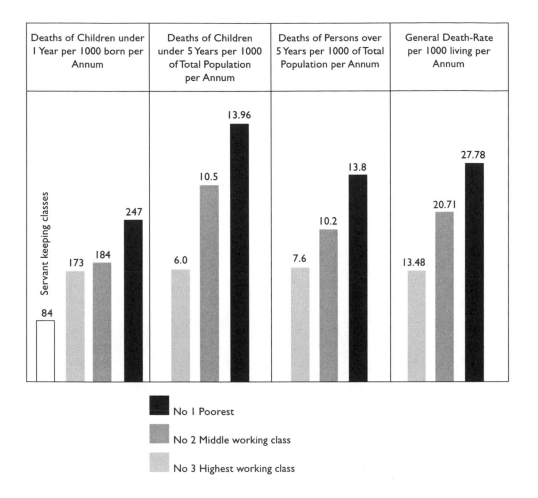

Deaths of Children under 1 Year per 1000 born per Annum	Deaths of Children under 5 Years per 1000 of Total Population per Annum	Deaths of Persons over 5 Years per 1000 of Total Population per Annum	General Death-Rate per 1000 living per Annum

No 1 Poorest

No 2 Middle working class

No 3 Highest working class

Charles Booth, 1840–1916 10

Photograph of Charles Booth with his family on the steps of
Gracedieu Manor 1902

C harles Booth was born into a rich Liverpool corn merchant's family. In 1864 he established a shipping line company. He married Mary Macauley, a cousin of Beatrice Potter (later Beatrice Webb) in 1871 and they moved to London in 1875. There he was greatly influenced by social debate on the state of the nation and in particular on poverty in London. Ten years after he arrived in the capital a report was published claiming that a quarter of workers in London were in receipt of wages not sufficient to maintain life. Booth did not believe the proportion could be so high and set out to disprove the report.

Booth's own study of the extent of poverty in London was planned to only take three years and to rely on Census returns about which he had already written. He recruited many people to help him, among them Beatrice Potter (who later worked with William Beveridge). In particular, the School Board visitors were suggested to him as a source of data. These visitors kept detailed records of every family with children in their area. His study began in 1886 and took 17 years to complete, in the end resulting in the publication of 17 volumes. By 1889 he had found that some thirty per cent of London's population lived below the poverty line which he devised – more than was claimed by the report he had originally set out to disprove as an exaggeration. He also wrote that it was the circumstances of irregular and poor employment, rather than matters of habit and character, which were the major causes of poverty.

Here we present extracts from *Life and labour of the people of London*.

Booth, C. (1902–3) *On the city: Physical pattern and social structure*

Introduction

The inquiry of which I am now able to publish the results, was set on foot in 1886, the subject being the condition and occupations of the inhabitants of London, and my grateful thanks are due to those friends who helped me at the outset in laying down the principles on which the inquiry has been conducted. It was decided to employ a double method, dividing the people by districts and again by trades, so as to show at once the manner of their life and of their work. Most of 1886 was occupied with preliminary work. 1887 sufficed to complete the district inquiry in East London, and 1888 was spent on the trades and special subjects.

The special subjects connected with East London have started into great prominence during the time I have been at work. On the question of the "Unemployed" we have seen a house-to-house inquiry instituted by Government, which took as one of its selected districts St. George's-in-the-East. On the influx of poor Jews, under the name of "Foreign Immigration," we have had a Committee of the House of Commons; and there has been the Committee of the House of Lords on the "Sweating system," which is still prolonging its labours. In addition, the whole question of Poor Relief has been laid open by another Committee of the House of Commons, and we have seen a succession of Mansion House inquiries on the same subject. To meet this evident demand for information I offer the pages which follow. The facts as given have been gathered and stated with no bias nor distorting aim, and with no foregone conclusions.

For the district inquiry, resulting in the division of the people into 8 classes, I have relied upon information obtained from the School Board visitors, of whom there are 66 in the East London district, and my tables are based on three assumptions:

1. That the numbers of married men with school children in each section by employment imply a similar proportion in the same sections of married men without school children, and of other male adults. For the choice of employment is made before the epoch of school children, and the period of employment continued long after; the fathers of the school children of the day are but a section of a block

which contains, all the while, old men and young, married and single, those with children and those without, in every trade. Hence, having scheduled the heads of families with school children, I feel justified in dividing the other male adults in similar proportions.

2. That likewise the number of children of school age in each section implies the existence of brothers and sisters, older and younger, to be found living under the same home conditions. Hence I have added children and young persons of 13-20 to each section in proportion to the number of school children scheduled.

3. That the condition as to poverty of those with children at school in each section will safely represent the condition of the whole section; the younger men in some employments, and the older men in others, earn less money than those of middle age who are the fathers of the children at school, but both are at less expense. On the whole, therefore, the condition of the bulk will be better than that of the part we are able to test.

I have, however, assumed that as is the condition of the tested part – which amounts to fully one half of the population – so is the condition of the whole population; and I may here say that I have throughout my inquiry leaned to the safe side, preferring to paint things too dark rather than too bright, not because I myself take a gloomy view, but to avoid the chance of understating the evils with which society has to deal.[1]

The School Board visitors perform amongst them a house-to-house visitation; every house in every street is in their books, and details are given of every family with children of school age. They begin their scheduling two or three years before the children attain school age, and a record remains in their books of children who have left school. The occupation of the head of the family is noted down. Most of the visitors have been working in the same district for several years, and thus have an extensive knowledge of the people. It is their business to re-schedule for the Board once a year, but intermediate revisions are made in addition, and it is their duty to make themselves acquainted, so far as possible, with new comers into their districts. They are in daily contact with the people, and have a very considerable knowledge of the parents of the school children, especially of the poorest amongst them, and of the conditions under which they live. No one can go, as I have done, over the description of the inhabitants of street after street in this huge district (East London), taken house by house and family by family – full as it is of picturesque details noted down from the lips of the visitor to whose mind they have been recalled by the open pages of his own schedules – and doubt the genuine character of the information and its truth. Of the wealth

[1] I undoubtedly expected that this investigation would expose exaggerations, and it did so; but the actual poverty disclosed was so great, both in mass and in degree, and so absolutely certain, that I have gradually become equally anxious not to overstate – C.B., 1902.

of my material I have no doubt. I am indeed embarrassed by its mass, and by my resolution to make use of no fact to which I cannot give a quantitative value. The materials for sensational stories lie plentifully in every book of our notes; but, even if I had the skill to use my material in this way – that gift of the imagination which is called "realistic" – I should not wish to use it here. There is struggling poverty, there is destitution, there is hunger, drunkenness, brutality, and crime; no one doubts that it is so. My object has been to attempt to show the numerical relation which poverty, misery, and depravity bear to regular earnings and comparative comfort, and to describe the general conditions under which each class lives.

For the trade inquires and special subjects, I have been fortunate in obtaining the aid of others, and their work will speak eloquently for itself.

If the facts thus stated are of use in helping social reformers to find remedies for the evils which exist, or do anything to prevent the adoption of false remedies, my purpose is answered. It was not my intention to bring forward any suggestions of my own, and if I have ventured here and there, and especially in the concluding chapters, to go beyond my programme, it has been with much hesitation.

With regard to the disadvantages under which the poor labour, and the evils of poverty, there is a great sense of helplessness: the wage earners are helpless to regulate their work and cannot obtain a fair equivalent for the labour they are willing to give; the manufacturer or dealer can only work within the limits of competition; the rich are helpless to relieve want without stimulating its sources. To relieve this helplessness a better stating of the problems involved is the first step. "We are a long way towards understanding anything under our consideration, when we have properly laid it open, even without comment."[2] In this direction must be sought the utility of my attempt to analyze the population of London.

In order that the true, and not more than the true, significance and value may be given to the facts and figures produced, it may be useful to explain exactly the method that has been adopted in collecting them.

The 46 books of our notes contain no less than 3400 streets or places in East London, and every house and every family with school children is noted, with such information as the visitors could give about them.

From notes such as these the information given in our schedules was tabulated, and from them also was coloured the map which now forms a part of that published in connection with these volumes. The people – that is those of them who had school children – were classified by their employment and by their apparent status as to means; the streets were classified according to their inhabitants. Such is the nature of our information, and such the use made of it. It was

[2] Autobiography of Mark Rutherford.

possible to subject the map to the test of criticism, and it was mainly for this purpose that it was prepared. It was exhibited at Toynbee Hall and Oxford House, and was seen and very carefully studied by many who are intimately acquainted, not with the whole, but each with some part, of the district portrayed. Especially, we obtained most valuable aid in this way from the Relieving Officers and from the agents of the Charity Organization Society. The map stood the test very well. There were errors, but on reference they were, in almost every case, found to be due to mistake in the transfer of verbal into graphic description, or consequent on our having made a whole street the unit of colour, whereas different parts of the same street were of very different character. The map was revised, and now equally represents the facts as disclosed by this inquiry, and as agreed to by the best local authorities.

Our books of notes are mines of information. They have been referred to again and again at each stage of our work. So valuable have they proved in unforeseen ways, that I only regret they were not more slowly and deliberately prepared; more stuffed with facts that even they are. As it was, we continually improved as we went on, and may be said to have learnt our trade by the time the work was done.

* St Hubert Street (Class A – coloured black on map) †

				Class	Section
1.	Casual labourer (Now gone hopping.)	1 room	2 school children	B	2
	Charwoman (The widow's sister also lives with her.)	1 room, widow	1 child at school and 1 baby	B	33
		1 room	1 family, no children at school		
2.	Bootmaker	1 room	Wife helps, 2 school children	C	11
	Casual labourer (Very low family. Also have one child at Industrial School.)	1 room	1 child at school and 2 babies	A	1
	?	1 room, widow	1 child at school	B	35
42.	Railway ticket collector		3 school children (1 an idiot)	F	13
43.	Carman		2 school children 2 babies	E	5
44.	Engineer		2 school children 1 baby	E	9
	Carman		1 child at school	E	5

General character – All the houses consist of 7 rooms and scullery and let at 13s per week. The people are all in good circumstances, and the houses well-built and commodious as a rule, but a few new houses are jerry built.

* The real names of the streets are, for obvious reasons, suppressed.

† Note. –The system of colour used on the map to indicate the class of each street is as follows:–

Black – the lowest grade; *Dark Blue* – very poor; *Light Blue* – ordinary poverty; *Purple* – mixed with poverty; *Pink* – working-class comfort; *Red* – well-to-do; and *Yellow* – wealthy.

At first, nothing seemed so essential as speed. The task was so tremendous; the prospect of its completion so remote; and every detail cost time. In the Tower Hamlets division, which was completed first, we gave on the average 19¾ hours work to each School Board visitor; in the Hackney division this was increased to 23½ hours. St George's-in-the-East when first done in 1886 cost 60 hours work with the visitors; when revised it occupied 83 hours. At the outset we shut our eyes, fearing lest any prejudice of our own should colour the information we received. It was not till the books were finished that I or my secretaries ourselves visited the streets amongst which we had been living in imagination. But later we gained confidence, and made it a rule to see each street ourselves at the time we received the visitors account of it. With the insides of the houses and their inmates there was no attempt to meddle. To have done so would have been an unwarrantable impertinence; and, besides, a contravention of our understanding with the School Board, who object, very rightly, to any abuse of the delicate machinery with which they work. Nor, for the same reason, did we ask the visitors to obtain information specially for us. We dealt solely with that which comes to them in a natural way in the discharge of their duties.

The amount of information obtained varied with the different visitors; some had not been long at the work, and amongst those who had been, there was much difference in the extent of their knowledge; some might be less trustworthy than others: but taking them as a body I cannot speak too highly of their ability and good sense. I also wish to express my warm thanks for the ready manner in which all – the Divisional Committees themselves, the District Superintendents, and the Visitors; lent themselves to my purpose. For without this nothing could have been done. The merit of the information so obtained, looked at statistically, lies mainly in the breadth of view obtained. It is in effect the whole population that comes under review. Other agencies usually seek out some particular class or deal with some particular condition of people. The knowledge so obtained may be more exact, but it is circumscribed and very apt to produce a distortion of judgment. For this reason, the information to be had from the School Board visitors, with all its inequalities and imperfections, is excellent as a framework for a picture of the Life and Labour of the People.

The population brought directly under the schedule – viz, heads of families and school children coming under the ken of the School Board visitors, with the proportion of wives and of older or younger children all partly or wholly dependent on these heads of families and sharing their life – amounts to from one half to two thirds of the whole population. The rest have been scheduled by other means or in proportion, according to the three assumptions already noted.

The special difficulty of making an accurate picture of so shifting a scene as the low-class streets in East London present is very evident, and may easily be exaggerated. As in photographing a crowd, the details of the picture change continually, but the general effect is much the same, whatever moment is chosen. I have attempted to produce an instantaneous picture, fixing the facts on my negative as they appear at a given moment, and the imagination of my readers must add the movement, the constant changes, the whirl and turmoil of life. In many districts the people are always on the move; they shift from one part of it to another like "fish in a river." The School Board visitors follow them as best they may, and the transfers from one visitor's book to another's are very numerous.[3] On the whole, however, the people usually do not go far, and often cling from generation to generation to one vicinity, almost as if the set of streets which lie there were an isolated country village.

The inquiry as to Central London was undertaken by a committee of six, and that for Battersea by Mr Graham Balfour; the method adopted in each case being the same as had been employed in East London.

[3] A return prepared by one of the School Board visitors, who has a fairly representative district in Bethnal Green, shows that of 1204 families (with 2720 children) on his books, 530 (with 1450 children) removed in a single year.

Statistics of poverty

Before giving the figures by which I have sought to measure the poverty existing in London, it may be well to refer once more to their validity. The methods employed in the collection and tabulation of the information have been already indicated. These methods were adopted as suited to the peculiarities of the subject and the materials with which we had to deal; but are doubtless open to criticism from many points of view. Not only is exactness in this case out of the question, but even the most general results obtained are open to dispute. At every turn the subject bristles with doubtful points. For each one of these, as it has arisen (if it has been observed) the best available solution has been sought, or what has seemed the most reasonable course has been taken.

But it is manifest that in an inquiry such as this, a very slight bias may lead to serious error, and the bias might be quite unconscious. I can only say we have done our best to keep clear of this danger.

It is to be remarked further that apart from bias two distinct mental attitudes continually recur in considering poverty; and either of these, if not safeguarded in some way, might prove very misleading. On the one hand we may argue that the poor are often really better off than they appear to be, on the ground that when extravagances which keep them in poverty are constant and immediate in their action, the state of things resulting cannot reasonably be called poverty at all. For instance, a man who spends ten or fifteen shillings in drink one week, cannot be called poor because he lacks the money for some necessity a few days later. In support of this it is certainly true that in many cases the homes appear no whit less poor whatever the earnings at the time may be. It often occurs too that the ordinary earnings are increased by accidental receipts capable, if judiciously applied, of meeting the occasional extra demands which keep men's pockets empty. On the other hand we may as logically, or perhaps more logically, disregard the follies past or present which bring poverty in their train. For how distinguish between degrees of folly more or less recent or remote? In this temper we prefer to view and consider these unfortunates only as they actually exist; constantly put to shifts to keep a home together; always struggling and always poor. And turning in this direction the mind dwells upon the terrible stress of times of sickness or lack of work for which no provision, or no adequate provision, has been made. According as the one or other of these two points of view is taken, thousands of families may be placed on one or the other side of the doubtful line of demarcation between class and class among the poor.

Of these two ways of looking at the same facts, the second is that which we have in theory adopted, and although in practice this theory will have been more or less modified, it is still probable that a good many families have been reported as poor, who, though they are poor, are so without any economic necessity. On the other hand it is likely enough that many a painful struggling life hidden under a decent exterior has passed in our books as "comfortably poor," to borrow a phrase used by one of the most sympathetic of the School Board visitors. Thus in the end, when I consider the figures, and the tale they tell, though I sway this way or that according to the mood of the moment, I am fully satisfied that the general conclusions are not very far from the truth, and I believe that my readers may fairly accept them in this light. In so far as there is any general error it will I think be found on the safe side; – that is, in overstating rather than understating the volume of poverty which exists, or existed when the inquiry was made; and it is satisfactory to know that since the inquiry was made, times have been good, and poverty less pressing, than was the case previously.

The inhabitants of every street, and court, and block of buildings in the whole of London, have been estimated in proportion to the numbers of the children, and arranged in classes according to the known position and condition of the parents of these children. The streets have been grouped together according to the School Board subdivisions or "blocks," and for each of these blocks full particulars are given in the tables of the Appendix. The numbers included in each block vary from less than 2000 to more than 30,000, and to make a more satisfactory unit of comparison I have arranged them in contiguous groups, 2, 3, or 4 together, so as to make areas having each about 30,000 inhabitants, these areas adding up into the large divisions of the School Board administration. The population is then classified by Registration districts, which are likewise grouped into School Board divisions, each method finally leading up to the total for all London.

The classes into which the population of each of these blocks and districts is divided are the same as were used in describing East London, only somewhat simplified. They may be stated thus:-

A   The lowest class – occasional labourers, loafers and semi-criminals.

B   The very poor – casual labour, hand-to-mouth existence, chronic want.

C and D   The poor – including alike those whose earnings are small, because of irregularity of employment, and those whose work, though regular, is ill-paid.

E and F   The regularly employed and fairly paid working class of all grades.

G and H   Lower and upper middle class and all above this level.

The Classes C and D, whose poverty is similar in degree but different in kind, can only be property separated by information as to employment which was obtained for East London, but which, as already explained, the present inquiry does not yield. It is the same with E and F which cover the various grades of working class comfort. G and H are given together for convenience.

Outside of, and to be counted in addition to, these classes, are the inmates of institutions whose numbers are specially reported in every census, and finally there are a few who, have no shelter, or no recognized shelter, for the night, elude official enumeration and are not counted at all.

The description of these classes given already as to East London, may be taken as applying with equal force to the whole population. Much might be added to make the description more complete, but nothing need be taken away. The numbers of the lowest class (A), it is admitted, are given at a very rough estimate; they are hardly to be counted by families and so partly escape the meshes of our School Board net. They are to be found in the common lodging-houses and in the lowest streets, and a very full description of their lives and habits is given in the special chapters which treat of these subjects. Class B is fairly counted, and of what it consists, many examples are given in the description of specimen streets, but neither it nor any of the working classes, C, D, E, or F, can be dealt with properly apart from their trades or employments, as the conditions under which these people live, depend mainly upon the conditions under which they work or fail to find work. An account of the life of each of the several classes that are grouped under the letters G and H would be very interesting, but is beyond the scope of this book. I am, however, able to make a division in the figures which answers pretty closely, though not quite exactly, to that between upper and lower middle class. This division is provided by the line of rental value, beyond which the School Board do not go in making their schedules. Out of the 750,000 people included in Class G and H, as nearly as possible 250,000 live in scheduled and 500,000 in unscheduled houses. These figures may be counted as representing roughly the lower and upper middle classes respectively. The wealthy classes are included with the upper middle class.[4]

Assuming that these figures are accepted as approximately correct, the view that is taken of them will depend partly upon what may have been pre-supposed. I imagine that bad as is the state of things they disclose it is better than was commonly imagined previous to the publication of the figures obtained for East London. On the other hand they are probably worse, especially in regard to the numbers of Classes C and D, than may have been anticipated by those who have studied and accepted the East End figures.

That is to say, the poverty of the rest of London as compared to East London is perhaps greater than most people have supposed. For myself it was so. In 1888 I made an estimate based on the facts as to East London, and the comparative density of population in other parts, on the theory that density would probably coincide with the degree of poverty. The result was to show a probable 25 per cent of poor for all London, or nearly 6 per cent less than we now get. South London and the district about Holborn are mainly responsible for the difference.

The 100,000 people counted in institutions belong rather to the whole of London than to the particular district in which they are found. They may be divided under four heads:–

1. Indoor paupers	45,963
2. Inmates of hospitals, asylums, homes, etc supported mainly by charitable donations, past or present	38,714
3. Inmates of prisons	5,833
4. Troops in barracks, etc	9,320
Total	99,830

These people do not belong to the active population, and have therefore been omitted from the percentages given, but if for some purposes it is desirable to introduce them, it will not be unreasonable to include the inmates of the prisons with Class A, the in-door paupers with Class B, those in hospitals, etc, with Classes C and D, and the troops, etc, with Classes E and F. The revised percentages would then stand as follows:– A, 1.0 per cent.; B, 8.4 per cent.; C and D, 22.7 per cent.; E and F, 50.5 per cent.; G and H, 17.4 per cent.

A picture of pauperism

The Rooney family and its connections MARTIN ROONEY, aged eighty-six, now in Bromley Workhouse, married Ellen King, and this family has been prolific in paupers.[5]

First there is Mary Rooney, the wife of Martin's brother James, who was deserted by him in 1867 and has had relief in various forms since, including residence in the sick asylum for several years. She also applied on behalf of her married daughter, Mrs Wilson, and her son Michael appears on the books; but with this branch we do not go at present beyond the second generation.

The old man Martin, who is now blind, applied for admission in 1878. His wife was then in hospital, having broken her leg when intoxicated. He had been a dock labourer, and had received £21 from the Company in 1857 on breaking a leg. He was admitted to Poplar Workhouse. A month later his wife, who is twenty-four years his junior, came out of hospital and was also admitted. The relieving officer made a note that he did not know a more drunken disreputable family than this one. He had seen the woman "beastly drunk" at all times of the day. From this time the old man remained in the house, but the woman went out several times, and when out was more than once seen in the streets in a drunken condition. She worked sometimes at the Lead Works, sleeping occasionally with her sons, at other times in various places – in water-closets, on stairs, etc. When her son Patrick was sent to prison for two months she went into the house. In 1888 she absconded, but in March, 1889, applied for readmission; she had fallen down and cut her face on the Saturday night before.

This couple had three children – Patrick, James, and Bridget. Patrick, born in 1853, by trade a stevedore is now in Poplar Workhouse. He was living with his mother in 1886, and she made application for medical attendance for him. He was suffering from rheumatism. He became worse and was sent to the sick asylum; was discharged, but again admitted a month or two later. Next year he was sent to Bromley Workhouse. He bears a bad character, and was in prison two months in 1888, and had one month in 1889 for attempting to steal some ropes. On coming out of prison he again applied for admission to the workhouse, and was sent to Poplar. He had a bad leg. He got work on the day he was discharged from the sick asylum, injured his leg, and was readmitted to workhouse. He served fourteen or fifteen years in the Royal Marines, and was discharged in 1885 for striking a petty officer. He was for this sentenced to six months' imprisonment by court-martial.

James, the second son, is a labourer, not married. He used to live with a woman name O'Reill, but left her, or she him, and is at present living with another woman.

Bridget, the eldest, born 1847, married John Murdock, a bricklayer's labourer, eight years older than herself, and there are four children, all boys. Murdock deserted his wife several times, and has been sent to prison for it. She in turn left him in 1877, and has been living with another man since. After this he was in Bromley House with the children. The two eldest were emigrated to Canada in 1880. The man's sister married Richard Bardsley, whose mother, a widow, is living at Bromley, and whose brother and brother's wife both had relief there.

Murdock had also a brother George, a general labourer, who lived with Anna Peel, a prostitute, whose parents are now in West Ham Workhouse. This woman applied in 1878 for sick asylum or medical relief for the man, and six months later wanted an order for the sick asylum herself. The relieving officer visited her two days later, but she had gone to her father at Stratford. In 1885 she came again and was admitted, suffering from syphilis. She had been living at a brothel in James Street for three years. George Murdock is now dead.

Murdock's mother married again, and both she and the man she married, Thomas Powles, are now in Bromley House. Powles, a dock labourer, had an accident, being burnt on a barge at Gravesend in 1875. He came to London then, and was admitted to the sick asylum. In 1877 he applied for relief, saying he had been knocking about, sleeping in barges, etc. He was admitted to the house. The next record was in 1883, when he asked for medicines for his wife. She had had a fall and was very ill. The relieving officer visited and found the home (one room) clean and comfortable; medical relief was given. In 1884 the man was admitted to the asylum, having met with another accident. He had been out of work some time then. In 1886 the man was ill again. He had not worked for five weeks, and they had lived by selling their things. He became worse, and was sent to the sick asylum in April. He did not stay long, but in two months' time applied again for relief outside. He had only earned 8*s* in the two months. Three days later the doctor recommended his removal to the sick asylum. Later in the same year his wife was taken ill: and finally they were both admitted to Bromley Workhouse.

We may now come to the relatives of Eliza King, Martin Rooney's wife. She had three sisters – Susan, Jane, and Sarah Anne. Of Susan we only know that she was in service at Guildford. Jane married Thomas Milward. In 1878 Milward applied for medical aid. He could not pay. Whatever money he gave his wife she spent in drink, and if he did not give her money she sold the furniture. Relieving officer made a note that he knew the woman as a notorious drunkard. On visiting he found her in the room drunk, while another woman (Mrs Harvey of Spring Street) was "reclining on a heap of something which served as a bed," speechlessly drunk. The sick man was sitting by the fire. He always found the room thus, with no furniture, although the man earned from 30s to 40s a week. A month later the woman came and said her husband was dead, and that she wanted him buried by the parish. During 1880 and 1881 Mrs Milward had medical relief frequently. She went to the Lead Works, and this work and drink seemed to be telling on her. Some time in 1882 she picked up with a man named Robert Belton, a carpenter, and she lived with him at intervals until 1885. This man was in Bromley Workhouse with a bad leg in 1879, and again later, and died in the sick asylum in 1885. Mrs Milward says he was a great drunkard, which was pot calling kettle black. After Belton's death she injured her shoulder, and having sold up Belton's home and spent the money, applied for admission. She was sent to Poplar Workhouse, and since then has been in and out several times. She hurt her shoulder three times when out from the workhouse, probably through falling while drunk. On two occasions she walked to Guildford to see her sister.

Sarah Anne, the remaining sister, married Thomas Searle, who broke his neck falling downstairs when drunk. It is even said that some of his relatives threw him down in a quarrel. The family was reported as utterly disreputable and very drunken. Left a widow, she kept herself by washing, and does not seem to have an assistance from the parish herself. She had three children – Edward, Martha, and Francis. Of Edward there is happily no record. Martha married Peter Connor, and her aunt, Mrs Milward, applied on her behalf for medical aid in 1882, she having hurt herself from falling from a ladder at the Lead Works. She had separated from her husband about three years before. He was a 'bus driver and lived at Notting Hill. After leaving him she lived a while at his sister's, and then went to her mother's in South London, and when her mother moved to this neighbourhood came with her. She was, however, living at the time with a dock labourer in a common lodging-house – a connection which did not last long.

Francis Searle cohabited with a woman named Augusta Hendy from 1877, he being then twenty-two, and he married her in 1885. They had three children. The woman asked for medical aid for her child Wilfrid in March, 1880. The relieving officer found the room filthy, with a bed on the floor. In May of the same year the man applied on behalf of the woman. She was found to be suffering from his ill-usage, had black eyes, and had been beaten much. From this time there were frequent applications for medical aid. In July, 1881, the woman was admitted to Poplar Workhouse, and was there confined of her third child Edith. In July, 1882, their landlady made application, saying that Francis Searle and Augusta Hendy were ill at her house.

The relieving officer visited with the doctor. The woman came downstairs without shoes or stockings, a miserable-looking creature. The man, woman, and child were sent to Poplar. After this there were no more applications till 1886, when the man came for medical aid for his child Constance. In 1887 the man applied for medicine for the children; he said he "was married now." During the greater part of 1888 the children were ill, and several applications were made by the parents, the last being in November, 1888. This woman, Augusta Hendy, was the daughter of old Benjamin Hendy, known as "Red Ben," who is now in the workhouse, and every one of whose family has had relief. Benjamin Hendy, the younger, age thirty, a dock labourer, not married, was sent to the sick asylum at the end of 1880, and in 1884 went into Poplar Workhouse. Margaret, another of them, was a servant. In 1879 she hurt her face while staying with Augusta, and had medical aid. In November, 1883, she went into Poplar Workhouse and was confined of a male child (Robert), born in 1884. With this workhouse child we come at last to the end of the Rooney family and its connections.

Stepney pauperism

The method adopted for tabulating the causes of poverty was as follows. To each cause I affixed an alphabetical symbol, using a capital letter where the cause given is the principal one, and a small letter where it is contributory, thus:

Cause	Principal	Contributory	Father or husband	Mother or wife	Both
Crime	C	c	c^1	c^2	c^3
Vice	V	v	v^1	v^2	v^3
Drink	D	d	d^1	d^2	d^3
Laziness	L	l	l^1	l^2	l^3
Pauper association	P	p	p^1	p^2	p^3
Heredity	H	h	h^1	h^2	h^3
Mental disease	M	m	m^1	m^2	m^3
Temper (queer)	Q	q	q^1	q^2	q^3
Incapacity	I	i	i^1	i^2	i^3
Early marriage (girl)	G	g	g^1	g^2	g^3
Large family	F	f	...	...	...
Extravagance	E	e	e^1	e^2	e^3
Lack of work (unemployed)	U	u	u^1	u^2	u^3
Trade misfortune	T	t	t^1	t^2	t^3
Restlessness, roving, tramp	R	r	r^1	r^2	r^3
No relations	N	n	...	...	...
Death of husband	W	w	...	...	...
Desertion (abandoned)	A	a	...	...	...
Death of father or mother (orphan)	O	o	o^1	o^2	o^3
Sickness	S	s	s^1	s^2	s^3
Accident	X	x	x^1	x^2	x^3
Ill luck	Y	y	...	...	...
Old age	Z	z	z^1	z^2	z^3

As a further indication of character when the opposite of a fault is intended, the letter can be enclosed in brackets thus: (I) for industry, (d) for known sobriety or teetotaller.

There are few stories that cannot be very forcibly expressed by married condition, age, and three letters. As for example:

Martin Rooney	M	86	I z d	Incapable old man, who drinks
Patrick Rooney	S	36	C h d	A criminal, hereditary pauper, and drunkard
Sarah Truelove	M	66	D z p	Drunken old woman of pauper associations
John Curtis	S	72	X z n	Single old man, without any relations, who has had an accident
Eliza Green	Ch	4	O^1 d^2	Child whose father is dead and mother drinks
Mary Carter	W	59(?)	(dl) S n z	Elderly widow of good character for sobriety and industry, with no relations, and ill
Eliza Knight	M	60(?)	(dl) M^1 S	Husband insane. This woman who is sick, has a good character for sobriety and industry

In the summary which follows a few words of history are added, but it will be found that the alphabetical cipher gives the gist of each case.

Summary of Stepney stories: Indoor relief

Note: + implies longer period unknown   d=days, m=months, w=weeks

Occupation in brackets those of husband or father.

[=Relations   {=Husband and wife

No.	Sex	Condition	Age	Occupation	Cause	Years	Story	Known pauper relatives
(Able-bodied)					*(Drink)*			
1	Male	Married	51	Pattern-maker	D	9	Wife had medicine in 1880. His family left him in 1884. Lost work through drink. In and out since.	Wife S d¹
2	Female	Widow	60	Lead worker	D p s	9	Drunken and immoral. Husband left her. Children are as bad. Often in and out of workhouse.	Son, S h d. Grandson, D3c. Daughter, Vsh. D'hter-in-law, Hw.
3	Female	Widow	54	None	D w	11+	Re-admitted in 1878. Had been sleeping in closets, on dust-heaps, and doorsteps. Drinks.	Late husband, S. Brother, L m. Niece's husband, No 1036
4	Female	Widow	56	Needle-woman	D w	5	Husband died 1878. She sold his shop 18 months after for £20. Was passed from Poplar 1884, and has been chargeable to one or other parish since.	
(Infirm)								
5	Male	Married	68	Customs Officer	D	12	Dismissed for drink and theft. Partially paralysed. Wife lives with friends, who are comfortably off.	
6	Female	Single	28	None	D	6+	Chargeable many years. First record (1883) is that leave is stopped for returning drunk.	Brother, S.
7	Male	Widow'r	69	Carpenter	D	6	Seized with paralysis a few days before admission. Had been a great drinker.	
8	Male	Widow'r	81	General labourer	D	8+	Wife died in Sick Asylum (1881). Man was messenger at Relief Office, but drank too much.	Late wife, Sz. Sister-in-law, X.
9	Male	Married	61	General labourer (formerly School-master)	D	10	Had medical attendance from 1879 to 1887, when he was admitted. When out he lives at common lodging-houses and begs.	Wife, S D¹

No	Sex	Condition	Age	Occupation	Class		Notes	Relations
10	Male	Widow'r	42	Potman	D	11	Had medicine in 1879. Wife died in June 1888. Man was admitted to Sick Asylum with a bad leg in April 1889. His children became chargeable during the same month. His sister says poverty is due entirely to drink.	Late wife, No 1072. Son, Sh.
11	Female	Child (In schools)	13		D^1	11		Children, Nos 11–13
12	Male	Child (In Schools)	9		D^1	17d+		Sisters, Nos 11–13
13	Female	Child (In schools)	5		D^1	17d+		Father, No 10
14	Male	Married	63	Cooper	D	9+	First recorded application in 1875. In 1880 man said his wife was dead. She returned to him in 1881, and they had had medical and other relief since.	Father, No 10
15	Female	Married	69	None	$D\,d^1$	7+		Father, No 10
16	Female	Widow			D	9 m	Husband died 1873, and woman lived with her sons. Asked for relief in 1887, and was buried by Union. One son died in 1887. Mother and this son go into workhouse in 1888. Both drink to excess and use foul language.	Father, No 10
17	Male	Single	26	Stallkeeper (Blind)	$I\,d$	9 m		
18	Male	Single	66	Coal work	$D\,v\,e$	9	Drunkard, has bad legs. Lived with No 22 for 30 years. She left him in 1879.	Paramour, No 22. Nephew's children, Nos 19–21
19	Male	Child	16		$O^1\,d^3\,h$	8	In 1881, the elder boy was sent to Smallpox Hospital with another brother and sister. Father died the same year, and mother got these three children into the schools.	Mother, No 1006
20	Male	Child	14		$O^1\,d^3\,h$	7		
21	Female	Child (In schools)	13		$O^1\,d^3\,h$	7		
22	Female	Single	59	None	$V\,p\,s$	8	Had fits in 1881, and was admitted. Relieved several times since. Stays with daughters when out of workhouse.	Paramour, No 18
23	Female	Child	5		$D^3\,v^3\,h$	5	These children have been frequently relieved with mother. Parents deserted them in April 1889, and they became chargeable. Father in prison for desertion.	Father, No 1043. Grandmother, P d. Mother, D a.
24	Male	Child (In schools)	11		$D^3\,v^3\,h$	10		
25	Male	Widow'r	61	Coal backer	$D\,v\,e$	2	Drunken immoral family. Turned wife out in 1877; she died 1884. Admitted homeless in 1887.	Daughter, V d.

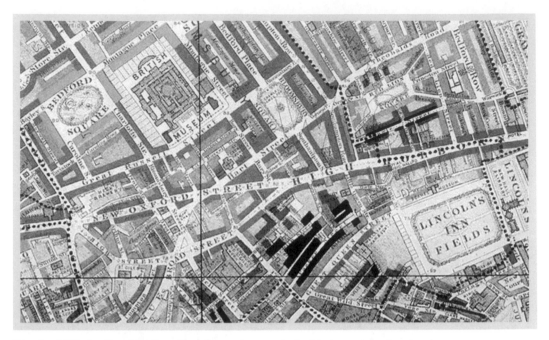

Details of Charles Booth's Map of London poverty, with the black sections showing the location of the poorest class.

Maud Pember Reeves, 1865-1953   **11**

S ocial reformer and feminist, Maud Pember Reeves was born in Australia and moved to London in 1896. Well-educated and middle class, she was on the committee of the Fabian Society from 1907. Pember Reeves was a founder member of the Fabian Women's Group (formed in 1908) which was concerned with equal rights and economic independence for women.

With fellow members of the Fabian Women's Group, from 1909 to 1913 Pember Reeves conducted a study of the daily lives of working class families in Lambeth. The study focused on the effect on the mother and child of sufficient nourishment before and after birth. This nourishment was provided as part of the study. The families were visited every two weeks, and the babies were weighed; the mothers kept detailed records as to how they provided for a family on "round about a pound a week".

The families included in the study were not the poorest in society. Pember Reeves described the men as "respectable, in full work, at more or less top wage, young, with families still increasing"; their wives were described as "quiet, decent, 'keeping themselves to themselves' kind of women".

Her book is the report of the study (originally published in 1912 as a Fabian pamphlet) and includes descriptions of the streets in which these people lived, their homes and daily activities. We read descriptions of their "drearily decent" homes and how the women cooked, washed, cleaned and scrimped to feed a family, and how they coped with cold, damp, vermin and sickness.

The report presented the realities of poverty to the public. Here, we have selected the chapter on 'The children', where we learn of the difficult material conditions of everyday life, and of the accumulation of deprivation which produces poor health. Elsewhere in the report Pember Reeves argues for a series of government reforms, including child benefit, free health clinics and the provision of school meals.

Pember Reeves, M.S. (1913)
Round about a pound a week

Chapter XIII
The children

In this investigation forty-two families have been visited. Of these, eight, owing to various reasons, were visited but for a short time. Three were given up after several weeks, because the husbands objected to the household accounts being shown to the visitor; and here it would be interesting to mention that in three other cases, not reckoned in the investigation, the husbands refused after the first week for the same reason as soon as they thoroughly realised the scope of the inquiry. In four cases the babies were born too soon, and lived but a few hours. The investigation was primarily on infantile mortality, so that it automatically ceased with the child's death. One family moved out of London before the child's birth. There remain, therefore, thirty-four babies who were watched and studied by the visitors for many months. In every case but one these children were normal, and thriving at birth. Only one weighed less than 6lbs; four more weighed less than 7lbs; fifteen more weighed less than 8lbs; ten more weighed less than 9lbs; and four weighed over 9lbs. The average weight at birth for the whole number was 7lbs 10ozs. The child which weighed 5lbs 12ozs at birth was always sickly, and died of diarrhoea and sickness during the hot August of 1911 at the age of six months. Her mother was a delicate woman, and had come through a time of dire stress when her husband was out of work for four months before this child was born. A baby born since, which does not appear in this investigation, is now about five months old. Not one of the others seemed otherwise than sound and healthy, and able to thrive on the nourishment which was provided for their special benefit by the investigation. One child, however, a beautiful boy of five months, who weighed 7lbs 12ozs at birth, and 14lbs 14ozs at twenty weeks, died suddenly of bronchitis in December, 1910. His mother's health record was bad. He was the sixth child she had lost out of eleven. She was an extraordinarily tidy, clean woman, and an excellent manager but her father had died of consumption, and she was one of those mothers who economised in rent in order to feed her flock more adequately. She paid 5s a week for very dark ground-floor rooms. The death of the child was so sudden and unexpected that an inquest was held. The mother was horrified and bewildered at the entrance of police officers into her home. She wrung her hands and repeated over and over, "I done all I could!" and never shook off the impression that some disgrace attached to her. The burial insurance money paid by the company was £1. Five shillings specially earned by the mother and 5s lent by a friend brought up the amount to the necessary 30s, and the humble funeral took place. The child was buried in a common grave with seven other coffins of all sizes.

With these two exceptions, the babies all lived to be over a year. They usually did fairly well, unless some infection from the elder children gave them a bad cold, or measles, or whooping-cough, when some of them had a hard struggle to live, and their convalescence was much retarded by the close air and overcrowding of their unhygienic surroundings. Compared with babies who were fighting such surroundings without special nourishment, they did well, but compared with the children of well-to-do people they did badly indeed!

The ex-baby, where such a person existed, was nearly always undersized, delicate, and peevish. Apart from such causes as insufficient and improper food, crowded sleeping quarters, and wretched clothing, this member of the family specially suffered from want of fresh air. Too young to go out alone, with no one to carry it now the baby had come, it lived in the kitchen, dragging at its mother's skirts, much on its legs, but never in the open air. One of the conveniences most needed by poor mothers is a perambulator which will hold, if possible, her two youngest children. With such a vehicle, there would be some sort of chance of open air and change of scene so desperately necessary for the three housebound members of the family. As it is, the ex-baby is often imprisoned in a high chair, where it cannot fall into the fire, or pull over the water-can, or shut its finger in the crack of the door, or get at the food. But here it is deprived of exercise and freedom of limb, and develops a fretful, thwarted character, which renders it even more open to disease than the rest of the family, though they share with it all the other bad conditions.

There is no doubt that the healthy infant at birth is less healthy at three months, less healthy still at a year, and often by the time it is old enough to go to school it has developed rickets or lung trouble through entirely preventable causes.

To take several families individually, and go through their history, many serve as illustration of the way in which children who begin well are worn down by the conditions round them: Mr A, whose house was visited all the year of 1909, was originally a footman in one of the houses of a large public school. He seemed at the time of visiting to be fairly strong and wiry. He was about 5 feet 8 inches in height, well educated, and very steady. His wife had been a lady's-maid, who had saved a little money, which she sank in a boarding-house kept by herself and her sister. The boarding-house did not pay, and when Mrs A married, the sister went back into the service of the lady with whom she had been before. Mr A left his position as foot-man, and became a bus conductor in one of the old horse-bus companies. When visited in 1909 he had been fifteen years in his position, but owing to the coming of motor traffic, his employers gradually ran fewer buses, and his work became more casual. He was paid 4s a day, and got four days' work a week, with an occasional fifth day. He had to present himself every morning, and wait a certain time before he knew whether he would be employed or not. All that he made he brought home. His wife, who by the time the visits began was worn and delicate, was a well-educated woman, and an excellent manager. She saved on all the 20s weeks in order to have a little extra for the 16s weeks. Her sister in service often came to the rescue when extra trouble, such as illness or complete unemployment, visited the household. There were five children after the baby of the investigation arrived. The eldest, a girl, was consumptive; the next, a boy, was short in one leg, and wore a surgical boot; the next, a girl, was the airless ex-baby, and suffered with its eyes; and only the new-born child, weighing 9lbs, seemed to be thriving and strong. The average per week for food was 1s a head for man, woman, and children. Presently the conductor's work stopped altogether. No more horse-buses were run on that particular route, and motor-buses did not come that way. Mr A was out of work. He used to bring in odd sums of money earned in all sorts of ways between tramping after a new job. The eldest girl was put into a factory, where she earned 6s a week; the eldest boy got up early one morning, and offered himself to a dairyman as a boy to leave milk, and got the job, which meant work from 6 am till 8 am, and two hours after school in the evening. Several hours on Saturday and Sunday completed the week's work, for which he was paid 2s 6d. His parents were averse to his doing this, but the boy persisted. The family moved to basement rooms at a cheaper rent, and then the gradual pulling down of the baby began. The mother applied to the school authorities to have the two boys given dinner, and after some difficulty succeeded. The elder boy made no complaint, but the short-legged one could not eat the meals supplied. He said they were greasy, and made him feel sick. He used to come home and ask for a slice of the family bread and dripping. The father's earnings ranged between 5s and 10s, which brought the family income up to anything from 13s 6d to 18s 6d. The food allowance went often as low as 8d a week. A strain was put upon the health of each child, which reduced its vitality, and gave free play to disease tendencies. The eyes, which had been a weak point in every child, grew worse all round. The consumptive girl was constantly at home through illness, the boy had heavy colds, and the younger children ailed. Work was at last found by the father at a steady rate of

20s a week. He took the consumptive girl from her work, and sent her into the country, where she remained in the cottage of a grandparent earning nothing. The boy was induced to give up his work, and the family, when last seen, were living on a food allowance of 1s 6d per head all round the family. The baby was the usual feeble child of her age, the children were no longer fed at school, and the parents were congratulating themselves on their wonderful good fortune.

Mr B, whose home was visited part of 1911 and all 1912, was a printer's labourer, and brought his wife 28s a week every week during the investigation. He had been in the army, and fought all through the South African war. He seemed to be a strong man. His wife was one of the few fairly tall women that were visited. She had been strong, but was worn out and very dreary. There were eight children, all under-sized, and increasingly so as they went down the family. The ex-baby was a shrimp of a boy, only eleven months old when the baby – another boy – was born. The third youngest was a girl, and was so delicate that neither parent had expected to rear her. She weighed less than many a child of a year old when she was two and a half. The chief characteristics of these three youngest children were restlessness, diminutiveness, and a kind of elfin quickness. The baby, which was a normal child weighing 7lbs at birth, caught the inevitable measles and whooping-cough at four months and six months, and at a year weighed just 15lbs. He could say words and scramble about in an extremely active way – so much so that his harassed mother had to tie him into the high chair at an earlier age than most children of his class. The eyes of all the children in this family needed daily attention, and showed great weakness. The eldest girl was supplied with spectacles at school, for the payment of which 2d a week appeared for months in the mother's budgets. There was no specific disease. The children were stunted by sheer force of circumstances, not, so far as could be ascertained, by heredity. The sleeping was extremely crowded, and the food allowance averaged 1s 2½d a week, or 2d a day for the mother and children.

A third family is interesting for the reason that the mother firmly believed in enough to eat, and, being a particularly hard-working, clean woman, she could not bear to take dark underground rooms or to squeeze her family of seven children into a couple of rooms. She solved her problem by becoming a tenant of the Duchy of Cornwall estate. She got four tiny rooms for 8s, and kept them spotless. Her husband, who was a painter's labourer and a devoted gardener, kept the tiny strip of yard gay with flowers, and kept the interior of the damp, ill-contrived little house fresh with "licks of paint" of motley colours and patches and odds and ends of a medley of papers. When work was slack, Mrs C simply did not pay the rent at all. As she said: "The Prince er Wales, 'e don't want our little bits of sticks, and 'e won't sell us up if we keeps the place a credit to 'im'". She seemed to be right, for they owed a great deal of rent, and were never threatened with ejection. She explained the principle on which she worked as follows: "Me and my young man we keeps the place nice, and wen 'e's in work we pays the rent. Wen 'e's out er work in the winter I gets twenty loaves and 2 lbs er sixpenny fer the children, and a snack er meat fer 'im, and then I begins ter think about payin' th' agent out er anythink I 'as left. I'd be tellin' a lie if I said I didn't owe a bit in the rent-book, and now and agen th' agent gets a shillin' er two extra fer back money, but 'e carn't 'elp seein' 'ow creditable the place is. That piece er blue paper looks a fair treat through the winder, so 'e don't make no fuss." The house they lived in, and many like it, have been demolished, and a number of well-built houses are appearing in their stead. The Lambeth people declare that the rents have gone up, however, and that the displaced tenants will not be able to return, but this rumour has not been inquired into. What happened to the C's overdraft when they were obliged to turn out is not known. The children of this family were short and stumpy, but of solid build, and certainly had more vigour and staying-power than those of the two other families already mentioned in this chapter. The baby flourished. She weighed 7lbs at birth, and at one year she weighed 18lbs 10ozs. She could drag herself up by a chair, and say many words. The system of feeding first and paying rent afterwards seemed to be justified as far as the children were concerned.

Another woman who lived in "the Duchy," as they all call it, and whose house has since been demolished, had not the temperament which had the courage to owe. She paid her 8s for rent with clockwork regularity, and fed her husband and four children and herself on a weekly average of 8s 6d a week. The average for herself and the children worked out at 1s a week, or less than 2d a day. All four children were very delicate. The baby, who weighed 8½lbs. at birth, weighed 16lbs 8ozs at one year. The ex-baby suffered from consumption of the bowels, and was constantly in and out of hospital. The two elder children were tuberculous. The father was a printer's labourer, and appeared to be fairly strong, though a small man. The mother was delicate and worn, but seemed to have no specific disease.

Some of the children in the different families had strong individuality. Emma, aged ten, stood about 4 feet 6 inches in her socks. Four years later, when she began to earn by carrying men's dinners backwards and forwards to them at work, she measured 4 feet 10 inches. At ten she was a queer little figure, the eldest of six, with a baby always in her arms out of school hours. She was not highly intelligent, but had a soothing way with children. Her short neck and large face gave the impression of something dwarf-like. But she was sturdy and tough to all appearance, and could scrub a floor or wring out a tubful of clothes in a masterly way. She had a dog-like devotion for a half deaf, half blind little mother, who nevertheless managed to keep two rooms, a husband, and six children in a state of extraordinary order, considering all things. When Emma's school shoes were worn out, her mother took them over and wore them till there was no sole left, and Emma was provided with a "new" fifth-hand pair, which were generally twice too big. Emma's mother found her a great comfort, and very reluctantly sent her to work in a factory at the age of fifteen. There she earned 6s. a week, and became the family bread-winner during the frequent illnesses of her father.

Lulu was ex-baby to the deserted wife, and was three years old when her mother was visited. She was a lovely child with brilliant dark eyes and an olive skin. She had round cheeks, which never seemed to lose their contour, though their poor little owner spent many weary weeks in hospital after four different operations for a disease which the visitor only knew by the name of inter-sections", pronounced by Lulu's mother with awe and respect. Lulu would be playing and suddenly she would be seized with violent pain and be hurried off in her mother's arms to the hospital. The visitor was present on one of these occasions, when it seemed as though the whole street knew exactly what to do. One neighbour accompanied the mother and child, one took over the baby, another arranged with a nod and a word to take the mother's place at work that afternoon, and in two minutes everything was settled. Lulu came out of hospital four weeks later, with pale but still round cheeks and a questioning look in her eyes which gave a pathetic touch to the baby face. She still lives – the very idol of her mother – to whom the two boys are as nothing in comparison.

Dorothy, a person of two and another ex-baby, was devoured with a desire to accompany her elder brothers and sisters to school. She was a fair, thin child, with a bright blue-grey eyes and straight, wispy tow-coloured hair. Her tiny body was seething with restlessness and activity. She spent her days in a high chair, from which place she twice a day shrieked and wailed a protest when the older, happier ones started for school. She was quick as a needle, and could spend hours "writing pictures" on a piece of paper with a hard, scratchy lead pencil. She had no appetite, and had to be coaxed to eat by promises, rarely fulfilled, of taking her for a walk as soon as her mother's work was done. She slept in the chair during the day, as her mother declared it was not safe to have her upstairs on the bed or she would be out the window or down the stairs directly she woke. She simply hated the baby, another girl, which had condemned her to second place and comparative neglect. At three, she was kindly allowed a place in a school near by, and her health visibly improved from that moment. She became almost pretty.

'Erbie was of an inquiring turn, and during fifteen months' visiting had at different times managed to mangle his thumb, fall into the mud of the river at low tide, and get lost for ten hours, and be returned by the police. He was excessively sorry for himself, on each occasion, while his diminutive mother took the catastrophes with infinite calm. He was eight years old and a "good scholar". Physically he was a small, nondescript person, thin, and fair with neat features and a shrill voice, which penetrated into the core of the brain.

Joey had a tragedy attached to him, which clouded a portion of his days. He was guilty of telling a "boomer" to his parents. he said that he had been moved out of the infant school into the boys' school when he hadn't. One day his mother accompanied him to the school gate because it was raining, and she was protecting him with the family umbrella. Then the horrid truth was discovered, as the entrance for boys is in a different street to that for infants. Joey urgently declared that he had only been "kidding" his parents, and that when they were so wildly delighted and took his news so seriously he had not had the courage to tell them it was "kidding". The net result was gloom and disgrace, which floated round Joey's miserable head for many days. In the middle of this awful time he *was* moved, and the strained atmosphere was consequently relieved. He distinguished himself in his new class, however, by his answer to a question his teacher put to him as to the origin of Christmas Day. "You get a bigger bit of meat on yer plate than ever you seen before", he replied, and after a pause he added, "and w'en 'E dies you gets a bun." The teacher had called round to complain of this way of looking at things, and Joey was in deep disgrace again. He was a nice, chubby thing, with earnest ways and some imagination. His "boomer" preyed on him, and made him thin and anxious till the climax was over. The second offence worried him not at all. He was the pride and delight of two very simple and devoted parents. His two little sisters, both younger than himself, were extremely attached to him.

Benny was twelve and very, very serious. He was the boy, who, without telling a soul of his plan, offered himself to the milkman as a boy who would leave milk on doorsteps. He earned 2s 6d a week for the job, and faithfully performed the duties for some weeks, till a man who kept a vegetable shop offered him the same money for hours which suited him better, and he changed his trade. He was a very small boy for his age, and had a grave, thin face with inflamed eyes. An overcoat, presented because the visitor could not bear to think of his doing his round in the rain and sitting all day at school afterwards in his wet clothes gave him the keenest flash of pleasure he had ever felt. He turned scarlet and then went white. He had a resolute mouth and a quiet voice and no constitution.

There is one little picture which must be described, though the child and its mother were unknown. The visitor in Lambeth Walk met a thin, decent woman carrying a pot of mignonette. By her side, a boy about seven years old was hopping along with a crutch under one arm. His other arm encircled a pot in which was a lovely blooming fuchsia, whose flowers swung to his movements. The woman was looking straight ahead with grave, preoccupied eyes, not heeding the child. His whole expression was one of such glorified beatitude that the onlooker, arrested by it, could only feel a pang of sharpest envy. They went on their way with their flowers, and round the next corner the visitor had to struggle through a deeply interested crowd, who were watching a man being taken to prison.

Questions are often asked as to how these children amuse themselves. They are popularly supposed to spend their time at picture palaces. As far as close observation could discover, they seemed to spend their play-time – the boys shrilly shouting and running in the streets, and the girls minding the baby and looking on. They played a kind of hop-scotch marked out in chalk, which reminded the visitor of a game much beloved by her in extreme youth. Boys whose parents were able to afford the luxury seemed to spend hours on one roller skate, and seemed to do positive marvels when the nature of the roadway and nature of the skate are considered. Girls sometimes pooled their babies and did a little skipping, shouting severe orders as they did so to the unhappy infants. One party of soldiers, whose uniform was a piece of white tape round the arm and a piece of stick held over the shoulder as a weapon, marched up and down a narrow street for hours on the first day of the August holidays, making such a noise of battle and sudden death that the long-suffering mothers inside the houses occasionally left their work to scream to them to be quiet. The pathways were full of hatless girls and babies, who looked on with interest and envy. Needless to state, no notice was taken of the mothers' remonstrance. The best game of all is an ambulance, but that needs properties, which take some finding. A box on wheels, primarily intended for a baby's perambulator, and with the baby inside, makes a wonderful sort of toboggan along the paved path. The boy sits on one corner and holds with both hands on to the edges, the baby occupies the centre, and off they go, propelled by vigorous kicks.

In holiday-time elder brothers or sisters sometimes organise a party to Kennington Park or one of the open spaces near by, and the grass becomes a shrieking mass of children, from twelve or thirteen years of age downwards. The weary mother gives them bread and margarine in a piece of newspaper, and there is always a fountain from which they can drink. When they come home in the evening, something more solid is added to their usual tea. On Bank Holiday these children are taken by their parents to the nearest park. The father strolls off, the mother and children sit on the grass. Nobody talks. There is scolding and crying and laughing and shouting, and there is dreary staring silence – never conversation.

Indoors there are no amusements. There are no books and no games, nor any place to play the games should they exist. Wet holidays mean quarrelling and mischief, and a distracted mother. Every woman sighs when holidays begin. Boys and girls who earn money probably spend some of it on picture palaces; but the dependent children of parents in steady work at a low wage are not able to visit these fascinating places – much as they would like to. Two instances of "piktur show, 2*d*" appeared in the budgets. One was that of a young, newly married couple. The visitor smilingly hoped that they had enjoyed themselves. "'E treated me," said the young wife proudly. "Then why does it come in your budget?", asked the visitor. The girl stared. "Oh, I *paid*," she explained; "he let me take 'im." The other case was that of two middle-aged people, of about thirty, where there were four children. A sister-in-law minded the children, they took the baby with them, and earnestly enjoyed the representation of a motor-car touring through the stars, and of the chase and capture of a murderer by a most intelligent boy, "not bigger than Alfie." Here again the wife paid.

The outstanding fact about the children was not their stupidity nor their lack of beauty – they were neither stupid nor ugly – it was their puny size and damaged health. On the whole, the health of those who lived upstairs was less bad than that of those who lived on the ground floor, and decidedly less bad than that of those who lived in basements. Overcrowding in a first-floor room did not seem as deadly as overcrowding on the floor below. It is difficult to separate causes. Whether the superior health enjoyed by a first baby is due to more food, or to less overcrowding, or to less exposure to infection, is impossible to determine; perhaps it would be safe to say that it is due to all three, but whatever the exact causes are which produce in each case the sickly children so common in these households, the all-embracing one is poverty. The proportion of the infantile death-rate of Hampstead to that of Hoxton – something like 18 to 140 – proves this to be a fact. The 42 families already investigated in this inquiry have had altogether 201 children, but 18 of these were either born dead or died within a few hours. Of the remaining 183 children of all ages, ranging from a week up to sixteen or seventeen years, 39 had died, or over one-fifth. Out of the 144 survivors 5 were actually deficient, while many were slow in intellect or unduly excitable. Those among them who were born during the investigation were, with one exception, normal, cosy, healthy babies, with good appetites, who slept and fed in the usual way. They did not, however, in spite of special efforts made on their behalf, fulfil their first promise. At one year of age their environment had put its mark upon them. Though superior to babies of their class, who had not had special nourishment and care, they were vastly inferior to children of a better class who, though no finer or healthier at birth, had enjoyed proper conditions, and could therefore develop on sound and hygienic lines.

Robert Tressell, 1870–1911 12

Robert Tressell's real name was Robert Nounan. He was a house painter who worked for builders in Hastings in the first years of the 20th century. After working all day he wrote this semi-autobiographical account of his life and the lives of the men he worked with. This vivid account of the opinions, politics and struggle of working people was only published by chance. Robert died of tuberculosis in 1911. His daughter was interested in the manuscript and happened to mention it to her employers. As a result it was published in 1914 and became inspirational reading for the Labour movement. A full version was published in 1955. The following extracts give an account of the struggle of a group of painters and decorators, focusing on the life of a young house painter, Easton, and his wife Ruth, bringing up a baby in poverty, with an account of why the socialist of the group – Owen – could not believe in good in the context of all this misery.

It is likely that much of Tressell's work was semi-autobiographical. It reads as if he is describing his own living conditions and it would have been very difficult to have written the accounts presented in the book without having experienced them himself. He describes a social world in Britain at the turn of the last century that was greatly modified over the subsequent two generations, partly because of the writing of people like him and the campaigning that these writings inspired.

Tressell, R. (1914) *The ragged trousered philanthropists*

The meaning of poverty

They walked softly over and stood by the cradle side looking at the child; as they looked the baby kept moving uneasily in its sleep. Its face was very flushed and its eyes were moving under the half-closed lids. Every now and again its lips were drawn back slightly, showing part of the gums; presently it began to whimper, drawing up its knees as if in pain.

"He seems to have something wrong with him," said Easton.

"I think it's his teeth," replied the mother. "He's been very restless all day and he was awake nearly all last night".

"P'r'aps he's hungry."

"No, it can't be that. He had the best part of an egg this morning and I've nursed him several times today. And then at dinner-time he had a whole saucer full of fried potatoes with little bits of bacon it in."

Again the infant whimpered and twisted in its sleep, its lips drawn back showing the gums: its knees pressed closely to its body, the little fists clenched, and face flushed. Then after a few seconds it became placid: the mouth resumed its usual shape; the limbs relaxed and the child slumbered peacefully.

"Don't you think he's getting thin?" asked Easton. "It may be fancy, but he don't seem to me to be as big now as he was three months ago."

"No, he's not quite so fat," admitted Ruth. "It's his teeth what's wearing him out; he don't hardly get no rest at all with them."

They continued looking at him a little longer. Ruth thought he was a very beautiful child: he would be eight months old on Sunday. They were sorry they could do nothing to ease his pain, but consoled themselves with the reflection that he would be all right once those teeth were through.

"Well, let's have some tea," said Easton at last.

Whilst he removed his wet boots and socks and placed them in front of the fire to dry and put on dry socks and a pair of slippers in their stead, Ruth half filled a tin basin with hot water from the boiler and gave it to him, and he then went into the scullery, added some cold water and began to wash the paint off his hands. This done he returned to the kitchen and sat down at the table.

"I couldn't think what to give you to eat tonight," said Ruth as she poured out the tea. "I hadn't got no money left and there wasn't nothing in the house except bread and butter and that piece of cheese, so I cut some bread and butter and put some thin slices of cheese on it and toasted it on a plate in front of the fire. I hope you'll like it: it was the best I could do."

"That's all right: it smells very nice anyway, and I'm very hungry."

As they were taking their tea Easton told his wife about Linden's affair and his apprehensions as to what might befall himself. They were both very indignant, and sorry for poor old Linden, but their sympathy for him was soon almost forgotten in their fears for their own immediate future.

They remained at the table in silence for some time: then,

"How much rent do we owe now?" asked Easton.

"Four weeks, and I promised the collector the last time he called that we'd pay two weeks next Monday. He was quite nasty about it."

"Well, I suppose you'll have to pay it, that's all," said Easton.

"How much money will you have tomorrow?" asked Ruth.

He began to reckon up his time: he started on Monday and today was Friday; five days, from seven to five, less half an hour for breakfast and an hour for dinner, eight and a half hours a day - forty-two hours and a half. At sevenpence an hour that came to one pound four and ninepence halfpenny.

"You know I only started on Monday," he said, "so there's no back day to come. Tomorrow goes into next week."

"Yes, I know," replied Ruth.

"If we pay the two week's rent that'll leave us twelve shillings to live on."

"But we won't be able to keep all that," said Ruth, "because there's other things to pay."

"What other things?"

"We owe the baker eight shillings for the bread he let us have while you were not working, and there's about twelve shillings owing for groceries. We'll have to pay them something on account. Then we want some more coal; there's only about a shovelful left, and-"

"Wait a minit," said Easton. "The best way is to write out a list of everything we owe; then we shall know exactly where we are. You get me a piece of paper and tell me what to write. Then we'll see what it all comes to."

"Do you mean everything we owe, or everything we must pay tomorrow."

"I think we'd better make a list of all we owe first."

While they were talking the baby was sleeping restlessly, occasionally uttering plaintive little cries. The mother now went and knelt at the side of the cradle, which she gently rocked with one hand, patting the infant with the other.

"Except the furniture people, the biggest thing we owe is the rent," she said when Easton was ready to begin.

"It seems to me," said he, as, after having cleared a space on the table and arranged the paper, he began to sharpen his pencil with a table-knife, "that you don't manage things as well as you might. If you was to make out a list of just the things you *must* have before you went out of a Saturday, you'd find the money would go much farther. Instead of doing that you just take the money in your hand without knowing exactly what you're going to do with it, and when you come back it's all gone and next to nothing to show for it."

His wife make no reply: her head was bent down over the child.

"Now, let's see," went on her husband. "First of all there's the rent. How much did you say we owe?"

"Four weeks. That's the three weeks you were out and this week."

"Four sixes is twenty-four; that's one pound four," said Easton as he wrote it down. "Next?"

"Grocer, twelve shillings."

Easton looked up in astonishment.

"Twelve shillings. Why, didn't you tell me only the other day that you'd paid up all we owed for groceries?"

"Don't you remember we owed thirty-five shillings last spring? Well, I've been paying that bit by bit all the summer. I paid the last of it the week you finished your last job. Then you were out three weeks – up till last Saturday – and as we had nothing in hand I had to get what we wanted without paying for it."

"But do you mean to say it costs us three shillings a week for tea and sugar and butter?"

"It's not only them. There's been bacon and eggs and cheese and other things."

The man was beginning to become impatient.

"Well," he said. "What else?"

"We owe the baker eight shillings. We did owe nearly a pound, but I've been paying it off a little at a time."

This was added to the list.

"Then there's the milkman. I've not paid him for four weeks. He hasn't sent a bill yet, but you can reckon it up; we have two penn'orth every day."

"That's four and eight," said Easton, writing it down. "Anything else?"

"One and seven to the greengrocer for potatoes, cabbage, and paraffin oil."

"Anything else?"

"We owe the butcher two and sevenpence."

"Why, we haven't had any meat for a long time," said Easton.

"When was it?"

"Three weeks ago; don't you remember? A small leg of mutton."

"Oh, yes," and he added the item.

"Then there's the instalments for the furniture and oilcloth- twelve shillings. A letter came from them today. And there's something else."

She took three letters from the pocket of her dress and handed them to him.

"They all came today. I didn't show them to you before as I didn't want to upset you before you had your tea."

Easton drew the first letter from its envelope.

CORPORATION OF MUGSBOROUGH

General District and Special Rates

FINAL NOTICE

Mr W. EASTON,

I have to remind you that the amount due from you as under, in respect of the above Rates, has not been paid, and to request that you will forward the same within Fourteen Days from this date. You are hereby informed that after this notice no further call will be made, or intimation given, before legal proceedings are taken to enforce payment.

By order of the Council.

JAMES LEAH.
Collector, No 2 District.

District Rate	.	.	£– 13	11
Special Rate	.	.	10	2
			£1 4	1

The second communication was dated from the office of the Assistant Overseer of the Poor. It was also a Final Notice and was worded in almost exactly the same way as the other, the principal difference being that it was 'By order of the Overseers' instead of 'the Council'. It demanded the sum of £11.5½ for Poor Rate within fourteen days, and threatened legal proceedings in default.

Easton laid this down and began to read the third letter −

J. DIDLUM & CO LTD
Complete House Furnishers
QUALITY STREET, MUGSBOROUGH
Mr W. EASTON,
  SIR:
We have to remind you that three monthly payments of four
shillings each (12/- in all) became due on the first of this month,
and we must request you to let us have this amount *by return of post*.
        Under the terms of your agreement you guaranteed that
the money should be paid on the Saturday of every fourth week. To
prevent unpleasantness, we must request you for the future to
forward the full amount punctually upon that day.
                                    Yours truly,
                            J. DIDLUM & CO LTD

He read these communications several times in silence and finally
with an oath threw them down on the table.

"How much do we still owe for the oilcloth and the furniture?" he
asked.

"I don't know exactly. It was seven pound odd, and we've had the
things about six months. We paid one pound down and three or
four instalments. I'll get you the card if you like."

"No; never mind. Say we've paid one pound twelve; so we still
owe about six pound."

He added this amount to the list.

"I think it's a great pity we ever had the things at all," he said,
peevishly. "It would have been much better to have gone without
until we could pay cash for them: but you would have your way, of
course. Now we'll have this bloody debt dragging on us for years,
and before the dam stuff is paid for it'll be worn out."

The woman did not reply at once. She was bending down over
the cradle arranging the coverings which the restless movements of
the child had disordered. She was crying silently, unnoticed by her
husband.

For months past − in fact ever since the child was born − she had
been existing without sufficient food. If Easton was unemployed
they had to stint themselves so as to avoid getting further into debt
than was absolutely necessary. When he was working they had to go
short in order to pay what they owed; but of what there was Easton
himself, without knowing it, always had the greater share. If he was
at work she would pack into his dinner basket overnight the best
there was in the house. When he was out of work she often pretended,
as she gave him his meals, that she had had hers while he was out.

And all this time the baby was draining her life away and her work was never done.

She felt very weak and weary as she crouched there, crying furtively and trying not to let him see.

At last she said, without looking round:

"You know quite well that you were just as much in favour of getting them as I was. If we hadn't got the oilcloth there would have been illness in the house because of the way the wind used to come up between the floorboards. Even now of a windy day the oilcloth moves up and down."

"Well, I'm sure I don't know," said Easton, as he looked alternatively at the list of debts and the three letters. "I give you nearly every farthing I earn and I never interfere about anything, because I think it's your part to attend to the house, but it seems to me you don't manage things properly."

The woman suddenly burst into a passion of weeping, laying her head on the seat of the chair that was standing near the cradle.

Easton started up in surprise.

"Why, what's the matter?" he said.

Then as he looked down upon the quivering form of the sobbing woman, he was ashamed. He knelt down by her, embracing her and apologising, protesting that he had not meant to hurt her like that.

"I always do the best I can with the money," Ruth sobbed. "I never spend a farthing on myself, but you don't seem to understand how hard it is. I don't care nothing about having to go without things myself, but I can't bear it when you speak to me like you do lately. You seem to blame me for everything. You usen't to speak to me like that before I – before – Oh, I am so tired – I am so tired, I wish I could lie down somewhere and sleep and never wake up any more."

She turned away from him, half kneeling, half sitting on the floor, her arms folded on the seat of the chair, and her head resting upon them. She was crying in a heartbroken helpless way.

[Note: This short extract is from later in the book and refers to Owen, who is the main character in the book.]

Why there is no God

As he hurried along he presently noticed a small dark object on the doorstep of an untenanted house. He stopped to examine it more closely and perceived that it was a small black kitten. The tiny creature came towards him and began walking about his feet, looking into his face and crying piteously. He stooped down and stroked it, shuddering as his hands came in contact with its emaciated body. Its fur was saturated with rain and every joint of its backbone was distinctly perceptible to the touch. As he caressed it, the starving creature mewed pathetically.

Owen decided to take it home to the boy, and as he picked it up and put it inside his coat the little outcast began to purr.

This incident served to turn his thoughts into another channel. If, as so many people pretended to believe, there was an infinitely loving God, how was it that this helpless creature that He had made was condemned to suffer? It had never done any harm, and was in no sense responsible for the fact that it existed. Was God unaware of the miseries of His creatures? If so, then He was not all-knowing. Was God aware of their sufferings, but unable to help them? Then He was not all-powerful. Had He the power but not the will to make His creatures happy? Then He was not good. No; it was impossible to believe in the existence of an individual, infinite God. In fact, no one did so believe; and least of all those who pretended for various reasons to be the disciples and followers of Christ. The anti-Christs who went about singing hymns, making long prayers and crying Lord, Lord, but never doing the things which He said, who were known by their works to be unbelievers and infidels, unfaithful to the Master they pretended to serve, their lives being passed in deliberate and systematic disregard of His teachings and Commandments. It was not necessary to call in the evidence of science, or to refer to the supposed inconsistencies, impossibilities, contradictions and absurdities contained in the Bible, in order to prove that there was no truth in the Christian religion. All that was necessary was to look at the conduct of the individuals who were its votaries.

Edgar L. Collis, 1870-1957 and Major Greenwood, 1880-1949

13

An illustration of protective clothing from *The health of the industrial worker*

Edgar Collis was Mansel Talbot Professor of Preventive Medicine at the Welsh National School of Medicine, a member of the Industrial Fatigue Research Board, a Medical Inspector of Factories and Director of Welfare and Health for the Ministry of Munitions. Major Greenwood came from a medical family who lived in a poor area of London. He himself went into medicine, and throughout his life maintained strong humanist interests and a dedication to social medicine. He was the first Professor of Medical Statistics and Epidemiology at the London School of Hygiene and Tropical Medicine.

The book *The health of the industrial worker* is not just about the diseases which are associated with particular occupations, but it is also about what the authors term the 'general hygiene of industry', by which they mean looking at issues of hygiene, health and safety in the context of the profound changes which had taken place as a consequence of the development of modern industry. Collis and Greenwood presented evidence of the influence of employment of health, in terms of accidents, sickness and death. But what was new about their approach was the emphasis on the role of preventive medicine for the industrial worker – pointing out that there were many potential ways of "improving the workaday lives of the productive classes". The book covers many topics, such as food, ventilation and lighting; here we have chosen an extract on tuberculosis.

Collis, E.L. and Greenwood, M. (1921) *The health of the industrial worker*

Chapter VI
Tuberculosis and industry

1. Epidemiology

Tuberculosis, or at least its pulmonary form, is a disease which has been familiar in all ages and to all civilised peoples; records of it exist which were made in the time of the Assyrian Empire; all the Graeco-Roman authors speak of it and hardly a mediaeval or modern physician whose works have survived failed to give a clinical account of pulmonary consumption.

Predisposition and Infection. – Although the possibility that consumption was an infectious disease had been discussed in more or less detail by such men as Aristotle, Galen,[1] Avicenna, Lommius, Morton and Morgagni, and fully examined by Thomas Young 100 years ago, the general trend of opinion before the days of Villemin, William Budd and Koch was to the effect that an inherited disposition, predisposition or diathesis (these terms as one of us has pointed out, are *not* synonymous) played the chief *roles* in the production of phthisis. After the unequivocal demonstration of the infective element by Villemin and Koch, opinion veered round completely, and in our own generation the hygienic problem of tuberculosis has been largely regarded as one of diminishing the opportunities for transferring the tubercle bacillus from man to man or from domestic animals to man. Although the practical measures inspired by the two theories were not necessarily or usually different, some change of emphasis has resulted. It was as fully accepted fifty years ago as it is now that tuberculosis was a *pestis pauperum*. But in pre-bacterial days the explanation was that the unfavourable environment of the poor, acting upon a population containing a relatively high percentage of physically inferior stocks, led to the manifestation of the innate physical vices of the constitution, and gave the predisposition its chance. It was thought that the only policy to pursue was to improve the general social and sanitary conditions of the working classes, thereby to

[1] The doctrine of contagion in ancient medicine was, however, essentially different from that entertained in modern times after the days of Fracastorius.

improve their general powers of resistance. In our time more attention has been devoted to attacking in detail particular evils associated with poverty, as, for instance, the purification of urban milk supplies or the segregation of "open" (ie actively infective) cases of phthisis in sanatoria, or again by the disinfection of the consumptive's discharges.

To crystallise tendencies into epigrams is always to overstate the antithesis, but we shall perhaps help the reader to grasp the distinction if we say our grandfathers believed that in the case of consumption what was the matter with the poor was poverty, and that consumption would not be eliminated without the eradication of poverty; since they did not believe that poverty could be eradicated, they did not expect to "stamp out" consumption. The latter-day view is less pessimistic (or, if we look at it from another point of view, more pessimistic) and suggests that consumption might be eliminated without any obliteration of the distinction between class and class.

From the point of view of the present work we have to try to ascertain which tendency of thought is in the true direction, and the problem we formulate for discussion in this chapter is whether the conditions of industry have any special effect in increasing or diminishing the toll taken by tuberculosis of human life. An attempt to answer this question will, however, involve a general examination of the epidemiological problems presented by the group of diseases due to the tubercle bacillus.

Effect of Poverty. — We said above that tuberculosis was always held to be a *pestis pauperum*; this statement must now be justified.

Two criteria may be appealed to: type of domicile, and occupational status.

The size of the house may be taken as a fair estimate of the poverty or affluence of the occupants; but, in instituting a comparison between the mortality from tuberculosis among the occupants, we are aware that poverty in this case may be held to stand for imperfect hygiene, general and personal, and also for overcrowding. The figures here quoted clearly show on this test that a close relation exists between poverty and the disease; and they may also be claimed in support of the view (to which we shall refer again later) that the home exerts a powerful influence in its dissemination.

Type of dwelling	Death rate per 100,000 from tuberculosis		
	Greenock (1913)	Glasgow (1913)	Edinburgh (1910-12)
Four or more rooms	87	70	56
Three rooms	106	120	111
Two rooms	179	180	146
One room	222	240	225

Occupational status provides further evidence. If we contrast the experience of the clergy on the one hand with that of general labourers (1900-2) we find that, although from nearly all causes of death, the latter died at a greater rate than the former, the contrast reaches an extreme in the matter of phthisis. The mortality of general labourers from cancer was 231 per cent that of the clergy; from all causes other than cancer and phthisis it was 344 per cent, but from phthisis no less than 849 per cent. In London metropolitan boroughs, while the death rate from phthisis varies with differentiae of poverty (such as the proportion of general labourers, or the proportion of pawnbrokers), the correlation between the (corrected) cancer rate and measure of poverty is not pronounced. Although the work of Maynard and of Brown and Lal suggests that there is a correlation between the incidence of cancer and lack of social well being, it is not very large; but the comparison for phthisis mortality between clergy and general labourers which we have made is representative of the general statistical relations observed in most kinds of data, eg the death rate from phthisis (1909-12) was 1.86 in the poor district of Shoreditch, and 0.57 in more prosperous Hampstead. Hence the close relation between a high death rate from tuberculosis and poverty may be deemed to be established.

Decline of Tuberculosis. – We shall now consider the course of tuberculosis mortality in England and Wales as a whole. In the past fifty years the rate of mortality in all areas has declined; taking the age standardised death rate of males 1851-60 for pulmonary tuberculosis – phythisis – as 100, we have the results shown in Table 1. The decline has been substantial in both sexes, but greater for women than for men; in 1851-60 the female death rate from pulmonary tuberculosis was 106 per cent of the male rate; in 1901-10 it was 70 per cent of the corresponding male rate. In the next table we give the death rates per million living at certain age groups of males and females in successive decennia recorded by the Registrar-General, contrasting groups of urban and rural counties. In Table 3 these are expressed as ratios. A noteworthy point is the greater death rate of women in the

Table 1: Comparative phthisis mortality of England and Wales since 1851

	Males	Females
1851-60	100	106
1861-70	97	96
1871-80	88	79
1881-90	73	62
1891-1900	61	46
1901-10	50	35

rural counties at the earlier ages. This has usually been explained by supposing that the migration to towns of healthy young women and the departure from the cities of pthisics have favoured the urban death rates. The decennial abstracts do not transfer deaths of non-residents from one registration area to another; but this has been done in the Registrar-General's annual reports since 1911. After this correction we find that although the rural death rate at fifteen to twenty (females) is less than the urban rate, in the three following quinquennial age groups the urban rate remains lower than the rural rate (Table 4). This transfer of deaths from the area in which they were registered to that of the home of the deceased possibly corrects one of the assumed errors; but the other, the migration to towns of healthy young women in search of employment, remains. This could only be effectively corrected by an elaborate process for which data are not available; but by the following considerations we may perhaps reach some approximate measure of its importance. In the enumerated population of England and Wales (1911) the ratio of women aged twenty to twenty-five to females under five was 0.872; of women aged twenty-five to thirty, 0.846; and of women aged thirty to thirty-

Table 2: Death rates per million – Pthisis

| Group | | Age periods | | | | | | |
		15-20	20-25	25-35	35-45	45-55	55-65	65 and over
Males	Urban 1891-1900	1,010	1,815	2,448	3,581	3,798	3,150	1,907
	Rural 1891-1900	1,039	2,195	2,269	2,248	2,116	1,995	1,349
	Urban 1901-1910	764	1,433	1,959	2,751	3,330	2,915	1,895
	Rural 1901-1910	755	1,796	2,049	1,907	1,839	1,656	1,174
Females	Urban 1891-1900	1,233	1,500	1,925	2,331	1,799	1,313	852
	Rural 1891-1900	1,557	1,967	2,108	1,849	1,409	1,155	826
	Urban 1901-1910	948	1,161	1,448	1,666	1,465	1,148	799
	Rural 1901-1910	1,182	1,585	1,681	1,383	1,078	964	754

Table 3: Urban mortality as percentage of rural mortality – Pthisis

| Group | | Age periods | | | | | | |
		15-20	20-25	25-35	35-45	45-55	55-65	65 and over
Males	(1891-1900	97	83	108	159	179	158	141
	(1901-1910	101	80	96	144	181	176	161
Females	(1891-1900	79	76	91	126	128	114	103
	(1901-1910	80	73	86	121	136	119	106

Table 4: Phthisis death rates per million, 1911 – Females

Age	Rural districts	All urban districts
15-20	972	1,031
20-25	1,273	1,227
25-30	1,480	1,316
30-35	1,463	1,344

five, 0.783. If we multiply the number of female children under five enumerated in the rural districts by these fractions we shall obtain the numbers of women in each age group who would be living in the rural districts if the ratio observed in the general female population were maintained. The numbers actually enumerated fell short by 47,783, 40,101 and 30,299 respectively of the computed numbers. If we suppose that these deficits represent the numbers of women who had passed from the rural to the town districts, and further suppose that their death rate from phthisis was negligibly small – all being by hypothesis selected lives – the deaths recorded in the urban districts (including London and county boroughs) divided not by the enumerated population, but by the enumerated population less the conjectured number of migrants, will give the true urban death rate; while the sum of deaths in rural districts divided by the enumerated population plus the migrants will give the true rural death rate.

This calculation gives for ages twenty to twenty-five, 1,275 per million for urban, and 1,106 for rural districts; for ages twenty-five to thirty, the figures are 1,361 and 1,311; and for ages thirty to thirty-five, 1383 and 1,327 respectively. The result tends to support the doctrine that the favourable rates at early ages in towns are really due to migration; but the method is very rough, and the point deserves a more detailed examination.

No such simple explanation will account for the more rapid decline of female phthisis mortality in the whole country in comparison with that of males. It is conceivable that the decline in birth rate has been a factor, in view of the unfavourable effect of childbirth upon the prognosis of pthisis; but female mortality was already declining faster than that of males in the decennium prior to that in which the decline of the birth rate began to be of serious import.

Male and Female Mortality. – Returning to Table 2, it will be noticed that from age thirty-five onwards, although the female mortality in the urban counties is considerably higher than in rural counties, the discrepancy between the urban and rural male rates is much greater, amounting to no less than 80 per cent excess in the age group forty-five to fifty-five. The same result is brought out in Table 5, which embodies the shorter series of more exact figures relating to the year 1911.

Table 5: Phthisis mortality, 1911 – ages thirty-five and over

| | Males | | | Females | | |
| | Rural | All urban | | Rural | All urban | |
Age	districts	districts	Ratio	districts	districts	Ratio
35-40	1,361	2,256	166	1,201	1,490	124
40-45	1,328	2,469	186	975	1,423	146
45-50	1,300	2,498	192	832	1,310	157
50-55	1,163	2,787	240	817	1,070	131
55-60	1,293	2,539	196	706	1,029	146
60-65	1,144	2,440	213	862	988	115

Sex ratios for urban and rural districts

Age	Rural districts	Urban districts
35-40	113	151
40-45	136	174
45-50	156	191
50-55	132	260
55-60	183	247
60-65	133	247

In these later age groups the factor of migration is of much less moment than at earlier ages, and to explain the facts we are led to choose between the following hypotheses:

(a) The heavier incidence upon males is a direct consequence of urban industrial employment; (b) home environment reacts more unfavourably upon males than upon females; (c) the physical selection of urban females is more stringent than that of males.

With respect to the third hypothesis, we have only to remark that there is no evidence at all that the struggle for existence is less keen or the physical criteria of survival less exacting among men than among women; young male adults are not subject to a lower death rate from all causes than are females.

Passing now to the other two direct environmental factors, (a) and (b), we have to examine the evidence that tuberculosis does affect with especial severity those engaged in occupations associated characteristically with urban life.

Assuming that this were the true explanation, the Great War led to a control experiment upon a large scale, because a vastly greater proportion of the female population than usual was suddenly plunged into factory life; if, then, industrialisation were a serious epidemiological factor we should expect, since the war, women in this country would die of tuberculosis at a higher rate than immediately before it. This actually happened and was noted by Dr Stevenson in his official review of the statistics of 1916; he pointed out that the increase of the order of 5 per cent) did not affect the women over forty-five, and might, therefore, be connected with munition factory work. In this country we have no statistical data of the incidence of tuberculosis upon women employed in industry; but such rates are available for the women of Leipzig, and, since it has been found by one of us that the Leipzig rates for males corresponded very closely with those of similarly employed English males, the probability is that the rates for females correspond equally closely. Now the distributions of women in industries just before the war and at the end of 1916 were known with some exactness. For instance, in July 1914, about 170,000 women were engaged in the metal industries; in January 1917, the number was 443,000; the numbers employed in chemical industries doubled in the same period; those employed in commerce increased 50 per cent, and so forth. Hence, to form a statistical appreciation of the magnitude of the industrial factor, we could proceed as follows: apply to the industrial groupings in 1914 and 1916 the Leipzig occupational death rates from tuberculosis and see how far the calculated numbers agree with the observations. The female tuberculosis death rate of Liepzig was 4.04 per 1,000 per annum in the metal industries, 3.13 in chemical industries, and 2.80 in textiles, as contrasted with 0.97 for domestic servants, etc (mainly women fifteen to thirty-five); so that substantial transfers would increase the mortality. In the result we reached the conclusion that there should by calculation be 22,446 deaths in 1914, and 23,986 in 1916, an increase of 1,540; the recorded numbers were 22,214 and 24,131, an increase of 1,917; the agreement is reasonably good, although the actual increase was larger than predicted. A further confirmation was afforded by a study of the proportion deaths due to pulmonary tuberculosis bore to all deaths in the great industrial centres since the war. It was found that this proportion had increased from under 35 per cent to over 42 per cent between 1913 and 1916 in the group of large towns (Birmingham, Coventry, Manchester, Newcastle and Sheffield) much affected by war influx of workers; it had increased less characteristically in towns less affected by war industries, such as Ipswich, Norwich, Stoke-on-Trent, York and Worcester; but it had not increased at all or even fallen in non-industrial towns like Bournemouth, Brighton, Oxford, and Great Yarmouth. This result is, of course, not decisive, because an increase in the proportion of deaths from a disease might be found although the absolute number of deaths declined, but this is unusual. Like all Nature's economic experiments, this of wartime was not planned on precisely the lines we desired, yet it does generally support the inference that industrial employment is a factor in the production of tuberculosis.

During the period considered no other relevant new factors were introduced; the country was well fed, and there was not among women any withdrawal of the healthy persons from the ambit of our civilian statistical records (which occurred in men, and, of course, rendered the wartime male rates of death from tuberculosis quite useless for any general epidemiological purpose). The one great factor which might have played a part was industrial employment itself inseparably connected with aggregation in urban districts.

The conclusion here suggested, that increased industrialisation has been the main factor determining the increased prevalence of phthisis among women which occurred during the war period, received some confirmation from the data for the year 1919.

Table 5a: Comparative mortality from Phthisis among women

Year	Age period			
	15-20	20-25	25-35	35-45
1913	100	100	100	100
1917	150	131	113	114
1919	130	120	103	94

The phthisis mortality experienced among women in the United Kingdom at different age periods in 1913 is, for comparative purposes, stated above as 100. The data for 1917 illustrate how the phthisis rate rose; while the data for 1919 show how a swing back took place as women came out from industry. This swing has actually carried the mortality below the 1913 standard for the older women, who naturally were the first to resume normal life, while the swing is less at younger ages, where the proportion of women still remaining in factories was considerable, and there are still probably more women in industrial employment than before the war.

Occupation and Male Mortality.—We shall now consider the occupational incidence of tuberculosis upon males, the problem being to learn whether there are any industries particularly associated with urban life which are unduly subject to tuberculosis.

This question has been investigated upon the following lines. We used the occupational mortality records compiled decennially by the Registrar-General and a similar set of data prepared in Holland, eliminating occupations to which a direct occupational risk attaches, viz, those forms of mining, quarry and metal work in which injury inflicted upon the pulmonary tissues by silica particles is known to enhance the tuberculosis death rate. The residue of occupations was then analysed and the death rate from tuberculosis correlated with that from all other causes. The equation connecting the death rate from other causes with that from tuberculosis was then computed, and those occupations noted which experienced a death rate from tuberculosis or from pulmonary tuberculosis at least 25 per cent greater than predicted from a knowledge of the death rate due to other causes. The reason for this proceeding was that we wished to find trades specially liable *in se*, not trades the followers of which were generally unhealthy, perhaps owing to some negative selection (such as might happen if bad wages bring together only the failures of other occupations, a factor which, no doubt, explains the high mortality of "general labourers"). In this way, bookbinders, printers, tailors and cabinetmakers emerged as on the black list of all the data (three English decennial returns and one Dutch record) used (see Table 6). Hosiery makers and shoemakers also in the English, but not the Dutch, experience, were unduly subject to tuberculosis. But these occupations are pre-eminently associated with the great urban aggregations of mankind, so that qualitatively the result reached is in good agreement with our geographical findings. We now come to a subtle point in the epidemiology. Assuming it to be proved that the higher incidence of male tuberculosis amongst town dwellers is due to industrial employment, is the effect a direct or an indirect one? It being certain that men employed in a printing works, say, suffer from tuberculosis at a higher rate than, say, agricultural labourers, is this because they are more likely to be infected in the indoor association enforced by their employment, and if so, do they infect their families?

Table 6: Comparative mortality figures, 1890-2 and 1900-2; Phthisis, 1910-12 – all forms of tuberculosis

Occupation	1890-2	1900-2	1910-12
Clergy	100	100	100
Agricultural labourers	175	155	156
Coal miners	147	160	163
Bricklayers, etc	338	355	273
Saddlers, etc	358	402	323
Commercial clerks	327	360	356
Cotton manufacturers	303	362	256
Wool and worsted manufacturers	287	296	262
Silk manufacturers	294	375	273
Hosiery manufacturers	286	398	377
Lace manufacturers	242	345	325
Carpet manufacturers	342	315	246
Tinplate goods manufacturers	327	394	263
Paper manufacturers	217	262	210
Cabinetmakers	373	409	412
Shoemakers	386	483	456
Tailors	408	445	383
Printers	491	547	421
Bookbinders	490	515	427

Or is it that the circumstances of the work make them more readily susceptible to deleterious influences in the home environment?

To test the point so far as it could be tested, Miss C. M. Thompson, working with one of us, has made a careful study of the inter-relations of the death rate from tuberculosis, the death rate from all other causes, the percentage of the population housed more than two to a room, and the proportions in age groups employed in factory industries in the twenty-eight metropolitan boroughs. If we accept the proportion more than two to a room as a fairly good measure of home conditions - which it probably is in the London boroughs – the proportion industrially employed as a criterion of the amount of factory work (the occupations taken out were those in which little home employment exists), and if we regard the death rate from other causes as some measure of general physique, the net, or in technical language, partial correlations of highest order, between the variables should tell us something about the respective importance of the different variables in the two sexes.

Taking first the overcrowding index. At ages fifteen to twenty-five this is negatively correlated with the tuberculosis death rate for both sexes, and is not significantly different in the two sexes. At ages twenty-five to forty-five the correlation becomes large and positive for males, but it is insignificant for women. At ages forty-five to sixty-five the correlation for males is still large, although smaller than for the previous group, and is also large for women. The deduction follows that at ages between twenty-five and forty-five the home environment factor is *more* important for males than for females.

The industrial factor is positively correlated with the death rate from tuberculosis at all ages, save that of women forty-five to sixty-five, and continuously decreases with age, being largest for the young adults and adolescents. The correlation with deaths from other diseases is positive at all ages, but much larger for women than for men in the age group twenty-five to forty-five, and also at forty-five to sixty-

Table 7: Co-efficients of partial correlation for each pair of the four variables shown, the remaining two being made constant. Data Twenty-eight London Boroughs, Years 1911-13

| | Ages | | | | | |
| | 15-25 | | 25-45 | | 45-65 | |
Variables	Males	Females	Males	Females	Males	Females
Tuberculosis and overcrowding	-.48± .10	-.38± .11	-.71± .06	-.05± .13	-.46± .10	-.60± .08
Tuberculosis and other diseases	- .21± .12	- .31± .12	- .15± .12	- .74± .06	- .19± .12	- .50± .10
Tuberculosis and factory employment	+.56±.09	+.48±.10	+.25±.12	+.19±.12	+.19±.12	+.40±.11

five. The apparent meaning of these coefficients is of so much epidemiological importance that they will need most careful testing upon larger collections of data, and our inferences are plainly subject to modification when knowledge is less fragmentary. That in the earliest age group there is actually an inverse relation between tuberculosis and overcrowding, which latter is a measure of bad home conditions, may reflect the circumstance that in the casual trades the most prosperous period is that of early manhood prior to marriage; at that age the blind alley trades often provide a better wage than is earned by apprentices to skilled trades. Of the relation between tuberculosis and underfeeding, the recently published statistics of Prussia, showing an increase of deaths from 56,861 in 1913 to 86,217 in 1917, are an impressive example. Again, the death rate from phthisis in the Registrar-General's occupational group of messengers and porters is below the average at the earliest age tabulated, although above the average subsequently. This group covers much "blind alley" work.

In adult life twenty-five to forty-five the greater effect of overcrowding upon the male than upon the female suggests that the influence of factory life is an indirect one. In London, the proportion of males employed in factories is much greater than that of women. In London, percentages in factories are:

	Men	Women
15-25	18	16.1
25-45	18	7.1
45-65	18	10.1

The suggestion is that the conditions of factory life render the male especially susceptible to unfavourable home conditions. The women, exposed nearly the whole time to the home conditions, do not respond so delicately to it; the chief cause of variation amongst them is their natural physique, hence the high correlation between the death rate from other causes and that from tuberculosis for women. This statistical surmise is borne out by the field investigation of Tebb in Birmingham. He found that no specific source of tubercular infection could be traced in any munition factories, good or bad; but the employees in the unhygienic factories did suffer much more from tuberculosis than those employed at good modern factories. The inference is that the factories act as sensitisers, making the operative particularly susceptible to home conditions; the epidemiological importance of the factory is indirect, that of the home direct. This finding is in agreement with the view expressed by Thomson, who, drawing his conclusion from different data, is emphatic that tuberculosis "is the morbid expression of unhealthy home conditions."

We provisionally answer the epidemiological question posed as to the relation between industrial employment and deaths from tuberculosis in the following terms: *The role of the factory is, by confinement in monotonously ventilated rooms and by causing general fatigue, to reduce the resistance of the operative to those sources of infection to which he is exposed in the natural course of life, to make him react more sharply to home influences than does his wife or sister.* The physiological basis of this lowered resistance has been explored by Dr Leonard Hill in his recent investigations. Dr Hill has shown that there is a considerable correlation between variations, not only of the sense of well-being, but of actual prevalence of sickness, and of the degree of stagnation of the air, and that stagnation of the air is revealed badly, if at all, by the time-honoured thermometer and hygrometer, but made patent by Hill's instrument, the katathermometer, which measures the rate of cooling of the air. Much is to be expected, not only from improvement of the dwellings of the working classes, but also from rational attention to the ventilation of workplaces; the fetish of a low CO_2 content must be replaced by the sound doctrine – long enough known instinctively to the people – that moving air, not a draught but a breeze, is health-giving.

Types of Phthisis. – So far we have discussed the epidemiology of tuberculosis as if it were necessarily one and the same disease everywhere. Naturally, one should distinguish between pulmonary tuberculosis and other clinical forms, and we have done so in some collections of data, but not always, because at the adult ages of life pulmonary tuberculosis is the predominating form; of the deaths assigned to tuberculosis in the decennium 1901-10 in persons between twenty and sixty-five, 90.9 per cent were due to pulmonary tuberculosis and (undefined) phthisis. But it is a pure assumption to say that all these clinically similar causes of death are epidemiologically identical. We are dealing with death records, and there are numerous instances of diseases, eg the typhoid group and the malaria group, which are clinically similar, and may even have a common bacteriological origin, but which none the less are epidemiologically different. Plague is a case in point. Persons dead of pneumonic plague may belong to two different epidemiological categories. In an epidemic of bubonic plague – the epidemiological features of which are non-transmission from human being to human being and maximum prevalence in moderately warm weather – deaths from a secondary pneumonia occur and the exudate teems with plague bacilli. But another epidemiological type, that of primary pneumonic plague, is known; here the disease prevails in cold weather and is probably, or certainly, transmitted from person to person. This is a rarer form, of which, however, the great Manchurian epidemic a few years ago provides a recent example. If we were furnished with statistics of plague deaths in a country subject to both epidemiological forms we might draw very erroneous conclusions from an analysis of the combined data. The question is, whether a form of this error has to be reckoned with in discussing pulmonary tuberculosis from the epidemiological side. Sub-divisions of the clinical types of pulmonary tuberculosis were effected years ago, and we most of us learn about them in our hospital courses – the galloping or florid consumption, the ordinary chronic phthisis, and the long-drawn-out fibroid phthisis. But, so far as we know, Dr John Brownlee was the first epidemiologist to attempt statistical analysis of phthisis into different forms. Brownlee's starting point was the great difference in shape of the curves of death rates at different ages in different parts of the country. For instance, in the Shetland Islands the death rate is at a maximum (5.85 per 1,000 living per annum) at the age twenty to twenty-five; in London the maximum, 5.47, is at the age group forty-five to fifty-five. Brownlee did not think that such great differences in the form of the death rate curves were due to migration, occupation or natural selection, and he attempted to explain them upon the hypothesis that pulmonary phthisis *sans phrase* is a mixture of three epidemiological types:

1. A type of phthisis which chiefly affects young adults, the commonest age of death being between twenty and twenty-five.
2. A type of phthisis which chiefly affects persons of middle age, the commonest age of death being between forty-five and fifty-five.
3. A type of phthisis which chiefly attacks persons in old age and most frequently causes death between fifty-five and sixty-five years.

Brownlees' first test of his hypothesis was an attempt to graduate the death rate curves for various parts of England upon the assumption that they were compounded of three elementary types, the death rate at any age being $aY + bA + cO$, where Y, A and O are the death rates at that age of the three pure types, and the small letters are constants to be determined. As it could not be expected that any one of these types existed pure anywhere, it was necessary to proceed by a method of approximation. Starting with the phthisis death rates of Ireland, of London and of coal miners as predominatingly appertaining to the three hypothetical types, Brownlee was ultimately able to approximate to the hypothetical types, and to graduate with success the composite death rate curves of different parts of England and Wales.

Phthisis and Environment. – We now come to an extremely important point. Brownlee correlated the death rate from phthisis with the death rate from other causes, and it proved to be .178 at twenty to twenty-five (males), .390 at thirty-five to forty-five, .272 at fifty-five to sixty-five (averages of ten districts or periods), while the value of the co-efficients varied with the proportion of the total distribution attributable to middle-age phthisis, being large when that was large, and *vice versa*. If then the death rate from other causes is taken as a measure of general unhealthiness, or, again, the general standardised death rate (which gave similar correlations), the middle-age type is more susceptible to environment than the others, and the fact that this is the predominant type in London, Lancashire and the great industrial districts explains why in these the phthisis rate becomes excessive in the later adult ages; in these districts that type most responsive to environment prevails[2]. There is a vicious circle. We need hardly remark that Brownlee's conception is of great importance and, if true, would explain more than one difficulty. For instance, take the variety of opinions held as to the clinical value of tuberculin. Nobody is surprised that a typhoid vaccine does not protect against para-typhoid, and it would on Brownlee's hypothesis be equally unreasonable to expect a tuberculin derived from the middle-age type to protect against the young adult form of pulmonary tuberculosis. In Glasgow, for instance, the middle-age type is unusual. In London it is common and predominant; if vaccines are usually made from the latter type they would give less satisfactory results in Glasgow than in London.

It must, however, be admitted that the evidence so far published by Brownlee, while consistent with the truth of his hypothesis, does not suffice to establish it. The test of effective graduation, although necessary, is not sufficient. It is a common enough experience in statistical practice to find that a set of data can be effectively graduated by mathematical formulae the bases of which are altogether disparate.

Before a hypothetical law can be accepted as the correct description of statistical phenomena we must *first* show that the law will adequately graduate the observations which were the starting point of the inquiry, but we cannot rest there. It is necessary to proceed inductively and to show upon a wide collection of examples that the graduation by the proposed law is definitely more effective than graduation by other formulae. It is no reproach to Brownlee that this condition has not yet been fulfilled by him; he has, at least, used all the data at present available.

The deductions from the co-efficients of correlation are also open to criticism[3]. It is perhaps doubtful whether either the standardised death rate or the death rate from causes other than tuberculosis at the same age is a really effective measure of environment; it might with at least equal plausibility, perhaps with with greater plausibility, be asserted that the residual death rate is a measure of individual resisting power, of natural physique. In any event the various measures used, crude death rate, death rate from causes other than tuberculosis, standardised death rate, are not independent one of another, so that the series of co-efficients does not really represent a like number of

[2] It may also explain why the method of p 136 [table 7] applied to a hetergenous collection of country boroughs leads to discrepant results.

[3] It is proper to add that our own use of coefficients of correlation is open to criticism, inasmuch as only three years' data were available, too short an experience for final deductions.

independent measurements of the phenomenon under study. Brownlee has perhaps rather slighted the probable effect of industrial employment. While recognising that the parallelism of the death rate curves of both sexes makes in favour of his contention, we still have to reckon with the much greater incidence upon urban males in contrast with the urban females (see Table 5); it is difficult to avoid the conclusion that this is really a function of industrial employment, whether direct or, as suggested by the investigation detailed above, implicit.

Summary. – We may now sum up the results of our epidemiological enquiry, not because these results are clear cut and decisive, but to help the reader to distinguish between the partly solved and the wholly unsolved problems.

Looking at the country as a whole and the changes which have taken place during the last fifty years, a period in which steadily increasing industrialisation and its associated effect of aggregation within urban areas has been accompanied with improvements of general sanitation, we find that the death toll of tuberculosis has diminished in both sexes, but has diminished faster among women than amongst men. When we make synchronous comparisons of urban and rural districts – whether the mass comparison of counties mainly urban with counties mainly rural without correction for deaths of non-residents, or the more detailed comparison possible after 1911 – we find that with advancing age the disadvantage of the town dwellers increases, and that the apparent advantage of young female city inhabitants can be accounted for more or less completely by immigration from the country of healthy females. At ages over thirty-five in both sexes the town dwellers die from phthisis at a much greater rate than the denizens of rural districts, but the excess if far greater amongst males than amongst females. This excess is most at the age periods of life at which the largest proportion of urban males are industrially employed and the smallest proportion of urban females – the age of married life. Hence we surmise that industrial employment is a great factor in producing the difference. In support of this we find that in great industries, such as printing and shoemaking, necessarily associated with urbanisation, the death rate from phthisis is extremely high, higher than is to be expected from the death rate due to other causes sustained by the members of the trade, and therefore can hardly be attributed to a generally low standard of physique attained by them.... Whether the deleterious influence of industry is direct and a result of factory produced infection, or indirect, has been investigated by comparing the correlation between tuberculosis rates and indices of employment and of home environment in the two sexes for the metropolis. The result has been to show that during the period of life when male industrial employment is at or near a maximum and female industrial employment at an absolute minimum, the period in which the greatest proportion of living persons are married, the index of bad home conditions varies closely with the male death rate from tuberculosis. From this the inference is drawn that the deleterious influence of factory life acts through the home environment. The males, whose vitality is lowered by factory conditions, become more susceptible to evils associated with the home itself; amongst women the factor of varying home conditions is less directly associated with variation of the tuberculosis death rate, which in them seems most closely correlated with the death rate from other causes than tuberculosis. Lastly, there is reason to believe that a full epidemiological analysis may involve the separation of the clinical entity phthisis into three types characterised by differences of age susceptibility, and, perhaps, differences in responsiveness to good or bad environmental conditions. Both the inferences as to the differential effect of home conditions and the epidemiological subdivision of phthisis are not yet to be accepted as proven; much more statistical work is needed thoroughly to test them.

In the light of what we do know, or more or less shrewdly guess, as to the essential epidemiology of phthisis, what are the practical measures to be taken to mitigate its ravages? Upon balance it appears that the general belief of our fathers and grandfathers is sound, and the policy which ought to have been, and to some extent was inspired by that belief is a sound policy. What is the matter with the poor is largely poverty. Not through any special intensive measures of campaigning against the tubercle bacillus, not even by the segregation of the actively tuberculous, does there seem any real hope of salvation. We have to improve the homes of the working classes in the first place – it is a sound popular instinct that inspires the popular outcry against urban and even rural housing conditions; in the second place, we have to ensure better factory conditions; here it is not so much sanitation in the popular sense as hygiene in the wider apprehension of the term. We require regulation of the hours and intensity of work, of the physical characters of the atmosphere, and of the quantity and quality of the meals taken, so that the workman returning home shall not reach it in a condition of definitely lowered resistance to an infection which must still be regarded as ubiquitous.

Frank W. White (dates unknown)   **14**

Darwin's theory of evolution rested on the notion of genetic inheritance, and Mendel characterised the process which transmitted properties from one generation to the next. In the early decades of the 20th century understanding of the basis of heredity greatly advanced. The term 'eugenics' refers to the manipulation of the processes of natural selection, in order to 'improve' the genetic stock of the population. This can be accomplished through 'negative eugenics', that is, taking steps to remove from the population those with genes or traits not seen as 'desirable', or through 'positive eugenics' whereby certain groups are selected for reproduction. Through such policies it was thought that diseases could be eradicated and the health of populations improved. As Francis Galton, who founded and named the discipline, said:

> Man is gifted with pity and other kindly feelings; he has also the power of preventing many kinds of suffering. I conceive it to fall well within his province to replace Natural Selection by other processes that are more merciful and not less effective.... Natural Selection rests upon excessive production and wholesale destruction; Eugenics on bringing no more individuals into the world than can be properly cared for, and those only of the best stock. (Galton, *Memories of my life*, 1908, p 323)

The Eugenics Society came to prominence in the early 1900s with many members in Britain and the US. Galton is known as the 'father of modern statistics'; another proponent of eugenics, Karl Pearson, also made an important contributions to the development of statistical methods. However, the extreme negative eugenicist policies, and genocidal practices, of Nazism in Germany in the 1930s and 1940s, discredited the 'science' of eugenics. New scientific developments concerning cloning, genetic engineering and the Human Genome Project mean that many of the ethical issues first raised by the development of eugenicist ideas a century ago are still pertinent today.

This article by Frank W. White, who was from Northumberland, was published in *Eugenics Review*, a journal of the Eugenics Society, in 1928.

White, F.W. (1928) 'Natural and social selection: a 'Blue–Book' analysis'

[1] 'Vital Statistics of Wealth and Poverty,'T.H.C. Stevenson, CBE, MD, in *Journal of the Royal Statistical Society*, Pt 2, 1928, and the Registrar-General's *Decennial Supplement for England and Wales*, Pt 2.

"Culture, extending to matters of hygiene," according to the Deputy Registrar-General[1], is the all-important agency in relation to death-rates.

He continues, "The power of culture to exert a favourable influence upon mortality, even in the complete absence of wealth, is well illustrated in the case of the clergy.

Their mortality is remarkably low. Of 178 occupation groups dealt with in the recently-published report on occupational mortality in 1921-23, Anglican clergy occupied second place."

But other factors are obviously at work in addition, since the report shows that the comparatively humble position of 90 is occupied by medical men – the admitted experts in matters of hygiene; whilst, in the same list, place 11 is taken by agricultural labourers, 27 by foremen at coal mines, 29 by bricklayers, 62 by coal hewers, 121 by barristers, 123 by above-ground colliery workers, 159 by undefined labourers, 165 by dock labourers, and 171 by costermongers and hawkers.

As it is claimed that occupation (males only, at ages 16-65) gives the surest guide to wealth, culture, and status, in a general way, social gradation on an occupational basis is adopted for the comparison of mortality. Every occupation distinguished in the census is assigned to one of five grades. They are: 1, Upper (Professional, etc); 2, Intermediate (between 1 and 3); 3, Skilled Workmen; 4, Intermediate; and 5, Unskilled Labourers. Grades 1, 3, and 5 are clearly defined, doubtful cases being put in 2 and 4.

Though admitting that the classification is somewhat rough-and-ready and empirical, Dr Stevenson says in evidence of its fundamental soundness, "The scheme yielded natality (1921) and mortality (1921-23) rates varying regularly with the social status, from a minimum for the highest class (1) to a maximum for the lowest (5). Taking the rate for all classes jointly as 100 in each case, natality (births per 1,000 married males under 55) varies as follows from Class 1 to Class 5: 70, 74, 101, 116, 127; and mortality as follows: 81, 94, 95, 101, 126"

Biological grading

The reader of this paper (and, indeed, of the *Decennial Supplement* also) is left to infer that different mortality rates are almost solely determined by the different environmental influences associated with, and corresponding to, the different occupations, and the groups into which they are gathered. But it seems to the present writer that the most essential factor, in the partial success of the classification, goes unrecognised. It is the underlying cause which has determined in the past, and which determines to-day, the actual personnel of the different occupations and social grades, that is of paramount importance. This cause is natural endowment–natural inheritance. And the reason why the five grades appear to have been built up upon the true lines is really because certain types of occupation, and certain degrees of wealth and culture, go *generally* (not always) hand-in-hand with corresponding degrees of natural endowment. Occupational grading, in fact, corresponds *roughly* with a grading in accordance with natural gifts. Consequently it happens that the higher grades contain (relatively to their total numbers) a much greater proportion of individuals of good inheritance, than do the lower. But every grade and occupation, of course, embraces an assortment; and this fact fully explains most of the anomalies exhibited in the Report.

Despite the modifications in the struggle for existence wrought by advancing civilization, the best-adapted (the fittest) still tend to rise, and the less fit to fall. This is indisputable; it is evidenced on every hand. There is, therefore, a continual circulation taking place throughout society: some going up in the scale, others down, according to their natural gifts. The different employments in the series mark the milestones; the principal stages are represented by the social grades. The occupations (and the grades constructed from them) select their men. In a general way, the higher and more desirable the occupation, the better are the natural endowments of those who gain admission to it; and *vice versa*. For to suppose the converse – that the average casual labourer, for example, possesses natural equipment superior to the average skilled craftsman – is obviously to plunge into absurdity.

But once a man has reached the higher grades he is subject to the advantages of a beneficent cycle – good inheritance and good environment – all making for good. And there he and his descendants would assuredly remain, were it not for the occurrence of unfavourable variations, the mating of fitness with unfitness, and excesses in eating, in drinking, and *in Venere*. In class 5, on the other hand, a man encounters all the adversities of the vicious circle – bad inheritance, bad surroundings – all tending to his early destruction. But even so, this unfortunate type of person does not die out, because it is not only artificially preserved at the expense of the rest of society, but allowed freely to reproduce its kind!

Occupational selection

For a confirmation of this view we have only to turn to the *Supplement*, which contains evidence in abundance. We will observe how an occupation selects its men according to their endowment, and how closely their rates of mortality correspond to their inheritance, *even in spite of unfavourable environment*. Let us examine the vital statistics of coal miners. The calling embraces a large number of men who are to a great extent segregated into colonies of their own; and the general standard of culture is practically the same for all – the hewers and others engaged below ground, as well as those employed above ground, all live together, side by side, lodging with each other, and so forth. As is well known, miners constitute a community of persons having singularly similar tastes, habits, and methods of life; their non-working environment is identical for all. But as workers they are divided broadly into three main groups, according to their natural gifts. The best-endowed are attracted to the occupation of hewing, which is much the most strenuous and exacting, but usually carries the highest remuneration. The two remaining occupations (ie, other workers below, and workers above ground) are of a lighter character, and are shared by the less vigorous men. In each group there are vast numbers continually employed – the largest being that of hewers, which accounts for some 460,000 individuals between the ages of 20 and 65.

The vital statistics show that mortality falls much more lightly upon those whose work is hardest and whose environment is the least favourable, not only for one particular age group, but, generally speaking, for all. Let us quote from the *Supplement*. The mortality-ratios at various ages are given as follows (included for comparison are corresponding figures for Anglican clergy, dock labourers, costermongers and hawkers):

Occupation	Ages 20-65	16-	20-	25-	35-	45-	55-
Hewers	93.8	86	84	91	88	84	105
Underground workers (not hewers)	120.3	134	130	132	119	120	116
Workers above ground	118.3	156	149	133	125	112	112
Anglican Clergy	56.1	–	–	50	62	56	63
Dock Labourers	153.2	135	128	135	178	162	145
Costermongers and Hawkers	166.0	181	139	172	202	180	142

The relative mortalities of coal miners from all causes are here clearly shown; and when one furthermore bears in mind the fact that hewers have a much higher mortality at all ages from *accident* than the above-ground workers, the part played by natural inheritance is strikingly manifested. Nothing else will explain these great differences. We must add that mortality rates for foremen in coalmining are lower still: the job of foreman exerting an even more severe selective action among competitors.

Again, the exceedingly high mortality rates (see table) for dock labourers and hawkers can only be accounted for as being in great part owing to their defective natural inheritance. Their occupational environment is not usually bad; much of their work is in the open air. But their remuneration is poor, their employment uncertain, and it is common knowledge that for these reasons their ranks are chiefly recruited from the constitutional derelicts of the large towns – improvidents, idlers, degenerates, 'unfits.' The same remarks apply to another large group, general undefined labourers. Here again we observe how the occupation selects the type, and how closely mortality corresponds to natural inheritance.

Class and longevity

The following figures (from the *Supplement*) present the mortality ratios at various ages for the five occupational grades (males):

Social grade	Ages 20-65	16-	20-	25-	35-	45-	55-	65-
1 Upper	81.1	57	67	65	76	85	87	94
2 Intermediate	94.2	83	87	94	92	94	96	99
3 Skilled	95.1	98	99	95	92	93	98	100
4 Intermediate	100.7	100	104	105	105	101	97	94
5 Unskilled	125.8	121	116	125	138	130	119	110

It is apparent from this table that as age increases mortality rates *tend* towards equality for all. This is clear evidence of the mixed character of each grade (and occupation) from the point of view of inheritance. In each, those of good endowment struggle successfully through the adversities of their respective environments, and tend to reach a very similar old age. But the constitutional weaklings, being far more numerous in the lower grades (relatively to total numbers), manifest their presence in the wide differences which are noticeable between grade-mortalities at the earlier ages.

One may fairly conclude that both environment and inheritance play their parts in determining mortality, but that by far the more important of the two is inheritance.

Child mortality

[2] Annual Report of the Ministry of Health, 1926-1927; Annual Report of Chief Medical Officer of Ministry of Health, 1926; Annual Report of the London County Council, 1926.

A careful study of the official volumes[2] relating to the health of our nation leaves one with a feeling of disappointment and oppression.

As evidence of achievement we are told to observe the vital statistics of today, and compare them with those of the past. Attention is drawn to the fall in the general death-rate, and especially to the fall in infant mortality and in the death-rates of young children. We are informed that these figures speak for themselves of a better state of things. But do they? And are we to accept them, without question, as proof of a satisfactory bill of health?

As we have already seen, with *occupied adults* exposed to ordinarily strenuous or even unfavourable environments, a low mortality rate (as compared with others at the same period) is closely associated with a relatively good natural inheritance and fitness. Under tolerably hard general conditions, in fact, a comparatively low death-rate in any group of persons can be relied upon always to point to a sound endowment. But under much softened conditions (when food and State reliefs are broadcast, and institutional care and nurture easily obtained), a precisely similar (or even reduced) death-rate might well be compatible with a considerably lower average of inherited gifts.

Accordingly, with infants, in particular, and with very young children, at different periods and under widely-different conditions, a falling death-rate may be altogether deceptive as indicative of an improvement in inherent healthfulness, since the life of a most wretchedly-endowed or even mortally-afflicted infant can be amazingly prolonged by a sedulous system of nursing and dietary.

For instance, during 1926 (the year especially under review) our general death-rate was 11.6 per thousand persons – the lowest yet recorded; and Sir George Newman (Chief Medical Officer, Ministry of Health) in his yearly report, makes the statement that "the expectation of life for a child born in this country today is not less than seventeen years longer than it was for a child born in 1846." The following table shows the decline in mortality which has actually taken place of late in each year up to five:

Period	Deaths per 1000 births	Deaths per 1000 survivors			
	Ages 0-1	1-2	2-3	3-4	4-5
1901-05	138	41	16	11	8
1926	70	18	8	5	4

The number of infants and young children, therefore, who are being saved today – at any rate for a while – is evident. But what is the *nature* of many of these children saved? In the majority of cases are they of the best stocks, or of the worst? The answer in view of the existing differential death and birth-rates is unfortunately only too obvious. They are, for the most part, physical and mental detectives who, under a sterner régime would unquestionably have been eliminated soon after birth by natural selection. And, unhappily, the more of such we save the worse becomes the outlook for the State.

In England and Wales, during 1926, there were 453,804 deaths from all causes at all ages. Of these, 24,564 were from old age, 18,620 from violence, and the rest from disease of some kind. 173,131 of the deaths were of individuals under 50 years of age. In spite of an ample supply of food and its liberal distribution to all, in spite of all that is being done for the nation by preventive medicine (more than was ever done in the past), in spite of pensions, doles, reliefs, welfare centres, venereal centres, and charities of every description, a very large percentage of those born every year are of such enfeebled constitutions that they are totally unable to reach a reasonably advanced age.

There were also 53,220 deaths from cancer during 1926. In other words, of every 1,000 deaths from all causes, 117 were from cancer. The steady increase in mortality from this disease in recent times is exhibited in the following table, which shows the actual deaths per million of population at various periods:

Period	Deaths	Period	Deaths
1847-50	274	1921	1,215
1866-70	403	1924	1,297
1886-90	632	1926	1,362
1906-10	939		

These figures, of course, show only the number of fatal cases recorded. The actual incidence of fatal cases recorded. The actual incidence of this terrible affliction must be considerably greater, since cure by early operation has to be taken into account; and at no time was surgical intervention so widely practised as it is today. Part of the increase is clearly due to improved diagnosis, and part to the higher age of death – since cancer is a disease of middle age. But its hereditary nature is becoming more and more recognized; and, it must be asked, are we snatching lives from the ailments of infancy only to reserve them for a worse fate in later life, after they have transmitted the fatal tendency to their children?

The tubercular burden

Although the mortality from tuberculosis is declining (mainly due to the better general standard of nutrition of the nation), yet its cost is annually increasing. Hosts of new cases still appear, and the rate of decline is slower than it used to be.

The total number of sufferers from tuberculosis (as under notification, December, 1926) was 358,133 in England and Wales. The deaths for the year were 37,525. In England alone there were 442 dispensaries; 482 residential institutions with 22,202 beds; besides special schools, etc, devoted to the treatment of the disease.

The chronicity and incapacitating effects are well known; the after results of institutional treatment are still discouraging. Sir George Newman says, "The proportion of patients who have responded well to sanatorium treatment but who relapse within a comparatively short time after return to ordinary conditions of life and work is unfortunately high."

That a very strong tendency to tuberculosis is hereditarily transmitted is notorious.

Mental disability

The following are the numbers of individuals who were *under care* for insanity on January 1st in certain recent years (England and Wales): 123,714 in 1922; 126,279 in 1923, 131,551 in 1925; and 133,883 in 1926. Also, 15,786 were *under care* for mental deficiency in 1923, and 19,376 in 1925.

But these figures greatly understate the real incidence of the mischief. Dr Tredgold believes that there are more MDs [sic: meaning people with mental disability deficiency] than insane in the country. He also says: "I think we shall be well within the mark in saying that the total number of persons suffering from certifiable mental disease in England and Wales is over 1 per cent, and perhaps nearer 2 per cent of the general population." This would amount to considerably more than half a million individuals. In addition, however, to this vast figure he thinks that there is an even greater number of border-line cases (uncertifiable), epileptics, neurasthenics, and the like.

There is every reason to believe that all these conditions are becoming more and more widely disseminated by intermarriage. Dr Tredgold further says: "An overwhelming proportion of cases of mental disease must be regarded as primarily due to innate and not to external causes." He estimates that about four-fifths of all cases of mental deficiency are hereditary in origin.

The death-roll from influenza has risen rapidly. The following table, in decennial periods since 1870, shows the average number of deaths per year in each period (England and Wales):

1871-80	1881-90	1891-1900	1901-10	1911-20
263	534	11,051	7,318	21,641

During the whole of the last period influenza accounted for nearly as many deaths as diphtheria, measles, scarlet fever, and whooping cough combined. In 1918 there were no fewer than 112,329 deaths from influenza. It is to be particularly noted that although all ages were attacked, yet the disease showed an especial ruthlessness to early adult life, a very high peak in the mortality occurring about age 30.

In view of these things the question naturally suggests itself – Are we rearing up to adult life a nation having a large percentage of highly vulnerable individuals with low general resisting powers, who, under the stress of slightly less favourable conditions, fall an easy prey to disease and perish prematurely by thousands?

The burden of pauperism

This table reveals the growing expenditure under the Poor Law:

Years ending March 31st	Total annual expenditure
1914	£15,055,863
1920	£23,501,241
1924	£37,882,282
1925	£40,083,455
1927	(estimated) £49,500,000

The sharp rise in 1926–27 was, of course, due to industrial troubles. But the following remark of the Minister of Health is well worth bearing in mind, "It is not generally realised that during the past six years numbers of young men, without employment and maintained on Poor Law relief, have married, securing thereby an increase in their income from relief, and have had families, each addition to the family bring its addition to the family income."

It must furthermore be remembered that huge and increasing sums are being paid out yearly in unemployment benefit, disablement benefit, widows' and orphans' and old age pensions. Thus:

Year	Unemployment benefit	Old age pension
1924	£37,874,490	£23,800,000 (approx)
1925	£45,814,762	£26,200,000 (approx)
1926	£50,201.758	£27,800,000 (approx)

This expenditure should cover the 'bad luck' cases and remove from the Poor Law all except the definitely defective. The National Health Insurance records show that during 1926 there was a loss of at least 28¼ million weeks' work owing to sickness, "or the equivalent of twelve months' work of upwards of 540,270 persons." "The total benefit payments under the scheme in 1926 for England and Wales, including medical benefit charges, amounted to £28,584,000, and in the same period the amount collected in contributions was £21,982,000, and the State grant was £6,255,000." These figures have been rising yearly.

Nearly 60 per cent of the total insured persons are under medical treatment every year for varying lengths of time. Clearly there is a great deal of unfitness even amongst the picked workers of the nation.

Readers will remember that in 1917-18 the discovery was made that of 2,425,184 men of military age, only three in every nine were perfectly fit. Since the War, from 60 to 80 per cent of those applying for army enlistment have been rejected as unfit; while it is significant that the height for admission to the Guards regiments has been increasingly lowered of recent years. Again, 95 per cent of those offering themselves for the Police Force are rejected.

In spite of 2,324 maternity and child welfare centres (In England alone costing nearly £2,000,000 per year), and of at least 3,963 health visitors, and of day-nurseries and the like, Sir George Newman tells us that about 35 per cent of children entering school have physical defects of some kind.

During 1926 about 1,000 children (at age 3) from various parts of England were officially examined in order to sample their general physical condition. In round figures, 49 per cent showed signs of rickets, about 22 per cent had enlarged tonsils, 10 per cent enlarged tonsils and adenoids, 7 per cent ear discharge, 24 per cent dental decay, 1½ per cent cardiac affection, etc.

The next facts relate to London school children, who, for practical purposes, may be taken as typifying school children in general. The following table shows the number found (in 1926) at routine medical inspection to require treatment for defects of some sort (excluding uncleanliness and dental disease):

Age group	Inspected	Requiring treatment	Percentage requiring treatment
Entrants (age 5)	74,948	12,975	17.3
Age 8	44,195	9,418	21.3
Age 12	64,553	14,018	21.7
Leavers (age 13¾)	63,099	11,112	17.6

The fluctuation is peculiar, but reveals that the percentage of children requiring treatment instead of declining after entering school, seems rather to increase, despite a death-rate in some degree selective.

Of the entrants, 46 per cent suffer from dental decay, 15 per cent have severe caries, with septic gums. It is stated in the Report that "these figures show no diminution."

Of the first three groups 5.5 per cent were referred for treatment for tonsils and adenoids; 5.2 per cent for enlarged glands in the neck – an increase of recent years (says the Report).

Of 8 year old children no less than 51.9 per cent of the boys, and 54.7 per cent of the girls failed to pass the test for normal vision.

Besides cases requiring treatment, many thousand others are marked as "requiring observation." Also, multitudes of instances of heart, lung, and nervous defects, as well as all kinds of deformities were brought to light during these routine inspections at the *ordinary elementary* schools.

But, it must be remembered, in estimating the total amount of unfitness in children, that there are now many special places for the reception of the more defective, schools for the blind and the partially blind, for the deaf and hard-of-hearing; open-air schools and camps; schools for the mentally defective; epileptic colonies,; and so forth. Furthermore, there exist a certain number who are altogether unfit for any kind of school.

In an article in the *English Review* (March, 1927) Mr Ludovici brought forward official statistics which demonstrated that, although general cleanliness and clothing had improved in school children, yet in recent years the percentage of AI individuals (both boys and girls) was definitely declining, also that sickness (especially rheumatic and heart trouble, chorea and nervous disorders) had increased following the decline in infant mortality.

"The school medical service," says the London school medical officer (Dr Menzies), "is a receiver of damaged goods and spends most of its time and energies in patching them up." But he appears to think that the 'damage' takes place between birth and the age of going to school. Then why has the 'damage' increased during the years when pre-school care has improved?

The invisible costs

That the cost of unfitness is each year rapidly increasing is evidenced on every hand. But the total amount cannot be precisely estimated, since some of it is borne by local authorities, some by State grants, and much again by voluntary aid. Besides actual expenditure, other factors have to be considered. Not only do the unfit require maintenance, but they are inefficient and unproductive – a dead loss to the State in every way. The labours of a great number of highly efficient persons needed for their care, are withdrawn from other purposes in consequence. This is true alike of paid State-officials, voluntary philanthropic workers, and relatives of 'unfits' in the home circle. Were it not for the existence of so many 'unproductives,' more fit individuals would unquestionably be born every year.

How long can any nation continue to bear the growing strain?

George C.M. M'Gonigle (1888-1939) and J. Kirby (dates unknown) **15**

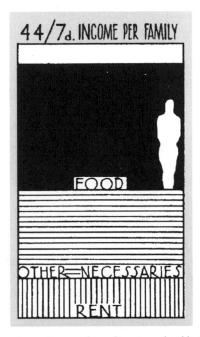

44/7d. INCOME PER FAMILY

FOOD

OTHER NECESSARIES

RENT

Section from diagram from *Poverty and public health*

George M'Gonigle was born in Monkwearmouth near Sunderland where his father was a Church of England clergyman. At the age of three he contracted polio which left him with a limp. He attended medical school in Durham and his subsequent appointments included being Schools Medical Officer in Durham and Medical Officer for Stockton-on-Tees. He also served in the RAMC in the First World War.

Poverty and public health by M'Gonigle and his co-author, J. Kirby, was published in a series by the Left Book Club, an organisation which aimed "to help in the terribly urgent struggle for World Peace and against Fascism by giving to all who are determined to play their part in this struggle such knowledge as will immensely increase their efficiency". In it they review a range of secondary statistical evidence concerning public health, including such sources as the results of routine medical examinations of schoolchildren and reports of Child Welfare Centres.

Here we present Chapter VII on 'Poverty, nutrition and the public health'. This chapter reports on the condition of a population in Stockton-on-Tees who were re-housed from slum dwellings into a "modern self-contained housing estate". They were compared in terms of their expenditure, nutrition and health. The results illustrate the importance of economics in determining family nutrition.

M'Gonigle, G.C.M. and Kirby, J. (1936) *Poverty and public health*

Chapter VII
Poverty, nutrition and the public health

In 1927 an "unhealthy area" in the Borough of Stockton-on-Tees was demolished. The inhabitants of this area (710 in number) were rehoused on a self-contained municipal housing estate, which had been specially built for the purpose. It was realised at the time that a study of the subsequent progress of this population would be of interest and might be of value in elucidating some of the problems which were then being investigated by the authors. Arrangements were accordingly made to keep careful records of the vital statistics of this group of people.

The "unhealthy area" which was demolished, formed, originally, a portion of a much larger area. It was decided that the original area was too large to be dealt with under one scheme, and it was therefore divided into two portions. For convenience a line of division was decided upon which ran along a street called "Smithfield." The portion lying to the south of this line was known as "The Housewife Lane Area," and that to the north of it as "The Riverside Area."

The Housewife Lane Area was dealt with under the usual procedure of an official representation followed by a public inquiry. The scheme was confirmed, after the public inquiry, by the Ministry of Health, and in the late autumn of 1927 the population, comprising 152 families and 710 individuals, was moved to the Mount Pleasant Estate. The portion of the original area which lay to the north of the boundary line running along Smithfield, and known as the Riverside Area, contained 289 families and 1,298 individuals. No official action under the Housing Acts was, at that time, taken in this area.

It will be seen that the conditions were very favourable for investigation. There was, in the first place, a population transferred from slum dwellings to a modern, self-contained housing estate, and kept intact without admixture with other populations. There was, further, a second population that continued to dwell in slum houses and served as a control.

Such favourable circumstances for human field research rarely occur.

In anticipation of action under the provisions of the Housing Acts, certain data as to death-rates, etc had been collected for these populations for the quinquennium 1923-1927, and these were of considerable value in making the investigation now to be described. *Crude death-rates* prior to transfer of the Housewife Lane Area population were as follows:–

Table 12

District	Crude death-rate quinquennium (1923-27)
England and Wales	12.00 per 1,000
Stockton-on-Tees	13.96 per 1,000
Housewife Lane Area	18.75 per 1,000
Riverside Area	22.16 per 1,000

The crude death-rate for the Riverside Area for this period was, as shown above, higher than that for the Housewife Lane Area, and both these rates were considerably higher than for the Borough of Stockton-on-Tees and for the whole of England and Wales.

The succeeding quinquennium (1928-1932) showed certain changes in these rates. The crude death-rate for the Borough of Stockton-on-Tees for this five-year period was 13.28 per 1,000 of the town's population; that of the population transferred from the Housewife Lane Area to the Mount Pleasant Estate had increased from 18.75 to 26.71 per 1,000, while that of the Riverside Area population decreased from 22.16 to 20.45.

The very considerable increase in the crude death-rate of the population which had been moved to the Mount Pleasant Estate obviously required careful investigation. It did not appear that the estate itself could be blamed for the higher mortality, for it possessed all the advantages of a carefully planned and well-built estate. The actual houses were soundly constructed and possessed up-to-date sanitary arrangements. Each house was fitted with a bath, an efficient kitchen range, a well ventilated food store, wash boiler, and so on. No fault could be found with the estate as a whole or with the individual houses.

Crude death-rates of a population do not necessarily give a record which can be truly compared with those of other populations; for, unless the age and sex distributions of the individuals forming the population are similar, a wrong impression may be given. For instance, the normal death-rate in a home for aged persons would be preposterously high in a residential school for boys. In order that comparisons may be made it is necessary to calculate the "standard death-rates." The fact that the general census was taken in the year 1931 was fortunate, in that it enabled standardising factors to be calculated for the populations here under review. A special local census was also taken of the populations of the Mount Pleasant Estate and the Riverside Area.

When 'standardised' the quinquennial death-rates were:

Table 13

	Stockton-on-Tees	Housewife Lane	Riverside Area
1923-27	12.32	22.91	26.10
		Mount Pleasant	
1928-32	12.07	33.55	22.78

Effects of standardisation

The effect of applying the standardising factor to the crude death-rate was to show that the fatality rate per 1,000 of the population on the Mount Pleasant Estate for the five-year period 1928-32, namely 33.53 per 1,000, was extraordinarily high. This rate represented an increase of 46.0% over the mean standardised rate for the same families in the previous quinquennium. Standardisation of the death-rates for the Borough of Stockton-on-Tees as a whole and for the Riverside Area showed a reduction in the second five-year period. It must be remembered that the population of the Riverside Area continued to dwell under slum conditions and that in the Housewife Lane Area people dwelt, during the second quinquennium, in environmental circumstances apparently approaching the ideal.

The population of the Mount Pleasant Estate contained a high proportion of young persons and consequently gave rise to the expectation of a low death-rate. Calculations based on the age and sex distribution of this group of people show that the "expected" mean death-rate for the five-year period 1928-32 would have been 8.12 per 1,000 of the population. Actually it amounted to 33.55. This constituted approximately a four-fold increase on a normal expected death-rate.

Birth-rates and infant mortality

One curious fact in the vital statistics of the population transferred to the Mount Pleasant Estate was a considerable increase in the birth-rate during the quinquennium 1928-32 compared with the previous five-year period. This increase occurred during a period of general decline in the birth-rate.

This is shown in Table 14.

This change in the birth-rate in this and certain other "closed" populations is at present the subject of study by the authors.

It may be stated here that the increase in the birth-rate was not consequent upon a higher marriage-rate, a larger proportion of first births, or an increase in the illegitimate birth-rate.

Table 14: Birth-rate per 1,000 population

Mean	England and Wales	Stockton-on-Tees	Housewife Lane	Riverside
1923-27	18.24	22.99	35.08	36.51

Mean			Mount Pleasant	
1928-32	16.27*	21.29	44.25	32.02

*Mean of 4 years.

Infant mortality rate

It is a matter of considerable interest that the very high birth-rate on the Mount Pleasant estate was not accompanied by an increase in the infant mortality rate as compared with the rate for the previous five years when the population was living in the Housewife Lane Area and when the birth-rate was lower. The Mount Pleasant Infant mortality rate for 1928-32 was considerably higher than for England and Wales during the same period, and also than the rate for the Borough of Stockton-on-Tees, but it did show a substantial reduction on the mean rate for the Housewife Lane Area.

Neo-natal mortality rate

The neo-natal mortality rate, expressed as a percentage of the total infantile mortality rate, was, for the five-year period 1928-32, 26.3% for the Mount Pleasant Estate (neo-natal deaths are deaths of infants occurring within four weeks of birth). This [rate] of 26.3 [per thousand] on the Mount Pleasant Estate compares favourably with the percentage for England and Wales, which amounts to 31.5, and with 34.2 for the Borough of Stockton-on-Tees during the same period. These figures are of some interest, in that they indicate that the viability of infants born on the Mount Pleasant Estate is not less than that of infants born elsewhere. No part of the increase in the general death-rate of the Mount Pleasant population can be attributed to an increase in the infant mortality rate.

The still-birth-rate was high and amounted to 61 per 1,000 live-births on the Mount Pleasant Estate, compared with 40.5 per 1,000 for England and Wales.

Table 15: Infant mortality rate per 1,000 live-births

Mean	England and Wales	Stockton-on-Tees	Housewife Lane	Riverside
1923-27	71.8	91.8	172.6	173.2
Mean			**Mount Pleasant**	
1928-32	66.2*	78.8	117.8	134.0

*Mean of 4 years.

Percentage of deaths in age-groups

It might have been expected that the increased fatality rate of the group of persons living on the Mount Pleasant Estate would have affected most severely individuals at the extremes of life. This expectation was not confirmed, for the increased fatality rate bore most heavily on those not at the extremes of life. There was a net increased death-rate of 9.2% among children from birth to 10 years of age; of 18.4% from 10 years of age to 65 years; and of 16.9 among those over 65 years old.

Morbidity and sickness rates

It would have been of interest to have obtained figures as to the morbidity and sickness rates of the Mount Pleasant and Riverside populations and to have compared them with the rates from other areas, but it was not found possible to collect reliable figures.

Extracts were made from the School Medical Inspection Schedule Cards of 160 children on the Mount Pleasant Estate and of 241 children on the Riverside Area. These extracts showed that the incidence of defects as ordinarily recorded at routine medical inspection was, in the case of both the Mount Pleasant Estate and Riverside Area children, rather more than double the figure for the whole of the elementary school children in the Borough of Stockton-on-Tees.

Consideration of the data summarised in the preceding pages made it appear reasonable to assume that the increase in the death-rate of the population of the Housewife Lane Area subsequent to its transfer to the Mount Pleasant Estate was a real increase and was beyond the probable extent of fortuitous variation. The data may further be assumed to be indicative of the operation among the Mount Pleasant population of some factor or factors inimical to the health of that population and, further, a factor or factors not operative among the population of the Riverside slum area.

It became a matter of importance to determine the nature of the factor or factors at work, and, consequently, investigations were made into several matters which, it was thought, might throw light upon the problem. Among those investigated were certain aspects of the economic circumstances of the two populations.

In both areas the families were poor, and the sums of money available for all purposes was so small as to bring them down to or below the poverty line.

Rents

Housewife Lane Area

The population of the old Housewife Lane Area enjoyed the advantage of low rents. In 1927 the mean "all in" rent (ie rent and rates) in that area was four shillings and eightpence (4s 8d) per family per week.

Riverside Area

In this area the rents paid in 1927 amounted to four shillings and sevenpence three farthings (4s 7¾d), a sum almost identical with the amount paid in the Housewife Lane Area at the same date.

Mount Pleasant Estate, 1928–1932

In 1928 the mean rent on the Mount Pleasant Estate was nine shillings (9s 0d) per family per week. On their transfer to Mount Pleasant the commitments of the translated families were, by reason of higher rentals, increased by four shillings and fourpence (4s 4d) per week.

Riverside Area, 1932

In 1932 the weekly rent per family amounted to four shillings and tenpence three farthings (4s 10¾d), an increase of threepence (3d) per week over the sum paid in 1927.

These facts concerning rents led to the detailed investigation of family budgets. (Consideration of known facts had led to the exclusion of such extrinsic environmental factors as housing, drainage, overcrowding or insanitary factors from responsibility for the increased death-rate on the Mount Pleasant Estate).

A large proportion of the families (over 90%) dwelling on the estate were, and in many instances had been for prolonged periods, unemployed. As a result of unemployment the weekly income available for all purposes was, among these families, strictly limited. Those families who continued to be domiciled in the Riverside Area were in a similar position, but they had the advantage over the Mount

Pleasant population in that the average amount of money which had, weekly, to be earmarked for rent was approximately half what the Mount Pleasant Estate families had to pay.

It was therefore decided to make an attempt to determine the sums of money available for the purchase of food by groups of families in each area and to assess, if possible, the quantity and quality of the foodstuffs purchased. It appeared that the best method of obtaining the desired information was to collect complete family budgets from each area of as many families as possible.

The obtaining of accurate and complete weekly budgets was dependent upon the goodwill and cooperation of the heads of the families concerned. Complete weekly budgets were obtained from 28 families on the Mount Pleasant Estate and from 27 in the Riverside Area. These numbers represented 18% of the families living at Mount Pleasant and 10% of those in the Riverside Area.

Analysis of these budgets yielded valuable information (see Table 16).

It will be noted that this table contains an item, "other necessary expenditure." This is made up of several items of which one is "fuel and light." The amount of money spent on fuel and light varied, being, in the case of the unemployed budget families on Mount Pleasant, 3s 1d per week, and rising to 3s 9½d among the employed budget families in the Riverside Area.

The next item included in "other necessary expenditure" was that of clothing and insurances. It is the custom in the North, and probably elsewhere, for the poor to purchase clothing and footwear by paying into a "clothing club" a weekly sum of one, two or more shillings per week. Insurances are nearly all small "industrial policies" which are maintained even at the cost of great personal sacrifice in order that a sum of money may be available at death sufficient to cover funeral

Table 16: Analysis of expenditure of income extracted from family budgets

| | Mount Pleasant Estate | | Riverside Area | |
| | 1 | 2 | 1 | 2 |
	Employed families	Unemployed families	Employed families	Unemployed families
Number of families	6	31	8	22
Mean man value	3.87%	3.8%	4.81%	3.5%
Mean income per family	47s 1d	30s 5d	44s 7d	30s 9d
Rent as % of income	20.5%	31.3%	14.7%	20.8%
Mean of other necessary expenditure	30.7%	29.3%	32.6%	33.3%
Food	42.9%	36.7%	46.3%	43.3%
Food per man per week in pence	62.6d	34.7d	51.5d	45.6d

expenses. Further, medical attention for dependants is usually obtained by weekly payments to a doctor's club, but with the unemployed families membership of these medical clubs has, in many instances, lapsed.

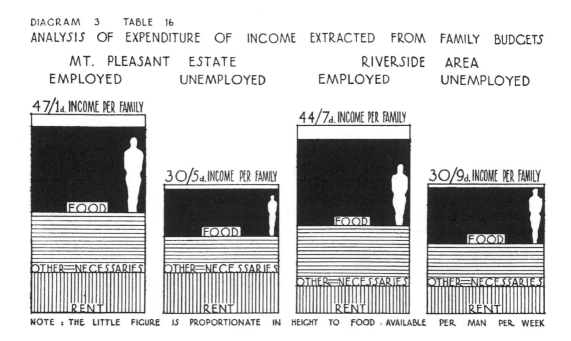

DIAGRAM 3   TABLE 16

ANALYSIS OF EXPENDITURE OF INCOME EXTRACTED FROM FAMILY BUDGETS

MT. PLEASANT ESTATE — RIVERSIDE AREA
EMPLOYED — UNEMPLOYED — EMPLOYED — UNEMPLOYED

47/1d. INCOME PER FAMILY

30/5d. INCOME PER FAMILY

44/7d. INCOME PER FAMILY

30/9d. INCOME PER FAMILY

FOOD — OTHER NECESSARIES — RENT

NOTE : THE LITTLE FIGURE IS PROPORTIONATE IN HEIGHT TO FOOD AVAILABLE PER MAN PER WEEK

Clothing and other club payments and insurances totalled 8s 1d with the employed budget families on Mount Pleasant and 7s with the Riverside Area employed families. The unemployed families had cut these amounts downs to 4s 3d on Mount Pleasant and 4s 2½d in the Riverside Area.

A further item which swells the total of "other necessary expenditure" was entered under the heading of "Etceteras" and varied from 1s 7d per week among the Mount Pleasant unemployed to 2s 10d in the case of the Riverside employed. The items entered under this heading consist of small household necessities such as crockery, pans, needles, thread and soap.

It will be seen that the items of rent, fuel and light, clothing clubs and insurances, and so on, absorbed a very considerable proportion of the family income; and it will be noted that the unemployed families on the Mount Pleasant Estate spent on food only 2s 10½d per man per week. Further consideration will be given in a subsequent chapter to the proportions of income expended on these items.

Table 17: Food purchased per man in grammes and total calories

"Normal diet"		Mount Pleasant		Riverside Area	
		Employed	Unemployed	Employed	Unemployed
First class protein	37	29.5	22.78	34.1	28.1
Total protein	100	87.4	65.79	82.9	74.6
Fat	100	117.4	73.72	101.1	85.2
Carbohydrates	400	573.5	410.8	496.3	452.6
Calories	3,000	4,277	2,696	3,223	2,910

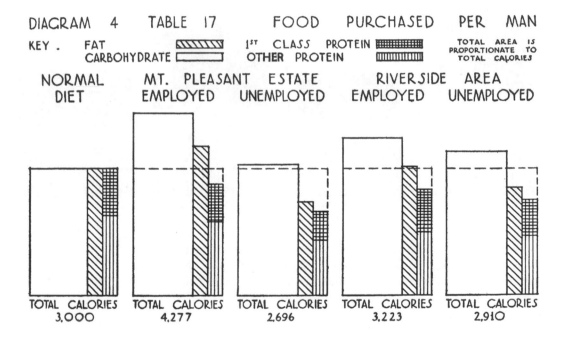

DIAGRAM 4 TABLE 17 FOOD PURCHASED PER MAN

KEY. FAT / CARBOHYDRATE / 1ST CLASS PROTEIN / OTHER PROTEIN / TOTAL AREA IS PROPORTIONATE TO TOTAL CALORIES

NORMAL DIET — MT. PLEASANT ESTATE EMPLOYED / UNEMPLOYED — RIVERSIDE AREA EMPLOYED / UNEMPLOYED

TOTAL CALORIES 3,000 — TOTAL CALORIES 4,277 — TOTAL CALORIES 2,696 — TOTAL CALORIES 3,223 — TOTAL CALORIES 2,910

Table 18: Quantities contained in Table 17 expressed as percentages of "Normal diet," after deducting 10 per cent for wastage

	Mount Pleasant		Riverside Area	
	Employed	Unemployed	Employed	Unemployed
First class protein	71.7%	55.4%	82.9%	68.3%
Total protein	78.6%	59.2%	74.6%	67.1%
Fat	105.6%	66.3%	91.0%	76.7%
Carbohydrates	129.0%	92.0%	111.0%	102.0%
Calories	128.0%	80.0%	97.0%	87.0%

Table 19: Quantities purchased as percentages of the British Medical Association scale of minimum diets

| | Mount Pleasant | | Riverside Area | |
	Employed	Unemployed	Employed	Unemployed
First-class protein	59.0%	45.5%	68.0%	56.0%
Total protein	87.0%	65.0%	83.0%	74.0%
Fats	117.0%	73.0%	101.0%	85.0%
Carbohydrate	114.0%	82.0%	99.0%	90.0%
Calories	125.0%	79.0%	94.0%	85.0%

Food purchased by the budget families

The next step in the analysis of the budgets was to determine the quantities of the various foodstuffs purchased. Table 16 sets out a summary of the quantities of first-class protein, total protein, fat and carbohydrates, and the number of calories calculated per "man value."

Some months after the publication of the report upon the Mount Pleasant Estate the British Medical Association appointed a Committee "To determine the minimum weekly expenditure on foodstuffs which must be incurred by families of varying size if health and working capacity are to be maintained, and to construct specimen diets." This Committee found it necessary to reconsider the question of a minimum "normal diet." After careful deliberation it decided that a total of 3,400 calories as purchased was necessary to maintain health and working capacity, and that the various constituents of the diet should be made up as follows: first-class protein 50 grammes, total protein 100 grammes, fat 100 grammes and carbohydrate 500 grammes. Table 19 sets out the percentages of the various constituents of the diets purchased by the budget families in relation to the British Medical Association scale.

Whether these dietaries be judged in comparison with the "normal" or the British Medical Association minimum scale, the conclusion cannot be avoided that there existed a serious shortage in the quantity of first-class protein in all the groups of family budgets analysed, and that the greatest deficiency occurred in those groups of families who were unemployed and who had less money available for the purchase of food than those who were fortunate in being in work.

The two groups of unemployed families show a woeful shortage of all dietary constituents except carbohydrates. These shortages were more extreme in the group of families living upon the Mount Pleasant Estate. The percentage of unemployed families on this estate was fully 90% and it was on this estate that the increase in the death-rate was noted.

The increased death-rate cannot be attributed to any devastating epidemic, such as influenza, for in the five-year period during which the population of the estate was kept under observation there was no undue incidence of infectious disease. During this period increased deaths were attributable to measles, cancer, heart conditions, bronchitis, pneumonia, diarrhoea, nephritis and puerperal sepsis. The increase in the death-rate due to measles amounted to 1.15 per 1,000 of the population of the estate; in the case of cancer to 0.87; heart conditions to 2.59; bronchitis and pneumonia to 3.74. Increases due to other causes of death were trifling. In each case the percentage increases shown above are relative to the rates for the same population during the five-year period prior to its removal to the Mount Pleasant Estate.

It is of interest to record that, during its five-year occupancy of the Mount Pleasant Estate, the population suffered fewer deaths from whooping cough, diphtheria, cerebro-spinal meningitis, tuberculosis, appendicitis and congenital debility than in the previous five years.

A point to be remembered is that the deficiencies in the diets cannot be attributed to temporary causes but that, owing to prolonged unemployment, the deprivations were, in the majority of cases, of long standing. By "long standing" is meant a period of two or more years.

It is difficult to come to any other conclusion than that the increased mortality was associated with the dietary deficiencies.

The findings of the investigation discussed in this chapter were included in a paper entitled "Poverty, Nutrition and the Public Health," which was read by one of the authors (G.C.M. M'G) before the Section of Epidemiology and State Medicine of the Royal Society of Medicine on February 24, 1933. The paper was published in full in the April number of the *Proceedings* of that Society in the same year.

This inquiry is of peculiar interest in that it was of a nature and scope which precluded the influence of personal bias. It is a matter for regret that no similar inquiry elsewhere has yet been undertaken. Certain inquiries into the vital statistics of Municipal Housing Estates have, it is true, been published, but they were planned on different lines, and so cannot, unfortunately, be used for purposes of comparison.

John Boyd Orr, 1880-1971   16

A family meal in the 1930s

John Boyd Orr was born in Kilmaurs, East Ayrshire, Scotland and studied theology at the University of Glasgow, later turning to nutrition and agronomy. He became director of the Institute of Animal Nutrition at the University of Aberdeen in 1914 and in 1929 founded the Imperial Bureau of Animal Nutrition. However, it is his work on human nutrition for which he is best known. His report *Food, health and income*, presented analyses of data from the early 1930s on nutrition in different income groups. It was the first time that such analyses had been conducted on a broad scale. It showed that the cost of a diet fulfilling basic nutritional requirements was beyond the means of half the British population and that ten per cent of the population was undernourished. This and other reports from the Rowett Research Institute formed the basis of the British food rationing system during the Second World War.

Boyd Orr became the Director of the United Nations Food and Agriculture Organisation in the late 1940s and was the architect of food policies aimed at helping poorly nourished nations. He advocated a world food policy based on need rather than on the interest of trade, and for this he was awarded the Nobel Peace prize in 1949. Boyd Orr was Knighted in 1935 and became a Baron in 1949.

Here we present an extract from *Food, health and income*, the most important finding of which Boyd Orr saw as: "the inadequacy of the diets of the lower income groups, and the markedly lower standard of health of people, and especially of the children in these groups, compared with that of the higher income groups" (1936, pp 11-12).

Boyd Orr, J. (1936) *Food, health and income*

Chapter VIII
Nutrition at different income levels

The examination of the diets of the different groups recorded in the preceding section shows that, on the standards taken, in the lower income groups the average diet is inadequate for perfect health. As income rises the average diet improves, but a diet completely adequate for health according to modern standards is reached only at an income level above that of 50 per cent of the population.

As income level falls other factors affecting health change as well as diet. These are referred to later [p 195]. Ignoring for the time being these other factors, one could predict from the nature of the diet of the different income level groups that there would be a good deal of ill health due to faulty diet, the incidence and degree being greater at the lower levels.

Owing to the requirement for new tissue formation in growth, children need a diet richer in first-class protein, in minerals and probably also in vitamins, than do adults. The evil effects of poor diet are, therefore, accentuated in children.

Nutrition of children

Owing to the difference in the nature of the diets, a comparison of the health of children of the lower income groups with that of children of the higher income groups, should show a slower rate of growth and a greater incidence of deficiency diseases in the former.

Rate of growth in children

It is well known that stature is largely determined by heredity. The extent to which a child will attain the limit set by heredity is, however, affected by diet. Certain deficiencies of the diet lead to a diminution in the rate of growth, with the result that the adult does not attain the full stature made possible by his inherited capacity for growth. Height and weight of children are therefore sometimes taken as an indication of the state of nutrition. On account of hereditary factors, figures applying to small groups are of little value. When applied to large groups of the same race, however, comparable figures for height and weight do give an indication of the relative adequacy of the diets of the groups.

Differences in the height of children and adolescents of different classes are depicted in the accompanying graph. Table IX shows the numbers of observations on which the averages are based. Further details are given in Appendix VII [not included here, Eds].

Table IX

	Dates of which measurements were taken	No of observations
I. Public School	1935	307
2. Christ's Hospital School	1926-29	16,031
3. Employed Males	1929-32	2,061
4. Council School, Boys	1927	12,605
5. Council School, Boys	1932-34	36,949

The children attending elementary council schools and the employed males may be taken as belonging mainly to groups I to IV; those attending Christ's Hospital School to groups III to VI. Those attending the public school belong almost entirely to group VI, where every constituent essential to health is present in abundance in the diet.

It is seen that there is a marked difference in the heights of boys drawn from different classes. Thus, at thirteen years of age the boys at Christ's Hospital School are on an average 2.4 inches taller than those of the Council Schools. At seventeen they are 3.8 inches taller than "Employed Males," who may be taken as belonging to the same class as the boys in the council schools. The most striking feature of the graph, however, is the average height of the boys of the public school drawn from group VI, the highest income group. Further figures are needed for other public schools of the same class to show whether the heights recorded here are true averages for boys in this class of school.

The British Association anthropometric data of 1883 showed that the average height of boys of thirteen and a half years in an industrial school was 2.6 inches below that of artisan boys of the same age, and 5.8 inches below that of boys of the professional class. It appears that in the last fifty years, though the average height for all classes has risen, there has been no marked change in the order of differences between the classes.

These differences in height are in accordance with what would be expected from an examination of the diets in common use in these classes. In the lower income groups the diet is relatively deficient in

Height of males by social groups: Compiled from various sources 1926-35

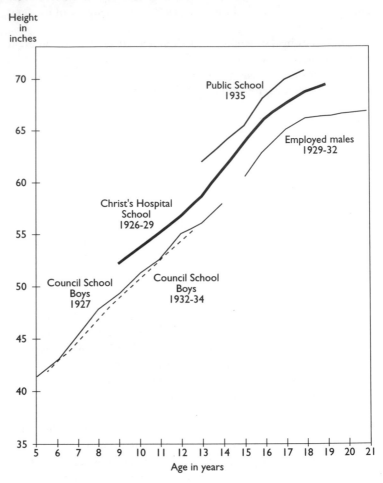

the constituents required for growth. Too high a proportion of the diet consists of carbohydrate rich foods, which contain very little bone and flesh forming material.

Of course tall and short individuals are found in all the groups. We are, however, considering here average diets and average heights. In each group some diets are better than the average and some worse. The better diets in the lower groups support a faster rate of growth. On the other hand no diet, however good, would enable an individual to exceed the limits of growth set by heredity. Short stature in the wealthier groups is in most cases inherited.

Incidence of deficiency disease in children

Owing to the varying standards of health assumed by different observers, those who accept the average as normal and regard as ill-health only what is markedly below the average, find little malnutrition or disease arising from it. On the other hand, those who adopt the physiological or ideal standard, as defined on page 18, recognise a great deal of preventable ill-health. There are no universally accepted standards of health based on agreed systems of measurements and clinical signs. Unfortunately there are too few observations on any reasonable standard. In the absence of sufficient comparable data, all that can be done is to give illustrative examples of observations of ill-health due to faulty diet.

It will be sufficient for the present purpose to consider three diseases: rickets, bad teeth and anaemia. It is known that diet is an important factor in the etiology of these.

Rickets. – Figures for the incidence of rickets given by different observers vary very widely owing to differences in the standard adopted and in the method of diagnosis. If the diagnosis be made on clinical examination only, the number found will usually be less than if a radiological examination be made, and in clinical diagnosis the number will depend on whether only obvious gross deformities are considered, or minor degrees of imperfect development are included. For this reason the figures given by different observers for the incidence of this disease are not comparable. Thus, for example, the incidence of rickets in L.C.C. schools was estimated at 0.3 per cent in 1933. On the other hand, in 1931 a special examination of 1,638 unselected school children showed that 87.5 per cent had one or more signs of rickets.

With such imperfect data it is impossible to make any accurate estimate of the incidence of this disease in the country generally, and still less of differences in incidence in different social classes. There is, however, no doubt that though minor degrees of rickets are still prevalent and probably more prevalent in the poorer classes, the incidence of gross rickets with marked bony deformities, which are obvious even to the lay observer, has markedly decreased in recent years. The deficiencies in the diet to which this condition is due are now well known, and this knowledge has been applied to the reduction of the preventable disease.

Bad Teeth. – It is now generally believed that there is a close correlation between dietary deficiency and dental caries. Though there is still some difference of opinion as to the relative importance of the dietary factors involved, there is no longer any doubt that the diets of the lower income groups, which are markedly deficient in minerals and vitamins, are not such as to promote the growth of sound healthy teeth. Whatever other causes of dental caries there may be, one would expect to find poorly developed teeth and a high incidence of caries in children reared on such diets.

About 80 per cent of the deciduous teeth of British children are imperfectly developed (hypoplastic). Since this defect may be established before birth, it may in part be due to dietary deficiency in pregnancy. But the fact that the incisors, which are in the most advanced state of development at birth, are usually better calcified than the later developed molars, suggests that the dietary deficiency may be even greater in early childhood than before birth.

Nutritional Anaemia. – Records of the incidence of nutritional anaemia would give a good indication of the adequacy of the diet. Unfortunately the incidence of anaemias and the extent to which they are due to causes other than diet, cannot be stated with any degree of confidence. Reports of School Medical Officers based merely on the appearance of the child show incidences of from 0.25 to 3.76 per cent in the children examined, but an examination based merely on appearance would not show minor degrees of anaemia such as could be caused by lesser degrees of malnutrition.

The haemoglobin content of the blood is the only true standard. In a special investigation in which the haemoglobin of the blood was determined in two groups of children: *(a)* in a routine medical inspection group, and *(b)* in a group selected because of poverty to be given a supplement of milk, 75 per cent of the children in (a), and only 51.5 per cent in (b) showed a haemoglobin value over 70. For a perfectly healthy child the value should be at least 90.

There are available the results of one investigation in which children of pre-school age of the poorest class are compared with children of the same age of the well-to-do class. Of the former, 23 per cent were definitely anaemic, and of the latter, none.

It is possible that a minor degree of anaemia, indicating a minor degree of ill-health in children, is more common than is generally supposed. An extensive enquiry to show the relative frequency of anaemia in the children of groups I and II compared with that in groups V and VI would throw much needed light on the relative state of health of the children of families at different economic levels.

We have considered three characteristic signs of malnutrition in children, rickets, bad teeth and anaemia. These are fairly wide-spread in the lower income groups, the only groups in which extensive observations have been made. In these groups growth is slower than in the high income groups. It is interesting to note that these diseases and stunted growth are attributable to lack of those dietary factors, viz, first class protein, minerals and vitamins which are the constituents of the diets shown to be deficient in the lower groups.

Incidence of infective disease in children

There is evidence to show that these same deficiencies affect resistance to some infectious diseases, such as pulmonary and intestinal disorders in young children. Children with rickets shown a higher incidence of complications and a higher death-rate from some common diseases, such as whooping-cough, measles, and diphtheria than do those in the same environment without rickets. A recent observation seems to indicate that non-pulmonary tuberculosis is less frequent in children who drink relatively large quantities of milk than in those who consume little milk.

Nutrition of adults

It has been established in nutritional studies that the constitution of the adult is affected by the state of nutrition in childhood. The rate of growth and the health of children have been shown to be below the optimum. The result of this should be traceable in poor physique in adult life. There is much evidence of the effect of malnutrition in selected groups of male adults, eg, in certain occupations and in army recruits. There are, however, few comparable data on adults at difference income levels. The state of nutrition of the adult is therefore not referred to at length. It will be sufficient to choose two diseases as illustrative examples, one infectious and one non-infectious, in which diet is an important factor.

The most significant infectious disease illustrating the influence of nutrition on susceptibility to infection, is tuberculosis. Infection is very widespread and in the great majority of cases it is the resistance of the individual which determines the extent to which the disease develops. Striking evidence of the influence of diet on resistance is afforded by the experience of Germany during the recent war. In the highly industrialised parts of the country where the food shortage was most severe the tuberculosis mortality showed an enormous increase. In Saxony it was almost doubled. This increase was accompanied by a change from the chronic to the acute type of the disease.

The Registrar-General's Report of 1927 shows that the mortality rate from tuberculosis amongst occupied males was nearly three times as high for unskilled labour as for the higher ranks of business and professional life. It is probable that the most effective line of attack on tuberculosis is by the improvement of diet.

For the health and physique of the rising generation the health of women is more important than that of men. One of the common results of malnutrition is anaemia, though, of course, anaemia may arise from other causes. It is much more common in women than in children and men. Its frequency in women is attributed to the extra demands for iron in women of the child-bearing age. In an investigation in Aberdeen in 1933, it was found that of about 1,000 women of the class of groups I, II and III, 50 per cent were anaemic, 15 per cent being classed as "severely anaemic". In 1935 in the examination of 368 London mothers of low economic status, it was found that less than 30 per cent had a normal haemoglobin level.

There are no comparable figures showing the incidence of anaemia in the higher income groups. Further, causes other than poor diet predispose to it. All that can be said, therefore, is that some degree of anaemia is common in the lower income groups, that it is, at least in part, preventable, and that diet is an important factor in its prevention.

Influence of factors other than diet

In considering the different types of ill-health referred to above, it has been difficult to assess the relative importance of diet and other factors. As income level falls, housing and other environmental conditions change. The importance of these for health is now fully recognised. Even apart from the known deleterious effect on health, the social evils of slums are so great that any suggestion that improvement of housing is of less importance than other social reforms is to be deprecated. The advantages to be obtained by better housing, as has been shown by M'Gonigle, are limited by inadequacy of diet, and the maximum advantage can only be obtained by improvements in both.

Hereditary differences also profoundly affect growth and susceptibility to some diseases. No individual can pass the limits set by inheritance. The most that can be done by diet or other environmental factors is to enable the individual to attain his full inherited capacity for growth and health.

Feeding tests with other factors controlled

The effect of diet can, however, be studied by feeding experiments with animals under conditions where diet is the only varying factor. Hundreds of such experiments have been made on closely related animals with, as far as possible, the same inherited characteristics and kept under the same environmental conditions. McCarrison, who has made a life study of nutritional problems, especially those relating to India, took several groups of rats and fed each group on a diet in common use by one or other of the various tribes in India. These rats were all kept under the same environmental conditions. He found that the physique and incidence of disease in each of the groups corresponded to an astonishing degree with those found in the tribes whose diets were copied and that there was a similar corresponding incidence even in the case of diseases which, at that time, were not usually thought to be connected with faulty diet.

A similar experiment with modifications to suit this country has since been conducted in Scotland. The rats in one group were fed on a diet somewhat similar to that of income group I in the present survey. Other closely related rats were fed on the same diet supplemented by an abundance of milk and as much green food as they cared to eat. These additions made good all the deficiencies of the average group I diet, making it as adequate for the maintenance of health as the diet of group VI. The following graph shows the relative rates of growth of the young animals of the two groups.

Not only were the rates of growth markedly divergent, but the death rates of the two groups differed correspondingly. The mortality to 140 days of age on the supplemented diet was 11.6 per cent, while for those on the experimental diet the rate was 54.3 per cent. This heavy death rate was due mainly to epidemic infections to which both groups were equally exposed.

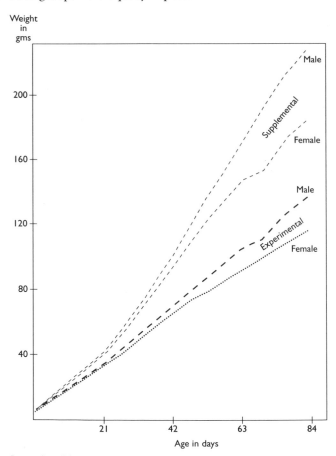

Reproduced from the *Journal of Hygiene* by courtesy of the Cambridge University Press

Such experiments with rats, of course, do not carry the same weight as observations on human beings. The dietary requirements of man and rats are not identical. Observations, however, have been made on two tribes, the Masai and the Kikuyu, living in Africa under the same climatic and housing conditions, but with very different diets. The diet of the Masai is rich in first-class proteins, minerals and most vitamins, though faulty in some other respects; the diet of the Kikuyu is rich in carbohydrates but relatively poor in most other constituents. The latter corresponds, roughly, to the average diet of groups I and II of our own population. A medical survey of the two tribes showed that the males in the tribe with the former diet were, on an average, five inches taller than the males of the latter tribe. There was also a striking difference in the incidence of disease in the two tribes. Bony deformities, somewhat similar to those found in children who suffer from rickets, carious teeth and pulmonary and intestinal diseases were more than twice as prevalent in the tribe on the diet poor in proteins, minerals and vitamins. These observations, though they do not refer to the people of this country, give confidence in accepting as substantially correct the general picture given here.

Effect of improvement of diet on rate of growth and health

Tests have also been carried out with children in this country. As far as they go these confirm the results obtained on animals and native tribes.

In 1926 observations were made on the effect of supplementing the diet of boys in an industrial school. The diet without the supplement was assumed to be adequate for health. It was found that the addition of milk increased the rate of growth for the period of the test, the increase per twelve months in boys on the diet alone being 1.84 inches, while in those receiving extra milk it was 2.63 inches.

These results, however, cannot be applied to children under home conditions. In 1927, therefore, a series of tests was carried out in Scotland in which about 1,500 children in the ordinary elementary schools in the seven largest towns were given additional milk at school for a period of seven months. Periodic measurements of the children showed that the rate of growth in those getting the additional milk was about 20 per cent greater than in those not getting additional milk. The increased rate of growth was accompanied by a noticeable improvement in health and vigour. This experiment was twice repeated by different observers who obtained substantially the same results on numbers up to 20,000 children.

Tests with even more striking results have been obtained in other countries, where the average diet is inferior to that in this country. Tsurumi has shown that in elementary schools in Tokyo the addition of 200cc (about one third of a pint) of milk to the diet for six months caused a marked acceleration in the rate of growth, the gain in weight being 86 per cent. and in height, 16 per cent more than in the controls. It was reported that the children who received milk "had improved complexions and glossy skins," and that "they became more cheerful, attended school more regularly, and were more successful in athletic contests than the corresponding control children". Turbott and Rolland, in New Zealand, found that a supplement of ½ to 1 pint of milk daily given to Maori children caused an increase in rate of growth such that they gained twice as much in height, and 2½ times as much in weight as the controls.

The results of these tests on animals under experimental conditions and children under ordinary conditions of everyday life, suggest that, to whatever extent heredity and environment account for differences in health and physique of different classes, it would be possible to effect a considerable improvement in the health of the children of lower income groups by improving the diet.

Chapter IX
Summary and conclusion

The food position of the country has been investigated to show the average consumption of the main foodstuffs at different income levels. The standard of food requirements and the standard of health adopted are not the present average but the optimum, ie, the physiological standard, which, though ideal, is attainable in practice with a national food supply sufficient to provide a diet adequate for health for any member of the community. The main findings may be summarized as follows:—

I. Of an estimated national income of £3,750 millions, about £1,075 millions are spent on food. This is equivalent to 9s per head per week.

II. The consumption of bread and potatoes is practically uniform throughout the different income level groups. Consumption of milk, eggs, fruit, vegetables, meat and fish rises with income. Thus, in the poorest group the average consumption of milk, including tinned milk, is equivalent to 1.8 pints per head per week; in the wealthiest group 5.5 pints. The poorest group consume 1.5 eggs per head per week; the wealthiest 4.5. The poorest spend 2.4d on fruit; the wealthiest 1s 8d.

III. An examination of the composition of the diets of the different groups shows that the degree of adequacy for health increases as income rises. The average diet of the poorest group, comprising 4½ million people, is, by the standard adopted, deficient in every constituent examined. The second group, comprising 9 million people, is adequate in protein but deficient in all the vitamins and minerals considered. The third group, comprising another 9 million, is deficient in vitamins and minerals. Complete adequacy is almost reached in group IV, and in the still wealthier groups the diet has a surplus of all constituents considered. (See Appendix IX [not included here, Eds].)

IV. A view of the state of health of the people of the different groups suggests that, as income increases, disease and death-rate decrease, children grow more quickly, adult stature is greater and general health and physique improve.

V. The results of tests on children show that improvement of the diet in the lower groups is accompanied by improvement in health and increased rate of growth, which approximates to that of children in the higher income groups.

VI. To make the diet of the poorer groups the same as that of the first group whose diet is adequate for full health, ie, group IV, would involve increases in consumption of a number of the more expensive foodstuffs, viz, milk, eggs, butter, fruit, vegetables and meat, varying from 12 to 25 per cent.

If these findings be accepted as sufficiently accurate to form a working hypothesis, they raise important economic and political problems. Consideration of these is outwith the scope of the investigation. It may be pointed out here, however, that one of the main difficulties in dealing with these problems is that they are not within the sphere of any single Department of State. This new knowledge of nutrition, which shows that there can be an enormous improvement in the health and physique of the nation, coming at the same time as the greatly increased powers of producing food, has created an entirely new situation which demands economic statesmanship. The prominence given to this new social problem at the Assembly of the League of Nations in 1935 and 1936 shows that it is occupying the attention of all civilized countries. It is gratifying that the lead in this movement was taken by the British Empire.

Wal Hannington (1896–1966)   **17**

The search for employment, 1930s

Wal Hannington trained as a toolmaker from the age of 14 and was a member of the London district committee of the Toolmakers' Society during the First World War. He joined the British Socialist Party at the end of 1915 and was a founding member of the Communist Party of Great Britain. In 1921 Hannington was one of the founders of the National Unemployed Workers' Movement in which he was the leading figure until its dissolution after the Second World War.

Hannington was a champion of the unemployed during the depression years of the 1930s. He saw the spread of unemployment as the price that capitalism exacts from society and the resulting inequalities as not only an economic but a moral issue. The Special (Distressed) Areas Act was passed in 1934 which allocated extra resources to areas suffering high unemployment. Hannington was familiar with the condition of 'distressed areas': South Wales, Cumberland, Durham, Nothumberland and West Scotland. He describes the plight of the unemployed, including suicides, malnutrition, the break-up of family life and broken ambitions. Here we present an extract from Hannington's book, which describes and presents remedies for these areas.

At one of the rallies of the notorious Hunger Marches in London's Hyde Park in the mid-1920s Hannington appealed to the police to display less brutality to the unemployed and to remember their own working-class origins. For these remarks, he was tried for 'creating disaffection amongst Her Majesty's police forces' and was sentenced to a year's hard labour.

Hannington, W. (1937) *The problem of distressed areas*

Chapter V
Scientists, diets, and realities

I do not know whether it was for humanitarian, social, or economic reasons, or on purely military considerations, or, again, whether it was due to the increasing pressure of the medical reports at this period, that the British Medical Association decided to appoint a committee with the following terms of reference: "To determine the minimum weekly expenditure on foodstuffs which must be incurred by families of varying size, if health and working capacity are to be maintained, and to construct specimen diets."

The report of this committee appeared in the *British Medical Journal* on November 25th, 1933. Their report produced no little uneasiness when it was found that the diet which they estimated as the minimum necessary for existence was such that the mass of the unemployed, and even a considerable proportion of employed workers, especially those in the Distressed Areas, had an income which prevented them from obtaining it. The minimum weekly cost of diets suggested by the BMA were as follows:

	s	d
Adult male	5	11
Male over 14 years	5	11
Adult female	4	11
Female over 14 years	4	11
Child 12 to 14 years	5	4
Child 10 to 12 years	4	9
Child 8 to 10 years	4	2
Child 6 to 8 years	3	7
Child 3 to 6 years	3	5
Child 2 to 3 years	3	1
Child 1 to 2 years	2	8

In preparing this table the committee took rock-bottom prices; in fact, it was found that they were too low as compared with prices which generally obtained throughout the country. The scale made no allowance for additional expenditure that might vary according to domestic problems, particularly sickness. The publication of the report led to a fierce controversy in medical circles, whilst the poor unemployed worker and his family looked on at this new capitalist game of treating human beings like so many test-tubes. There was much talk of calories, alphabetical vitamins, proteins, carbohydrates, fats, and grammes, which all sounded like a foreign language to the ordinary unemployed worker whose family was having to exist on a diet composed chiefly of potatoes, bread, margarine, tea, and condensed milk.

Then the Ministry of Health, the guardian of the public's well-being, waded into the controversy and claimed that the BMA minimum diets were too high. The experts of this Ministry prepared their own minimum diet, and they found that it was possible for an adult man to exist on food valued at 5s 1½d a week, not 5s 11d. They estimated that 3,000 calories a day instead of 3,400, as recommended by the BMA, were sufficient for a male, and, for a housewife, 2,600 as against 2,800.[1] The controversy led to a joint conference being held between the BMA and the Ministry of Health experts, and they issued their report in May 1934, which did little to clear up the mystification to which the earlier reports had given rise.

There is one important point that needs to be brought out in connection with the Ministry of Health scale of 5s 1½d, namely, that they based this upon bulk purchases of food in institutions and not on the purchase of food by a single family. There is a great difference between the economy that can be derived from bulk purchase and that of the housewife buying her penn'orths and ha'porths. The irony of the whole business is brought forcibly home to us when we remember that this calculation of the minimum diet to the decimal calorie was not occasioned by the need of rationing because of a shortage in foodstuffs, for, on the contrary, as everybody knows, there was an abundance of food, so much so that from time to time one reads of large quantities of food being destroyed because there is a glut in the market. We read of fish being thrown back into the sea again because the harvest of the fisherman has been so abundant. We read of milk being used for pig food at the time when little children are literally dying for the want of fresh milk.

It is surely a terrible reflection upon present-day civilisation when one finds on the one hand the medical experts indulging in controversy about the minimum upon which a human being can exist, whilst on the other hand those human beings are reading of the destruction of food which they require and which they cannot get. Now, I cannot lay claim to a sufficient knowledge of medical science to entitle me to embark upon scientific polemics with the wise men of the BMA and the experts of the Ministry of Health.

[1] Ministry of Health White Paper, *Nutrition.*

Against their scientific minds I can only pit my common and everyday experiences of the way the unemployed and the low-paid workers live. My political work as leader of the unemployed movement in this country over the last fifteen years has brought me into the closest personal touch with the living-conditions of the workless, and I know that the kinds of food which were proposed by the BMA and the Ministry of Health, and which are necessary to provide the vitamins and calories which have been specified as the minimum requirements, are not being eaten in the homes of the workless, for the simple reason that they cannot afford to buy them. For instance, it has been estimated that juveniles and children under sixteen years of age should have at least one pint of fresh milk a day. A pint of fresh milk costs 3½*d*, so that if they had only this minimum of one pint a day there would be an expenditure on milk of 2*s* 0½*d* a week. Deduct that from the 2*s* 8*d*, for instance, prescribed in the BMA scale for a child of one to two years, or from the 3*s* 1*d* for the child between two and three years of age, and we see what a ridiculously low amount is left over for other food. Sir George Newman, in his annual report for 1933 as Chief Medical Officer of Health for England and Wales, estimated that a pregnant mother needed at least two pints of milk a day; that would cost 4*s* 1*d* per week out of the 4*s* 11*d* minimum prescribed by the BMA for all foods. It would, indeed, be interesting to know how the Minister of Health would spend the odd tenpence on buying three meals a day for seven days a week.

If we take the higher of the two scales, viz that of the BMA, which prescribes 5*s* 11*d* for an adult male and 4*s* 11*d* for a female, assuming that the unemployed were eating three meals a day – which they are certainly entitled to – it would work out at approximately 3¼*d* a meal for a male and 2¾*d* for a female.

But, terribly inadequate as those figures undoubtedly are, we know that the great mass of unemployed workers are not able to spend even that low amount. This has been shown by the investigations of such experts as Dr G.C.M. M'Gonigle, Medical Officer of Health for Stockton-on-Tees, and Sir John Boyd Orr, the eminent nutrition expert, in their respective well-known publications, *Poverty and Public Health* [see Chapter 15] and *Food, Health, and Income* [see Chapter 16]. They prove conclusively that most of the people are existing on a diet far below either the BMA scale or the Ministry of Health scale, and that this is producing grave physical deterioration and ill-health amongst the people.

Sir John Boyd Orr gave us the benefits of his knowledge, based upon careful investigations,[2] which showed that he classified the population of this country as follows:

[2] *Food, Health, and Income.*

4,500,000 persons spending an average of 4s week on food

9,000,000 persons spending an average of 6s week on food

9,000,000 persons spending an average of 8s week on food

9,000,000 persons spending an average of 10s week on food

9,000,000 persons spending an average of 12s week on food

4,500,000 persons spending over 14s week on food

In Group 1 he includes families living at about the economic level of unemployment benefit or of the lowest paid wage-earners, and he tells us bluntly that the diet is inadequate in all respects. Group 2 he estimates may be receiving adequate diet in total proteins and fats, but not in first-class proteins or fats. In Group 3 the diet is adequate in energy value, proteins, and fats of all sorts, but below standard in vitamins and minerals. Sir John arrives at the conclusion that complete adequacy of diet is only found in Group 4 and upwards, where the family income per head reaches at least 20s to 30s a week, and the average food expenditure per head is not less than 10s a week. If these conclusions are correct, only 50 per cent of the population are receiving a diet completely adequate for health and physical and mental well-being.

According to a report which appeared in the *Daily Herald* on September 10th, 1935, Sir John Boyd Orr, speaking at Norwich to a conference of medical men, is reported to have claimed that there were 20,000,000 people in this country living below the economic level which ensures adequate diet and proper health, and that the diet of those who fall below the cost of 10s per head per week was markedly deficient from a health point of view. The scale of the BMA was based upon rock-bottom prices in 1932. By the middle of 1935, Dr M'Gonigle estimated that the increase in the price of certain commodities of food meant that 7s 1d per week was needed to buy the diet which in 1932 the BMA estimated could be bought at 5s 11d; since this statement was made we all know that, particularly during the years 1936 and 1937, a very considerable increase has taken place in the prices of certain foodstuffs, so that the unemployed are even worse off than the reports of Dr M'Gonigle and Sir John Boyd Orr have indicated.

We frequently come up against insidious propaganda, which I believe has been encouraged by the Ministry of Health, to the effect that it is not the amount of income to the household that is too low, but that it is the ignorance of the average working-class housewife in regard to food values and in the art of cooking, resulting in the loss of the nutritive qualities of the food, which is responsible for the present ill-health that pervades so many working-class homes. It is, indeed, interesting to read of the well-to-do woman assuming the right to instruct the working-class mother on the way she shall spend the 4*s* or less on twenty one meals a week. Sir John Boyd Orr effectively answered this slander on the housewife at the medical conference in Norwich on September 10th, when he said:

> "Give the workers sufficient income to enable them to have a free choice of food and they will eat food which will bring them to the proper health level."

Dr M'Gonigle, in a letter to *The Times* on March 26th, 1936, replied to this attempt to throw the blame for the under-nourishment of working-class families on to the housewives by declaring:

> "Beware all dicta of persons who for long denied the existence of any considerable amount of malnutrition, and who now attribute its existence to the housewives' ignorance of food values and cooking. Insufficient purchasing power, and not the ignorance of food values, is the dominant cause of malnutrition."

Those who are pretentious enough to take upon themselves the right to instruct the working-class housewife on laying out her small amount of money might do well to remember that the working out of diets on the basis of their calorie-content and their value in vitamins is an entirely different thing from buying food which will satisfy the hunger of the family.

I have been in the homes of unemployed workers and seen the little children asking for a slice of bread before they went to bed, only to be informed by the mother that "if you eat it now you can't have it for breakfast tomorrow." When the average housewife goes out to spend her very limited means on food, she does not work out whether this or that food contains this or that amount of calories or vitamins. She has a general knowledge of what is nutritious, but at the same time she has to plan her expenditure in such a way that if possible she can put food on the table for her family which satisfies their hunger – even if it may not contain the same amount of calories as a smaller and less satisfying amount of food.

I think the workers are entitled to be indignant at the patronising insults of those who suggest that the ill-health of their families is due to the ignorance of the harassed housewife. We have a right to protest vehemently against the whole principle of minimum diets and against the idea that it is possible to determine the minimum diet compatible with health without making allowances for the hundred and one other possible items of expenditure which can completely upset the scales of the experts.

The continuous under-feeding of working-class families through long unemployment and insufficient income has so reduced their stamina that they fall easy victims to physical ailments and disease. Especially do they become susceptible to tubercular and pulmonary infection, anæmia and dental decay. Dr M'Gonigle records in his book, *Poverty and Public Health*, that during the year 1933 the dental inspections carried out amongst elementary school children totalled 3,303,983, and that of this number 2,263,135 were recorded as requiring dental treatment. This represents 68.5 per cent of the children inspected.

The sacrifice of the mother for the child is quite a common thing amongst working-class families. When there is not enough food in the home to satisfy all, the mother will go without in order to allow her child to have more. In 1934 a sanatorium superintendent stated to a Press correspondent, when asked for his impressions about the type of patients being admitted to the sanatorium:

> "Among the adults there has been an increase in the number of young people admitted, especially women, suffering from an acute type of tuberculosis. They appear to have no immunity, and their resistance seemed to be completely overcome."

In spite of the alarming evidence which poured out in 1933, 1934, 1935, and which I believe can in a large measure be traced to the effects of the means test, the National Government has refused to make adequate provision for the unemployed or materially to relive their appalling position. The discussions about minimum diets, and the proof that so many workers' families were below these levels, seem to had had little effect upon the Ministers of the National Government. It is almost as though the whole question was viewed by them in an entirely detached way; one might almost imagine that the discussion and evidence about diets were related to some almost forgotten race of long ago, and not about contemporary society.

But let us hear from the mother of today in her own simple language of the conditions under which she and many thousands of others have to exist. The Committee Against Malnutrition called a public meeting in the Essex Hall, London, on November 10th, 1936, at the time when the hunger marchers were in London. Many important men in the medical profession attended. The committee invited some of the women hunger marchers to speak about their own family conditions, and Mrs Harley, of Greenock, gave the following evidence:

She said she was the wife of an unemployed man who had worked only nine months in the last twelve years. Her husband was a shipbuilder, and there were many shipbuilders in Greenock who had been out of work almost continuously for ten or twelve years, with the exception of two or three short periods of work. Mrs Harley said that she and her husband and four children – aged between six and twelve years – were allowed in unemployment allowance 38*s* a week to live on. They lived in one room, and she, her husband, and the three boys had to sleep in the same bed, whilst, as there was no room for the twelve-year-old daughter, she slept with an aunt two miles away. The room was in a building which had only two lavatories for the use of sixty-five people. Mrs Harley stated that in the same building was a room occupied by ten people, the ages of the children in the family ranging from five to eighteen years. A new housing estate had been built, but the rents were too high for the majority of the unemployed families, and they therefore had to remain in the squalor of slum property. Mrs Harley went on to describe her budget; she said that 17*s* out of her 38*s* was spent on groceries – tea, sugar, bread, margarine, etc. She could buy no fresh milk. The rent for her one room was 4*s*, and clothing and boots for the family cost on an average 5*s* a week. On three days a week she bought minced meat at 2½*d* a pound and 3½lbs of potatoes for 5*d*. This mixed together was not particularly palatable. On the other four days of the week she bought half a pound of sausage for 2*d*. She could not afford vegetables every week. One of her boys had twice been admitted to hospital for mastoids, but because he had received treatment from the public assistance authority he was not allowed to go to a convalescent home.

Following Mrs Harley came Mrs Holliday, of Chopwell, co Durham. She spoke as the wife of a Durham miner who had been out of work for twelve years. They had to exist on the UAB [Unemployment Assistance Board] scale. There were two daughters, one eleven and one fourteen, both of whom suffered from anæmia and had to receive half a pint of milk a day at school. Mrs Holliday said when her children had pneumonia the health visitor informed her that they must have stockings, and wool next to their skin, but she hadn't the money to buy these things. She said that the staple meals of the family consisted of mashed potatoes, bread, and tea. She said that the family were badly in need of clothing; their clothes had been worn threadbare long before the clubs had been paid up. She said that after having paid her rent she had 15*s* 9*d* left for clothing and feeding four persons. They only had one pint of fresh milk on Sundays, and the rest of the week they had condensed. She had to buy pennyworths of bones to boil down for soup. She could manage no more than one blanket on each bed, yet she knew of people in worse circumstances even than herself.

Mrs Nelson of Blackburn, one of the Lancashire women marchers, made a statement on her domestic conditions. She said that she was a widow with a son aged seventeen and two daughters aged nineteen and twenty. All three of her children had won scholarships, and she had scraped and saved to send them to a central school, yet now there was nothing better for her girls to do than domestic service, and her boy worked for a wage of 13*s* a week. She said she was allowed 15*s* a week unemployment allowance, but when her son worked overtime her scale was cut down by 3*s* 6*d*. She spoke bitterly about the way in which the means test affected the workers in her area, and said that the public assistance committees made a point of asking if mothers fed their new-born babies from the breast; if they did this was taken into consideration and a lower allowance given.

These simple statements about the actual living-conditions which these women marchers had to endure in their homes reveal more poignantly the position of the unemployed than any scientific explanation could do. In January 1937, special evidence was collected by the National Unemployed Workers' Movement in various parts of the country by means of a *questionnaire* headed *The Housewives' Minimum*. The evidence collected in this *questionnaire* was in every case verified by the signature of either a doctor, a responsible trade union leader, or a county councillor. Here are a few examples taken from many that reveal the appalling conditions of poverty to which so many of our people have been reduced, especially in the Distressed Areas. For obvious reasons we do not use the names of the persons concerned, but the evidence, verified by responsible public men, is available should it ever be challenged:

Example 1

Mr E.P. of Aberdare, Glamorgan. Number in family, man, wife, and four children, aged two, four, six, and nine years. Income per week from unemployment allowance is 38*s*. Conditions in the home are that all cooking has to be done on an open fire; there is no gas-stove. There are no decent cupboards or meat safes. By way of utensils the family have one kettle with a broken spout, three saucepans, one frying-pan, and one pot. There are two bowls with holes stopped up with pieces of rag. No dinner-plates, no bread-knife. Only four cups and two saucers for six in the family, two knives and two spoons, three forks and four small plates. The floor of the kitchen in which they live is bare stone, with no lino or carpet covering. There is only one blanket in the family, no sheets, no pillow-cases. Articles of clothes such as old coats are mostly used for bed-covering. A rent of 8*s* 6*d* a week is paid, 1*s* 3*d* insurance, 3*s* 4*d* coal, 1*s* 6*d* light, and an average of 2*s* for boot repairs, etc, leaving £1 1*s* 5*d* for food, clothes, and miscellaneous expenditure for six people. There are only three chairs for six people. Two spring mattresses in the bedroom are broken, and the room has no furniture in it besides the bed, not even a table on which to place a candle. There is electric light in two out of the four rooms, but one is completely empty.

Example 2

Mrs D.A. of Liverpool, who is a widow. There are five in family, including four children aged seventeen, fourteen, eleven, and seven. One child is a cripple. They have no gas-stove or oven in the house. The food is stored in a small cupboard. Cooking utensils consist of one small kettle, one frying-pan in a very bad condition, one saucepan with no lid and which, because of a hole in the side, can only be used for boiling milk or eggs. No bowl for baking, only two lead spoons, two dessertspoons, and one knife – fingers are used for eating food most of the time. The only bowl they have has to be used for washing crockery and toilet purposes. There are three cups without handles, two small bread-and-butter plates, no dinner-plates, no basins. They cannot all drink tea at the same time but have to wait until the first two who have the cups are finished. The floor is covered with cheap oilcloth, and, whilst every effort is made to keep it clean, they are afraid to scrub it for fear of wearing it out and being unable to replace it. In the matter of bed-clothing, there are only two beds, two sheets, one flannelette blanket, three pillow-cases, and one bolster. The deficiency in bed-covering has to be made up by using old coats. This woman receives 36s to keep a family of five. The rent for one living-room and a boxroom is 5s. The weekly check for clothing for the family is 3s, burial club 9d, coal 3s 6d. The girl aged seventeen, who is a cripple, suffering from chronic tuberculosis, sleeps in the boxroom by herself, but it is not possible for her to keep her own cup and plate because there are not sufficient to go round. The sick girl has no bedclothes on her bed and is only covered up by old coats and skirts. The mother is also under the doctor and is in a weak state of health. She has to sleep with her young child in the same bed. Eating, cooking, and sleeping are all done in the same room.

Example 3

Mrs E.M.W. of Pontypool, Monmouth. There are nine in the family, the ages of the children being fourteen, thirteen, eleven, seven, five, three, and two. The income from all sources is £2 7s a week. Living-conditions in the home are that all food has to be cooked on the open fire – there is no gas-stove or oven. There is only one small cupboard for food and no meat safe. In regard to cooking utensils, the family has only one kettle, one small frying-pan, two small saucepans. Utensils for preparing food consist of only one bowl, which is used for making puddings and to wash up in. They have only seven cups and saucers between nine persons, two knives, six small spoons, six forks, and eight plates. The family live in three rooms, one living-kitchen and two small bedrooms. The kitchen has a stone floor and the bedrooms have bare boards; no lino. There are two full-size beds and one small bed. In bedclothes the family have only two flannelette blankets on each bed, one quilt and one sheet, three pillow-cases. All bed-clothing is very threadbare and has little warmth. The small bed does not belong to them; they have it only on loan. Four boys sleep in one bed and two boys sleep in the small bed. Husband and wife and child two years of age sleep in the other bed. The springs in one of the beds are badly broken and there is no money to get a new mattress. The house is old and very damp and cold. In a statement appended by the signatory who verifies the correctness of the above, he says: "I have known the family for a number of years. Both parents are very sober and industrious persons and the mother strives very hard to keep her children clean and respectable. The family endeavoured to get a special grant from the UAB in order that they could make good the deficiency in household goods, but this was refused. The mother is now suffering from a skin disease which is considered to have been brought on by poor quality food and nervous tension."

Example 4

Mr W.C. of Jarrow. There are seven in the family – father, mother, and five children, whose ages are thirteen, eleven, nine, seven, and three. The total income of the family to maintain them all is 40s a week. Whilst they have sufficient cups and saucers and plates to go round, they have only three knives, three forks, and five spoons, so some have to wait whilst the others finish their food. There are only three beds, and on each bed there is one blanket and one sheet; there are no pillow-cases – the sheet is laid over the bolster in place of a pillow-covering. When the bed-clothing needs washing it has to be washed in the morning and dried for the same night. When the housewife applied for a grant from the UAB to get bed-clothing she was told that she ought to be able to buy it out of the 40s income to the family and no assistance was given.

Example 5

Mrs M.J. of Swansea. The family consists of father, mother, and eight children, aged fourteen, thirteen, twelve, ten, seven, five, three, and five months. Income from all sources is £2 5s a week. For this family of ten there is only one kettle, one saucepan, one frying-pan, and no other cooking utensils. There is only one washing-up bowl which has to be used for various purposes. In table utensils they have six cups and saucers, two knives, three forks, four teaspoons, one tablespoon, and eight plates. There is no lino on the floor, but odd bits of coco-matting. The scrubbing-brushes have been worn out and the family is too poor to buy new ones; there are no boot-brushes and only one pail. The whole family is badly in need of wearing apparel of all descriptions. The children have had to be kept home from school frequently on very wet days because of the state of their shoes. Ms M.J. in her statement on the *questionnaire* says: "It is impossible to state within a small space our real position. Our whole family is definitely under-fed and under-clothed. Rent, light, fuel, and insurance, etc takes 20s weekly, leaving us 25s to maintain the whole family in every other respect." This family of ten live in two rooms. Repeated application has been made to the local housing authorities for a Council house, but without result, although, as Mrs M.J. says, "our rent is, and ever has been, paid regularly."

Example 6

Mrs K.J.E. of Upper Loughor, Glamorgan. This family of husband, wife, and daughter of eleven years has a total income of 29s from the Public Assistance Committee. This family suffers particularly from lack of wearing apparel, especially under-clothing. The wife's clothing consists of no more than one petticoat, one pair of stockings, one working skirt, and one skirt for outdoors – no nightdresses and only one pair of shoes. The daughter has very little underclothing, no nightdresses, but she has one good pair of stockings and one pair that has been heavily darned. She has two jerseys – one very much worn and thin. The husband has only one pair of pants, two khaki shirts almost worn out, one singlet which is threadbare and patched, a cap which he has been wearing for over two years, one second-hand raincoat, one pair of shoes. Mrs K.J.E. in her declaration says: "After rent, fuel, insurance, and hospital are paid weekly, eightpence per head per day remains to purchase all other necessities." This woman is waiting for admission to hospital for an operation, and when she goes she will have to borrow clothes for entry.

These examples are not isolated; they are typical of the conditions that exist in tens of thousands of working-class homes in the Distressed Areas of this country. In fact, one only needs to reflect upon the position for a moment to realise that it can hardly be otherwise when the breadwinner in the family has been unemployed for years and where the income to the family has been so low that, as Sir John Boyd Orr says, "More than four and a half million persons are unable to obtain more than four shillings' worth of food per week."[3]

In the *Public Assistance Journal* for May 21st, 1937, the following tragic report appeared concerning workhouse cases at Gateshead-on-Tyne:

> "The minutes of the Management Committee stated that the public assistance officer, Mr E. Waton, had intimated

[3] *Food, Health, and Income.*

that there were cases of men who were eligible for discharge to the UAB, who had been admitted to the institution after having attempted suicide owing to lack of employment. Several of these men had requested to be allowed to remain in the institution, as they were afraid that the same thing might happen after they were discharged. The public assistance officer intimated that, subject to the confirmation of the committee, he had agreed to this course. The action of the public assistance officer was confirmed."

When persons in fairly comfortable circumstances read in the newspapers from time to time of men and women driven to suicide through the operation of the means test and poverty, or of a father going insane and attempting to murder his children, or of a mother stealing a bottle of milk or a loaf of bread because her children are starving, they probably experience a deep sense of pity towards the person whose case has been brought before their attention by the Press. But I wonder how many of them realise that the conditions which give rise to these offences are conditions which obtain in tens of thousands of other homes stricken by unemployment, and that it is only by the exercise of the greatest self-control on the part of the unemployed that similar crimes are not committed on a vast scale?

Well might ex-King Edward VIII on the occasion of his visit to South Wales call upon the unemployed "not to lose heart, and to rest assured that their troubles are not forgotten." Such sentiments have been freely handed out to the unemployed for years, but, as the old proverb says, "Kind words butter no parsnips" – or bread. Sir Thomas Inskip, the Minister for Defence, was the guest of honour at the annual dinner of the Honourable Society of Cymmrodorion at the Mayfair Hotel, Park Lane (it is noticeable that this Welsh society, patronised by the wealthy, chose the West End of London as the venue for their dinner and not the Distressed Areas). In reply to the toast of "Our Guests," Sir Thomas Inskip made, according to the report which appeared in *The Times* on November 24th, 1936, the following statement:

> "We have heard a little too much about depressed Wales, and not quite enough of what the unconquerable spirit of Wales is helping to achieve in bringing about her own recovery.... Wales has never yet suffered defeat, and I join with you, as we look for the dawn which is bound to come, in saluting the unconquerable spirit of the Welsh nation."

I find it difficult to forgive a Minister of the Baldwin Government for talking about saluting the unconquerable spirit of the Welsh nation when that Government has consistently done its utmost to break that spirit, or at least that section of the nation which have either to toil in the mines or be unemployed.

Homes have been broken up by the policy of the Government, and the most abject poverty has been created. One could go into the homes of unemployed workers today and find that all the best portions of the furniture have been sold, and in the place of cabinets and sideboards boxes are used, which the wife drapes with some cheap material in order to make then look something like furniture. I have been into the homes of the unemployed in the Distressed Areas where all the household utensils have been worn out, and where, when they have succeeded in getting an egg, it has to be boiled in an old tin that has been picked from a garbage heap. Parents are often unable to buy leather shoes or boots for their children, even in winter-time, and it is not uncommon to see a child in the streets on a wet day with only cheap plimsolls. Old and broken boots often have to be soled with pieces cut from old motor-tyres. Lack of clothing in the unemployed families is a terribly serious problem. We can remember the Press reports which appeared at the time of the 1936 Trades Union Congress about a delegate from South Wales who, when urging that the trade union movement should do something to compel the Government to remedy the problem of the Distressed Areas, said that he had had no new suit of clothes for ten years. He explained how the expenses which he had been allowed by the Miners' Federation to attend the Congress had been spent on a new suit in order to make it possible for him to go to the Congress, as he only had rags to wear.

One thing that will strike the observer in the winter-time in the Distressed Areas is the number of men who even on a cold day are to be seen without an overcoat. Take a look at a funeral procession in South Wales these days. The custom is for the relations and friends to walk behind the hearse to the cemetery, and the miners, who in times of good trade always had a preference for smart blue serge suits, would turn out in their best apparel and bowler hats, and present an exceedingly respectable appearance. But not so today. A funeral procession in the Rhondda Valley bears the mark of extreme poverty. The few serge suits which are seen can be marked out by their cut as pre-war or immediate post-war, because for years no new clothes have been bought.

People who were once too dignified to look at second-hand clothing now scramble for it when it is sent into the mining villages by patronising organisations. I know of a particularly cheap brand of cigarette which, when introduced into the Distressed Areas, was eagerly taken up because of its cheapness. They were vile things to smoke, and even those who smoked them would joke about their asphyxiating effects. But they went on smoking them because they could afford nothing better. The poverty of the people in the Distressed Areas is reflected in the literature sales of working-class organisations. The Welsh workers were particularly great readers of working-class books and pamphlets, but today they have been reduced to a condition of planned poverty where the spending of a penny on a new pamphlet completely upsets their budget.

To add to the sufferings inflicted upon the unemployed by their long unemployment and scanty financial resources, there are also the shocking housing conditions, which have steadily become worse during the depression. The value of property in the Depressed Areas has fallen considerably. New housing property is not being built because of the state of bankruptcy in which many of the local authorities find themselves, and because private landlords are not prepared to invest in houses to let at rents which they know the population cannot pay. The houses of the workers, particularly in the mining areas, are in a grave state of disrepair. Landlords refuse to put them in order and the tenants cannot afford to do their own repairs. Where gas or electric light is laid on in the house it is not an uncommon thing to find the family using candles because they say gas or electricity is too dear and they go to bed early in order to save light. There are working-class mothers grown prematurely old through poverty and worry. Many have silently starved themselves for years in an effort to try and give the children a chance. There are women who for ten, twelve, and fifteen years have had no relief from household drudgery and the worries of keeping a family on the labour exchange or UAB pittance. The publicity that starts in the spring about holidays at the seashore is a mockery to them. There are men of strong and independent character whose vitality has been so sapped by long unemployment and insecurity that today, when they are summoned to appear before a court of referees or UAB investigators, they go in fear and trembling – scared lest the last mean dregs of existence be taken from them. I have seen men, when waiting to go before such investigators, trembling and on the verge of collapse. It is a fear not so much for their own fate as that of those who are dependent upon them. One so often hears the remark by such men: "It's the wife and kids that worries me." Family happiness is destroyed by lack of prospects and security. The paleness and shabbiness of the wife, the continual ailments of the child, the debility and ill-health and nervous strain caused in the parents by long under-nourishment, the drab monotony of idleness and no variety of life, produce frayed nerves, outbursts of intolerance, angry words that often lead to violent quarrels in families which under better circumstances would be bright and happy.

Such is the plight of the people in the Distressed Areas – a plight which this National Government has never yet made any attempt to dispel, but, on the contrary, as though the cup of suffering is not already full to the brim, the Government seeks to plague still further the wretched lives of the unemployed and has now introduced the new scales under the Unemployment Assistance Board for all persons who have exhausted their statutory benefit at the labour exchange.

At the moment of writing the Government has been prevented by the mass demonstrations of 1935 and the great Hunger March of 1936 from operating these scales fully, but if ever it is allowed to do so it will mean further terrible reductions, particularly for the workers in the Distressed Areas, where whole families are unemployed. For instance, the scale laid down under the UAB for an adult son living with his parents is 10s a week, being a reduction from 17s as at present. For a daughter over twenty-one the scale is reduced from 15s to 9s a week, for a son between the ages of eighteen and twenty-one from 14s to 8s, for a daughter of that age, from 12s to 8s, for a son seventeen to eighteen from 9s to 8s.

In the Distressed Areas it is not an uncommon thing to find a family of father, mother, and two or three sons and daughters all unemployed. The sons have reached adult age and have avoided marriage because they see no prospects of security before them, and the daughters likewise have avoided marriage because they do not wish to take the risk of bringing children into the world in the conditions of poverty which surround their own lives. Take the case of a family where there is a father, mother, and three sons over twenty-one years of age. The father would have his benefit reduced by 2s, and each son by 7s, making a total reduction in the family income of 23s a week. Where there are two sons and one daughter, all over twenty-one years of age, the reduction would be 22s a week. If there were two adult daughters and two sons, the reduction would be 28s a week. If there were four adult sons, the reduction would be 30s a week.

One requires little imagination to realise what such terrible reductions in the family income would mean to families who are already reduced to the bare subsistence level, and in some cases below. It is not surprising, therefore, that when these cuts were first attempted by the Government on January 7th, 1935, tremendous mass demonstrations of protest swept the country. In the Distressed Areas there was grave alarm, not only amongst the unemployed, but amongst the employed workers and professional people. The demonstrations, particularly in the South Wales coalfields, took on a mass character representative of all sections of the working community. The united front of all progressive thinking elements was forged almost overnight, and expressed itself in mighty marches through the Welsh valleys. Doctors and others concerned with public health, who knew how difficult their task already was in resisting the effects on health of poverty, felt indignant about this new attack, and in many cases openly associated themselves with the workers' demonstrations. School-teachers who had constantly seen the children come into their schools badly clothed, ill-shod, and so under-nourished that they had difficulty in concentrating upon their lessons, knew how much more difficult the work of the teacher would be unless these cuts were prevented; they joined with the rest of the working class in the mighty marches. Shop-keepers who knew that their businesses were failing, and had already seen many of their fellow-tradesmen driven out of business because of the poverty of the people and their inability to buy, likewise joined in the common protest against the new starvation scales. Right-Wing trade union leaders, who for years had, in committee and on the public platform, opposed the idea of the united front against the Government, were caught up in the avalanche of mass activity and impelled into the stream. Within a month the National Government was compelled to climb down and to withdraw the new scales for further consideration; and, shortly after, Mr Oliver Stanley, the Minister of Labour, resigned his post and Mr Ernest Brown was appointed in his place.

But again the scales were brought forward with only minor modifications, and were fixed for operation on November 16th, 1936. Again the unemployed had to drive the Government back, and win a temporary respite, by the great 1936 Hunger March. It can truly be said that the unemployed, particularly in the Distressed Areas, are fighting with their backs to the wall, literally fighting to live, because they know that any further worsening of their present conditions means another terrible blow against the health and lives of themselves and their children.

But the lowering in their standards is already taking place in another form, namely the steady rise in the cost of living, so that the small amount of purchasing-power which they already have is reduced, and less can be bought. Capitalism, which has taken huge profits and wealth from the sweat and toil of these people in the basic industries of this country, is now crucifying them, while the Government outdoes the Pharisee by smiting the victim and passing on.

Margery Spring Rice, 1887–1970 **18**

Children of the 1930s (photograph by Edith Tudor Hart)

Margery Spring Rice read for an MA in Moral Sciences at the University of Cambridge. Throughout her life she worked passionately in the area of social welfare and reform, particularly relating to the health of women and children. She was Treasurer of the Women's National Liberation Foundation and an active worker for Women's Health Services. She was co-founder of the North Kensington Women's Welfare Centre, which was a voluntary clinic for women.

Working-class wives reports the work of the Women's Health Enquiry Committee, formed in 1933. Spring Rice was a member, along with other middle-class women from various women's organisations who volunteered their time. The Committee sought to provide an account of the living conditions and health of working class women, particularly married women. The research consisted of a questionnaire which was completed by 1,250 married women living in different districts, social conditions and occupations, as well as 60 unmarried women. As Dame Janet Campbell says in her introduction:

> The stories upon which this book is based have been gathered from different parts of the country and are completely unedited. They describe in the words of the women themselves, most poignantly and movingly, the life which is the lot of many; and they reveal plainly the claims which these patient, courageous, inarticulate mothers might well make to a greater share in the benefits which medical services, public health administration, and facilities for physical education are bringing to the community as a whole. (1933, p xii)

Here we present an extract which describes the day's work.

Spring Rice, M. (1939)
Working-class wives:
Their health and conditions

Chapter V
The day's work

"I believe myself that one of the biggest difficulties our mothers have is our husbands do not realise we ever need any leisure time. My life for many years consisted of being penned in a kitchen 9 feet square, every fourteen months a baby, as I had five babies in five years at first, until what with the struggle to live and no leisure I used to feel I was just a machine, until I had my first breakdown, and as dark as it was and as hard as it was it gave me the freedom and privilege of having an hour's fresh air. And so I truly know this is the lot of many a poor mother. I know my third baby had rickets, but what could I do, I was expecting another little one and already had a baby three years of age and one two years. So many of our men think we should not go out until the children are grown up. We do not want to be neglecting the home but we do feel we like to have a little look around the shops, or if we go to the Clinic we can just have a few minutes…. It isn't the men are unkind. It is the old idea we should always be at home."

Not many of the women go into such detail as this about the trials of their lives, but the record given of hours spent at work, the size of the family, the inability to pay for any help outside, the inconvenience of the house, the lack of adequate utensils and of decent clothes – let alone any small household or personal luxury – yields a picture in which monotony, loneliness, discouragement and sordid hard work are the main features, – a picture of almost unredeemed drabness. It is not that all of the women are unhappy as the writer of the above letter manifestly is. Taken as a whole, their vitality must be prodigious, for, in spite of every possible embarrassment, life goes on undiminished in bulk, even if with a lessening vigour and enjoyment. Happiness, like health, can suffer an almost unperceived lowering of standard, which results in a pathetic gratitude for what might be called negative mercies, the respite for an hour a day, for instance, from the laboriousness of the other eleven, twelve or thirteen the help that a kind husband will "occasionally give on washing days, when he comes home from work," the relief when a major disaster which threatened one of the children (in the case of a woman in Leeds whose eldest some lost one eye in an accident and was threatened with the loss of the other) was "miraculously overcome".

It is little comfort that these women have learnt to accept their lot with so little complaint, often with such cheeriness and apparent satisfaction. For they are the mothers of the new generation and their outlook must to a certain extent be passed on to their daughters who will harbour no more than a vague hope that somehow, and through no direct action of their own, matters will have improved by the time they embark on the business of wife and mother. But that they do not raise the banner outside their own homes is neither surprising nor discreditable. Throughout their lives they have been faced with the tradition that the crown of a woman's life is to be wife and mother. Their primary ambition is therefore satisfied. Everyone is pleased when they get married, most of all the great public, who see therein the working of Nature's divine and immutable laws. If for the woman herself the crown turns out to be one of thorns, that again must be Nature's inexorable way. It would be presumptuous on her part to think that she could or should do anything to change it. It is little short of a miracle that some women, even some of the most hard-worked, find time and mental energy to belong to such organisations as the Women's Co-Operative Guild, the Salvation Army or a branch of their political party where they can hear and talk about the wider aspects of their own or other people's problems. It is, however, very rare to find amongst the active members of these organisations, the women whose poverty and consequent hard work demand the greatest measure of consideration and carefully planned reform. The poorest women *have no time* to spare for such immediately irrelevant considerations as the establishment of a different system, a better education, a more comprehensive medical service, or some sort of organised co-operation. They are not themselves going to be given the second chance, whatever reforms may be introduced, and meantime they have their twelve or thirteen or fourteen hours' work to do every day and their own day to day life to lead. It cannot stop, it cannot be interrupted; no-one else can do any of their jobs; and even if there is anyone else, like an adolescent daughter or a kind husband, this would mean losing time at any rate for a little while the pupil was learning; it might mean one meal at least being spoilt, one saucepan allowed to boil over, and there is no margin whatever for such waste, such loss of time; it requires less thought, even less physical energy to do the job oneself.

This is not a question of health. Whatever the condition of fitness, the mother who does the work for a whole family of husband and three or more children has a titanic job under present conditions. If she is fortunate enough to be abnormally strong, she will manage to keep up with it, as long as her daily routine is not checked by some unusual misfortune. But if the ordinary round is harder than her body is strong her health must surely suffer with the result that she will find the course more and more difficult to hold; the less able she is to get through her task, the harder it will become … a circle of peculiar and tragic viciousness.

For the majority of the 1,250 women under review the ordinary routine seems to be as follows. Most of them get up at 6.30. If their husband and/or sons are miners, or bakers, or on any nightshift, they may have to get up at 4 (possibly earlier), make breakfast for those members of the family, and then, if they feel disposed to further sleep, go back to bed for another hour's rest. The same woman who does this has probably got a young child or even a baby, who wakes up early, and sleeping in the same room will in no case give his mother much peace after 6 am. If there is a suckling baby as well, (and it must be remembered that the woman who has had seven or eight children before the age of 35 has never been without a tiny baby or very young child,) she will have had to nurse him at least as late as 10 the night before. There are many complaints of children who for some reason or other disturb the night's rest. Her bed is shared not only by her husband but, in all probability, by one *at least* of her young family. Sleeplessness is not often spoken of in this investigation, because it is not considered an ailment, but it is quite clear that a good night's rest in a well-aired, quiet room and in a comfortable, well-covered bed, is practically unknown to the majority of these mothers. A woman can become accustomed to very little sleep just as she can to very little food.

When once she is up there is no rest at all till after dinner. She is on her legs the whole time. She has to get her husband off to work, the children washed, dressed and fed and sent to school. If she has a large family, even if she has only the average family of this whole group, four or five children, she is probably very poor and therefore lives in a very bad house, or a house extremely inadequately fitted for her needs. Her washing up will not only therefore be heavy, but it may have to be done under the worst conditions. She may have to go down (or up) two or three flights of stairs to get her water, and again to empty it away. She may have to heat it on the open fire, and she may have to be looking after the baby and the toddler at the same time. When this is done, she must clean the house. If she has the average family, the rooms are very "full of beds", and this will make her cleaning much more difficult than if she had twice the number of rooms with half the amount of furniture in each. She lacks the utensils too; and lacking any means to get hot water except by the kettle on the fire, she will be as careful as possible not to waste a drop. The school-children will be back for their dinner soon after 12, so she must begin her cooking in good time. Great difficulties confront her here. She has not got more than one or two saucepans and a frying pan, and so even if she is fortunate in having some proper sort of cooking stove, it is impossible to cook a dinner as it should be cooked, slowly and with the vegetables separately; hence the ubiquitous stew, with or without the remains of the Sunday meat according to the day of the week. She has nowhere to store food, or if there is cupboard room, it is inevitably in the only living room and probably next to the fireplace. Conditions may be so bad in this respect that she must go out in the middle of her morning's work to buy for dinner. This has the advantage of giving her and the baby a breath of fresh air during the morning; otherwise, unless there is a garden or yard, the baby, like herself is penned up in the 9ft square kitchen during the whole morning.

Dinner may last from 12 till 3. Her husband or a child at work may have quite different hours from the school-children, and it is quite usual to hear this comment. Very often she does not sit down herself to meals. The serving of five or six other people demands so much jumping up and down that she finds it easier to take her meals standing. If she is nursing a baby, she will sit down for that, and in this way "gets more rest". She does this after the children have returned to school. Sometimes the heat and stuffiness of the kitchen in which she has spent all or most of her morning takes her off her food, and she does not feel inclined to eat at all, or only a bite when the others have all finished and gone away. Then comes the same process of washing up, only a little more difficult because dinner is a greasier meal than breakfast. After that, with luck at 2 or 2.30, but sometimes much later, if dinner for any reason has had to go on longer, she can tidy herself up and REST, or GO OUT, or SIT DOWN.

Leisure is a comparative term. Anything which is slightly less arduous or gives a change of scene or occupation from the active hard work of the eight hours for which she has already been up is leisure. Sometimes, perhaps once a week, perhaps only once a month, the change will be a real one. She may go to the Welfare Centre with baby, or to the recreation ground with the two small children, or to see her sister or friend in the next street, but most times the children don't give her the opportunity for this sort of leisure, for there is sewing and mending and knitting to be done for them; and besides there is always the shopping to be done, and if she possibly can, she does like to rest her legs a bit and sit down. So unless there is some necessity to go out, she would rather on most days stay indoors. And she may not have any clothes go to out in, in which case the school children will do the shopping after school hours. (Clothes are a great difficulty, "practically an impossibility".)

Then comes tea, first the children's and then her husband's, when he comes home from work; and by the time that is all over and washed up it is time the children began to go to bed. If she is a good manager she will get them all into bed by 8, perhaps even earlier, and then at last, at last, "a little peace and quietude!". She sits down again, after having been twelve or fourteen hours at work, mostly on her feet, (and this means *standing* about, not *walking*,) and perhaps she then has a "quiet talk with hubby", or listens to the wireless, "our one luxury". Perhaps her husband reads the paper to her. She has got a lot of sewing to do, so she doesn't read much to herself, and she doesn't go out because she can't leave the children unless her husband undertakes to keep house for one evening a week, while she goes to the pictures or for a walk. There is no money to spare anyhow for the pictures, or very seldom. She may or may not have a bite of supper with her husband, cocoa and bread and butter, or possibly a bit of fried fish. And so to her share of the bed, mostly at about 10.30 or 11.

This is the way that she spends six days out of seven, Sundays included, although Sunday may bring a slightly different arrangement of her problems because the shops are shut, the children and husband are at home. If she has been able to train her family well, and has got a good husband, they will relieve her of a little of the Sunday work, but it must be remembered that the husband is the breadwinner and must have his rest – and the children are young and will have their play. With luck, however, the mother will get "a nice quiet read on Sundays" – or a pleasant walk, or a visit to or from a friend; sometimes, if she is disposed that way, a quiet hour in church or chapel. But for her the seventh day is washing day, the day of extra labour, of extra discomfort and strain. At all times and in all circumstances it is arduous, but if she is living in the conditions in which thousands of mothers live, having to fetch water from the bottom floor of a four-storied house or from 100-200 yards or even a quarter of a mile along the village street; if she has nowhere to dry the clothes (and these include such bed clothes as there may be) except in the kitchen in which she is cooking and the family is eating, the added tension together with the extra physical exertion, the discomfort of the house as well as the aching back, make it the really dark day of the week. There is no avoidance of it. Even if she could raise the money to send the washing out – she hasn't got the second set of clothes or bed coverings which this necessitates. The bed clothes have to be used again, possibly on the same day as washing.

There is also no avoidance of the other great labour which is superimposed on the ordinary round, the labour of child-bearing. The work will have to be done in the same way for those nine months before the baby comes and for the two or three months after she is about again but still not feeling "quite herself". The baby will probably be born in the bed which has already been described, the bed shared by other members of the family, and in the room of the use of which, even if she can get the bed to herself for a week, she cannot possibly deprive the family for more than a few hours. It is out of the question, she thinks, to go to hospital, and to leave her husband the children either to fend for themselves – or to the care of a stranger, or of an already overworked but friendly neighbour. Even if she is in bed, she is at least in her own home; and can direct operations, even perhaps doing some of the "smaller" jobs herself – like drying crockery, ironing[1], and of course the eternal mending. How is it possible that she should stay in bed for long enough to regain her full physical strength, the strength that has been taxed not only in the actual labour of child-birth, but in six or seven of the preceding months, when every household duty has been more difficult to accomplish and has involved a far greater strain than it does when she is in her "normal" health? If she is sensible, she will have got help from the Clinic, extra milk if she is very poor, and tonics and, perhaps, if she is fortunate enough to live in an enlightened municipality, a good meal once a day for herself. But her scene and her work will not have changed, and unless she goes into hospital for the confinement, it cannot bring that rest and comfort which she needs and deserves, but only extra difficulties for everyone in the family and very often serious ill-health for herself.

So the days, the weeks, the months, the years go on. There may be a break for an hour or two in the month when she attends some Guild or Women's Institute meeting. Once a year there may be a day's outing; but a holiday in the sense of going away from home, eating food she has not herself cooked, sleeping in another bed, living in a different scene, meeting other people and doing the things she can never do at home, – this has been unheard of since the family arrived. She cannot go without the family, and there can be no question of taking them too. Possibly the children are somehow or other got into the country for a few days in the summer, if they live in the town; but it is without mother, unless she will go hop-picking, taking the small children with her. But it is only a very, very few who get the chance of even this "holiday". There is – again for the very few – another possibility of a holiday – convalescence. If the mother has been "really ill" she may be sent away by the hospital or under some insurance scheme, or by the Salvation Army or by one of the agencies whose merciful function it is to procure this kind of intermission for the woman whose strength has at last given way. She is sent away ... away from her home, away from the smell of inferior and inadequately prepared food, away from the noise and worry of her family, away to the sea, for a fortnight or even three

[1] The writer found one woman sitting up in bed three days after the birth of her sixth baby ironing on a tray across her knees; the iron was handed to her by a neighbour who was washing up the dinner.

weeks. It may be that she is too ill to get much active enjoyment out of it, but oh, the blessedness of the rest, the good food, the comfortable bed, the difference of scene for her eyes, the glorious feeling of having nothing to do. "As dark as it was and as hard as it was, it gave me the privilege of having an hour's fresh air."

But if illness has been so severe as to merit this magnificent atonement, it has meant months probably of crippling indisposition which has added enormously to the burden of work, and robbed it of all that potential satisfaction that can be found in the fulfilment of her task. She has had to let things slide, and she has slipped back so far that it will take months and months to catch up again even to her old standard of order and efficiency. This, in her eyes, is probably the worst disaster that can happen – her own illness. Other disasters are bound to come in the ordinary course of family life; the sickness of a child – the unemployment of her husband – the care of an old and perhaps tiresome grandparent. But if she can keep fit, she will meet the extra burden. She may even voluntarily adopt another child, whose parents are dead; or she will augment the family income by going out to work herself, somehow or other squeezing her own house-work into shorter hours. It may be a little less efficient, but the compensation is that she has a little more money for food, and can get better cooking utensils. At whatever cost of labour and effort a little more money is what she really wants; that is the magic which unties the Gordian knot. But there is little opportunity for this, and the poorer she is, the more difficult it is to arrange things in her own home so as to make it possible to leave it for even a couple of hours a day. Where it *must* be done, as in the case of a widow, or a woman with an invalid husband, the strain is nearly always almost insupportable.

Naturally there are some who seem to get more out of life than others; but almost without exception it is those women who have very few children, one, two or at the most three, and who for this or some other reason are in much better financial circumstances, who are able to get more real rest and change of scene and to employ their leisure in some way which suggests an interest in outside things. But there are not more than half a dozen who speak of politics, literary interests, study of any sort or music. The cinema is very rarely mentioned, and many women say that they have *never* been to the pictures. A few who live in the country speak of walking and gardening; others of going to chapel or church on Sundays. An overwhelming proportion say that they spend their "leisure" in sewing and doing other household jobs, slightly different from the ordinary work of cooking and house cleaning.

The subject of husbands could form a thesis by itself. They are not very often specifically mentioned in the answers to this interrogatory, except in regard to their occupation and the money with which they provide their wives for housekeeping. But when a man adds to the embarrassments of life by bad temper or drunkenness, or is exasperatingly impatient with the wife's ill-health or unsympathetic with her difficulties, he generally appears in the list of her grievances directly or by implication. It is more often the visitor than the wife who makes special note of him. Equally, great solicitude for or sympathy with his wife is specially commended in a husband. Many instances are given of the husband carrying heavy tubs or coals for his wife – keeping watch over the children one evening a week, so that she can go out – reading aloud to her – or – if she is really ill – looking after her with great care, as far as his occupation allows. But the impression given in general of the attitude of the husbands in this enquiry is that of the quotation at the head of this chapter: – "our husbands do not realize we ever need any leisure". With the best will in the world, it is difficult for a man to visualise his wife's day – the loneliness, the embarrassments of her work, the struggle to spend every penny of his money to the best advantage. In most cases he can count upon her devoted service to himself and to their children, – and he feels instinctively that her affection gives a pleasant flavour to her work which is absent from his own – and that she is fortunate in not being under the orders of an employer, and subject to regulations of time and speed of work etc etc. If he is unemployed and therefore spends more time at home, the additional worry for both of them will take precedence of all other difficulties, and if he then notices the harassing conditions of her life, he will attribute them largely to this cause. Besides, the unemployed man can and does generally give his wife some help in the housework, which does much to lighten her physical burden, although it is little compensation for the additional mental worry.

Note is sometimes made in the women's accounts of the help given to them by the older of their schoolchildren. It is very usual to find mention of a child being kept back from school to do some of the work that the mother is too ill to do. Only a few mothers speak of training their children to help in the house as part of a regular routine – but this is probably less rare than it appears to be. It must be realized, however, that any help that a child under twelve can give costs so much in supervision and probably worry for a careful mother, that she feels it is easier to send the child out of the way and get on with the job herself. This may be a short-sighted policy, but it is easily forgiven in the woman who has no time to organise or plan.

It may be said that, even granting that there is no exaggeration in the above account of the working-class mother's life, there is no ground for giving special consideration to her case as apart from that of the father and the children; that their lot is just as hard as hers, and that the want from which she suffers is equally severe for them. That in many respects this is so, cannot be denied; but it is abundantly clear from the accounts given by the women themselves in this investigation that they are subject to many hardships from which circumstance or they themselves protect their families. To begin with, the working mother is almost entirely cut off from contact with the world outside her house. She eats, sleeps, "rests", on the scene of her labour, and her labour is entirely solitary. However arduous or unpleasant the man's work has been, the hours of it are limited and he then leaves not only the work itself but the place of it behind him for fourteen or sixteen hours out of every twenty-four. Even if he cannot *rest* in this time, he changes his occupation and his surroundings. If he is blessed with a capable hard-working wife, his home will represent to him a place of ease and quiet after an eight or ten hour day spent in hard, perhaps dangerous toil. He will have had ample opportunity for talking with his fellows, of hearing about the greater world, of widening his horizon. The children have equally either been out at work or at school, where for many hours of the day they have lived in airy well-lighted rooms, with ample space for movement and for play. They too have met and talked with their fellows, and whatever the deprivations of their home, they go there to find that someone else has prepared their food, mended their clothes, and generally put things in order. Natrually they suffer, as the father does too, from the poverty of the home, the lack of sufficient food and clothes and warmth and comfort, but it is undoubtedly true that even in these respects the mother will be the first to go without. Her husband *must* be fed, as upon him depends the first of all necessities, money. The children must or will be fed, and the school will if necessary supplement. Equally husband and children must be clothed, not only fairly warmly but for school or work fairly decently. She need not be; she need not even go out, so it is not *absolutely* necessary for her to have an outdoor coat. And lastly, whatever the emotional compensations, whatever her devotion, her family creates her labour, and tightens the bonds that tie her to the lonely and narrow sphere of "home". The happiness that she often finds in her relationship of wife and mother is as miraculous as it is compensatory.

William Beveridge, 1879-1963   19

William Beveridge was an economist whose first well-known work on poverty involved a collaboration with Beatrice Webb on the 1909 Poor Law's report for the Liberal Prime Minister David Lloyd George. Beveridge became director of Labour Exchanges after helping their establishment through his government research on unemployment and during the First World War. He was responsible for devising the system of rationing in Britain (later influenced by John Boyd Orr). From 1919 to 1937 he was director of the London School of Economics, after which he moved to the University of Oxford. At the request of the British government he produced the *Social Insurance and Allied Services* report in 1942 which proposed 'cradle to the grave' social security for all. This quickly became known as the 'Beveridge Report' and it is from the first few pages of this influencial report that the Summary that follows is taken.

The report detailed how child allowances should be created and paid, how a comprehensive health service should be established and employment could be maintained. It resulted in the 1945 Family Allowances Act and the National Insurance Act of 1946, and was influential in the establishment of the National Health Service. William Beveridge was very much a member of the establishment; he was knighted in 1919 and made Baron Beveridge of Tuggal in 1946. Beveridge was highly influenced by Fabian Socialists but stood, himself, as a liberal, being a Member of Parliament between 1944 and 1945. The Beveridge Report was written to appeal to Conservative as well as Liberal and Labour thinking.

Beveridge, W. (1942) *Social Insurance and Allied Services* (The Beveridge Report)

Introduction and summary

1. The Inter-departmental Committee on Social Insurance and Allied Services were appointed in June 1941, by the Minister without Portfolio, then responsible for the consideration of reconstruction problems. The terms of reference required the Committee "to undertake, with special reference to the inter-relation of the schemes, a survey of the existing national schemes of social insurance and allied services, including workmen's compensation and to make recommendations." The first duty of the Committee was to survey, the second to recommend. For the reasons stated below in paragraph 40 the duty of recommendation was confined later to the Chairman of the Committee.

The Committee's Survey and its results

2. The schemes of social insurance and allied services which the Inter-departmental Committee have been called on to survey have grown piece-meal. Apart from the Poor Law, which dates from the time of Elizabeth, the schemes surveyed are the product of the last 45 years beginning with the Workmen's Compensation Act, 1897. That Act, applying in the first instance to a limited number of occupations, was made general in 1906. Compulsory health insurance began in 1912. Unemployment insurance began for a few industries in 1912 and was made general in 1920. The first Pensions Act, giving non-contributory pensions subject to a means test at the age of 70, was passed in 1908. In 1925 came the Act which started contributory pensions for old age, for widows and for orphans. Unemployment insurance, after a troubled history, was put on a fresh basis by the Unemployment Act of 1934, which set up at the same time a new national service of Unemployment Assistance. Meantime, the local machinery for relief of destitution, after having been exhaustively examined by the Royal Commission of 1905-1909, has been changed both by the new treatment of unemployment and in many other ways, including a transfer of the responsibilities of the Boards of Guardians to Local Authorities. Separate provision for special types

of disability – such as blindness – has been made from time to time. Together with this growth of social insurance and impinging on it at many points have gone developments of medical treatment, particularly in hospitals and other institutions; developments of services devoted to the welfare of children, in school and before it; and a vast growth of voluntary provision for death and other contingencies, made by persons of the insured classes through Industrial Life Offices, Friendly Societies and Trade Unions.

3. In all this change and development, each problem has been dealt with separately, with little or no reference to allied problems. The first task of the Committee has been to attempt for the first time a comprehensive survey of the whole field of social insurance and allied services, to show just what provision is now made and how it is made for many different forms of need. The results of this survey are set out in Appendix B describing social insurance and the allied services as they exist today in Britain. The picture presented is impressive in two ways. First, it shows that provision for most of the many varieties of need through interruption of earnings and other causes that may arise in modern industrial communities has already been made in Britain on a scale not surpassed and hardly rivalled in any other country of the world. In one respect only of the first importance, namely limitation of medical service, both in the range of treatment which is provided as of right and in respect of the classes of persons for whom it is provided, does Britain's achievement fall seriously short of what has been accomplished elsewhere: it falls short also in its provision for cash benefit for maternity and funerals and through the defects of its system for workmen's compensation. In all other fields British provision for security, in adequacy of amount and in comprehensiveness, will stand comparison with that of any other country; few countries will stand comparison with Britain. Second, social insurance and the allied services, as they exist today, are conducted by a complex of disconnected administrative organs, proceeding on different principles, doing invaluable service but at a cost in money and trouble and anomalous treatment of identical problems for which there is no justification. In a system of social security better on the whole than can be found in almost any other country there are serious deficiencies which call for remedy.

4. This limitation of compulsory insurance to persons under contract of service and below a certain remuneration if engaged on non-manual work is a serious gap. Many persons working on their own account are poorer and more in need of State insurance than employees; the remuneration limit for non-manual employees is arbitrary and takes no account of family responsibility. There is, again, no real difference between the income needs of persons who

are sick and those who are unemployed, but they get different rates of benefit involving different contribution conditions and with meaningless distinctions between persons of different ages. An adult insured man with a wife and two children receives 38/- per week should he become unemployed; if after some weeks of unemployment he becomes sick and not available for work, his insurance income falls to 18/-. On the other hand a youth of 17 obtains 9/- when he is unemployed, but should be become sick his insurance income rises to 12/- per week. There are, to take another example, three different means tests for non-contributory pensions, for supplementary pensions and for public assistance, with a fourth test – for unemployment assistance – differing from that for supplementary pensions in some particulars.

5. Many other such examples could be given; they are the natural result of the way in which social security has grown in Britain. It is not open to question that, by closer co-ordination, the existing social services could be made at once more beneficial and more intelligible to those whom they serve and more economical in their administration.

Three guiding principles of recommendations

6. In proceeding from this first comprehensive survey of social insurance to the next task – of making recommendations – three guiding principles may be laid down at the outset.

7. The first principle is that any proposals for the future, while they should use to the full the experience gathered in the past, should not be restricted by consideration of sectional interests established in the obtaining of that experience. Now, when the war is abolishing landmarks of every kind, is the opportunity for using experience in a clear field. A revolutionary moment in the world's history is a time for revolutions, not for patching.

8. The second principle is that organisation of social insurance should be treated as one part only of a comprehensive policy of social progress. Social insurance fully developed may provide income security; it is an attack upon Want. But Want is one only of five giants on the road of reconstruction and in some ways the easiest to attack. The others are Disease, Ignorance, Squalor and Idleness.

9. The third principle is that social security must be achieved by co-operation between the State and the individual. The State should offer security for service and contribution. The State in organising

security should not stifle incentive, opportunity, responsibility; in establishing a national minimum, it should leave room and encouragement for voluntary action by each individual to provide more than that minimum for himself and his family.

10. The Plan for Social Security set out in this Report is built upon these principles. It uses experience but is not tied by experience. It is put forward as a limited contribution to a wider social policy, though as something that could be achieved now without waiting for the whole of that policy. It is, first and foremost, a plan of insurance – of giving in return for contributions benefits up to subsistence level, as of right and without means test, so that individuals may build freely upon it.

The way to freedom from want

11. The work of the Inter-departmental Committee began with a review of existing schemes of social insurance and allied services. The Plan for Social Security, with which that work ends, starts from a diagnosis of want – of the circumstances in which, in the years just preceding the present war families and individuals in Britain might lack the means of healthy subsistence. During those years impartial scientific authorities made social surveys of the conditions of life in a number of principal towns in Britain, including London, Liverpool, Sheffield, Plymouth, Southampton, York and Bristol. They determined the proportions of the people in each town whose means were below the standard assumed to be necessary for subsistence, and they analysed the extent and causes of that deficiency. From each of these social surveys the same broad result emerges. Of all the want shown by the surveys, from three quarters to five-sixths, according to the precise standard chosen for want, was due to interruption or loss of earning power. Practically the whole of the remaining one-quarter to one-sixth was due to failure to relate income during earning to the size of the family. These surveys were made before the introduction of supplementary pensions had reduced the amount of poverty amongst old persons. But this does not affect the main conclusion to be drawn from these surveys: abolition of want requires a double re-distribution of income, through social insurance and by family needs.

12. Abolition of want requires, first, improvement of State insurance that is to say provision against interruption and loss of earning power. All the principal causes of interruption or loss of earnings are now the subject of schemes of social insurance. If, in spite of these schemes, so many persons unemployed or sick or old or widowed are found to be without adequate income for subsistence according to the standards

adopted in the social surveys, this means that the benefits amount to less than subsistence by those standards or do not last as long as the need, and that the assistance which supplements insurance is either insufficient in amount or available only on terms which make men unwilling to have recourse to it. None of the insurance benefits provided before the war were in fact designed with reference to the standards of the social surveys. Though unemployment benefit was not altogether out of relation to those standards, sickness and disablement benefit, old age pensions and widows' pensions were far below them, while workmen's compensation was below subsistence level for anyone who had family responsibilities or whose earnings in work were less than twice the amount needed for subsistence. To prevent interruption or destruction of earning power from leading to want, it is necessary to improve the present schemes of social insurance in three directions: by extension of scope to cover persons now excluded, by extension of purposes to cover risks now excluded, and by raising the rates of benefit.

13. Abolition of want requires, second, adjustment of incomes, in periods of earning as well as in interruption of earning, to family needs, that is to say, in one form or another it requires allowances for children. Without such allowances as part of benefit – or added to it, to make provision for large families, no social insurance against interruption of earnings can be adequate. But, if children's allowances are given only when earnings are interrupted and are not given during earning also, two evils are unavoidable. First, a substantial measure of acute want will remain among the lower paid workers as the accompaniment of large families. Second, in all such cases, income will be greater during unemployment or other interruptions of work than during work.

14. By a double re-distribution of income through social insurance and children's allowances, want, as defined in the social surveys, could have been abolished in Britain before the present war. As is shown in para 445, the income available to the British people was ample for such a purpose. The Plan for Social Security set out in Part V of this Report takes abolition of want after this war as its aim. It includes as its main method compulsory social insurance, with national assistance and voluntary insurance as subsidiary methods. It assumes allowances for dependent children, as part of its background. The plan assumes also establishment of comprehensive health and rehabilitation services and maintenance of employment, that is to say avoidance of mass unemployment, as necessary conditions of success in social insurance. These three measures – of children's allowances, health and rehabilitation and maintenance of employment-are described as assumptions A, B and C of the plan; they fall partly within and partly

without the plan extending into other fields of social policy. They are discussed, not in the detailed exposition of the plan in Part V of the Report, but in Part VI, which is concerned with social security in relation to wider issues.

15. The plan is based on a diagnosis of want. It starts from facts, from the condition of the people as revealed by social surveys between the two wars. It takes account of two other facts about the British community, arising out of past movements of the birth rate and the death rate, which should dominate planning for its future; the main effects of these movements in determining the present and future of the British people are shown by Table XI in para 234. The first of the two facts is the age constitution of the population, making it certain that persons past the age that is now regarded as the end of working life will be a much larger proportion of the whole community than at any time in the past. The second fact is the low reproduction rate of the British community today: unless this rate is raised very materially in the near future, a rapid and continuous decline of the population cannot be prevented. The first fact makes it necessary to seek ways of postponing the age of retirement from work rather than of hastening it. The second fact makes it imperative to give first place in social expenditure to the care of childhood and to the safeguarding of maternity.

16. The provision to be made for old age represents the largest and most growing element in any social insurance scheme. The problem of age is discussed accordingly in Part III of the Report as one of three special problems; the measures proposed for dealing with this problem are summarised in paras 254-257. Briefly, the proposal is to introduce for all citizens adequate pensions without means test by stages over a transition period of twenty years, while providing immediate assistance pensions for persons requiring them. In adopting a transition period for pensions as of right, while meeting immediate needs subject to consideration of means, the Plan for Social Security in Britain follows the precedent of New Zealand. The final rate of pensions in New Zealand is higher than that proposed in this Plan, but is reached only after a transition period of twenty-eight years as compared with twenty years suggested here; after twenty years, the New Zealand rate is not very materially different from the basic rate proposed for Britain. The New Zealand pensions are not conditional upon retirement from work; for Britain it is proposed that they should be retirement pensions and that persons who continue at work and postpone retirement should be able to increase their pensions above the basic rate. The New Zealand scheme is less favourable than the plan for Britain in starting at a lower level; it is more favourable in some other respects. Broadly the two schemes for two communities

of the British race are plans on the same lines to solve the same problem of passage from pensions based on need to pensions paid as of right to all citizens in virtue of contribution.

Summary of plan for social security

17. The main feature of the Plan for Social Security is a scheme of social insurance against interruption and destruction of earning power and for special expenditure arising at birth, marriage or death. The scheme embodies six fundamental principles: flat rate of subsistence benefit; flat rate of contribution; unification of administrative responsibility; adequacy of benefit; comprehensiveness; and classification. These principles are explained in paras 303–309. Based on them and in combination with national assistance and voluntary insurance as subsidiary methods, the aim of the Plan for Social Security is to make want under any circumstances unnecessary.

18. A plan which is designed to cover so many varieties of human circumstance must be long and detailed. It must contain proposals of differing orders of certainty and importance. In preparing the Report, the question arose naturally as to how far it was necessary at this stage to enter into details, and whether it might not be preferable to deal with principles only. For two reasons it has appeared desirable, in place of giving an outline only, to set the proposals out in as much detail as the time allowed. The first reason is that the principles underlying any practical reform can be judged only by seeing how they would work in practice. The second reason is that if a Plan for Social Security is to come into operation when the war ends or soon after, there is no time to lose in getting the plan prepared as fully as possible. The many details set forth in Part V are neither exhaustive nor final; they are put forward as a basis of discussion, but their formulation will, it is hoped, shorten subsequent discussion. Even among the major proposals of the Report there are differences of importance and of relevance to the scheme as a whole. There are some proposals which, though important and desirable in themselves, could be omitted without changing anything else in the scheme. Three in particular in the list of major changes in para 30 have this character and are placed in square brackets to indicate it. This does not mean that everything not bracketed is essential and must be taken or left as a whole. The six principles named above and all that is implied in them are fundamental; the rest of the scheme can be adjusted without changing its character: all rates of benefit and all details are by nature subject to amendment.

19. The main provisions of the plan may be summarised as follows:

   i. The plan covers all citizens without upper income limit, but has regard to their different ways of life; it is a plan all-embracing in scope of persons and of needs, but is classified in application.

   ii. In relation to social security the population falls into four main classes of working age and two others below and above working age respectively, as follows:

   I   Employees, that is, persons whose normal occupation is employment under contract of service.
   II Others gainfully occupied, including employers, traders and independent workers of all kinds.
   III Housewives, that is married women of working age.
   IV Others of working age not gainfully occupied.
   V   Below working age.
   VI Retired above working age.

iii. The sixth of these classes will receive retirement pensions and the fifth will be covered by children's allowances, which will be paid from the National Exchequer in respect of all children when the responsible parent is in receipt of insurance benefit or pension, and in respect of all children except one in other cases. The four other classes will be insured for security appropriate to their circumstances. All classes will be covered for comprehensive medical treatment and rehabilitation and for funeral expenses.

iv. Every person in Class I, II or IV will pay a single security contribution by a stamp on a single insurance document each week or combination of weeks. In Class I the employer also will contribute, affixing the insurance stamp and deducting the employee's share from wages or salary. The contribution will differ from one class to another, according to the benefits provided, and will be higher for men than for women, so as to secure benefits for Class III.

v. Subject to simple contribution conditions, every person in Class I will receive benefit for unemployment and disability, pension on retirement, medical treatment and funeral expenses. Persons in Class II will receive all these except unemployment benefit and disability benefit during the first 13 weeks of disability. Persons in Class IV will receive all these except unemployment and disability benefit. As a substitute for unemployment benefit, training benefit will be available to persons in all classes other than Class I, to assist them to find new livelihoods if their present ones fail. Maternity grant, provision for widowhood and separation and qualification for retirement pensions will be secured to all persons in Class III by virtue of their husbands' contributions; in addition to maternity grant, housewives who take paid work will receive maternity benefit for thirteen weeks to enable them to give up working before and after childbirth.

vi. Unemployment benefit, disability benefit, basic retirement pension after a transition period, and training benefit will be at the same rate, irrespective of previous earnings. This rate will provide by itself the income necessary for subsistence in all normal cases. There will be a joint rate for a man and wife who is not gainfully occupied. Where there is no wife or she is gainfully occupied, there will be a lower single rate; where there is no wife but a dependant above the age for children's allowance, there will be a dependant allowance. Maternity benefit for housewives who work also for gain will be at a higher rate than the single rate in unemployment or disability, while their unemployment and disability benefit will be at a lower rate; there are special rates also for widowhood as described below. With these exceptions all rates of benefit will be the same for men and for women. Disability due to industrial accident or disease will be treated like all other disability for the first thirteen weeks; if disability continues thereafter, disability benefit at a flat rate will be replaced by an industrial pension related to the earnings of the individual subject to a minimum and a maximum.

vii. Unemployment benefit will continue at the same rate without means test so long as unemployment lasts, but will normally be subject to a condition of attendance at a work or training centre after a certain period. Disability benefit will continue at the same rate without means test, so long as disability lasts or till it is replaced by industrial pension, subject to acceptance of suitable medical treatment or vocational training.

i. Pensions (other than industrial) will be paid only on retirement from work. They may be claimed at any time after the minimum age of retirement, that is 65 for men and 60 for women. The rate of pension will be increased above the basic rate if retirement is postponed. Contributory pensions as of right will be raised to the full basic rate gradually during a transition period of twenty years, in which adequate pensions according to needs will be paid to all persons requiring them. The position of existing pensioners will be safeguarded.

ii. While permanent pensions will no longer be granted to widows of working age without dependent children, there will be for all widows a temporary benefit at a higher rate than unemployment or disability benefit, followed by training benefit where necessary. For widows with the care of dependent children there will be guardian benefit, in addition to the children's allowances, adequate for subsistence without other means. The position of existing widows on pension will be safeguarded.

x. For the limited number of cases of need not covered by social insurance, national assistance subject to a uniform means test will be available.

xi. Medical treatment covering all requirements will be provided for all citizens by a national health service organised under the health departments and post-medical rehabilitation treatment will be provided for all persons capable of profiting by it.

xii. A Ministry of Social Security will be established, responsible for social insurance, national assistance and encouragement and supervision of voluntary insurance and will take over, so far as necessary for these purposes, the present work of other Government Departments and of local Authorities in these fields.

Richard Titmuss, 1907-73 20

Richard Titmuss trained in bookkeeping and worked as an insurance clerk. From early in his life he developed an interest in poverty, populations and the potential of welfare. During the Second World War he advised the Ministry of Information on social surveys and was a statistical adviser to the Ministries of Health and Economic Warfare. He was appointed to the position of official historian of the war cabinet in 1942.

Along with colleagues such as Peter Townsend and Brian Abel-Smith he made a key contribution to the study of social policy and welfare provision in the postwar period. He was appointed Professor of Social Administration at the London School of Economics and Political Science, as well as sitting on many government committees and being an adviser to the Labour Party. He had a firm belief that while welfare systems could not eradicate inequality, they could go a long way to alleviating poverty and other social problems.

Here we present an extract from *Birth, poverty and wealth: A study of infant mortality*, published in 1943. Using various sources of secondary data Titmuss describes, compares and synthesises data, the results showing a clear and unrelenting social class gradient in infant mortality which is persistent over time. As well as this, causes are considered and remedies suggested.

Titmuss, R. (1943)
Birth, poverty and wealth

Chapter I
A measurement of human progress

"A strict investigation of all the circumstances of these children's lives might lead to important discoveries and may suggest remedies for evils of which it is difficult to exaggerate the magnitude."

Dr W.M. FARR,
*Supplement to the XXVth Annual
Report of the Registrar-General,*
pp xii and xiii, 1864

Infant mortality provides society with the first major index of the reaction of a new human life to its surroundings. It is a measure of man's ability and willingness to control his environment. The characteristics of a community in all gradations from the aboriginal of Australia to the civilised Scandinavian begin to impress themselves as soon as the child starts its separate existence apart from its mother. This existence begins with explosive force. At no period in after life does there occur any shock like that accompanying birth. For in the great systems of the body, in the physiological processes of respiration, circulation, heat regulation and digestion, there is an instantaneous and drastic change, and the failure of the child to meet the new demands on him – or of the community to provide adequate protection – can only result in death. Infant mortality is indeed the price of adaptation paid by each generation when entering life, and the toll of infant deaths is today, just as it has always been, a broad reflection of the degree of civilisation attained by any given community. "Health", declared René Sand, "is purchasable ... Each country, within certain limits, decides its own death rates."[1] In the British colony of Gambia in West Africa life for the native is both brutal and brief, with infant deaths at the rate of 370 to every 1,000 births. At the other extreme there are districts of New Zealand where the rate has fallen to below 20. Or we may compare modern Glasgow and its rate of 109 in 1936 with pre-1939 Amsterdam and a rate of

[1] *Health and Human Progress* 1935.

only 30. These wide differences in the risk of death bear out Sir Arthur Newsholme's view that "Infant Mortality is the most sensitive index we possess of social welfare and of sanitary administration, especially under urban conditions".[2]

"Progress", wrote Herbert Spencer, "is not an accident", and it is no accident that the infant death rate for England and Wales has fallen from over 150 to around 50 in one hundred years. It was not, however, until about 1900 that the rate began to fall rapidly, and the ensuing 30 years witnessed the greatest decline. It is instructive to note that public attention – as seen in the flow of commissions and inquiries after 1900 – was directed to the high infant mortality chiefly by the disclosures of physical ill-health and inefficiency during and after the South African War.[3] There is perhaps something rather shocking in the idea that it took a war to focus public attention on a wastefully high infant death rate. Whatever our reaction, it remains true that our concern for national health has followed the course of our military fortunes. Just as the South African war focussed attention on the physique and health of the nation (impelling the Inspector-General of Recruiting to speak of "the gradual deterioration of the physique of the working classes from which the bulk of the recruits must always be drawn"), so did the war of 1914-18, with its revelations of ill-health and the first appearance of the phrase "a C3 nation"; and now once again, the present war – pressing closely on the whole population – sharply reminds us that we tend to forget communal fitness when the threat of mass destruction is not upon us. As F. Le Gros Clark wrote, "The fact is that most of our standards are still very crude and pragmatic;" and he added that "Usually at the back of our minds hangs the vision of war as the supreme test of stamina".[4] We have yet to formulate a standard of positive health as an absolute good in itself unrelated to industrial or military considerations. To do so, however, demands an understanding of the fundamental causes of ill-health and premature death.

The termination of an individual life is the product of an enormous number of complex and inter-related forces; from a Government's policy in international affairs to the local methods of refuse disposal and from a coal-owner's decision to close the pits to a mother's intake of calcium. Reducing this diversity to identity, to find the causation of infant mortality, we can distinguish two main factors operating in the past to produce a high death rate. One can be summed in the word poverty; the other is insanitary urbanisation.

As an illustration of the latter we may compare Norway's infant mortality rate of 105 during 1851-55 with Glasgow's rate of 109 in 1936. In the middle of the nineteenth century Norway and Ireland were considered to be, in comparison with England, poor countries. While ignorance, lack of personal hygiene and a higher degree of poverty contributed to produce a rate above 100, these countries did

[2] Supplement to 39th Annual Report of the Local Government Board, 1909-10.

[3] The first detailed statement of Infant Mortality in the Registrar-General's Reports appeared in 1905.

[4] Le Gros Clark, F. and Titmuss, Richard M. (1939) *Our Food Problem.*

not suffer from the dirt and infection manufactured by industrialisation and rapid urban growth. During 1891-95, just before a rapid decline in the rate occurred in each country, England and Wales had a rate of 151, Ireland 102 and Norway 98. The purely economic differences between these countries were, however, masked by the factor of population density; and for that reason by standards of sanitation involving air and water-borne infection. While Ireland and Norway were, in the main, poverty stricken at the end of the last century, their poor were not crowded together in an insanitary environment. The people of England and Wales who, at that time probably stood at a somewhat higher standard of living, were nevertheless subjected to the factor of high population density. This factor, when superimposed on poverty, thus contributed to produce an infant death rate 50 per cent higher than that obtaining in poorer, but sparsely populated agricultural communities. If however the urban populations of the three countries are compared we find Dublin with the highest rate of 169, then Oslo with 158 and lastly London with 156. In the reversal of the rates for English, Irish and Norwegians we see the influence exerted in the nineteenth century by the forces of density and industrialisation. It was Farr who first pointed out that mortality was a function of the density of the population. His formula of 1843 showed the mortality to vary with the sixth root of the density.[5] In the sixties he found that the relation was expressed approximately by the eighth root of the density.

Thus in Farr's day the public health administrator was faced with two main problems, poverty and drains. But although both were indubitably present only one was recognised as a problem – poverty was part of the natural order of things – and all the emphasis was concentrated on drains. While the Royal Commissions on sewage policy succeeded one another with monotonous regularity, the treatment of the impoverished sick was dominated by the simple Poor Law maxim that "People must not be encouraged to be ill by the knowledge that they could be treated free at the expense of the State". To most, poverty, or the inequal distribution of wealth, was quite natural in an age when every man was taught to promote his own self-interest. The poor were part of the landscape. The phrase "the labouring poor", so beloved of official reports in those days, is rich in social implications.[6] Equally expressive was Young's tranquil observation, as of one enunciating a commonplace, that "everyone but an idiot knows that the lower classes must be kept poor or they will never be industrious". In such an age when, under the leadership of the new class of self-centred, self-confident, god-fearing and money-worshipping entrepreneurs, Britain was becoming the workshop of the world, it was not perhaps unnatural that to many the provision of drains conflicted with the principle of self-seeking.

"The beneficent private war" (to quote Sir Henry Maine) "which

[5] Farr, W. (1843) Appendix to Registrar-General's Fifth Annual Report.

[6] See Simon, John (1890) *English Sanitary Institutions* and *General Report on the Sanitary Condition of the Labouring Population of Gt Britain,* 1842.

makes one man strive to climb on the shoulders of another and remain there" was hardly conducive to equality in the realm of clean water, drains, water-closets and other sanitary necessities. *The Times* in 1858 summarised its opposition to sanitation when it wrote, "The English people would prefer to take the chance of cholera rather than be bullied into health". It is necessary to read the lives of men like Farr, Chadwick and Simon to understand how long and bitter was the battle for drains. Just as the mass of the working class suffered from an inequal distribution of wealth, so, until the turn of the twentieth century, did they have to endure pail closets, privy middens and ash-pits, while existing

> long in populous city pent
> Where houses thick and sewers annoy the air.

It was not until the rich were forced to the conclusion that sanitation was economic sense and would save them, the rich, from contracting much infectious disease (witness the influence of the cholera epidemics) that water-closets and clean water were provided. Thus the winning of the battle for drains and the effective control over sanitary urbanisation were the chief factors in the lowering of infant mortality to one-**third** of its former level. It has now been abundantly proved that mortality need not increase at all with the density of the population so long as other influences are not active at the same time. This is notably true so far as infant mortality is concerned; and it may be said that in most advanced countries the infants have now little to suffer from the struggle for adaptation to an urban mode of life.[7] Stocks, for instance, has shown that up to middle life the importance of crowding per room as a factor in mortality would appear to be now almost double that of density per acre.[8] He arrived at this conclusion by measuring the change in mortality according to the two types of density, one factor being held constant in each case. To distinguish between the two factors of density is important; the one (per acre) is an index of success or failure in combating insanitary evils such as water-borne infection, the other is a measure of the effects of overcrowding *per se* (including the transmission of disease by droplet infection) and/or other social factors with which overcrowding is inextricably related.

Improved sanitation having amputated the nineteenth century peak in infant mortality, there now became apparent the contours of a new peak largely formed on the dynamics of poverty. It was not, however, until 1911 that the first official attempt was made to measure the different rates of mortality in different social classes.[9] Before this a few unofficial investigations had been made, mainly actuarial in purpose, and concerned to find out the expectation of life of different

[7] See for example the discussion on the changes since 1871 in the relative healthfulness of town and country by R. S. Barclay, W.O. Kermack and A.G. McKendrick (1940) ('Comparison of the Specific Mortality Rates in Town and Country Districts of Scotland since 1871', *J. Hyg., Camb., 40,* 423). The authors "conclude that the relative healthiness of the town is now at roughly the same level as that of the country. The balance of advantage may still be with the latter, but, if so, it cannot be very great".

[8] Stocks, P. (1934) 'The Association between Mortality and Density of Housing', *Proc. R. Soc. Med.* (Epid. Section), 27, ii, 1127.

[9] The earliest investigation of occupational mortality among adult males relates to 1851 (14th Annual Report of the Registrar-General).

[10] *Treatise on Annuities.*

[11] *Observations on the Mortality among the Members of the British Peerage.*

[12] Farr, W. (1837) *British Annals of Medicine.*

[13] *Lancet,* 1838, 39, 867.

[14] Article 'Vital Statistics' in McCulloch's *Account of the British Empire,* 1837.

[15] First Report of the Commissioners for Inquiry into the State of Large Towns and Populous Districts, 1844, *I.*

[16] *On the Rate of Mortality prevailing amongst the Families of the Peerage during the 19th century,* J. Inst. Actu., 9, 305.

social groups. But such work had to be done with most inadequate statistics, and the results were thus not very reliable. As early as 1815 Milne[10] concluded that "There can ... be no doubt but that the mortality is greater among the higher than the middle classes of society". In 1832 Farren[11] thought that members of the peerage had a lower expectation of life than the general population. Farr[12] in examining the life span of kings and peers drew attention to the great insecurity surrounding the lives of the noble. This great pioneer of English statistics later compared the work of Edmonds[13] on the mortality at different ages of English peers with that of labourers employed by the East India Company. After excluding from the peers' mortality those deaths (5 per cent) due to violence – hardly an occupational risk – he found that the labourers had the lower mortality. Farr's comment runs: "Are we to infer that the mortality among peers is now higher than among labourers, crowded within the metropolis? Should we not rather infer, that as the investigation extends far back into the centuries of bloodshed and pestilence, that the lives of peers were then shorter, and are now longer, than the lives of labourers? The plague, which was born in huts, and nursed by famine, rioted in luxurious halls, and smote the high-born".[14] And it was not only in huts that the plague was born. At royal Windsor the footmen suffered from perpetual sore throats until in 1844 more than 50 unemptied cesspits were discovered beneath the castle. It seems then that Farr's inference of a change in the differences in mortality experienced by distinctive social groups was the truth; for a "gentleman" in London, the Commissioners of 1844 were told, lived on the average twice as long as a "labourer", while the corresponding figures for Leeds were forty-four and nineteen years, and for Liverpool thirty-five and fifteen. In York City, during the years 1839-41, the average age at death for "gentry and professional persons and their families" was 48.6; for "tradesmen and their families" 30.8; and for "labourers and their families" 23.8.[15]

Clearly the industrial revolution had something to do with this trend in differential mortality. "It is a melancholy fact," wrote, as late as 1865, the most distinguished of contemporary economists, "that the whole structure of our wealth and refined civilisation is built upon a basis of ignorance and pauperism and vice, into the particulars of which we hardly dare to inquire.... We are now in the first morning of our national prosperity and are approaching noon, yet we have hardly begun to pay the moral and the social debts to millions of our countrymen which we must pay before the evening". In 1861 Bailey and Day[16] found that the mean duration of life at birth in Peerage Families was greater than that for the general population, greater indeed than for Farr's "Healthy Districts" of England and Wales. The difference was apparently largely due to lower death rates during childhood, for, as Bailey and Day pointed out, "the advantage in favour of the families of the peerage is most remarkable in infancy and childhood – the mortality under the age of 10 years being little more than one-third of that of the general population". This class difference was again confirmed when, in 1874, Ansell found that the expectation of life at birth in the upper and professional classes was 53 years indicating an advantage of about 10 years over the expectation for the general population.[17] Thus it would seem that even in those early days wealth triumphed over the handicap of inferior drains. To enquirers at that time such as Farr and Chadwick, concerned with the riddle of varying death rates, nothing was known of the functions of nutrition, but to the more far-sighted it seemed that some important factor, other than drains, was at work. Bailey and Day, for instance, concluded that, "A consideration of the characteristic features, both of these and of other observations on persons in affluent circumstances, may suggest to another class of enthusiasts that there are many other causes affecting the mortality of mankind besides the sanitary condition of their habitations; and that although ventilation, drainage and water supply are all very necessary things, they are not 'all the law and the prophets' notwithstanding". They went on, "Despite all that has been written on the subject we remain of opinion that the law of mortality of the human race is yet undiscovered".

Twenty-two years were to pass before Sir Francis Galton published in 1883 his conclusions as to the parts played by heredity and environment in determining human qualities. His verdict was: "We may, therefore, broadly conclude that the only circumstance, within the range of those by which persons of similar conditions of life are affected, that is capable of producing a marked effect on the character of adults is illness or some accident that causes physical infirmity. The impression that all this leaves on the mind is one of some wonder whether nurture can do anything at all, beyond giving instruction and professional training. There is no escape from the conclusion that nature prevails enormously over nurture when the differences of nurture do not exceed what is commonly to be found among persons of the same rank of society and in the same country'.[18]

The study of heredity preceded nutritional research for it was not until 1897 that Eijkman, concerned with the outbreaks of beri-beri in the jails of the Dutch East Indies, carried out his classical experiments with chickens and decided that some important factor was missing from the polished rice the native prisoners were receiving. Since these two men first spoke there has accumulated a vast amount of evidence on the relative influence of nature and nurture, and the period following the 1914 war has produced results which emphasise the great importance of the qualitative aspects of nutrition. We shall attempt to summarise some of this material when we come to interpret the statistical data on infant mortality. In the meantime we may note that in a few parts of the world infant mortality has been reduced to

[17] Ansell, C. (1874) 'Vital Statistics of Families in the Upper and Professional Classes'. Discussion in *J.R. Statist. Soc.*, *37*, 464.

[18] *Inquiries into Human Faculty*, 1883.

[19] *Health and Wealth.*

below 20 deaths per 1,000 live births. Dublin, in 1928, suggested that a rate of 30 was feasible.[19] Today, in this dark hour of a gifted age, we may suggest that there are no medical, social or economic reasons why advanced communities should not achieve a rate of 15, for the knowledge formerly lacking is now abundantly available. The saving of 100,000 lives of English infants every four years would be no small achievement particularly as, in the coming decades, the problem of declining numbers, and possibly of even further declining birth rates, is one which may before all others condition our national life and colour all our social thinking. When the crisis comes many will no doubt rush in with population policies modelled on the Nazi technique of the enslavement of parenthood. It would be as well therefore if those who have visions of a democratic approach to the problems of population realise in time that they cannot adequately be solved without reference to handicaps and inequalities in infancy. They would also be helped if they appreciated that these handicaps and inequalities are not isolated phenomena, but an integral part of an unequal society, pervading and invading the activities of men from the cradle to the grave. If the beginning be sordid can life be full, abundant and generous?

J.N. Morris, 1910– **21**

Professor J.N. Morris was born in Liverpool and studied in Glasgow and London. Throughout his career he has been at the forefront of epidemiological research in a range of areas, including juvenile heart disease, infant mortality and investigating the influence of exercise on cardiovascular disease. In 1948 he became the first director of the newly formed Medical Research Council Social Medicine Unit. In the postwar period he made, along with colleagues Richard Titmuss and Brian Abel-Smith, a major contribution to the development of health policy and the establishment of community medicine. He has been a member of various committees of influence, including the first Royal College of Practitioners committee on smoking and air pollution in the 1950s and the Black Report committee in the late 1970s.

Despite formally retiring in 1975, Professor Morris continues to publish in the field of public health and social medicine and is an active member of the Health Promotion Research Unit at the London School of Hygiene and Tropical Medicine. Here we reproduce in full his pamphlet entitled simply *Health*, which was published in 1944 by the Association for Education in Citizenship.

Morris, J.N. (1944) *Health*

How well are we?

Everyone seems agreed that Health wants Reconstruction. This enthusiasm for a new order in health derives from dissatisfaction that has long been maturing with the gulf that exists between what is and what might be, between our immense knowledge and the little use we make of it. It expresses the growing confidence in our ability to create such health for the many as the few have hitherto enjoyed.

Health – a social function

Most of us are born with a long expectation of life, with an immense capacity to be healthy. What matters is less the *inherited* constitution than what is done with it. For health – "wholeness," "haleness" – man needs many things: the A B C of food, fresh air and shelter, and, only next in urgency, work to do, rest and recreation, security, freedom from anxiety, harmonious human relationships, care in sickness and infirmity. For ages man has recognised the association of famine and pestilence; today we see the same sort of association in over-crowding and tuberculosis, slums and the dirt diseases, insanitation and enteric fevers, malnutrition and anaemia, insecurity and neurosis, fatigue and accidents, speed-up and dyspepsia. We have learned to associate health with an *environment* that satisfies man's needs, ill-health with one that distorts and denies them. Whether our needs are satisfied and how they are satisfied is, more and more, *socially* determined; so that if we speak of health and ill-health as *social* functions we are not far from the truth. As social functions they at once become social responsibilities. Society largely determines health; ill-health is not a personal misfortune due often to personal inadequacy, but a social misfortune due more commonly to social mismanagement and social failure.

Human experiments

Many human "experiments" have taught us the needs of man. The smaller stature of the working class was once attributed to their inferior origins. Today we know that it is largely due to the inferior nutrition of poor children. The following figures are from a famous experiment at an Industrial School:–

The effects of good diets on the physique of schoolboys

Average annual gain in weight and height

Boys on ordinary diet	3.85 lbs	1.84 ins
Boys on ordinary diet plus 1 pint of milk daily	6.98 lbs	2.63 ins

Such an experiment explains why London elementary school entrants in 1938 were two inches taller and five pounds heavier than children entering the same schools in 1905-12, and why boys leaving school at 14 in Sheffield were 13¼ pounds heavier and 3¼ inches taller in 1937 than boys leaving the same schools in 1920.

Another experiment illustrates even more clearly our new powers over health and sickness. Three Canadian doctors tried improving the diets of poor mothers during the latter half of pregnancy to see whether their health and that of their infants was benefited. They compared two groups: one remained on their ordinary (and deficient) diet, the other was given extra milk, eggs, fruit and vegetables, together with concentrated vitamins:–

> "During the whole course of pregnancy the mothers on the good diet enjoyed better health, had fewer complications, and proved to be better obstetrical risks than those left on poor diets. The incidence of miscarriages, stillbirths and premature births in the women on poor diets was much greater.... In a large proportion one could tell the diet group of a mother by looking at her baby.... The incidence of illness (eg anæmia, rickets and frequent colds) in the babies up to the age of 6 months ... was many times greater in the poor diet group."

The additional foods cost about 1*s* a day in English pre-war prices.

In South Wales during 1935-7 over 10,000 expectant mothers were given an improved diet, including a pint of milk daily and a small amount of special foods rich in vitamins and minerals. For every thousand babies born the death-rate among these mothers was 1.63, including one death from infection; infant mortality was 57 per 1,000 born alive. In those who subsisted on their ordinary diets, the death-rates were 6.15 per 1,000 deaths for the mothers (including 46 deaths from infection), and 102 per 1,000 for the babies.

Nutrition is only one instance. Clearing a Glasgow slum reduced child mortality by half. Children brought up in the hygienic and anything but luxurious life of the Poor Law Schools were found to suffer very little from rheumatism, one of the worst afflictions of the poor child living in his own home. Children with tuberculous parents living in special settlements like Papworth do not contract the disease.

Another kind of experiment comes from the over-enthusiastic engineering firm which achieved 26,000 hours more overtime in 1940 than in 1939 – and lost 23,800 extra hours in sickness.

Where do we stand now?

Immense progress has been made in recent years. The average expectation of life has risen during the last 100 years from just under 40 to just over 60 years. Death-rates show the improvements already gained, improvements that coincide with a period of great social advance. Contrast the 1860s and 1930s: in every age-group there has been an encouraging fall in the death-rate, though as expected the decline is smaller from middle-life onwards:–

The death-rate at seven ages (deaths per 1,000 people in each age-group)

Periods	All ages	0-5 years	5-10	15-20	20-35	45-55	65-75
1861-70	21.3	68.6	8.0	6.4	9.8	17.4	62.8
1921-30	10.6	22.9	2.4	2.5	3.7	10.0	51.9

How much there is still left to do can be seen from figures like the following:–

Deaths in the social classes (1930-32)

(Class 1 represents the upper and middle classes, Class 3 the skilled workers and Class 5 the unskilled labourers)

Ages   20 to 65

Men ■

Women ☐

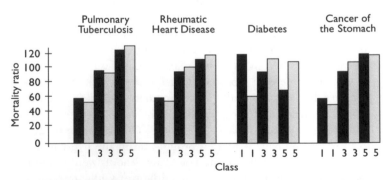

This diagram shows the differences between three social classes in their death rates from certain diseases. Diabetes – for men – is one of the few diseases, mortality from which is greater for the rich than the poor.

Sickness, too, reflects the stresses and strains of our life:–

Weekly family income per adult male	Days of sickness per year	
	Males	**Females**
26s and over	4.7	7.3
18s to 26s	7.3	8.6
Less than 18s	14.9	11.1

These are recent figures from the USA, but conditions are similar in Britain.

Insured workers in England and Wales lose more than 30 million weeks a year on account of sickness. In spite of falling death-rates, there is still an enormous accumulation of ill-health, much of it only remotely measurable by death statistics. In addition to the well-recognised "diseases", subnormal vitality, "debility," unfitness are the burden of so many lives that they are often accepted as normal. Much of this subnormal health is probably due to malnutrition, much to "nervous" disturbance. In war and peace alike, the blight of neurosis expresses much that is wrong in our social life with its lack of security and peace of mind, its restless acquisitiveness, its lack of faith and its frustrations, its unceasing rush that in the end seems to lead nowhere. Our strange society has too few children, yet motherhood so often spells only progressing drudgery, and half our working-class children are condemned to spend their most impressionable years in the shadows of poverty.

Our health services

The war is making so many changes from day to day, and much of the new legislation is so obviously of a temporary and experimental nature, that it will be best to consider the pre-war position. Our object will be rather *to discover what was wrong, so that in Reconstruction the mistakes will not be repeated.*

An unequal society

Pre-war England was rather a failure in its provision of the basic health services, the foundations of good health. Sir John Orr's work in 1936 showed that a third of the population were in some degree malnourished, including a half of the children. Crawford and Broadley in their survey found that 16 millions could not afford the "minimum diet for health and working efficiency" prescribed by the British Medical Association; on the League of Nations "optimum" or really first-class diet, the figure rose to 23 millions. In the doctor's surgery these cold statistics were translated into general unfitness, excessive liability to infections, slow recovery from illness, and into anaemia, rickets and decaying teeth.

How consumption of the better foods depended largely on income may be judged from figures like these:–

Food consumption per week per head

Class	Approx annual income	Bread	Meat	Milk	Eggs	Fruit	Potatoes
AA	£1,000 and over	48 oz	53 oz	5.3 pts	6.6	19d	73 oz
A	£500-999	48	50	5	6.2	17	56
B	£250-499	50	43	4.4	5.5	13	67
C	£125-249	55	35	2.7	3.8	6	62
D	Under £125	62	30	1.6	2.6	3	62

Class AA represents 1 per cent of the population, Class C 6 per cent, Class D 15 per cent. Beneath a certain income level it just was not possible (even for a professor of nutrition) to buy a satisfactory diet.

There is nothing new in our housing problem, which dates from the Industrial Revolution. It is an appalling thought that in all these 150 years, with the uncountable wealth that was produced and poured into this country, at no time could it be said that the people were decently housed. Great progress was made between the two wars: 4 million new houses were built. Yet an official survey in 1936 found almost 10 per cent overcrowded in England and Wales on a none too generous standard; the situation was much worse in some parts, notably the Industrial North-East, and of course in Scotland housing conditions were truly disgraceful, with probably more than half the population affected. Bradford had 30,000 back-to-back houses, Birmingham 38,772, Sheffield 60,000, and Leeds 70,954. During 1936 one dwelling-house out of every fifty in Leeds had to be treated for bugs. In bad housing, a great authority (Sir George Newman) wrote, there are three evils:–

> "There is *diminished personal cleanliness and physique* leading to debility, fatigue, unfitness, and reduced powers of resistance. A second result of bad housing is that the *sickness rates* are relatively high, particularly for infectious, contagious, and respiratory diseases. Thirdly, the general *death-rates* are higher and the expectation of life is lower. The evidence is overwhelming, and it comes from all parts of the world – the worse the people are housed the higher will be the death-rate."

Nutrition and the homes of the people reflect the size of the wage packet. Inequalities of income were summed up in the different social class mortalities already mentioned, in an infant death-rate of 25 at Welwyn and 120 in the Manchester slums, in Titmuss's shocking conclusion that "54,000 deaths would not have occurred in the single year 1936 if the standard of health reached by the prosperous Home Counties applied to all England and Wales." Perhaps a million died unnecessarily between the two wars.

Preventive medicine

The Public Health Services were created to deal with epidemic diseases due largely to lack of elementary sanitation. They have been so successful that typhoid, dysentery and cholera, together with some other now forgotten features of the "good old days," have been blotted out entirely, or almost so. We expect clean water and food as a right, and can have clean milk and no deaths from Bovine Tuberculosis if we want. As the service expanded, the sanitary work more and more became routine, and emphasis shifted to prevention of *individual* illness as well as *community* infections. Maternity and Child Welfare Centres and School Clinics were developed, and have been progressively extending their influence to all the medical needs of the groups they cover.

These personal health services are mostly *adoptive, permissive,* ie, Parliament has *permitted* the Local Authorities to *adopt* these measures, but does not compel them to do so, or, anyhow, to reach a definite standard of excellence. The intention was to allow full scope for local initiative, and it has been fully justified, for example, in Dudley's efforts for diphtheria immunisation, in Cambridge's dental schemes, in Rochdale's campaign to reduce maternal mortality. But the general result is an extraordinary disparity between the best, the average and the worst in activities where nothing less than the best ought to satisfy. Many of the Local Authorities were too poor, or their ratepayers too apathetic, to extract the full possibilities from the *permissive* legislation. These are the sums per head in pence spent by 80 County Boroughs in the year 1933-4 on some of the most important services coming within the control of Local Authorities:–

	Maternity and child welfare	School medical inspection	Tuberculosis
Highest	37.5	40.3	39.5
Average	15.9	15.1	22.0
Lowest	6.3	6.3	8.0

In 1934 all the County Boroughs had Ante-Natal Clinics, but only 53 had any dental service there; only 24 provided home-helps; 15 of the 80 ran toddlers' clinics; only 30 had complete school dental schemes; 7 were enterprising enough to establish Child Guidance Clinics; less than half the authorities used their powers to provide for the after-care of the tuberculous, only one spending as much as the Government permitted.

The provision of school meals was even more neglected and haphazard before the war. Sir John Orr estimated that 25 per cent of all children in the country had a diet which was deficient in *every* respect, because their parents could not afford to provide a better one; but only about 2.5 per cent of children got free solid meals from their Local Authorities. The milk in schools scheme was more successful, but it provided only $^1/_3$ of a pint and less than 60 per cent of the children received it. Happily in the last two years the problem has been tackled with a new enthusiasm, and over 700,000 children are receiving dinners and over 3½ million milk.

Health education

In an invaluable activity like Health Education pre-war efforts were half-hearted. Only in the last year or two has diphtheria immunisation been pressed and wireless and newspaper publicity been exploited. A great reduction in the death-rate from diphtheria has been achieved in recent years in New York as a result of large-scale immunisation. When the death-rates for New York and London were compared, it was found that in 1906 10.7 deaths occurred in New York for every one in London, and in 1940 8.6 deaths in London for every one in New York. There can be no question of introducing compulsory immunisation till a full and fair trial has been given to voluntary methods. On kindred subjects like patent medicines and quackery in general a discreet silence was maintained. The patent medicine traffic reached £30,000,000 a year. Based often on fantastic claims and selling usually at fantastic prices, the trade met next to no opposition from those responsible for the education of a public opinion which too often views Medicine as magic, mystery and mumbo-jumbo.

The care of the sick

The technical knowledge and skill of many of our doctors and nurses is so great, the excellence of many of our hospitals so undoubted, that it is rather startling to discover how inadequately in many respects the sick *were* treated in pre-war Britain.

We could all give instances where treatment fell short of the patient's needs. And an enormous amount of *untreated* sickness was revealed by the few examinations that were made of the presumably healthy. "The nation's teeth," declared the Minister of Health a year or so before the war, "are rotten": yet 24 million people were unprovided with any dental service. The neglect of common ailments like rheumatism and dyspepsia and minor post-natal complications was equally unfortunate.

More than 200,000 cases of fractured bones were treated annually, but only a quarter of these in properly equipped fracture clinics. In a series of cases specially studied it was found that permanent disability persisted in only 1 per cent of the patients treated in organised clinics, but in no less than 37 per cent of patients not so treated. Since the outbreak of war the Ministry of Health has been making strenuous efforts to remedy this state of affairs. Likewise, the Ministry of Labour is *now* attempting to establish a proper rehabilitation service to carry on where fracture clinics must leave off, arranging for such re-education as may be indicated till final replacement in suitable jobs.

Even the best treatment may be of little avail if the standard of living of the sick is not at the same time safeguarded. Illness, any illness, means more expense, not less. Yet citizen A, who breaks his leg getting off the bus outside his factory, receives 18/- a week (plus possibly a few shillings more if he belongs to a prosperous Approved Society). Citizen B more wisely breaks his leg while at work; he may receive 35/- a week under Workmen's Compensation. If A and B are married and have three children, A's 18/- remains 18/-, but B now gets 45/-. By comparison, citizen C who is merely unemployed receives 41/-, and he and all his family are naturally as fits as fiddles on this.

After spending 6 months in a sanatorium, at a cost to the community of £5 or £6 a week, a worker with tuberculosis returns home crammed with good advice on diet, fresh air and the sort of life he should lead during what may be quite a prolonged convalescence. From National Health Insurance he receives 10/6 a week, and usually has to depend for the rest on Public Assistance. Small surprise if he takes the first job that is going, and within a few weeks or months will be ready once again for the sanatorium. The Beveridge Plan would do much to abolish these discrepancies in cash incomes.

A system without system

Our Health Services represent the English genius for improvisation or muddling through, or what you will, in full flower. There are at least two of everything, and often more: Public Hospitals and Voluntary Hospitals, private practice and Health Insurance, Municipal Clinics and doctors' surgeries. Dr Douglas Hubble, writing in the *Lancet*, illustrates the inevitable overlapping by a "characteristic example":–

"A pregnant woman is attended in sickness by a Dr A, though Dr B is doing the ante-natal examinations and midwife C will conduct the confinement. After delivery, Dr A attends both mother and child in sickness, but the child is taken to an infant-welfare centre for advice on diet, and is there supervised by Dr D; either Dr A or D may, and often does, refer the child to a local hospital, where it is seen by Dr E, who may refer it back to Dr A; or the child may become a chronic out-patient under a succession of house physicians, Dr F^n. At school medical inspections the child is examined by Dr G and possibly later by Dr H. At the age of 14 he is given the right to choose his own doctor, and with characteristic independence discards the family doctor, old A (of whom it is true he has seen woefully little) in favour of Dr I."

Dr A was probably the husband's panel doctor, B and D were very likely employed by the district Council, E and F^n by the local Voluntary Hospital, G and H by the County Council. Dr I may well have been a newly-settled private practitioner, trying his luck in a neighbourhood quite well supplied with doctors already. At present, apart from occasional meetings of the local medical society, there is no reason why these doctors should ever meet, not to say pool their experiences.

Planning for health

In the Reconstruction of Health we want a society with equal opportunity for health. We want medical services to keep people healthy, to prevent disease, or to detect in its earliest stages. We want all who are ill to have the best treatment that modern knowledge can offer. We assume a society cured of its disinclination to plan by a war won only through planning on a gigantic scale.

A national minimum

Freedom from want, freedom from fear take first place in a Health Charter. The most perfect medical services would only be wasted effort in a society that did not provide its citizens the wherewithal to be healthy. "The really essential Health Services of the Nation," wrote PEP,

"are the making available of ample safe fresh milk to all who need it, the cheapening of other dairy produce, fruit and vegetables, new accommodation to replace slums and relieve overcrowding, green-belt schemes, playing fields, youth hostels and physical education, social insurance which relieves the burden of anxiety on the family, advances in employment policy which improve security of tenure or conditions of work, and finally education in healthy living through training and propaganda. Health problems are frequently the result of social and industrial conditions, and the attempt to deal with these problems piece-meal results in a lop-sided development of the health services. It is necessary to remember that there are often alternative policies for dealing with ill-health – either to go on indefinitely treating the cases or to deal with the social and economic conditions producing the cases."

Intensive research into human needs, and into the means of satisfying them continues, but we know enough already to build an environment that promotes health, to stamp out the diseases of malnutrition, overcrowding and social insecurity. An undernourished child today is no more an act of God than the hunchbacked dwarf of the early years of the Industrial Revolution. Discussion of the roads that could lead to this anything but utopian goal involves the largest issues of politics and economics, and these are outside the scope of this pamphlet. But one road has been mapped out in detail by the Beveridge Report.

The medical service indivisible

There has never been in this country a truly national policy on health, never a general staff whose responsibility it is to conduct a *whole* campaign. The Royal Commission of 1869 already saw the need for a powerful central authority consolidating within itself all central Government departments concerned with health, and equally that "all powers requisite for the health of town and country should in every place be possessed by *one* responsible Local Authority ... so that no area should be without such an authority, *or have more than one*." We may not have been ready for this in Chadwick's time, but today we see nothing necessarily undemocratic in such organisation. The co-ordination of all medical agencies, preventive and curative, hospital and domiciliary is a primary need, for all are a single social service. Today the Beveridge Plan *assumes* that a "comprehensive national health service will ensure that for every citizen there is available whatever medical treatment he requires, in whatever form he requires it, domiciliary or institutional, general, specialist or consultant, and will ensure also the provision of dental, ophthalmic and surgical appliances, nursing and midwifery and rehabilitation after accidents." A big reconstruction job is waiting to be done. Will the Ministry of Health, the doctors and the man in the street rise to the occasion?

The family doctor

One of the most depressing of recent trends in medicine has been the decline in the prestige of the family doctor. The general practitioner carries health education into the home; should become expert in the early diagnosis of all types of disease; should conduct periodic health examinations of all the family. He treats much illness himself, and mediates between the family and the diverse agencies concerned with health in our complicated society. These functions are basic. If he is no longer the family counsellor and friend as well, the loss is mutual.

Various tendencies have led to this falling of the family doctor in the public esteem. In part the gradual encroachment of Public Health's personal services is responsible, in part the development of specialisation and the glamourisation of "men in white" at the big hospital. The general practitioner is, moreover, greatly handicapped by a system that makes him more and more of a black-coat tradesman. He buys his practice, often borrowing heavily in the process. His running expenses are so high that he is forced to charge for all manner of petty offices like shillings for certificates. He is perpetually bothered by financial conflicts that have no place in *anyone's* idea of the right doctor-patient relationship. He is a professional man with no time that he can call his own, who finds it intensely difficult to take off the few odd weeks a year for post-graduate study that mean so much to his professional life. Above all, his own ability to diagnose and treat disease is gradually contracting, simply because medicine has now outdistanced the powers of one man with a stethoscope.

The health centre

Team work in medicine has become inevitable with the extension of knowledge in so many directions and the consequent growth of specialism in diagnosis and treatment. In hospitals, in many middle-class general practice partnerships, wherever in fact high quality medical work is done, consultation and co-operation are the established routine. In the present state of general practice among the great mass of the population the family doctor finds this almost impossible to attain. It is complicated as well as expensive to discuss cases with colleagues, to employ such elementary diagnostic methods as the X-Ray and blood examination if patients are not to be sent to hospital, which often means losing them entirely.

To meet this situation the idea of centralising and developing local health services in a Health Centre is becoming increasingly popular. All the everyday work of medicine would be done there. The family doctors would each have their consulting rooms, and all patients fit to get about would be seen there. Night work would be done by a rota, but each doctor would visit his own patients at home during the day if they were too sick to come to the Centre. X-Rays and a pathological laboratory would be provided. Periodic health examinations could be properly carried out, and there would be little difficulty, eg, in X-Raying all young people from time to time to detect tuberculosis before it had gone too far. There would be a properly staffed theatre for minor operations, a dispensary, and dental, ophthalmic and physiotherapy clinics. The maternity, infant and child welfare and school medical services would, of course, be conducted there, and as far as possible by the family doctors. Consultants could visit unless the hospital was near. Medical records would be kept by a *clerical* staff. Welfare workers would attend to all the social and domestic complications of being ill. Health Visitors also would logically operate from such a Centre.

Doctors would be limited to about 2,500 patients. Up to this maximum there would be a free choice of doctors. Beyond, the most popular would probably have a waiting list. The Health Centre could thus incorporate some dozen separate doctors' surgeries and dispensaries, the personal public health services, the essential minor specialities. It would enormously increase the efficiency of general practice, and it would take over a large part of the burden now imposed quite unfairly on hospital out-patients' departments.

Re-mapping England

Health Centres would naturally work together with the hospitals where more severe and obscure illness could be investigated and treated, and on whose staff would be found the various specialists. The anarchy of two parallel and independent hospital "systems" functioning busily, often overlapping clumsily, yet between them leaving many gaps, had already become absurd before the outbreak of war, and when war broke out the Ministry of Health had to establish a degree of control over both. It has attempted since to co-ordinate their activities and to make good their joint deficiencies, without interfering with the individual set-up of the public and voluntary systems.

More and more do patients want to go to hospital for treatment; more and more do they need to go there if they are to have the full benefit of modern medical science. Health Centres are essentially local, district affairs, but the area of a large general hospital should cover about 100,000 people. The more specialised services, like Tuberculosis Sanatoria or radium treatment or plastic surgery, can be supplied economically only for very much larger units of population, which vary widely with the particular service in question. If all the varying services are to be made accessible to the individual citizen we shall have to remap the country in terms of large hospital regions, each of which could undertake with some hope of success to provide its citizens with a complete service. The concentration of consultants in the Harley Streets of the University towns would give way to a more logical distribution. Special services of the types mentioned, involving expensive apparatus and a very high degree of technical skill, would be placed in town or in country, whichever was more suitable.

In such regions, bureaucracy need never be allowed to rear its head. It would not be a case of abolishing Local Government, merely of adapting it to changing circumstances. Democratic control could be as active as ever and provide the stimulus of local knowledge, local interest and local competition. The distances would not be goo great for out-patients and ambulances, for consultants and general practitioners and for the elected representatives on the various Boards of Management. The Government has already accepted Regionalism as a principle of post-war hospital policy.

Industrial health

The factory doctor personifies the modern outlook in medicine, aiming at prevention first and treatment second. The worker, from the age of 14, spends two-thirds of his waking hours at his job, in getting there and coming home. The day's work colours all his life. Excess and monotony can deprive it of all savour; a nagging foreman can turn it sour, just as badly arranged machinery bends his back or gives him rheumatism. Making and keeping people healthy in a factory is a very practical enterprise. Protection of the worker from specific industrial hazards like dermatitis and silicosis is only one, and a small, part of the doctor's day. Lighting, ventilation, sanitation, noise, canteens, shift hours are the medical officer's concern. Cuts and bruises, sore feet, indigestion, and a thousand one strains are sufficient challenge to all his art and science. Physical and psychological selection of personnel, routine examinations particularly of young workers, rehabilitation of the convalescent to maximum usefulness – there is no more fruitful field for the new humanism. Before the war there were less than 100 doctors in the whole of England engaged full-time in industrial medicine, including the staff of the Industrial Health Research Board, the Medical Inspectors of Factories, and the solitary Medical Inspector of Mines. The service is expanding rapidly under the stress of war. Whether it is to develop as a branch of Public Health or Factory Welfare, or whether it can be left to individual employers with some form of State supervision, is the sort of question that is nowhere near settlement.

£300 millions

This was the sum spent annually before the war on health: £100 millions on environmental sanitation and amenities, £13 millions on Public Health's personal services, £185 millions on the care of the sick. Of these £300 millions, rates and taxes provided more than a half, private payments less than a third, and National Health Insurance less than a sixth. Workmen's Compensation and the various contributory schemes represented a small fraction.

Private charity has failed. The voluntary hospitals were finding it increasingly difficult to pay their way, and the Government has already undertaken to subsidise them after the war through contributions from the "major" Local Authorities. It is accepted by all that some new means must be found of providing a complete medical service for the workers, their wives and dependants.

The insurance principle

Many doctors, while realising, and better than any, its defects, have hitherto been anxious to maintain National Health Insurance as the basis for the creation of a comprehensive health service. The long experience embodied in these views entitle them to the most careful scrutiny. These doctors consider that

> "the continuance of personal relationship between doctor and patient, each being free to choose, would be ensured. The general practitioner would remain primarily responsible for the health of the patient, having been freely chosen by the patient as the best doctor for him. Practitioners would do their best work if allowed to settle, as at present, where and in what type of practice they please. The incentive of fair competition (both for panel patients and practice among the minority not covered by insurance) with legitimate economic reward, ought not to be disgarded." As the machinery of National Health Insurance already exists, its extension "would give the largest number of people a nearly complete service ... without drastic alteration of ... general methods."

A fundamental issue is raised here. The Royal Commission on National Health Insurance (1926), in discussing the need for a "unified health service on a single local basis in which all varieties of preventive and curative work would find their appropriate place," reached the conclusion that

> "the wider the scope of these services the more difficult
> would it be to retain the insurance principle. The ultimate
> solution will lie, we think, in the direction of divorcing the
> medical service entirely from the insurance system and
> recognising it along with all the other public health activities
> as a service to be supported from the general public funds."

And now Sir William Beveridge endorses this conclusion.

The point at issue can be stated quite simply. What is to be the
criterion for medical services? The people's needs or the up-to-
dateness of their contributions? It is hard to resist the conclusion in
the words of seven members of the Committee on Scottish Health
Services (1936), that "it is not defensible, assuming the existence of a
national health policy, that the care of an individual's health should
be made to depend on the number of stamps affixed to a card in
respect of his employment."

The expansion of National Health Insurance would only serve to
enhance what should be an entirely irrelevant factor. And retaining
the insurance principle to pay for the medical care of the insured,
their wives and children, would now mean the maintenance at great
expense of elaborate machinery covering 90 per cent of the population,
merely to exclude the remaining 10 per cent. Is this not too easy a
start for the old snobbery in the new Britain?

In any case, to make so greatly swollen an insured population the
basis of national medicine would merely mean for doctors the *substance*
of a State medical service (nearly all income being derived from
central funds) without the *shadowy* disadvantages of enrolment in the
Government Service. For the public it would mean the shadow of a
State medical service (with the persistent nuisance of the insurance
element), yet without the *substance* of a single and really comprehensive
national health organisation.

State medical service

The alternative to an enlarged and improved insurance system is that
the State should provide Health Services as it provides Elementary
Education – or the Royal Navy. As at present advocated, it would be
run on the following lines:–

1. The family and the family doctor would remain the essential unit.

2. The service would be distributed according to the needs of each
   district, not the ability of its citizens to pay nor the personal fancies
   of doctors or their wives. (Slums till they were eradicated would
   have more doctors, not less as at present.)

3. The service would be complete, incorporating preventive medicine, home, hospital and convalescent treatment, midwives and health visitors, home helps and welfare workers, the provision of dentures, surgical and other appliances.

4. There would be no economic barrier between the citizen and health. However paid for, whether by taxation or contribution or both, there would be no actual charge for medical care.

5. The service would be provided for the whole community and not for the poor or any other section as such. It would not be possible, after an inevitable period of transition, for anyone to obtain in any way different facilities from those provided by the community for all its citizens.

6. Doctors, nurses, welfare workers and all auxiliaries would be whole-time salaried officers with promotion by merit and experience.

One Service. One policy on health, on prevention and cure. The advantages are obvious and the possibilities would be immense. The drawbacks and the difficulties inherent in such a change must be weighted with care. It need not mean a violent break with the past if introduced with intelligence and step by step, but it would demand a complete reorientation of outlook for many citizens, doctors, health officers and civil servants. It must mean less freedom and less privilege for many: would it mean more democracy? The invitation to political jobbery must be balanced against a system that permits the highest bidder, whatever his ability, to purchase any practice. Some hold that guaranteed salaries and pensions would remove a major incentive to good work; that initiative and enterprise are inevitably choked by Administration. Many are afraid that it would be difficult if not impossible to maintain the personal intimate and confidential doctor-patient relation within the necessarily "more rigid mould" of a Government service.

A plea

Millions of wage-earners now pay taxes as well as rates, so that Health could be paid for in this way *or* by contributions which are merely an indirect form of taxation. There is no reason for either method to involve much complication if we can grasp the simple enough ideas we have been discussing in this pamphlet. Does not Reconstruction – and the Beveridge Plan in particular – present us with a great opportunity? Life is becoming so cluttered up with Societies and insurance, with claims, applications, assessments, with orders, advices and demands, with allowances and deductions, that we are in danger of becoming a nation of form-fillers, with one half the population engaged in administering the other half, to say nothing of the small army of interpreters who try to keep the ring. This is *not* just a War Casualty. A single tax for health, granting in return and without further ado the right to all health services, would be a giant stride towards simpler living and a healthier and better Britain.

To the reader

Investigation

The best way to make a further study of these subjects is to find out all you can about health conditions and health services in your own community. How many doctors and dentists? How are they distributed? How many clinics, how many hospitals? What is it like to be an out-patient? How many factories have medical officers? How many children are immunised against diphtheria or smallpox? How much of the milk is pasteurised or tuberculin tested? What does your council spend on health services? What has it done with its permissive powers? How much smoke in the air? How much overcrowding? How many parks, swimming pools, playing fields? How much does it cost and how long does it take to get into the country for a day's outing? How many factories and shops give holidays with pay? What are the local death-rates – infant mortality, tuberculosis in young persons, diphtheria, etc? In all these respects how does your community compare with neighbouring districts, with the whole country, with the best areas? Why are there such differences?

John Hewetson, 1913–90   **22**

John Hewetson was a medical practitioner who hailed from a wealthy background but spent his life working with patients in poor areas. He was a spirited character who in the 1930s did his rounds in a white Rolls Royce, but also attended anarchist meetings. In the 1940s he was jailed twice, once as a conscientious objector and then a second time as a 'disaffecter of the Forces'.

In the 1950s he spent much time working for freely available birth control and abortion, and made particular efforts to make contraceptives available to working-class women so that they could enjoy their sex lives uninhibited by the fear of becoming pregnant. He was also involved with getting birth control materials into France, where they were illegal until the 1970s. While in practice at the Elephant and Castle he made a range of alternative medicines available to all patients. He was also a Visiting Medical Officer at The Spike – a 'resettlement unit' for homeless people – for over 30 years.

John Hewetson wrote *Ill-health, poverty and the state* in jail, and had to rewrite it on release as his manuscript was confiscated. It was published by the anarchist Freedom Press in 1946. This was a damning indictment of capitalist and authoritarian society. In it he proposes that the abolition of poverty should be the basis of any measures to ameliorate social conditions and that nothing short of a radical attack on the problem of poverty itself would be adequate to remove the ill-health, pain and premature deaths which economic pressures inflict. The extract we have chosen refers to nutrition, infant mortality, maternal mortality and the persistence of poverty.

Hewetson, J. (1946) *Ill-health, poverty and the state*

Chapter Nine
Reformism and the abolition of poverty

"It is fair to say that there is no problem of nutrition in England today. So much research work has been done in the laboratories and so many precise dietary surveys have been made that we know all we need to know about the food requirements of the people and the extent to which they are or could be provided. The real problem is how to make it possible for those whose health is being adversely affected by faulty diet to obtain not only the knowledge of the right kinds of food to eat but the food itself. The position is perfectly clear-cut."

DRUMMOND AND WILBRAHAM[1]

[1] *The Englishman's Food,* 1939, p 543.

In each of the foregoing sections it has been stressed and stressed again that the question of ill-health is inextricably bound up with the question of poverty. This is not simply a propaganda point; its truth is now recognized by all those who are working at what has come to be called "Social Medicine." And an editorial article in a leading medical journal, the *Lancet,* commenting on the Beveridge Report, declared: "The greatest single cause of ill-health and sub-optimal health, mental and physical, is not a virus or a bacterium but poverty. So it is the doctor's duty to fight poverty with even greater vigour than he fights the diphtheria bacillus."[2] This clear cut declaration is in line with the conclusion, already quoted, of various social investigations which state that the only practical way to attack the problem of ill-health is by raising the standard of living.[3] What has reformism in the past achieved in this direction? The answer is – very little indeed.

[2] *Lancet,* 5th December, 1942.

[3] Even the *Times* remarked (30 June 1938) that "a close relationship is known to exist between the incidence of tubercle and the size of 'real' wages."

Mr Seebohm Rowntree, to whose valuable surveys we have referred several times already, gave his general opinion just after the last war on how conditions at that time compared with those of twenty years earlier. "At the present moment," he wrote, "in spite of the abnormal amount of unemployment, there is somewhat less acute destitution than there was twenty or even ten years ago, and ... this improvement is due to factors which will continue to operate when trade becomes normal. *There are, indeed, today extraordinary numbers of families living, not in positive destitution, but barely above, or just under, the poverty line. Among these are countless households which have never before experienced actual privation.*"[4]

[4] B. Seebohn Rowntree: Preface to 1922 ed. of *Poverty: a Study of Town Life* [see Chapter 10].

Rowntree's impressions were not isolated ones. In the same winter of 1921-22, Toynbee Hall carried out an enquiry into the condition of the East London workers. *They concluded that the increase in distress was comparatively small*, but added:

> "It must not be imagined from this conclusion that East London is not suffering from distress. The standard of living is normally low and conditions are normally miserable. The fact that conditions have not become worse means only that the unemployed have not as a rule fallen from poverty to destitution ... Trade Union benefit, savings, and charity have taken some part in the work of relief, but the contributions from these sources is almost negligible, compared with the enormous calls made on the payers of rates and taxes. If these calls had not been made, distress and destitution would have been common and would have increased as long as the depression in trade lasted, workpeople would have become demoralized and lost their ability to work, and children would have been weakened by privation with results on mind and body which might have lasted through their whole lives."

A.W. Humphrey, who quotes the above, comments: "These statements are of great significance. In the first place, it must be observed that, thirty-five years after Charles Booth made his great inquest into the lives of London's people, the standard of living in East London was still 'normally low' and conditions 'normally miserable.' Mass poverty had persisted."[5] Such was the position twenty years ago.

[5] A.W. Humphrey: *The Workers' Share, A Study in Wages and Poverty*, 1930, pp 69-70.

But the end of the same decade – only fifteen years ago – showed no improvement in conditions. Drummond and Wilbraham[6] wrote: "A report of the Ministry of Health in 1929 described the terrible food conditions in the Welsh coalfields, but the same distressing details were true of a thousand other areas in the country. The diets of the poor working people had become almost as bad as they had been in the worst years of Queen Victoria's reign: white bread, margarine, jam, sugar, tea and dried fish. Meat was seldom eaten more than once a week, while fresh vegetables, other than potatoes, were rarely bought. Fresh milk was hardly ever seen."

[6] Drummond and Wilbraham: *The Englishman's Food*, 1939, p 539.

Since then the world has known the most devastating economic depression in history. It would be difficult to say that any significant change had taken place since the last war, certainly not for the better.

Thus despite various so-called reforms the workers' lot remains substantially unaltered over the past fifty years. This view has been confirmed by studies on wage trends during the present century. The following figures, for example, are taken from Jurgen Kuczynski.[7]

[7] Jurgen Kuczynski: *A Short History of Labour Conditions in England*, 1942, p 113.

Year	Net real wages per unemployed and employed worker
1900	100
1905	94
1910	93
1914	96
1917	75
1920	100
1925	89
1930	95
1935	95
1939	94

Another source, the Balfour Committee, which cannot be accused of socialist sympathies, reported in 1929 that "Such figures as are available indicate that over a period of forty years (1888–1928) the weekly rates of money wages for similar grades of work have advanced by about 120 per cent, and the cost of living by about 90 per cent, showing an advance in 'real' weekly wages of about 16 per cent." Thus even on the most favourable estimate (the Cost of Living Index of the Ministry of Labour has been under criticism for more than a quarter of a century) can only show an advance – spread over forty years – of sixteen per cent!

With poverty virtually unchanged it is not surprising to find ill-health also as pervading as ever, even if the mortality from certain diseases has shown a steady decline. The curing of disease depends less on taking medicine than on altering the conditions which make a man ill. But whereas it is an easy matter to recommend a wealthy man to winter abroad, to go for a cruise, or even simply to keep warm or take a rest, these things are often impossible to working men and women. Often enough the house is damp, or they cannot afford more fuel, or they cannot take time off from work without disorganizing the family's finances. All too often one's treatment is frustrated by a man's material inability to carry it out. No amount of increased medical facilities will alter these factors; only the sweeping away of the whole system whereby a man is dependent solely on selling his labour in order to secure a minimum degree of food, clothing and shelter for himself and his family; only when a man is free from restricting conditions and is assured of the primary necessities, will he begin to enjoy the possibility of full health.

With poverty still the rule for the vast majority of people, they are debarred from making full use of whatever health facilities the State or private charity provides. It follows that health facilities benefit those whose economic position makes them comparatively free, but ability to use such facilities diminishes in proportion as poverty reduces freedom of action down to the point of virtual slavery which is destitution. And this conclusion, bizarre and unnatural as it may seem, is borne out by the facts regarding the effects of health reforms during the past thirty years.

Titmuss[8] recently examined the figures of the Registrar-General with regard to Infant Mortality rates during the years since 1911 – that is during the period since Lloyd George's National Health Insurance Act inaugurated the modern period of health reforms. During this period the mortality rates have been steadily falling, a fact which the adherents of gradualism are never tired of continuously pointing out. But Titmuss showed that the Infant Mortality rate *has fallen much more sharply among the children of the well-to-do than among poorer children*, a finding of the utmost importance in assessing the value of reforms.

[8] Richard M. Titmuss: *Birth, Poverty and Wealth*, 1943 [see Chapter 20].

It has been the expressed intention of reformers that the measures they seek to introduce shall iron out the anomalies which occur in a society in which wealth is unequally distributed. They try to mitigate the effect of the economic system, and reduce the gap in health which exists between the rich and the poor. Infant Mortality rates are generally regarded as the most sensitive index of social and environmental conditions; yet, during the reform period, so far from being narrowed, the gap between the worst and the best figures has actually widened.

Titmuss illustrates this by comparing the "worst" infant death rates with the "best," using the Registrar-General's figures. For 1911 the worst figures for the second six months of the first year of life exceeded the best by 173 per cent, but by 1921–3 the worst exceeded the best figures by 324 per cent and in 1930–32 they were 439 per cent greater. This means that the rates have improved much faster in the Registrar-General's Class I than in Class V. Using the mortality figures according to certain trades (of the father) the worst in 1911 exceeded the best by 299 per cent whereas in 1930–2 the excess was 498 per cent. Titmuss gives the following illuminating table for these figures, using those for certain trades for 1911 and 1930-2, and the Registrar-General's figures for 1921-23.

Infant mortality. Percentage excess of Class I over Class V			
Age	1911	1921-3	1930-2
0-1 month	106	58	66
1-3 months	180	263	239
3-6 months	253	312	330
6-12 months	299	324	498
1-2 years	–	–	408

"This Table," says Titmuss, "expresses something more than the great and widening gulf that separates one class of the people from another. The separation can be measured both by the increases in the percentages – reading across the table – or by noting that inequality *increases with age* – reading down each column. In 1911 an excess of 106 per cent rises in stages to one of 299 per cent; twenty years later an initial excess of 66 per cent grows to 498 per cent. These statistics epitomize the chances of death of two infants; one born of well-to-do parents, the other of poor parents, both potential citizens of Britain. During the first few weeks of life, little separates the two children in their chances of death, but slowly at first and then with increasing effect, as week succeeds week, the gulf widens."

Moreover, the comfortable reformist illusion that a measure like the National Health Insurance Act of 1911 has "of course" been effective in reducing class differences in health is seen to be simply an illusion. Even the *Times* was compelled to say in a leading article on Titmuss' work:

> "Mr Titmuss's startling conclusion is that between the census years 1911 and 1931 a 50 per cent reduction in the national average infant death rate was accompanied by a widening of the difference between the economically favoured and the economically handicapped.... There is thus a strong *prima facie* case for believing that one-third of the nation's parents, and half the nation's children, did not benefit to anything like a proportionate extent from the important social advances of the period since 1911, notwithstanding the great expansion, precisely during those years, of social services intended primarily for their well-being."

The only conclusion possible from these figures is that the decline in mortality rates is due to advances in medicine. The rich are not affected to any great extent by reforms; it is not they who use the hospitals and the National Health Insurance schemes. Yet the mortality rate for their children fell much more than those of the children of the poor, despite the reforms designed to bring the mortality amongst the latter nearer the level of the former. The reformist measures, just because they leave the fact of poverty untouched, have failed of their object.[9]

In conclusion, it is possible, on the basis of the above findings, to assess the value of the new National Health and other post-war reforms. Both the Beveridge Report and the Government's White Paper on Social Insurance presuppose the continued existence of rich and poor. We can, therefore, say with conviction that they have not attempted to remove the root cause of ill-health - poverty. These reforms will be as ineffective as those introduced since 1911.

[9] "The object of 'la médicine sociale'," wrote Dr Et. Burnet, "may be described as the equalization of classes, rich and poor, in respect of health." Quoted by W.R. Aykroyd: *Human Nutrition and Diet*, 1937, p 184. Dr Burnet was, until 1937, a member of the Health Section of the League of Nations.

Chapter Ten
The abolition of ill-health

"Tomorrow a man attired in rough clothes will come to fetch you to see a sick woman. He will lead you into one of those alleys where the opposite neighbours can almost shake hands over the heads of the passers-by; you will ascend into a foul atmosphere by the flickering light of a little ill-trimmed lamp; you climb two, three, four, five flights of filthy stairs, and in a dark, cold room you find the sick woman lying on a pallet covered with dirty rags. Pale, livid children, shivering under their scanty garments, gaze with their big eyes wide open. The husband has worked all his life twelve or thirteen hours a day at no matter what; now he has been out of work for three months. To be out of employment is not rare in his trade; it happens every year, periodically. But, formerly, when he was out of work, his wife went out as a char-woman − perhaps to wash your shirts − at the rate of fifteen-pence a day; now she has been bed-ridden for two months, and misery glares upon the family in all its squalid hideousness.

"What will you prescribe for the sick woman, doctor? you who have seen at a glance that the cause of her illness is general anæmia, want of good food, lack of fresh air. Say a good beef steak every day? a little exercise in the country? a dry and well-ventilated bedroom? What irony! If she could have afforded it this would have been done long since without waiting for your advice!"

KROPOTKIN: *An Appeal to the Young*, 1880

In general, conditions today are not so very different from when Kropotkin wrote, more than sixty years ago. Yet, with the immense advances in medical science, there is far less excuse for them. The mortality from particular diseases may have fallen remarkably; but the main burden of ill-health still falls most heavily on the poor. Indeed, as Titmuss has shown, the poorer sections of society are, *relative to the well-to-do*, actually less healthy than they were thirty years ago.

The usual attitude in the face of all this misery of sickness is one of optimistic fatalism. "Improvements are constantly being made. Rome wasn't built in a day" – etc, etc. It has been one of the purposes of this pamphlet to show, however, that though progress in medical science has never, perhaps, been more rapid than now, an increasing proportion of ill-health is directly due to purely economic causes, *and is therefore preventable*. Yet these economic causes have hardly been touched.

The recognition of such a position inevitably leads to the demand for action to remedy the economic organization which has kept the majority of people poor and, therefore, relatively unhealthy for centuries. Many writers on social medicine do, in fact, recognize this necessity. But they quail before the task of removing the evil of economic and social inequality. They, therefore, feel compelled to be vociferous supporters of *reforms* in health services, family allowances, social insurance schemes and the like. They are afraid to advocate the abolition of poverty, or feel hopeless about it, and so fall back on these lukewarm plans for merely attempting to mitigate its worst aspects. Such reformers were rightly ridiculed by Kropotkin in the quotations placed at the heads of Chapters Seven and Ten [not reproduced here, Eds] in the present pamphlet. The fact that Kropotkin's remarks were made sixty years ago, and yet still have force, is itself a sufficient comment on the inept optimism of piecemeal reformers.

In the preceding chapters some grounds have been given for rejecting reformism as being no solution at all. In this section, therefore, some examples will be given which indicate the kind of result which may be expected when malnutrition ceases to be the lot of the majority of our fellow-countrymen.

Even the *Times* recognizes the potentialities of economic well-being on the future of health, for on 17th February, 1938, it remarked of tuberculosis that "what *keeps it in check* is probably good food." (Our italics.) And here is how Drummond and Wilbraham point the essential lesson from the famous experiment of Corry Mann:[10]

> "Meanwhile there is one simple test for malnourishment which can be used in every case and which seldom, if ever, fails, but which, unfortunately, is very rarely applied; improve the diet and watch the result. This was how Dr Corry Mann

[10] Drummond and Wilbraham: *The Englishman's Food*, 1939, p 546. Corry Mann's results were published as Special Report Series No 105, *Diets of Boys During the School Age*, by the Medical Research Council. In addition to the gains in height and weight of the boys in the milk group over the control groups, they also had much less illness, particularly in regard to colds and coughs, they had less chilblains, and the condition of their skin was much better.

demonstrated the inadequacy of the diet of children at an institution where the food had long been regarded as ample. A pint of milk a day for a year increased the average height of the boys by nearly one inch and their weight by over three pounds. Even more important was the improvement in physical vigour and mental alertness. There could be no further argument; the boys had been undernourished before the supplement of milk was given."

Similar results were reported in 10,000 children in Lanarkshire who received milk supplements.[11] We have already seen that the value of milk is officially recognized by the Ministry of Education. It is interesting to note, however, that compared with 1914, the price of milk has risen more than the price of food generally[12] – that it has become less accessible as a food to those sections of the population who stand most in need of it.

The ease with which food will make unfit people fit was demonstrated in the army several years ago. Thirty-three recruits who were not fit for army service (by peacetime standards, that is) were selected for treatment by special diets and exercises. After two weeks ten were up to standard; at four weeks, 19; at six weeks 21; at nine weeks 23, and after three months, twenty-four out of the thirty-three had reached a standard of fitness such that they were now acceptable to the army.[13] These men had been taken out of the "normal" life of wage labour, and were introduced to a healthy régime, with plenty of rest, fresh air, and exercises, such as their civilian life could not possibly provide them with. They were also well fed. The cost of their extra food is instructive; it amounted to 7/6 per head per week[14] – and that at the wholesale prices which only the army can command. A small sum, but as Orr's figures show – one which is right outside the capacity of the majority of the ill-nourished to pay, and one, moreover, which reformists would hesitate to saddle the rates with. Thus even in men who had reached adult life, and showed effects of malnutrition which one might have expected to be permanent, good food could still go a long way towards rectifying their ill-health and underdevelopment. This army experiment confirms a finding of hospital practice; that often the only treatment which improves the tired out housewives who attend for more or less vague chronic ailments, is a period of several weeks convalescence. In the convalescent home they get the rest which their overworked home life denies them, and better food than they are accustomed to. The improvement is sometimes startling. Similar improvement is noted in the children of the very poor who, too often, are obviously undernourished. A sickly, pale, languid and dispirited child can quickly be turned by good food and surroundings into a healthy, high spirited creature hardly recognizable as its former self. Paul de Kruif, in his

[11] Leighton and McKinley: *Milk Consumption and the Growth of School Children.* Report on an investigation in Lanarkshire Schools, Edinburgh. Department of Health for Scotland. HMSO, 1930. See also Leighton and McKinley, *Lancet,* 1929, I, p 40.

[12] H.M. Vernon: *Health in Relation to Occupation,* 1939, p 153.

[13] Capt. P.J.L. Capon: *Journal of the RAMC,* May, 1937. Capon's results have since been confirmed on a larger scale. A group of 874 young recruits rejected because of underdevelopment and other defects usually considered as due to malnourishment, were placed in a camp under optimum conditions of nutrition, exercise and rest. After several months of such treatment, 87 per cent of the group passed the physical tests which they had previously failed. Crawford: *Journal of the RAMC,* July, 1939.

[14] Margery Spring Rice: *Working class wives,* 1939, p 158, ff [see also Chapter 18].

highly coloured, but sincere and arresting book on the economic background of child ill-health in America, *Why Keep Them Alive?*, gives several examples of this kind of change. In recent years a good deal of evidence has accumulated about the relationship between subnutrition – that is, not getting enough to eat – and deaths in child-birth. A short account of some of this work will be given, for it shows what an immense advance follows from economic wellbeing.

Unlike the figures for many diseases, the maternal mortality rates, until recently, showed an obstinate refusal to decline. It was hoped that an improvement would follow the Registration of Midwives Act at the beginning of the century; but these deaths in child-birth, having their root in economic causes, in poverty, proved indifferent to Acts of Parliament. The following table shows how slight was the improvement.[15]

Maternal deaths per 1,000 births

1911	3.87
1912	3.98
1913	3.96
1936	3.65

In some districts in England there was even a rise in the Maternal Mortality rate between 1935 and 1936. Though the general rate for the country as a whole fell, in the North it rose from 4.34 in 1935 to 4.36 in 1936. The North of England contains one-third of the total population. In the depressed areas of the North the rate rose from 4.68 to 4.78.[16]

Since about 1937, however, there has been a fall in the total mortality, mainly due to a decline in the mortality rates from infection (puerperal fever) following childbirth, which fell between 1934 and 1938 by about half. This reduction is considered to be due to the new sulphonamide group of drugs. Here, once again, progress is due almost solely to the advance in medicine which these drugs constitute. The gynæcologist, Aleck Bourne, remarks: "If, however, we subtract the deaths from infection in which there has been so much improvement, from the total maternal mortality, we find there has been comparatively little improvement. In 1934 there were 1,241 deaths from other conditions and in 1938, 1,185 deaths, or expressed as rates per 1,000 births, 1.99 and 1.84 respectively."[17]

As might be expected the maternal mortality rates vary from district to district according to the economic status of the inhabitants. The following table shows the rates for various districts.[18]

[15] Richard M. Titmuss, *Poverty and Population, a Factual Study of Contemporary Social Waste*, 1938, p 150.

[16] *Ibid*, p 141.

[17] Aleck Bourne: *Health of the Future* (Penguin), 1942, p 37

[18] Titmuss, *op. cit.*, p 144. The *Pilgrim Trust Unemployment Enquiry Report* states (Interim Paper No IV): "We may estimate the number of human victims of depression unemployment (ie, from 1928 to 1934) among mothers dying of puerperal disease as 3,200."

Maternal mortality per 1,000 births (1936)	
Wales	5.17
Bermondsey	5.04
Paddington	5.02
North of England	4.36
England and Wales	3.65
Greater London	2.16
Westminster	1.81
Kensington	0.86

(In the depressed areas of the North and of Wales, the figures were 4.78 and 5.29 respectively.)

Titmuss remarks of these figures that "according to the Test of the Registrar-General's Review for 1934, no year or group of consecutive years, as far as the statistics go back to 1891, produces a higher maternal mortality rate than that for South Wales for 1936." This shows how far advances in medicine sink through the social layers to the poorest sections of the population. On the other hand, Letchworth, a relatively prosperous garden city with 10,000 insured workers out of a total 17,000, had no maternal deaths at all in the five years prior to 1938. In the island of Tristan da Cunha, where food supply is plentiful, deaths in childbirth are unknown. It is clear, therefore, that to all intents and purposes all maternal deaths are preventable, and the death rate, given favourable economic circumstances, could be reduced virtually to nil. Let us see what further positive evidence we can bring forward in support of this view.

In an experimental enquiry carried out in Toronto recently, a group of women "from a low income group" were given supplementary food during pregnancy, and were compared with a similar group whose diet was not supplemented. The investigators summarize their finds thus:

> "During the whole course of the pregnancy, the mothers on a good or supplemented diet enjoyed better health, had fewer complications, and proved better obstetrical risks than those left on poor prenatal diets. The incidence of miscarriage, still-births and premature births in the women on poor diets was much increased. The incidence of illness in the babies up to the age of six months and the number of deaths resulting from these illnesses were many times greater in the poor diet group. While it is recognized that there are other important factors in the successful outcome of pregnancy, this study suggests that the nutrition of the mothers during the prenatal period influences to a

[19] Ebbs, Tisdal and Scott: *The Influence of Prenatal Diet on the Mother and Child, Journal of Nutrition*, 22, 515-526 (No 5, November), 1941.

[20] Green, Pinda, Davis and Mellanby: *Brit. Med. Journ*, 1931, 2, 595.

[21] Lady Juliet Williams, *Times*, 8th December, 1937. See also H.M. Vernon: *Health in Relation to Occupation*, 1939, p 127; also Titmuss: *Poverty and Population*, 1938, p 153. *The Medical Officer*, in an editorial comment on these results, caustically remarked that a reduction in the "exceptional maternal mortality in Wales" was "more likely to be achieved by a herd of cows than by a herd of specialists." (*The Medical Officer*, 29 May 1937). This dictum might well be born in mind by those earnest reformers who imagine that an extension of the existing medical services will materially reduce the general level of ill-health.

[22] Margaret I. Balfour: *Supplementary Feeding in Pregnancy, Lancet*, 1944, I, 208.

considerable degree the whole course of the pregnancy, and, in addition, directly affects the health of the child during the first six months of life."[19]

Similar results had already been obtained ten years before, when 275 women attending an ante-natal clinic were given doses of a concentrated Vitamin A preparation for only a month before delivery. They had a sickness rate of 1.1 compared with 4.7 in a similar group of 275 women who were given no Vitamin preparations, but were otherwise similarly treated.[20]

But the most interesting of these enquiries was that undertaken by the National Birthday Trust in South Wales. The provision of specialist obstetric services, and educational propaganda to pregnant women had not been at all effective in reducing the maternal mortality rate. But during the period 1935 to 1937 more than 10,000 expectant mothers in the poorer districts of South Wales were given special food supplements during pregnancy. As a result the death rate in this group was only about a quarter as great as that in 18,000 who received no food supplements. Here are the actual figures:

Number of mothers	Maternal death rate per 1,000 births	Number of deaths from Sepsis
10,384 receiving special food	1.63	1
18,854 not receiving special food	6.15	46

The infant death rate was also substantially reduced. For the 3,064 cases fed during the first six months of 1937 it was 57 per 1,000, as compared with 102 per 1,000 in the 4,781 who were not fed.[21]

The food supplement in this experiment consisting of quite a small amount, but containing a high proportion of vitamins and mineral salts (they also had a pint of milk a day), cost only 13s 4d per head. The Government has realized the value of this experiment for pregnant women can now obtain extra milk (not free, but at a reduced cost of 2d a pint) and vitamin supplements at Ante-Natal Clinics. An inexpensive reform.

The Birthday Trust continued its work in other depressed areas with similar results during 1937, 1938 and 1939. It closed in March, 1939, not from choice on the part of the investigators, but because the Treasury grant from the Commissioner for Special Areas (Government euphemism for Distressed Areas) was withdrawn. In this experiment the women on supplementary food were all very poor, whereas the control group was, on the whole of slightly better economic status. Nevertheless, the former were rendered substantially healthier. Some insight into the conditions behind the figures is given by the following description of the supplementary food group.[22]

"The women of the fed class were all in very poor circumstances. They were the wives of unemployed men or of low wage earners. In some of the areas rents were high and when all expenses had been met there was not sufficient to meet the BMA standard of diet, far less to provide special foods for expectant mothers. It has to be remembered in this connection that the mother of the family distributes the income and finds it hard to satisfy the hunger of the children and to keep her husband in good physical condition. She thinks of herself last or not at all. When asked about her diet a common reply is 'Oh, I can do with anything.' Towards the end of the week a cup of tea and a bit of bread might be her dinner, this even when she was pregnant. It did not seem to occur to her that the foetus would be affected by her diet, or if it did she thought more of the children actually there than of the child coming. Many of these mothers were living under slum conditions, overcrowded and insanitary. Those with large families were living under a great strain, constantly trying to make sixpence go as far as a shilling, and failing. There were many individual cases of hardship and distress; one mother had had six children in eight years and found another coming. She described the difficulty of getting enough food for the hungry children and of sending them to school respectable and well shod. She *could not* have another. Would the nurse help her? Another in somewhat similar circumstances found herself unable to cope with the urgent demands of the school authorities to keep her children tidy, better shod and especially less verminous. She said, with calm despair, "I just can do *no more*, nurse.' Such cases were scattered through the fed class and the strain left its mark on the mothers."

Against such a picture let us place the complacent remarks of Sir George Newman, in his Annual Report as Chief Medical Officer to the Ministry of Health in 1932, on the subject of maternal mortality. "After all, sound nutrition in a pregnant woman is obviously the only way of sustaining her health and that of the forthcoming child. She should become accustomed (*sic*) to a diet which includes ample milk – two pints a day – cheese, butter, eggs, fish, liver, fruit and fresh vegetables which will supply the body with essential elements, salts and vitamins…." Fourteen pints of milk at fourpence halfpenny a pint comes to 4/6 a week.

"Sound nutrition in a pregnant woman is obviously the only way of sustaining her health and that of her forthcoming child…." Obviously. Yet all these grim food supplementing experiments show that a tremendous number of mothers are deprived of this obvious necessity. The truth of Sir George Newman's remarks, which our society makes such a gruesome mockery of, is shown by the startling effects of even comparatively short periods of supplementary feeding. They give one a glimpse of the darkness and terror of our social system. Yet at the same time they show that ill-health is not inevitable, that it can be attacked by quite simple means. The possibility of stamping out all this terrible and unnecessary suffering and loss is clearly exposed. Economic well-being is the key to positive health.

All the evidence presented in this pamphlet shows how much the incidence and severity of ill-health depends on economic factors and especially on the factor of inadequate food. It follows that improvement in economic conditions, bringing with it an improvement in dietary intakes, will be an immense factor in improving health. In fact it will almost certainly remove the majority of those universally found causes of illness and chronic discomfort, to say nothing of removing the commonest causes of premature death among the largest section of the world community, the working class. That this is no idle utopian hope is shown by the evidence from feeding experiments outlined above. It matters little that these experiments are rare and isolated phenomena, and in themselves make no sensible difference to the death rates and sickness rates. What does matter is the fact that they show clearly how those rates *could* be reduced if the peoples of the world got enough to eat, if in fact our economic system aimed at the satisfaction of the needs of all, instead of being dictated by the likelihood (or otherwise) of producing a profit for the few.

We have already seen that governments, and the League of Nations, have recognized the importance of the economic factor in the question of health or ill-health. We have also seen how grudgingly they have introduced legislation in the matter, and how that legislation is largely self-stultifying because it makes no attempt to obliterate poverty. Now we can see that what is fundamentally required is an enormous increase in the food intakes of populations. Yet at the very moment when their own committees were deploring the low dietary standard of the peoples, governments all over the world were ordering the destruction of "surplus" food, in order to maintain agricultural prices. Not only destroy the food, but do so in order to see to it that the price of such food as capitalist economics did permit to reach the market should be kept up – that is, kept beyond the reach of the largest sections of society. The destruction of food for the purposes of maintaining prices has often been described; but those who look to governments to remedy current ill-health (and there are plenty of partisans of State control in the matter) must face the facts of governmental action in destroying the very commodity in which their peoples stood most in need of.

Bearing in mind the evidence presented in foregoing chapters [of

Hewetson's book, Eds], consider the following remarks by the Food Research Institute of Stanford University, California, on the market position at the end of the 1934 season.

"To observers concerned with the improvements in the world wheat situation the crop year 1933-34 was one of disappointed hopes and expectations. Early indications pointed towards a world wheat crop ex–Russia *small enough to assure a substantial reduction of the world wheat surplus, and to foreshadow a rise in wheat prices,* with an accompanying measure of relief to wheat producers and to Governments deeply engaged in assisting producers.

"Week by week as the season progressed, however, the crop forecasts and estimates made larger and larger world totals; and appraisals standing in December, 1934, were some 300 million bushels – nearly 10 per cent above forecasts current in August and September, 1933. World wheat prices, low when the crop year opened, tended to fall rather than rise in the early months...."[23]

[23] Quoted by C.E. McNally: *Public Ill-Health*, 1935, p 57. (Our italics.)

In our society it is a disaster if a commodity, even though it be the most basic commodity of all – food – is available in "too large" amounts. For then prices fall, and the only way to make them rise again is to create a scarcity. Is it surprising that lack of food is the great outstanding feature of our social life when scarcity is a fundamental necessity to our market economy?

In the teeth of the now recognized malnutrition, the various States did not scruple to create a scarcity by destroying food. Wheat was burnt, other crops ploughed in again, stock slaughtered and their carcasses burnt all over the world because there was no market for them. "It is a tragic irony," wrote the *News Chronicle* (17 October 1933), "that men and women in New York should be suffering the tortures of hunger while tens of thousands of pigs in farrow are being slaughtered in Iowa by the command of the Government, and farmers in Kansas and Nebraska are burning their grain." *The Economist* (30 December 1933) published the figures for the expenditure under the American Agricultural Adjustment Administration for the restriction of agricultural production: – 33 million dollars to be paid as compensation to farmers for destroying and burning their pigs; 350 million dollars on corn and hay production control; 120 million dollars for the purpose of reducing wheat acreage. And so on. Examples could be multiplied indefinitely. The destruction, or deliberate restriction of production of food went on – and still goes on. A fisherman told a *Reynolds News* reporter (16 January 1944): "You read of a woman being fined a pound for throwing away stale

24 Much the same thing was happening in Russia. During the ghastly famine of 1933-34 the Soviet Government continued to export foodstuffs. "1933 was a particularly critical year for the food supply of the Soviet Union. Nevertheless, 1.8 million tons of grain and other foodstuffs were exported. During the first eight months of the year 466,905 tons of grain, worth 13.2 million roubles (here and below the roubles referred to are gold roubles, worth at par 9.46 roubles to the £), were exported, together with fodder and other foodstuffs worth 29.9 million roubles. In the first eight months of 1934, during which period the acute lack of foodstuffs continued, the export was even more considerable; 591,833 tons of grain, worth 13.6 million roubles, were exported, as well as foodstuffs and fodder to the value of 34.5 million roubles. These goods were mostly sent via the Black Sea ports in the immediate vicinity of which millions were at that time dying of starvation pure and simple. It is obvious that a great number of them could easily have been saved if the export of foodstuffs had been abandoned." Ewald Ammende: *Human Life in Russia*, 1936, p 46.

25 Quoted by McNally, *op. cit.*, p 61.

bread, and yet we have to see tons of food wasted here." He was referring to the dumping of sprats. Another declared, "Its time something was done about this wicked waste. I see tons of good food thrown away year after year. When I think what some people would give for this food! Even if it wasn't eaten fresh, it could easily be salted and dried."[24]

Nor is food the only commodity which is restricted. In India the famine is complicated by widespread outbreaks of malaria which the public health authorities are powerless to control because of the shortage of quinine. Yet the *Daily Herald* could write more than ten years ago (1 January 1933): "While 2,000,000 people are dying every year from malaria, supplies of quinine, the most valuable medicine for the prevention and cure of the disease, are being deliberately and drastically curtailed to keep up the price. 'The world needs at least 1,400 tons of quinine a year, but gets 600 tons,' says a special report issued by the Health Organization of the League of Nations.

The growers have greatly improved on the old methods of obtaining the bark of the cinchona tree, from which quinine is extracted, and the trees have been improved by careful cultivation. If the growers liked, all the world's needs could be supplied in a few years and the death roll from malaria at least halved."[25] But even the needs of the dying must take second place to the need to keep prices up.

It must be remembered that the State, the Government, represents the interests of the propertied class in society, the class which benefits from high prices because they are the class which sells the commodity. The State is there to look after the interests of these captains of industry. Small wonder, therefore, that it lays aside a considerable proportion of the taxpayers' money in schemes for the restriction of production in order to keep prices up. It is, therefore, useless to look to the State for radical reforms. Capitalists' interests demand scarcity, and they expect their State to provide it for them.

No doubt, it will still be objected that the shortage of food is caused through there being "simply too many people for the amount of food that can be produced." This good old Malthusian hobby horse is still brought out to justify inaction and the defence of the *status quo*. And it will doubtless be added that anyway the evidence for malnutrition is "greatly exaggerated." Sir Edward Mellanby, some years ago, wrote that: "In Tristan da Cunha, where the main articles of diet are milk, mutton, fish, eggs, and potatoes, *there is no rheumatism or arthritis, there has never been a death in childbirth*, and the teeth are relatively free from caries and incomparably better than in Great Britain." The very fact that Governments have undertaken measures to *restrict* production of food shows that food production can be vastly increased. And during the restrictive phase of capitalist production scientific methods of increasing production have tended to be set aside and neglected. If they were put into operation, there is no doubt that immense output increases could be achieved. "It would scarcely be an exaggeration," wrote Dr Enid Charles, "to say that the world's good production could be increased many times without increasing the area of cultivation."[26]

Remarkable increases in production were in fact effected by the voluntary collectives of the Spanish peasants after the revolution of 1936. In Aragon they increased the wheat crop by an average of 30 per cent. A somewhat smaller increase was obtained with other cereals – potatoes, sugar, beet, lucernes, etc. Increased production of animal stock was even more startling in Aragon, where the numbers of cows and pigs were tripled over a period of eighteen months.[27] But it required a revolution to achieve these results, and the free initiative of liberated peasants. When a powerful centralized government was established again in the summer of 1937, it set to work to destroy the peasant collectives with the result that food production fell once more, so that by the winter of 1938–39 famine conditions prevailed. Nevertheless the Spanish peasants had proved that it can be done.

*   *   *   *

What then is our conclusion? The achievement of full health demands a radical change in our economic system. It requires nothing short of the abolition of poverty, the placing of production on a basis of needs. Let us so organize our economy that when people need a commodity, that commodity is produced. It is necessary to destroy altogether the form of economic organization which only produces when there is a prospect of selling, and which, therefore, inevitably deprives the working class, who cannot afford to buy, and who form the bulk of the community, of the basic necessities of life. This organization lies at the root of contemporary ill-health. Full health is a mirage until profit economy is swept away. But it will be easily realized when the means of life are freely available to all.

[26] *The Twilight of Parenthood*, 1934. Quoted by Burnet and Aykroyd: *Nutrition and Public Health, Quarterly Bulletin of the Health Organization,* League of Nations, Vol IV, No 2, June, 1935. Geneva. For an extended discussion of the problem of increasing agricultural output, see Kropotkin, *Fields, Factories and Workshops.*

[27] Gaston Leval: *Social Reconstruction in Spain,* Freedom Press (Spain and the World), 1938, pp 13, 14. Reprinted in abridged form as 'Collectivizations in Spain'. Freedom Press, 1945.

Aneurin Bevan, 1897-1960   **23**

Aneurin (Nye) Bevan was born in Tredagar, Monmouthshore, Wales in 1897. He worked as a miner from the age of 13 and later became a local leader of the South Wales Miners Federation and a local councillor. He was a committed socialist and strongly influenced by *The Communist Manifesto*. He was elected Member of Parliament for Ebbw Vale in 1929, and held his seat until his death in 1960. As a member of the Socialist League he stood at the left wing of the Labour Party.

As the architect of the National Health Service, Bevan was one of the most influential Labour politicians of the 20th century. Here we present an extract from his book *In Place of Fear*, where he laid out his blueprint for the NHS. It was his intent that the NHS should be a free service, and when prescription charges were first introduced for false teeth and spectacles by Chancellor Hugh Gaitskill (in order to pay for armaments for the cold war), he resigned from the government.

The spirit of Nye Bevan's beliefs and the force with which he conveyed them continue to inspire those who defend the NHS today.

Bevan, A. (1947) *In place of fear*

Chapter Five
A free health service

The field in which the claims of individual commercialism come into most immediate conflict with reputable notions of social values is that of health. That is true both for curative and preventive medicine. The preventive health services of modern society fight the battle over a wider front and therefore less dramatically than is the case with personal medicine.

Yet the victories won by preventive medicine are much the most important for mankind. This is so not only because it is obviously preferable to prevent suffering than to alleviate it. Preventive medicine, which is merely another way of saying health by collective action, builds up a system of social habits which constitute an indispensable part of what we mean by civilisation. In this sphere values that are in essence Socialist, challenge and win victory after victory against the assertions and practice of the Competitive Society.

Modern communities have been made tolerable by the behaviour patterns imposed upon them by the activities of the sanitary inspector and the medical officer of health. It is true, these rarely work out what they do in terms of Socialist philosophy; but that does not alter the fact that the whole significance of their contributions is its insistence that the claims of the individual shall subordinate themselves to social codes that have the collective well-being for their aim, irrespective of the extent to which this frustrates individual greed.

It is only necessary to visit backward countries, or the backward parts of even the most advanced countries, to see what happens when this insistence is overborne. There, the small well-to-do classes furnish themselves with some of the machinery of good sanitation, such as a piped water supply from their own wells, and modern drainage and cesspools. Having satisfied their own needs, they fight strenuously against finding the money to pay for a good general system that would make the same conveniences available to everyone else.

The more advanced the country, the more its citizens insist on a pure water supply, on laws against careless methods of preparing and handling food, and against the making and advertising of harmful drugs. Powerful vested interests with profits at stake compel the public authorities to fight a sustained battle against the assumption that the pursuit of individual profit is the best way to serve the general good.

The same is true in relation to contagious diseases. These are kept at bay by the constant war society is waging in the form of collective action conducted by men and women who are paid fixed salaries. Neither payment by results nor the profit motive are relevant. It would be a fanatical supporter of the Competitive Society who asserted that the work done in the field of preventive medicine shows the enslavement of the individual to what has come to be described in the USA as "statism", and is therefore to be deplored. The more likely retort is that all these are part of the very type of society I am opposing. That is true. But they do not flow from it. They have come in spite of it. They stem from a different order of values. They have established themselves and they are still winning their way by hard struggle. In claiming them, capitalism proudly displays medals won in the battles it has lost.

When we consider the great discoveries in medicine that have revolutionised surgery and the treatment of disease, the same pattern appears. They were made by dedicated men and women whose work was inspired by values that have nothing to do with the rapacious bustle of the Stock Exchange: Pasteur, Simpson, Jenner, Lister, Semelweiss, Fleming, Domagk, Roentgen – the list is endless. Few of these would have described themselves as Socialists, but they can hardly be considered representative types of the Competitive Society.

The same story is now being unfolded in the field of curative medicine. Here individual and collective action are joined in a series of dramatic battles. The collective principle asserts that the resources of medical skill and the apparatus of healing shall be placed at the disposal of the patient, without charge, when he or she needs them; that medical treatment and care should be a communal responsibility; that they should be made available to rich and poor alike in accordance with medical need and by no other criteria. It claims that financial anxiety in time of sickness is a serious hindrance to recovery, apart from its unnecessary cruelty. It insists that no society can legitimately call itself civilised if a sick person is denied medical aid because of lack of means.

Preventable pain is a blot on any society. Much sickness and often permanent disability arise from failure to take early action, and this in its turn is due to high costs and the fear of the effects of heavy bills on the family. The records show that it is the mother in the average family who suffers most from the absence of a free health service. In trying to balance her domestic budget she puts her own needs last.

Society becomes more wholesome, more serene, and spiritually healthier, if it knows that its citizens have at the back of their consciousness the knowledge that not only themselves, but all their fellows, have access, when ill, to the best that medical skill can provide.

But private charity and endowment, although inescapably essential at one time, cannot meet the cost of all this. If the job is to be done, the State must accept financial responsibility.

When I was engaged in formulating the main principles of the British Health Service, I had to give careful study to various proposals for financing it, and as this aspect of the scheme is a matter of anxious discussion in many other parts of the world, it may be useful if I set down the main considerations that guided my choice. In the first place, what was to be its financial relationship with National Insurance; should the Health Service be on an insurance basis? I decided against this. It had always seemed to me that a personal contributory basis was peculiarly inappropriate to a National Health Service. There is, for example, the question of the qualifying period. That is to say, so many contributions for this benefit, and so many more for additional benefits, until enough contributions are eventually paid to qualify the contributor for the full range of benefits.

In the case of health treatment this would give rise to endless anomalies, quite apart from the administrative jungle which would be created. This is already the case in countries where people insure privately for operations as distinct from hospital or vice versa. Whatever may be said for it in private insurance, it would be out of place in a national scheme. Imagine a patient lying in hospital after an operation and ruefully reflecting that if the operation had been delayed another month he would have qualified for the operation benefit. Limited benefits for limited contributions ignore the over-riding consideration that the full range of health machinery must be there in any case, independent of the patient's right of free access to it.

Where a patient claimed he could not afford treatment, an investigation would have to be made into his means, with all the personal humiliation and vexation involved. This scarcely provides the relaxed mental condition needed for a quick and full recovery. Of course there is always the right to refuse treatment to a person who cannot afford it. You can always "pass by on the other side". That may be sound economics. It could not be worse morals.

Some American friends tried hard to persuade me that one way out of the alleged dilemma of providing free health treatment for people able to afford to pay for it, would be to fix an income limit below which treatment would be free whilst those above must pay. This makes the worst of all worlds. It still involves proof, with disadvantages I have already described. In addition it is exposed to lying and cheating and all sorts of insidious nepotism.

And these are the least of its shortcomings. The really objectionable feature is the creation of a two standard health service, one below and one above the salt. It is merely the old British Poor Law system over again. Even if the service given is the same in both categories there will always be the suspicion in the mind of the patient that it is not so, and this again is not a healthy mental state.

The essence of a satisfactory health service is that the rich and the poor are treated alike, that poverty is not a disability, and wealth is not advantaged.

Two ways of trying to meet the high cost of sickness are the group insurance, and the attachment of medical benefits to the terms of employment. Group insurance is merely another way of bringing the advantages of collective action to the service of the individual. All the insurance company does it to assess the degree of risk in any particular field, work out the premium required from a given number of individuals to cover it, add administrative costs and dividends, and then sell the result to the public. They are purveyors of the law of averages. They convert economic continuity, which is a by-product of communal life, into a commodity, and it is then bought and sold like any other commodity.

What is really bought and sold is the group, for the elaborate actuarial tables worked out by the insurance company are nothing more than a description of the patterns of behaviour of that collectivity which is the subject of assessment for the time being. To this the company adds nothing but its own profits. This profit is therefore wholly gratuitous because it does not derive from the creation of anything. Group insurance is the most expensive, the least scientific, and clumsiest way of mobilising collective security for the individual good.

In many countries the law implicitly recognises this because the insurance company is required to invest some, if not all, its income in trustee stock, national bonds and debentures. In other words, the company must invest in those properties which bear the strongest imprint of continuous communal action. The nearer the investment approaches to those forms of property which are most characteristic of competitive capitalism, the less the element of collective security, and therefore the less desirable from the point of view of insurance. There never can be a clearer case of the private exploitation of a product publicly produced.

Where medical benefits are attached to employment as a term of the contract the situation is somewhat different. Here is an instance where the workers, as occupational groups, succeed in accomplishing what they have failed to do or not tried to do as enfranchised citizens. It has the one advantage that the employer in such a case will be less eager to Lobby against legislation for a national health scheme. He may be inclined to support national proposals because these will make others share part of his burden. As a political tactic, therefore, occupational medical benefits have something to be said for them; and the workers enjoy some protection in the meantime whilst the national scheme is being held up.

But they are no substitute for a national scheme. An industrial basis is too narrow for the wide range of medical needs which should be met, both for the worker and for his family. The incidence of sickness vary from industry to industry and so do the rates of economic obsolescence and unemployment. We had experience of this in Britain where certain of the Approved Societies under the old National Health Insurance recruited a disproportionate number of members from industries with a high degree of sickness and accident rate, and affected by serious industrial depression. The result was that these Approved Societies were compelled to curtail benefits to their members, whilst other Societies with a different industrial composition were able to distribute the full benefits. That situation consequently helped the strong and hurt the weak.

There are two final objections to the methods I have been describing. They create a chaos of little or big projects, all aiming at the same end; assisting the individual in time of sickness. A whole network of strong points emerge, each with a vested interest in preventing a rational national scheme from being created. Thus to the property Lobby is added the Lobby of those who stand to lose under the national project. In the end they may have to be bought out at great cost in time, effort and money.

The second objection is even more serious. These schemes all have for their aim the consumption of the apparatus of health. But they leave the creation of that apparatus without plan and central direction. In place of a rational relationship between all its parts, there arises a patch–quilt of local paternalisms. My experience has taught me that there is no worse enemy to the intelligent planning of a national health service, especially on the hospital side. Warm gushes of self-indulgent emotion are an unreliable source of driving power in the field of health organisation. The benefactor tends also to become a petty tyrant, not only willing his cash, but sending his instructions along with it.

The other alternative is a flat rate compulsory contribution for all, covering the full range of health treatment, or a limited part of it. There is no advantage whatever in this. It is merely a form of poll tax with all its disagreeable features. It collects the same from the rich and the poor, and this is manifestly unjust. On no showing can it be called insurance.

One thing the community cannot do is insure against itself. What it can and must do is to set aside an agreed proportion of the national revenues for the creation and maintenance of the service it has pledged itself to provide. This is not so much insurance as a prudent policy of capital investment. There is a further objection to a universal contribution, and that is its wholly unnecessary administrative cost; unless it is proposed to have graduated contributions for graduated benefits, and I have already pointed out the objections to that. Why should *all* have contribution cards if *all* are assumed to be insured? This merely leads to a colossal Record Office, employing scores of thousands of clerks solemnly restating in the most expensive manner what the law will already have said; namely, that *all* citizens are in the scheme.

The means of collecting the revenues for the health service are already in the possession of most modern states, and that is the normal system of taxation.

This was the course which commended itself to me and it is the basis of the finance of the British Health Service. Its revenues are provided by the Exchequer in the same way as other forms of public expenditure. I am afraid this is not yet fully understood. Many people still think they pay for the National Health Service by way of their contribution to the National Insurance Scheme. The confusion arose because the new service sounded so much like the old National Health Insurance, and it was launched on the same date as the National Insurance Scheme. Some part of the misunderstanding was caused by the propaganda of the BMA, which warned the people at one time that, although they would be paying their contributions, the Health Service would not be there to meet their needs. There was a certain irony about this, because when the time came for enrolment in the Health Service more than ninety per cent of the population hastened go get their names in; some under the impression, helped by the BMA itself, that they had started paying for it. This gave me some quiet satisfaction.

Brian Abel-Smith, 1926–96 and Peter Townsend, 1928–   **24**

Brian Abel-Smith was born in London in 1926. After postwar army service, he obtained his education at Cambridge and joined the London School of Economics where he remained until his retirement in 1991. He spent most of his career in the Department of Social Administration and became professor in 1961. He was also a member of the Fabian Society and advised Labour governments in Britain on social policies. As a consultant of the World Health Organisation, he advised more than 60 countries on how to set up and consolidate social security and health systems. Brian Abel-Smith died in 1996.

Peter Townsend has written extensively on poverty, health, social policy and old age. He was a founding member of the Child Poverty Action Group in 1965 and its chair from 1969-89. He was a member of *The Black Report* working party, which reported in 1980 (see Chapter 27). He continues to work on issues of poverty – increasingly on its global eradication. He is Emeritus Professor and Senior Research Fellow of Social Policy at the University of Bristol and Visiting Professor of Social Policy at the London School of Economics.

Together Abel-Smith and Townsend wrote *The poor and the poorest*, first published in 1965. This was a study reviewing secondary sources on income and expenditure data in order to uncover social aspects of the relationship between poverty and income distribution. In the tradition established by Seebohm Rowntree, they looked at the extent of poverty and the distribution of income using data from two surveys conducted by the Ministry of Labour, making a concerted effort to look at the evidence rather than be swayed by 'general assumptions'. Here we present 'Chapter 5: Conclusions'. Despite the complexity of some of the statistical detail, which is openly described, the conclusion is simple: that greater affluence has not led to greater equality.

Abel–Smith, B. and Townsend, P. (1965) *The poor and the poorest*

Chapter 5
Conclusions

The limited object of the work upon which this report is based was to find out from data collected in government income and expenditure surveys in two postwar years as much as possible about the levels of living and the social characteristics of the poorest section of the population in the United Kingdom. In the process we have defined and used a national assistance standard of living, have reapplied a subsistence standard adopted in an earlier study of poverty (by Rowntree and Lavers in 1950), and have given some account of the extent to which households range in income and expenditure from the average for their type. In this chapter we will first of all discuss whether the evidence for 1953-54 and 1960 allows us to draw conclusions about changes in living conditions between the two years. We will then discuss briefly some of the implications of this report for future research, for government information services and for government action.

Changes between *1953-54* and *1960*

Chapters 3 and 4 describe the proportions of the population found in 1953-54 and 1960 to have low levels of living, defined as less than 140 per cent of the basic national assistance scale plus rent and/or other housing costs. It is a tenable view that the basic assistance scale, with the addition of *actual* housing expenditure and a modest margin for special needs and disregards, represent the officially defined minimum level of living at a particular time. The data for 1953-54 were calculated from expenditure and the data for 1960 from income. We set out below the results for the two years and discuss *in detail how closely they can be compared*. The matter is complex, not only because expenditure is taken into account in the one year and income in the other but also for the methodological reasons advanced in Chapter 2. It is worth reviewing carefully because the data represent the best available information about the living standards of poor households in the postwar years.

Table 25 shows the percentages and numbers of the total population recorded as having low levels of living in the two years. The crude figures *suggest* a large increase in both the proportion and number of persons with low levels of living. Under 140 per cent of the basic national assistance scale were 10.1 per cent of the survey households in 1953-54 and 17.9 per cent in 1960. The percentage of persons in these households was 7.8 per cent in 1953-54 and 14.2 per cent in 1960. The largest increase took place at the lower levels and it was at these lower levels that the increase in household size was at its greatest. Under the basic assistance rates, the proportion of households increased from 2.1 to 4.7 per cent and the proportion of persons from 1.2 to 3 8 per cent. The estimated total of persons in households

Table 25: Percentage of households and persons and number of persons with low levels of living, 1953-54 and 1960

Total expenditure*	Percentage of households		Percentage of persons		Estimated persons in United Kingdom (000s)	
	1953-54	1960	1953-54	1960	1953-54	1960
Under 80	0.5	1.3	0.3	0.9	152	471
80-89	0.6	1.0	0.2	0.9	101	471
90-99	1.0	2.4	0.7	2.0	354	1,048
100-109	1.9	4.7	1.4	2.8	709	1,467
110-119	1.7	3.1	1.4	2.4	709	1,257
120-129	2.0	2.7	1.8	2.5	911	1,310
130-139	2.4	2.8	2.0	2.7	1,012	1,414
140 and over	89.9	82.1	92.2	85.8	46,663	44,945
Total	100.0	100.0	100.0	100.0	50,611	52,383

*(1953-54) or income (1960) as percentage of basic NA scale plus rent/housing.

with low levels of living increased from nearly 4 million to nearly 7½ million. The estimated total of persons in households living below the basic assistance scale increased from about 600,000 to about 2,000,000.

In considering these increases let us first review the comparability of the samples for the two years. Both under-represented the sick and aged (and therefore national assistance recipients). But, as shown earlier, the under-representation was greater in 1953-54 than in 1960. The crude figures suggest that the proportion of the population living at less than 40 per cent above the basic assistance scale increased from 7½ to 14.2 per cent. We calculate that a quarter to a third of the difference can be explained by the difference in the extent to which the two samples represented the United Kingdom population of the two years.

Expenditure and income

Second, was any of the recorded increase in the proportion of households with low levels of living due to adopting an expenditure basis for the analysis of the 1953-54 data and an income basis for the 1960 data? In general it has already been shown that expenditure tends to be overstated and income understated in inquiries of this kind, particularly among low income households.[1] Thus one would expect to find too few persons recorded as having low levels of living in 1953 and too many in 1960. Moreover, the aged, who were heavily represented among the poorer households, tend to be dissavers. Again, one would expect expenditure figures recorded over a three week period to be less widely dispersed than income figures, even possibly than *'normal'* income figures. Thus there would be a higher proportion of households recorded as having *temporary low* income in 1960 than a *more permanently low* expenditure in 1953-54.

Ideally we would have wished to examine for 1960 the relationship between expenditure and 'normal' income for each individual household in the sample. In practice we could only examine this relationship for a sub-sample of 152. In addition we were able to take into account a special analysis of the 60 households in the sample of that year with an income of under 60s, which had been produced by the Ministry. On the basis of the results from this sub-sample we were able to make broad estimates for the whole sample. These are compared with the income figures and with the 1953-54 expenditure figures in Table 26. Instead of 17.9 per cent of households, and 14.2 per cent of persons, living below or just above the national assistance standard it emerges that there would have been 15.9 per cent and 12.4 per cent respectively if current expenditure instead of normal income had been taken as the criterion. Instead of nearly 7½ million persons being in poverty or on its margins there would have been about 6½ millions. The basis for the expenditure figures given for 1960 in the table is explained in Appendix 4 [not reproduced here, Eds].

Although the 1960 expenditure estimates must be treated with caution since they are based on a small sub-sample of households investigated in the 1960 survey (percentages are therefore placed in brackets), two broad conclusions can be drawn from the table. First, the expenditure data confirm the income data in showing an increase between 1953-54 and 1960 in the numbers and proportion of the population living below or just above the national assistance 'standard'. Second, the evidence suggests a marked increase in the proportion living *below* the basic national assistance rates. Although the overall percentage living in poverty or on the margins of poverty is lower according to the expenditure than according to the income criterion, the percentage *below* the scale rate is higher.

[1] See Chapter 2 above [not reproduced here, Eds].

Table 26: Percentage of households and persons with low expenditure, 1953-54, and low income, 1960

Total income/ expenditure as percentage of national assistance scale plus rent/ housing	1953-54			1960		
			Estimated nos of persons in the UK			Estimated nos of persons in the UK
	Households	Persons	(000s)	Households	Persons	(000s)
Income						
Under 100	–	–	–	4.7	3.8	1,990
100 and under	–	–	–	13.3	10.4	5,448
140	–	–	–			44,945
140 and over	–			82.1	85.8	
Total	–	–	–	100	100	52,383
N =		–	–	3,540	10,765	–
Expenditure						
Under 100	2.1	1.2	607	(5.8)	(4.3)	2,250
100 but under 140	8.0	6.6	3,341	(10.1)	(8.1)	4,843
140 and over	89.9	92.2	46,663	(84.1)	(87.6)	45,290
Total	100	100	50,611	100	100	52,383
N =	3,225	10,270	–	212*	418*	–

Note: *Sub-sample of 152 households plus data for 60 households with income of under £3. See Appendix 4 for further details* [not reproduced here, Eds].

Table 26 also suggests that possibly a third of the increase between 1953 and 1960 in numbers of persons at low levels of living is due to our having taken an income basis for measurement in the second but not the first of these years. It is disappointing that the Ministry has not yet published information about this important matter, showing the distribution around the average and the disparity between income and expenditure for each household type

Reasons for more people living at low levels of living

Part of the increase in the proportion of households with low levels of living seems however to be genuine. The most obvious reason for this is that the proportion of the aged (and particularly the proportion of the very aged) in the population increased between the two years. Between 1953 and 1960, the proportion of the population of the United Kingdom who were aged 65 and over increased from 11.1 to 11.7 per cent. We found that over two-thirds of the households with low expenditure in the 1953-54 survey had retired heads. A second reason is the increase in the proportion of large families in the population.

In Table 27 we show the percentage of households of different size recorded as having low levels of living in the two years.

Table 27: Percentage of households of different size with low levels of living, 1953-54 and 1960

Number of persons in household	1953-54 (low expenditure)	1960 (low income)
1	38.6	52.1
2	9.6	18.2
3	4.9	7.5
4	4.6	6.4
5	5.4	10.0
6+	11.5	25.2
All sizes	10.1	17.9

Among households of every size the proportion with low levels of living increased. The proportion of two-person households nearly doubled. The proportional increase was smaller for households of three or four persons and smallest for one-person households where the proportion with low expenditure was already nearly 39 per cent in 1953-54. The largest increase was among the very large households with six or more persons. There were 11½ per cent of such households with low levels of living in 1953-54 and 25 per cent in 1960.

The age distribution of persons in households with low levels of living is shown in Table 28.

In general there was a modest increase in the proportion of children

Table 28: Age distribution of persons with low levels of living 1953-54 and 1960

Household expenditure*	Year	Age			
		Over 16	5-15	Under 5	All ages
Under 100	1953-54	83.1	10.5	6.4	100.0
	1960	66.9	21.1	12.0	100.0
100-119	1953-54	68.3	23.2	8.5	100.0
	1960	79.7	14.6	5.7	100.0
120-139	1953-54	69.1	19.6	11.3	100.0
	1960	62.2	25.3	12.5	100.0
All under 140	1953-54	70.9	19.5	9.6	100.0
	1960	69.9	20.2	9.9	100.0

* (1953-54) or income (1960) as percentage of basic national assistance scale plus rent/housing.

in the sampled households with low levels of living from 29.1 to 30.1 per cent. This concealed bigger changes at the different levels. There was in fact a fall in the proportion of children at and just above the assistance level from 31.7 to 20.3 per cent. This was more than balanced partly by an increase in the proportion of children at the higher level but also, and perhaps more importantly, by a greater increase in the proportion of children in households under the assistance level – from 16.9 to 33.1 per cent. Too much weight should not however be placed upon these figures in view of the small numbers, involved in many of these categories.

Between 1953 and 1960, the proportion of children increased by about 0.5 per cent in both the total population and in the samples. The proportion of children in households with low levels of living increased by 1 per cent. These modest changes conceal much larger changes in family size. While the total population increased by 3.5 per cent between the two years, the number of families with four dependent children increased by about 20 per cent, with five children by about 26 per cent and with six or more children by 45 per cent.[2] Moreover, the economic position of large families was relatively worse in 1960 than in 1953. While we have shown that the general level of incomes of the country increased by just over 50 per cent in money terms, the family allowance for the second child remained at 8*s* in both years, while the family allowance for a third or subsequent children increased from 8*s* to 10*s* – an increase of only 25 per cent. No doubt the failure of family allowances to keep pace with the living standards of the community contributed to the higher proportion of households found to have low levels of living in 1960 than in 1953-54. But in view of the fact that only 14 per cent of low income households were found in 1960 consisting of a man, woman and three or more children, the changing size and economic position of the family can only have accounted for an increase of 3 or 4 per cent in the proportion of households with low levels of living. A third reason for the recorded increase in the proportion of the population with low levels of living was the increase in the proportion dependent for long periods on sickness benefits. This is partly due to the relative increase in the proportion of the population aged between 55 and 65 and also to the relative increase in the proportions of men in this age–group who are chronically sick.[3] In addition to the increases in the proportions of the aged, of large families and of the chronic sick, we cannot exclude the possibility that although *average* earnings increased by about 50 per cent, the lowest earnings increased by less than 50 per cent.

[2] Calculated from statistics on family allowances given in the Ministry of Pensions and National Insurance Reports for 1953 and 1960.

[3] Between 1951 and 1960 "there was ... an appreciable rise of chronic sickness among men in their late fifties, and a very substantial one, amounting to 30 per cent, in men in their early sixties." The proportion of insured men aged 61-63 who were absent sick from work for over three months increased from 9 per cent in 1953-54 to 10.6 per cent in 1960. Morris, J.N. *Uses of Epidemiology*, 2nd edition, Edinburgh & London, Livingstone, 1964, p 11.

Definitions of poverty

What implications does this analysis hold for the future? First, much more thought needs to be given to concepts of poverty. The subsistence standards used by earlier writers on poverty seem at first sight to lend themselves to comparisons over time. This approach allows a basket of foodstuffs and other goods to be defined as necessary to provide subsistence. The cost of purchasing these goods can be calculated for different years and the number of households with insufficient income to purchase the goods can be ascertained. Although the principle seems easy to state, there are problems of applying it in practice. For example, the goods on the market at the later period may not be the same as at the earlier period. The cumbrous garments which convention required women to wear at the beginning of this century were unlikely to be found on the market in the nineteen-thirties let alone today. Electricity has replaced oil lamps and candles. Even food habits have changed. These are among the problems which face those who attempt to apply the same poverty line at different periods. Again, the choice of goods that are selected initially cannot be defended in narrowly 'physical' or 'nutritional' terms. In laying down what articles of clothing and items of food are necessary for physical efficiency those in charge of the surveys have been unable to prevent judgments about what is conventional or customary from creeping into their lists and definitions.

There are further kinds of difficulties. There is, for example, a difference between defining poverty in any objective or partly objective sense and defining it subjectively – as felt by the individual or by particular social groups. In any objective sense the word has no absolute meaning which can be applied in all societies at all times. Poverty is a relative concept. Saying who is in poverty is to make a relative statement – rather like saying who is short or heavy. But it is also a statement of a much more complex kind than one referring to a unilineal scale of measurement. It refers to a variety of conditions involving differences in home environment, material possessions and educational and occupational resources as well as in financial resources – most of which are measurable, at least in principle. Income or expenditure as defined in this paper should be regarded as only one of the possible indicators. We need to develop other indicators of the command of individuals and families over resources. Our frame of reference can be local, national or international society, according to our interests. In saying all this we are saying nothing new. The fact that poverty is essentially a relative concept and essentially one which refers to a variety of conditions and not simply a financial condition has been accepted overtly or implicitly by leading writers on the subject almost as long as poverty studies have been undertaken.

Implications for government information and research

Reports on government surveys of the population still contain far too little social information about the poorest sections of the population. This is true not only of the family expenditure surveys, but also of nutrition surveys.[4] Despite searching public criticisms of the analysis of nutritional data the National Food Survey Committee has failed to provide information about families with children, particularly large families, falling short of the standards recommended by the British Medical Association.[5] No government can expect to pursue rational policies in social security and welfare unless information about living conditions, particularly the living conditions of the poor, is regularly collected, analysed and reported.

The first aim should be to develop various standards which indicate need or poverty. Budgets necessary to purchase minimum nutrition, of the kind developed by the United States Department of Agriculture,[6] might be worked out. The environmental, including housing, resources of families might be more carefully assessed, as also the social and other resources, they require to overcome disability.

The second aim should be to collect information regularly and publish annual reports. It would of course be possible to publish a report complementary to that on the Family Expenditure Survey, showing the sources of income, incomes and expenditures of households receiving certain kinds of social benefits, or of particular kinds of household known to have exceptional social and financial problems – fatherless families, large families or the families of the long-term unemployed. The Central Statistical Office has carried out some useful analyses of redistribution, based on the expenditure surveys, but they give emphasis to overall trends rather than the particlar circumstances of poor families as related to middle-income or wealthy families.[7] Government sources in the United States are now publishing very informative analyses of poverty in that country.[8] Perhaps in time the same might be possible in the United Kingdom.

The third aim should be to carry out some immediate inquiries into the information about the relationship between income and expenditure, as collected in family expenditure surveys. In addition, more needs to be known about non-respondents. We believe that such inquiries would help to ensure that future family expenditure surveys can be reliably used to depict the socio-economic conditions of particular groups of the population.[9]

[4] See, for example, the latest Annual Report of the National Food Survey Committee, *Domestic Food Consumption and Expenditure: 1962*, London HMSO, 1964.

[5] Lambert, R, *op cit.*

[6] Though we hope certain technical criticisms might be overcome. See US Department of Agriculture, Agricultural Research Service, *Family, Food Plans and Food Costs*, Home Economics Research Report, No 20, Nov 1962; and Household Food Consumption Service, *Food Consumption and Dietary Levels of Households in the US*, Spring 1955, ARS 62-6, Aug 1957.

[7] See 'The Impact of Taxes and Social Service Benefits on Different Groups of Households', *Economic Trends*, Nov 1962, and 'The Incidence of Taxes and Social Service Benefits in 1961 and 1962', *Economic Trends*, Feb 1964. See also Nicholson J.L. *Redistribution of Income in the United Kingdom in 1959, 1957 and 1953*, London, Bowes & Bowes, 1965.

[8] Especially Orshansky M. 'Counting the Poor: Another Look at the Poverty Profile', *Social Security Bulletin*, Vol 28, Jan 1965.

[9] A number of improvements have been made in the family expenditure surveys in recent years. We understand that a study of *individual* discrepancies in income/expenditure totals is now in hand and that statistical analyses other than those which are already published are passed on to the Ministry of Pensions.

Implications for policy

One conclusion that can be drawn from both surveys is that national assistance is inefficient. While it is impossible to give precise figures it is clear that substantial numbers in the population were not receiving national assistance in 1953-54 and 1960 and yet seemed, *prima facie,* to qualify for it. In the latter year, for example there were nearly one million persons who had pensions or other state benefits and whose incomes fell below assistance rates plus rent.

This national evidence is extremely important and confirms what has been concluded from independent studies, particularly of the aged, in recent years.[10] It is given greater force by the unambiguous statement in the recent report of a Government committee of inquiry into the impact of rates on households: "We estimate that about half a million retired householders are apparently eligible for assistance but not getting it."[11]

This is not the place for a searching discussion of reforms in social security. All that we wish to point out is that there is a two-fold implication for social policy of the evidence in this report – not only that a substantial minority of the population in addition to those receiving national assistance live at or below national assistance standards, but also that a substantial minority are not receiving national assistance and yet appear to qualify for it. The legitimacy of the system of national assistance is therefore called into question.

Possibly the most novel finding is the extent of poverty among children. For over a decade it has been generally assumed that such poverty as exists is found overwhelmingly among the aged. Unfortunately, it has not been possible to estimate from the data used in this study exactly how many persons over minimum pensionable age were to be found among the 7½ million persons with low income in 1960. However, such data as we have suggest that the number may be around 3 million. There were thus more people who were not aged than were aged among the poor households of 1960. We have estimated earlier that there were about 2¼ million children in low income households in 1960. Thus quantitatively the problem of poverty among children is more than two-thirds of the size of poverty among the aged. This fact has not been given due emphasis in the policies of the political parties. It is also worth observing that there were substantially more children in poverty than adults of working age.

There is a simple if relatively expensive remedy for the problem of poverty among children – to substantially increase family allowances, particularly for the larger family. Alternatively, part of the problem could be dealt with at relatively low cost by allowing national assistance to be drawn despite the fact that the breadwinner is receiving full-time earnings. Such a proposal would mean over-riding more than

[10] Cole D. with Utting J. *The Economic Circumstances of Old People,* Occasional Papers on Social Administration No 4, Welwyn, The Codicote Press, 1962; Townsend P. and Wedderburn D. *The Aged in the Welfare State,* Occasional Papers on Social Administration No 14, London, Bell, 1965.

[11] This was a conservative estimate made after consultations with the National Assistance Board. *Report of the Committee of Inquiry into the Impact of Rates on Households* (The Allen Report), Cmnd 2582, London, HMSO, 1965, p 117 and pp 221-225. The Government Social Survey carried out a special survey for the Committee in 1963 which was in all major respects identical to the family expenditure survey.

a century of conventional wisdom about incentives. However assistance is paid to families receiving full-time earnings in several States in the United States and this policy enoys the tacit support of the American trade unions.[12] The acceptance of this principle would make it possible to deal with the problem of poverty among 'wage stopped' families already receiving assistance and among large families with a breadwinner in full-time work. In the case of the latter group, however, there would remain the problem of families who were not prepared to apply to the Board for help.

[12] Sinfield A. 'Supplementation of Earnings by Public Assistance in the United States' (unpublished paper) University of Essex, 1965.

Summary

In summary, we have in this chapter brought together the statistics about low levels of living which we presented respectively in Chapter 3, for 1953-54, and in Chapter 4, for 1960. Although we have tried to apply definitions and procedures which would allow the statistics for the two years to be compared, we realise that it is difficult, for technical reasons, to draw firm conclusions. Between 1953 and 1960 the Ministry of Labour surveys suggest that the number of persons living at low levels increased from 7.8 per cent to 14.2 per cent. Of the difference of 6.4 per cent we would estimate that about 1½ per cent was due to a better representation in the sample of aged persons in 1960 than in 1953 and another 0.5 or 1 per cent to a fuller representation in the sample of national assistance recipients other than the aged. Very little of the difference seems to be due to a change, relative to wages, in the definition of 'low levels of living', but part of it (about 2 per cent) seems to be due to the fact that the definition was based on income in 1960 and expenditure in 1953-54. Nonetheless, some part of the apparent increase from 7.8 to 14.2 per cent seems atrributable to (a) the relative increase in the number of men in late middle age who are chronically sick, and (c) the relative increase in the number of families with four or more children, at a time when family allowances have increased much less than average industrial earnings and when the wages of some low-paid workers may not have increased as much as average industrial earnings. On the whole the data we have presented contradicts the commonly held view that a trend towards greater equality has accompanied the trend towards great affluence.

In general, we regard our figures for 1960 to be the more accurate even though we believe that they understate the numbers of the population with low levels of living because of the under-representation of the aged and the sick. We may summarise our findings for that year by saying that about 5-6 per cent of the population were in low income households because wages, even when supplemented by family allowances, were insufficient to raise them above the minimum level. A further 3-4 per cent were in households receiving social insurance benefits (principally pensions) but the latter were insufficient. Many such households would probably be entitled to national assistance but for various reasons had not applied for it. A further 4–5 per cent of the population were in low income households because, under various regulations, they were not entitled to the full scale of national assistance grant or because the minimum we have taken is considerably above the *basic* national assistance scale.

Even if we take a substantially lower base line – the basic assistance scale plus rent – we find that about 2 million people (3.8 per cent of the population) were living in households with exceptionally low incomes. For about a quarter of them the problem was inadequate earnings and family allowances; for nearly half of them the problem was inadequate social insurance benefits coupled with unwillingness to apply for national assistance and for the remainder the amount of national assistance being received was apparently inadequate.

In terms of national information we conclude from the evidence that steps should be taken by the government to ensure that regular surveys are made of the living conditions of the poorest households in our society and that reports should be published showing their sources of income and how their social characteristics compare with those of other households.

Finally, we conclude that the evidence of substantial numbers of the population living below national assistance level, and also of substantial numbers seeming to be eligible for national assistance but not receiving it, calls for a radical review of the whole social security scheme. Moreover, the fact that nearly a third of the poor were children suggests the need for a readjustment of priorities in plans for extensions and developments.

Robert Roberts, 1905-74

A cornershop in Salford

Robert Roberts was born in Salford in 1905. The fourth of seven children he left school at 14 and though serving an apprenticeship in engineering he joined the ranks of the unemployed. He undertook further study and subsequently became a language teacher at a commercial college. He began to write while recovering from TB and his short stories won several awards. Roberts was deeply involved with the labour movement and he also taught illiterate and educationally deprived prisoners at Strangeways prison in Manchester.

The classic slum is an autobiographical account of Salford life in the first half of the 20th century. Rather than being the report of a study by a wealthy, educated middle-class philanthropist, this is a first-hand account of poverty. Robert Roberts lived the grinding poverty of the slums of Salford, where his family ran a corner shop. The book is a finely detailed account of the condition of the day-to-day lives of those who lived in the area and their cultural mores, from a perspective of personal reminiscence. This is combined with social history and references to secondary sources to give a background of broader economic and social conditions and how these affected life in the slums. The book covers topics such as class structure, possessions, and manners and morals. Here we extract sections from chapters called: 'The common scene' and 'Food, drink and physic'.

Roberts, R. (1971) *The classic slum: Salford life in the first quarter of the century*

Chapter 5
The common scene

> I heard the sighs of men that have no skill
> To speak of their distress, no, nor the will.
> WILFRED OWEN

Whatever it was that went to make the lower-working-class home 'cosy', parents had first, often sole, rights in it. They took, of course, the best bed and bedding and the two cushioned armchairs nearest the fire. In some families children were forbidden to sit on these at any time; during parental absence they had to remain vacated thrones of power. To many people the idea of sharing food and possessions equitably with their children would have seemed preposterous; yet adult life with all its little prerogatives was often no more than a stake in common poverty.

The homes of the very poor contained little or no bought furniture. They made do with boxes and slept in their clothes and in what other garments they could beg or filch. Of such people there were millions. Seebohm Rowntree's *Poverty: a study of town life* (1901), for example, showed that 'one in four of the inhabitants of York lacked the bare necessities of life'. Our village, like so many others that went to make the cities of thriving industrial Britain, was stamped with the same poverty, and this right to the outbreak and beyond of the first world war. In among the respectable rows of 'two up and two down' houses we had the same blocks of hovels sharing a single tap, earth closet and open midden: each house with a candle for light, an oil lamp or a bare gas jet. Coal the 'low class' and 'no class' rarely bought; they picked or stole it from spoil heap and wharf, or, in bad times, dragged the canals for droppings from barges. The more fortunate rolled home a hundred-weight or so weekly in an iron-wheeled wagon from coal yards, dark, temple-like sheds where great cones of fuel rose among the gloom like a miniature volcanic range. Any customer wanting less than half a hundredweight was denied a vehicle and had to bear off his load in a sack over the shoulder. People like publicans who bought the stuff a ton at a time gave by this an impressive display of affluence. Few were so fortunate.

In 1906 the Board of Trade figures showed that half the women in industrial Britain earned under 10s for a week's work of seldom less than fifty-four hours. The Sweated Industries Exhibition organized by the *Daily News* in 1907 shocked at least the more sensitive visitors into realizing the conditions in which so many of the poor were living. Women, they learned working fourteen hours a day, made artificial violets and geraniums for 7d a gross, buttercups for 3d and roses for 1s 3d a gross. They put 384 hooks on cards for one penny and spent eighteen hours at it to earn 5s a week.[1] Matchbox makers got a similar sum. In sweated sewing shops machinists made pinafores and babies' bonnets for 2s a dozen and ran up a gross of ties to earn 5s. Shirt manufacture brought them in less than a penny an hour. These were but a few examples in a massive chronicle of brutal exploitation. What it meant in terms of human suffering could be glimpsed, at times, only too terribly, in the columns of the local news-sheet. There was Emily Hughes, now.

One January day in 1913 Mrs Hughes, living in a street close by ours, found herself short of fuel. She went into the back yard and left her young daughter in the kitchen, where there was a small fire but no guard. When the mother returned her child was in flames. A neighbour ran in and wrapped a rug about her, but the little girl died the same day in hospital.

At the coroner's court the mother was questioned:

Coroner:	'You had a fireguard?'
Woman:	'I had no guard.'
Coroner:	'But one was seen on the same day as the accident before your fire.'
Woman:	'Someone came into my house and put it there while I was at the hospital. I don't know who. It did not belong to me.'
Coroner:	'You know the police can prosecute you?'
Woman:	'Yes.'
Coroner:	'You know you can be sent to gaol?'
Woman:	'Yes'
Coroner:	'It is very creditable of you to have spoken in this way.'
Woman:	'I could not afford a guard. I have had no fire for many days, but occasionally I managed to get a few cinders and make one to keep the children warm.'

A verdict of accidental death was returned and the woman put into touch with an officer from the NSPCC.

[1] Of 304 women imprisoned in Strangeways between 4 August and 4 September 1914, forty-three were 'chars', thirty-two 'laundresses' (in court every washerwoman called herself a laundress), twenty-four 'servants' and thirty-seven 'hawkers'. At regular intervals the police made drives against 'illegal street traders' – those who tried to get a living by selling bootlaces and similar articles from door to door. Pedlars without licence, like the hawker with his hand-cart, they haunted the ways, a permanent part of the common scene.

The local newspaper, in an earlier year, had reported too on a woman, unnamed, found lying by some workmen on bare boards in a property boarded off as derelict and insanitary. By her side lay a baby, two days old. She was living on the food brought to her by neighbours, the poorest of the poor. 'Mother and child were removed to the workhouse', where she was visited later by a member of the Ladies' Health Society, who, 'not seeing the infant, inquired for it'.

> The mother said, 'God has been good and taken it.'
> 'Is that the way you view it?' the lady asked.
> '*Yes,*' she said. 'I have had nine, but thank the Lord I've buried six, and hard work I've had to find food for those left.'

The Ladies' Health Society worked bravely among us, especially in the early years of the century. Together with the 'Sanitary Society', they visited the 'lowest classes' and found

> much that is saddening: but there are bright spots – clean homes, pretty little sitting-room kitchens, pictures on the wall, clean hearths, chests of highly polished mahogany drawers, a steady husband, a tidy wife and children.

> The lime and whitewash brushes have done excellent service and have been in constant demand. They were lent out thirty-six times last year, thus sweetening and purifying the houses.

(Brushes were loaned by the corporation.) The Society also sold ten hundredweights of carbolic soap and distributed six hundredweights of carbolic powder. One woman who kept her windows dirty so that people couldn't mark her poverty was promised a blind if she would only clean them. Light was certainly needed by her neighbour: she was engaged in hemming handkerchiefs at sevenpence a gross (no cotton provided) and had to fetch and carry her materials to and from the warehouse.

The corporation lent out its whitewash brushes, distributed free bags of lime and bottles of a preventive medicine popularly known as 'diarrhoea mixture', and urged hygiene on all the populace. And no wonder. In summer house-flies and bluebottles swarmed, every kitchen alive: sticky, foul-smelling paper traps dangled about, dark with their writhing bodies. And the bed bugs! With the warm days they appeared in battalions, first in the hovels, then in the better-class houses, where people waged campaigns against their sweet-odoured, sickening presence. They lime-washed bedrooms ('bug binding' was the delicate term for this) and drenched them with 'Klenzit Kleener' disinfectant.[2] The blue flames of blowlamps licked spring mattress, floorboard, cracked walls and ceilings: but still they came, creeping along joists and through party walls until even the valiant cleanly housewife gave up in despair and prayed for cold weather. Through summer days one saw the 'fever' van carrying off some child, who only too often would be seen no more. In school, inspection showed whole classes of children infested with head vermin; many had body lice. The worst would sit isolated from the rest in a small sanitary cordon of humiliation. They would later be kept at home, their heads shaven, reeking of some rubbed-in disinfectant. Their status did not suffer from this treatment: they had already reached rock-bottom.

One saw a quarter of a class sixty 'strong' come to school barefoot. Many had rickets, bow legs or suffered from open sores. It is true that from the early years of the century the health of the people as a whole was improving steadily. Infant mortality, for instance, in the first decade decreased by 40 per cent and there was a considerable decline in the number of deaths from children's diseases generally. Nevertheless, in great slum pockets the late nineteenth-century social and economic pattern still persisted and it is doubtful whether the health of their inhabitants was much better than it had been twenty years before.

In 1899, of 12,000 men from the city who volunteered for service in the South African war, 8,000 were rejected outright and only 1,200 accepted as completely fit, though army pass standards had been lowered to those of 1815.[3] The figures did not take into account the 'large number' who applied and who looked so obviously unfit that doctors 'did not even bother to examine them'. Fifteen years later, at the start of the first world war, men poured again in thousands from the ginnels eager to serve and again they were turned down in vast numbers, the authorities being shocked at their wretched physical standard. The new century, it seemed, had done little as yet to improve Britain's slum manhood.

Our medical officer's report to the education committee in 1905 noted outbreaks among children of 'small-pox, typhus fever, enteric fever, scarlet fever and diphtheria', only a few of the diseases mentioned. 'A large proportion of the pupils', the report added, 'show signs of rickets.' There had been considerable distress during the winter, but the children had 'much appreciated the free breakfasts provided'. Some went hungry every day. In our own school the more ravenous were know as 'bread horses'. At play-time the bread horse would stagger across the yard with another boy on his back in return for a scrap to eat from the rider's lunch. At the local mission hall, where scores of men went for a night's rest, those with twopence were asked to go to a doss house, so that the entirely destitute could have a mission bed. Yet no one in public seemed unduly depressed by it all.

[2] A local firm – 'Bed Cleaners & Purifiers' – promised short-term immunity as 3s a bed, but this was considered exorbitant.

[3] In 1902 the minimum height for entry into the army was reduced from 5ft 3in to 5ft, the smallest soldiers later forming the 'Bantam' regiments.

Our village, like the rest, had its quota of feeble-minded, dummies (deaf mutes), hydrocephalics, grotesque cripples, and its elderly women, broken like horses, who could be hired to drag a hundredweight of coke in a wagon a mile or more for threepence. One knew others, the unnamable, mere living bags of rags who existed mostly on local charity and who stood draped in a creeping subservience that only years of beggary could confer. These were they who came shuffling into the shop late Saturday night pleading for the day's scraps of cheese and bacon to make Sunday's only meal: the economic lowest of the low. They and their like are all gone now from our 'dull' Welfare State. In the England of 1912, according to official statistics, a mere ninety people died through 'starvation or privation due to destitution'. Judging by the number of those in our own world of the time who did 'not strive, officiously to keep alive', the figure seems a little conservative. There was, for instance, Albert J. Ainsworth, who according to a report in the local news, typical of many not unlike it, was found

> leaning against a wall in Brook Street. He told Constable Hare that he was ill and destitute. The kindly policeman took him to the infirmary, where he was treated by the doctor and removed to the workhouse. He had slept the previous night, he told the Resident Medical Officer, on a bundle of paper. He remained in a comatose condition until 11 pm on Friday, when he died. His body was much diseased. The man had a brother residing in the district, but personally had nowhere to lay his head.

Chapter 6
Food, drink and physic

> Pinched and poor are we, while they, the knaves, are rich and fat!
>
> SONG

Man seems to have adulterated food ever since he began to sell it. In industrial England of the nineteenth century its sophistication became both widespread and highly profitable. By 1900 government action had stamped out most of the blatantly dishonest practices, but even in that year public health analysis proved that 13 per cent of coffee and 9.9 per cent of milk were adulterated, and this in spite of vigilance and innumerable prosecutions. In one working-class district alone one in every five samples of beer examined was found to have been watered. A favourite trick of some publicans, well enough known to our imbibers, was to dilute their ale, then add salt[4] to 'flavour it up' and stimulate thirst. My father, who loved liquor as he loved life, considered this to be a crime that called for the ultimate penalty.

The minds of the very poor of the time were constantly preoccupied with feed – where was it to come from tomorrow, or even today? How best could a pittance be spent? Board of Trade figures for 1904 give the bald facts.

The majority in our area came within the first group listed, with a weekly income of less than 25s, but a good twenty per cent of the whole lived at a much lower standard; their income each week reached 18s or less. As the century grew older we know that the poor grew poorer; real wages fell and rumblings of discontent increased. by 1912 the workhouses of England held 180,000 paupers: an all-time record. Some of our neighbours went there, honourable men and women, after a lifetime's work; old Mr Molson, a one-time waiter; Mrs Gray, char for the 'Live and Let Live', and her husband, degraded beyond measure. At least in the 'Union' they would get food, such as it was.

[4] They sell the salt now with potato crisps.

[5] Farthings in the shop were common currency. They bought, among other things, one of those slim candles which served at night to make darkness visible in the bedrooms ands sculleries about us (often only the living room of a house would have gaslight), and down the ways when day had gone what a dim, flickering world it was! For some reason my mother always segregated the farthings from other cash; they ranged in a series of martello towers rising and diminishing along a shelf by the shop window. All the rest of her takings (up to 30s on good days) she dropped into a double-pouched calico 'till' taped about her waist, tipping it on the table each night for counting. Out of the larger pocket slid a mass of pence and half-pence and from the other, a mere slit, a patter of silver; poverty did business through the copper coin. Those customers finding a half sovereign in their wages on Saturday would often come in at once to get it 'changed down' for fear of losing it. Any money at all passed over by one of our 'regulars', a big, slow-moving woman, my mother washed immediately. Once I watched her and opened my mouth. 'Ask no questions!' she ordered, 'and mention it to no one!' Only years later did I learn that this customer, a bookmaker's mistress, had been suffering in the later stages of syphilis.

Average weekly cost and quantity of certain articles of food consumed by urban workmen's families

	Under 25s		25s and under 30s	
Number of returns	261		289	
Average weekly family income	21s	4½d	26s	11¾d
Average number of children living at home	3.1		3.1	
	s	d	s	d
Bread and flour	1	0½	3	3¾
Meat (bought by weight)	1	8	3	4¾
Other meat (including fish)		7½		8¾
Bacon		8¾		9
Eggs		5¾		8½
Fresh milk		8		11¾
Cheese		4¾		5½
Butter	1	2	1	7
Potatoes		8¾		9¾
Vegetables and fruit		4¾		7
Currants and raisins		1½		1¾
Rice, tapioca, oatmeal		4½		5
Tea		9¼		11¼
Coffee and cocoa		2		3¼
Sugar		8		10
Jam, marmalade, treacle, syrup		4¼		5¼
Pickles and condiments		2		2¼
Other items	1	0½	1	3¾
	14s	4¾d[5]	17s	10¼d

The Board of Trade list of provisions gives little idea in human terms of how people eked out their earnings. Many varieties of 'fancy' food common in middle-class grocery stores were quite unknown in the slum. What 'luxuries' people bought at a corner shop often figured only in the father's diet, and his alone. 'Relishes' consisted of, brawn, corned beef, boiled mutton, cheese, bacon (as little as two ounces of all these), eggs, saveloys, tripe, pigs' trotters, sausage, cow heels, herrings, bloaters and kippers or 'digbies' and finnan haddock. Most could be bought from the cornershop. These were the protein foods vital to sustain a man arriving home at night, worked often to near-exhaustion. When funds were low a pennyworth of 'parings', bits from a tripe shop (sold by the handful in newspaper), staved off hunger in many a family. Another meal in such times, long known and appreciated, was 'brewis'. It consisted merely of a 'shive' of bread and salted dripping broken up and covered with boiling water.

Boiled ham on the bone we highly esteemed and ate it so often after funerals (provided the 'late lamented' had been 'well backed' with the insurance) that to be 'buried with 'am' became a comic's cliché. Many children yearned for the taste of it. One urchin of our day was sent to the shop to get two ounces of the delectable stuff for his father's Saturday tea. Returning, the Devil tempted. He tore off the tiniest morsel. 'It tasted', he said ruefully fifty years after, 'like the food of the gods! I took a little more and, terrified, found I was hooked! Two ounces went down to a piece about the size of a postage stamp. I swallowed that too and fled!'

The very poor never fell into debt; nobody allowed them any credit.[6] Paying on the nail, they bought in minimal quantities, sending their children usually for half a loaf, a ha'p'orth of tea, sugar, milk or a scrap of mustard pickled cauliflower[7] in the bottom of a jar. Generally, two ounces of meat or cheese was the smallest quantity one could buy; to sell less, shopkeepers said, was to lose what tiny profit they got through 'waste in cutting'. Yet poor folk would try again and again, begging for smaller amounts – 'Just a penn'orth o' cheese – to fry with this two ounces o' bacon.' My father would not deign to attend to any of these 'shipping orders', as he called them; an elder sister took indigent pence. 'It's all cash,' she said briskly. Nor would Lipton, or 'Sir Thomas', as my mother named him, have truck with any who tried to buy a single boot-lace or asked him to divorce a pair of kippers.[8] Such things, he seemed to believe, came to man in natural pairs, binary as bosoms.

Customers always preferred my mother to cut their meat because she could slice it so finely that 'two ounces looked like half a pound' and it 'spread plenty on the plate'. When Mother sold a quarter of anything it weighed exactly one fourth of a pound: the old man's 'quarter' varied from three and a half to five ounces, according to the customer's face, reputation and antecedents. Whenever I or any

[6] In the early days of his career as 'mixed' grocer Father took down a card hanging on the wall by the boot and stay laces. 'Please Do Not Ask For Credit', it begged, 'As Refusal Might Offend'. He turned the notice over and, using a stick of Berry's Blacking, daubed on it for the benefit of simpler natives a translation in basic English – 'NO TICK'!

[7] Some families who dealt with us had male members (all un-skilled workers) who had soldiered in the outposts of empire during the late nineteenth century and after. Their experience seemed to have gained them little beyond a contempt for lesser breeds, a love of family discipline and a passion for hot pickles.

[8] Later Father banned kippers, swearing that their 'pong' as he called it, amalgamated with the odour from tarry firelighters under the counter to give a certain *je ne sais quoi* to the milk. At times, too, Mother thought she detected in it the distinct flavour of 'Lively Polly', a pervasive washing powder we stocked. 'This isn't milk,' I heard her say once, dabbing her lips in distaste, 'it's more of a disinfectant!' Still, the liquid, highly esteemed in the neighbourhood for its 'creamy taste', went on selling in large quantities. And each day the family did their best, scrubbing and scalding every milk bowl and measure in the endless war against infesting dirt.

member of the family saw a heavy, cold-eyed man in the neighbourhood we sped home on the instant – 'Weights 'n' Measures!' The one nearest rushed to the scales and slid off a piece of fat bacon attached under the pan. But once the ogre arrived without warning! Both parents knew their peril. While the old man engaged him in converse, Mother, in the kitchen, grabbed me by the arm. 'Get in there!' she ordered. 'Crawl on your stomach and knock it off!' That ten-foot journey was among the longest of my life. At last I lay under the scale pan, reached clumsily, hooked with my finger at the meat and missed. The scales trembled. I stretched again, hooked, and it fell, to bounce once before the cat, whipping round, snatched it and fled. Yet this 'equalizer', though strictly against the law, of course, did no more than balance our decrepit scales; Mother was painfully honest.

'That little lot's not right, yer know!' the inspector would say, feeling again the scales and testing with weight and finger. 'Not by a long chalk! You're yer own worst enemy!'

'We don't mind givin' a bit of "over",' Father would smirk hypocritically.

'That's not it,' the inspector told him. 'Give what's the weight, see! No more an' no less. Then you won't be in no trouble. Now let's have them scales down at our place today!'

Here I could groan silently. This meant that the heavy iron balance, weights and pans would be pushed into a sack and I would have to hump them a mile or more, for adjustment in a dark little room under some railway arches, then carry them all back. And only a few months later, there he would be again! – 'That little lot's not right!...'

Cockles and mussels bought from buckets or off pushcarts were a common delicacy; but in the early years of the century only the 'low' in the working class ate chips from the shops. Good artisan families avoided bringing them, or indeed any other cooked food, home: a mother would have been insulted. Fried fish without chips one could already buy from cook shops. One could eat at these shops or take out a fourpenny hot dinner in a basin. Many working women among our three thousand or so inhabitants took advantage of the basin meal; engaged as they were all day in the weaving, spinning and dyeing trades, they had little time to cook,[9] or indeed to learn how to, since their mothers before them had often been similarly occupied in the mills. This contributed, I think, to the low culinary standards which existed in the Lancashire cotton towns before the first world war. Most cooking was done, of course, on the open fire, though single gas rings had come rapidly into general use. The frying pan, because of the case and speed with which it produced cooked food, was the most esteemed utensil despite the medical profession's pronunciamento that fried foods were ruining the health of the working classes. One local doctor whenever he called upon our

[9] In the forty years before 1914 a new eating habit developed in the industrial areas of Britain, especially in those towns which used female labour. After 1871 and compulsory military service in a united Germany, thousands of Bavarians emigrated, mostly to North America, but some arrived in Britain. Among them came a steady stream of young pork butchers, humble followers in the wake of the German cotton merchants and woollen men long established in Manchester and Bradford. The newcomers saw at once that the kind and variety of pork products they could make for sale far exceeded anything on show in the conservative English shops. Establishing themselves first in Hull and other east coast ports, they slaved, prospered, married – usually other German pork butchers' daughters – and set up their sons in the same business. By the outbreak of the first world war it is doubtful if there was a single Northern town, large or small, that did not have its German pork butchers. Each one, versed in Continental culinary skills, introduced a range of new tastes in cooked meats to the British working class, and incidentally established the image of the 'typical German' for the next several generations.

humbler neighbours with stomach troubles would demand the family frying pan, then go outside and smash it to pieces against a wall; a gesture which compelled the housewife to borrow one from next door until she could afford to buy another. She made no protest at the act: a doctor was a demi-god.

Among us there was still a great deal of prejudice against corned beef and boiled mutton in tins (not shared by the very poor), though condensed milk and tinned salmon were readily accepted; but a dietary revolution was on the way. Until the mid-nineteenth century and the coming of railway transport the working classes ate very little fresh fish, though the salt variety and pickled herrings were popular enough. The introduction of deep sea trawlers in later decades and the use of ice as a preservative brought vast quantities of cheap Icelandic cod into the country. Towards the end of the century new cotton seed oils, often vile smelling when heated, came on to the market; neighbourhoods were polluted by still another odour and a further 'offensive trade' was added to the official list. Well before 1914 'chip' shops had mushroomed all over working-class areas and fish and chips became an integral part of proletarian diet. Many of the elité, however, still rejected this new-fangled food, but not so the poorest; they would buy, and gladly, even a farthingsworth of 'scratchings' – scraps of cooked potato and the broken bits of batter which had fallen from frying fish.

Dining precedence in the homes of the poor had its roots in household economics: a mother needed to exercise strict control over who got which foods and in what quantity. Father ate his fill first, to 'keep his strength up', though naturally the cost of protein limited his intake of meats. He dined in single state or perhaps with his wife. Wage-earning youth might take the next sitting, while the younger end watched, anxious that any titbit should not have disappeared before their turn came. Sometimes all the children ate together: a basic ration of, say, two slices (and no more) of bread and margarine being doled out. There was, however, a tremendous resistance to eating 'Maggie Ann' (margarine[10]): it stood as the very symbol of a poverty-stricken diet. Whenever they could, even the poorest would try to buy butter. This reluctance to substitute margarine for butter has persisted in Britain, though not in other European countries, far into the twentieth century. In the apportioning of food, small girls often came off very badly indeed: mothers felt that they didn't need much – 'not the same as lads'. In the streets, therefore, none looked more pathetically 'clemmed' than the little schoolgirl. Through ingrained habit this stinting could continue even after she had started work. If women generally possessed a stronger will to live than men some certainly needed it!

[10] From 1909 to 1913 the annual consumption of butter per head in the United Kingdom stood at 16lbs, that of margarine 6lbs.

Julian Tudor Hart, 1927- **26**

'Pentre diwaith' ('Village without work') by Julian Tudor
Hart

Julian Tudor Hart was born into a medical family, both his parents being doctors. He followed in their footsteps and studied medicine at Cambridge and St George's Hospital in London. However, his values were not those of the typical middle-class professional; he tried three times to become a Communist MP. He chose to practise in Glyncorrwg, a mining village in South Wales, where he could make his contribution to medicine according to his strong left-wing principles. He was committed to studying the lives of his patients, working tirelessly with them to make their conditions healthier.

Tudor Hart is still writing and lecturing and wrote in a talk given at the King's Fund in January 2000:

> "At 72 I'm less interested in the speed of social change than in its direction. Since 1979, society has bowled forward on an accelerating causal cycle: things get bigger and better, by making people smaller and worse."

As well as being a practising doctor Tudor Hart has made invaluable contributions to epidemiology. He is perhaps best known for his paper on the 'inverse care law', which states that those in need of medical care are least likely to receive it, and it is this that we have reproduced here.

Tudor Hart, J. (1971) 'The inverse care law'

Summary

The availability of good medical care tends to vary inversely with the need for it in the population served. This inverse care law operates more completely where medical care is most exposed to market forces, and less so where such exposure is reduced. The market distribution of medical care is a primitive and historically outdated social form, and any return to it would further exaggerate the maldistribution of medical resources.

Interpreting the evidence

The existence of large social and geographical inequalities in mortality and morbidity in Britain is known, and not all of them are diminishing. Between 1934 and 1968, weighted mean standardised mortality from all causes in the Glamorgan and Monmouthshire valleys rose from 128% of England and Wales rates to 131%. Their weighted mean infant mortality rose from 115% of England and Wales rates to 124% between 1921 and 1968.[1] The Registrar General's last Decennial Supplement on Occupational Mortality for 1949-53 still showed combined social classes I and II (wholly non-manual) with a standardised mortality from all causes 18% below the mean, and combined social classes IV and V (wholly manual) 5% above it. Infant mortality was 37% below the mean for social class I (professional) and 38% above it for social class V (unskilled manual).

A just and rational distribution of the resources of medical care should show parallel social and geographical differences, or at least a uniform distribution. The common experience was described by Titmuss in 1968:

> "We have learnt from 15 years' experience of the Health Service that the higher income groups know how to make better use of the service; they tend to receive more specialist attention; occupy more of the beds in better equipped and staffed hospitals; receive more elective surgery; have better maternal care, and are more likely to get psychiatric help and psychotherapy than low-income groups – particularly the unskilled."[2]

These generalisations are not easily proved statistically, because most of the statistics are either not available (for instance, outpatient waiting-

[1] Hart, J.T., *J.R. Coll. Gen. Practnrs* (in the press).

[2] Titmuss, R.M. *Commitment to Welfare*. London, 1968.

lists by area and social class, age and cause specific hospital mortality-rates by area and social class, the relation between ante-mortem and post-mortem diagnosis by area and social class, and hospital staff shortage by area) or else they are essentially use-rates. Use-rates may be interpreted either as evidence of high morbidity among high users, or of disproportionate benefit drawn by them from the National Health Service. By piling up the valid evidence that poor people in Britain have higher consultation and referral rates at all levels of the NHS, and by denying that these reflect actual differences in morbidity, Rein[3,4] has tried to show that Titmuss's opinion is incorrect, and that there are no significant gradients in the quality or accessibility of medical care in the NHS between social classes.

3 Rein, M.J. *Am. Hosp. Ass.* 1969, 43, 43.

4 Rein, M. *New Society*, Nov 20, 1969, p 807.

Class gradients in mortality are an obvious obstacle to this view. Of these Rein says:

> "One conclusion reached ... is that since the lower classes have higher death rates, then they must be both sicker or less likely to secure treatment than other classes ... it is useful to examine selected diseases in which there is a clear mortality class gradient and then compare these rates with the proportion of patients in each class that consulted their physician for treatment of these diseases...."

He cites figures to show that high death-rates may be associated with low consultation-rates for some diseases, and with high rates for others, but, since the pattern of each holds good through all social classes, he concludes that

> "a reasonable inference to be drawn from these findings is not that class mortality is an index of class morbidity, but that for certain diseases treatment is unrelated to outcome. Thus both high and low consultation rates can yield high mortality rates for specific diseases. These data do not appear to lead to the compelling conclusion that mortality votes can be easily used as an area of class-related morbidity."

This is the only argument mounted by Rein against the evidence of mortality differences, and the reasonable assumption that these probably represent the final outcome of larger differences in morbidity. Assuming that "votes" is a misprint for "rates", I still find that the more one examines this argument the less it means. To be fair, it is only used to support the central thesis that "the availability of universal free-on-demand, comprehensive services would appear to be a crucial factor in reducing class inequalities in the use of medical care services". It certainly would, but reduction is not abolition, as Rein would have quickly found if his stay in Britain had included more basic fieldwork in the general practitioner's surgery or the outpatient department.

Non-statistical evidence

There is massive but mostly non-statistical evidence in favour of Titmuss's generalisations. First of all there is the evidence of social history. James[5] described the origins of the general-practitioner service in industrial and coalmining areas, from which the present has grown:

[5] James, E.F. *Lancet*, 1961, i, 1361.

> "The general practitioner in working-class areas discovered the well-tried business principle of small profits with a big turnover where the population was large and growing rapidly; it paid to treat a great many people for a small fee. A waiting-room crammed with patients, each representing 2s 6d for a consultation ... not only gave a satisfactory income but also reduced the inclination to practise clinical medicine with skilful care, to attend clinical meetings, or to seek refreshment from the scientific literature. Particularly in coalmining areas, workers formed themselves into clubs to which they contributed a few pence a week, and thus secured free treatment from the club doctor for illness or accident. The club system was the forerunner of health insurance and was a humane and desirable social development. But, like the 'cash surgery', it encouraged the doctor to undertake the treatment of more patients than he could deal with efficiently. It also created a difference between the club patients and those who could afford to pay for medical attention ... in these circumstances it is a tribute to the profession that its standards in industrial practices were as high as they were. If criticism is necessary, it should not be of the doctors who developed large industrial practices but of the leaders of all branches of the profession, who did not see the trend of general practice, or, having seen it, did nothing to influence it. It is particularly regrettable that the revolutionary conception of a National Health Service, which has transformed the hospitals of the United Kingdom to the great benefit of the community, should not have brought about an equally radical change in general practice. Instead, because of the shortsightedness of the profession, the NHS has preserved and intensified the worst features of general practice...."

[6] Collings, J.S. *ibid.* 1950, i, 555.

This preservation and intensification was described by Collings[6] in his study of the work of 104 general practitioners in 55 English practices outside London, including 9 completely and 7 partly industrial practices, six months after the start of the NHS. Though not randomly sampled, the selection of practices was structured in a reasonably representative manner. The very bad situation he described was the one I found when I entered a slum practice in Notting Hill in 1953, rediscovered in all but one of five industrial practices where I acted as locum tenens in 1961, and found again when I resumed practice in the South Wales valleys. Collings said:

> "the working environment of general practitioners in industrial areas was so limiting that their individual capacity as doctors counted very little. In the circumstances prevailing, the most essential qualification for the industrial GP.... is ability as a snap diagnostician – an ability to reach an accurate diagnosis on a minimum of evidence ... the worst elements of general practice are to be found in those places where there is the greatest and most urgent demand for good medical service.... Some conditions of general practice are bad enough to change a good doctor into a bad doctor in a very short time. These very bad conditions are to be found chiefly in industrial areas."

In a counter-report promoted by the British Medical Association, Hadfield[7] contested all of Collings' conclusions, but, though his sampling was much better designed, his criticism was guarded to the point of complacency, and most vaguely defined. One of Collings' main criticisms – that purpose-built premises and ancillary staff were essential for any serious up-grading of general practice – is only now being taken seriously; and even the present wave of health-centre construction shows signs of finishing almost as soon as it has begun, because of the present climate of political and economic opinion at the level of effective decision. Certainly in industrial and mining areas health centres exist as yet only on a token basis, and the number of new projects is declining. Aneurin Bevan described health centres as the cornerstone of the general-practitioner service under the NHS, before the long retreat began from the conceptions of the service born in the 1930s and apparently victorious in 1945. Health-centre construction was scrapped by ministerial circular in January, 1948, in the last months of gestation of the new service; we have had to do without them for 22 years, during which a generation of primary care was stunted.

Despite this unpromising beginning, the NHS brought about a massive improvement in the delivery of medical care to previously deprived sections of the people and areas of the country. Former Poor Law hospitals were upgraded and many acquired fully trained specialist and ancillary staff and supporting diagnostic departments for the first time. The backlog of untreated disease dealt with in the

[7] Hadfield, S.J. *Br. Med. J.* 1953, ii, 683.

first years of the service was immense, particularly in surgery and gynæcology. A study of 734 randomly sampled families in London and Northampton in 1961[8] showed that in 99% of the families someone had attended hospital as an outpatient, and in 82% someone had been admitted to hospital. The study concluded:

[8] Family Needs and Social Services. Political and Economic Planning, London, 1961.

> "When thinking of the Health Service mothers are mainly conscious of the extent to which services have become available in recent years. They were more aware of recent changes in health services than of changes in any other service. Nearly one third thought that more money should be spent on health services, not because they thought them bad but because 'they are so important', because 'doctors and nurses should be paid more' or because 'there shouldn't be charges for treatment'. Doctors came second to relatives and friends in the list of those who had been helpful in times of trouble."

Among those with experience of pre-war service, appreciation for the NHS, often uncritical appreciation, is almost universal – so much so that, although most London teaching hospital consultants made their opposition to the new service crudely evident to those students in 1948 and the early years, and only a courageous few openly supported it, few of them appear to recall this today. The moral defeat of the very part-time, multi-hospital consultant, nipping in here and there between private consultations to see how his registrar was coping with his public work, was total and permanent; lip-service to the NHS is now mandatory. At primary-care level, private practice ceased to be relevant to the immense majority of general practitioners, and has failed to produce evidence of the special functions of leadership and quality claimed for it, in the form of serious research material. On the other hand, despite the massive economic disincentives to good work, equipment, and staffing in the NHS until a few years ago, an important expansion of well-organised, community-oriented, and self-critical primary care has taken place, mainly through the efforts of the Royal College of General Practitioners; the main source of this vigour is the democratic nature of the service – the fact that it is comprehensive and accessible to all, and that clinical decisions are therefore made more freely than ever before. The service at least permits, if it does not yet really encourage, general practitioners to think and act in terms of the care of a whole defined community, as well as of whole persons rather than diseases. Collings seems very greatly to have underestimated the importance of these changes, and the extent to which they were to overshadow the serious faults of the service – and these were faults of too little change, rather than too much. There have in fact been very big improvements in the quality and accessibility of care both at hospital and primary-care level, for all classes and in all areas.

Selective redistribution of care

Given the large social inequalities of mortality and morbidity that undoubtedly existed before the 1939-45 war, and the equally large differences in the quality and accessibility of medical resources to deal with them, it was clearly not enough simply to improve care for everyone: some selective redistribution was necessary, and some has taken place. But how much, and is the redistribution accelerating, stagnating, or even going into reverse?

Ann Cartwright's study of 1370 randomly sampled adults in representative areas of England, and their 552 doctors,[9] gave some evidence on what had and what had not been achieved. She confirmed a big improvement in the quality of primary care in 1961 compared with 1948, but also found just the sort of class differences suggested by Titmuss. The consultation-rate of middle-class patients at ages under 45 was 53% less than that of working-class patients, but at ages over 75 they had a consultation-rate 62% higher; and between these two age-groups there was stepwise progression. I think it is reasonable to interpret this as evidence that middle-class consultations had a higher clinical content at all ages, that working-class consultations below retirement age had a higher administrative content, and that the middle-class was indeed able to make more effective use of primary care. Twice as many middle-class patients were critical of consulting-rooms and of their doctors, and three times as many of waiting-rooms, as were working-class patients; yet Cartwright and Marshall[10] in another study found that in predominantly working-class areas 80% of the doctors' surgeries were built before 1900, and only 5% since 1945; in middle-class areas less than 50% were built before 1900, and 25% since 1945. Middle-class patients were both more critical and better served. Three times as many middle-class patients were critical of the fullness of explanations to them about their illnesses; it is very unlikely that this was because they actually received less explanation than working-class patients, and very likely that they expected, sometimes demanded, and usually received, much more. Cartwright's study of hospital care showed the same social trend for explanations by hospital staff[11]. The same study looked at hospital patients' general practitioners, and compared those working in middle-class and in working-class areas: more middle-class area GPs had lists under 2000 than did working-class area GPs, and fewer had lists over 2500; nearly twice as many had higher qualifications, more had access to contrast-media X-rays, nearly five times as many had access to physiotherapy, four times as many had been to Oxford or Cambridge, five times as many had been to a

[9] Cartwright, A. Patients and their Doctors. London, 1967.

[10] Cartwright, A., Marshall, J. *Med. Care*, 1965, 3, 69.

[11] Cartwright, A. Human Relations and Hospital Care. London, 1964.

London medical school, twice as many held hospital appointments or hospital beds in which they could care for their own patients, and nearly three times as many sometimes visited their patients when they were in hospital under a specialist. Not all of these differences are clinically significant; so far the record of Oxbridge and the London teaching hospitals compares unfavourably with provincial medical schools for training oriented to the community. But the general conclusion must be that those most able to choose where they will work tend to go to middle-class areas, and that the areas with highest mortality and morbidity tend to get those doctors who are least able to choose where they will work. Such a system is not likely to distribute the doctors with highest morale to the places where that morale is needed. Of those doctors who positively choose working-class areas, a few will be attracted by large lists with a big income and an uncritical clientele; many more by social and family ties of their own. Effective measures of redistribution would need to take into account the importance of increasing the proportion of medical students from working-class families in areas of this sort; the report of the Royal Commission on Medical Education[12] showed that social class I (professional and higher managerial), which is 2.8% of the population, contributed 34.5% of the final-year medical students in 1961, and 39.6% of the first-year students in 1966, whereas social class III (skilled workers, manual and non-manual), which is 49.9% of the population, contributed 27.9% of the final-year students in 1961 and 21.7% of the first-year in 1966. The proportion who had received State education was 43.4% in both years, compared with 70.9% of all school-leavers with 3 or more A-levels. In other words, despite an increasing supply of well-qualified State-educated school-leavers, the over-representation of professional families among medical students is increasing. Unless this trend is reversed, the difficulties of recruitment in industrial areas will increase from this cause as well, not to speak of the support it will give to the officers/other ranks' tradition in medical care and education.

The upgrading of provincial hospitals in the first few years after the Act certainly had a geographical redistributive effect, and because some of the wealthiest areas of the country are concentrated in and around London, it also had a social redistributive effect. There was a period in which the large formerly local-authority hospitals were accelerating faster than the former voluntary hospitals in their own areas, and some catching-up took place that was socially redistributive. But the better-endowed, better-equipped, better-staffed areas of the service draw to themselves more and better staff, and more and better equipment, and their superiority is compounded. While a technical lead in teaching hospitals is necessary and justified, these advantages do not apply only to teaching hospitals, and even these can be dangerous if they encourage complacency about the periphery, which

[12] Report of the Royal Commission on Medical Education 1965-68; p 331. London, 1968.

is all too common. As we enter an era of scarcity in medical staffing and austerity in Treasury control, this gap will widen, and any social redistribution that has taken place is likely to be reversed.

Redistribution of general practitioners also took place at a fairly rapid pace in the early years of the NHS, for two reasons. First, and least important, were the inducement payments and area classifications with restricted entry to over-doctored areas. These may have been of value in discouraging further accumulation of doctors in the Home Counties and on the coast, but Collings was right in saying that "any hope that financial reward alone will attract good senior practitioners back to these bad conditions is illusory; the good doctor will only be attracted into industrial practice by providing conditions which will enable him to do good work". The second and more important reason is that in the early years of the NHS it was difficult for the increased number of young doctors trained during and just after the 1939-45 war to get posts either in hospital or in general practice, and many took the only positions open to them, bringing with them new standards of care. Few of those doctors today would choose to work in industrial areas, now that there is real choice; we know that they are not doing so. Of 169 new general practitioners who entered practice in under-doctored areas between October, 1968, and October, 1969, 164 came from abroad.[13] The process of redistribution of general practitioners ceased by 1956, and by 1961 had gone into reverse; between 1961 and 1967, the proportion of people in England and Wales in under-doctored areas rose from 17% to 34%.[14]

Increasing list size

The quality and traditions of primary medical care in industrial and particularly in mining areas are, I think, central to the problem of persistent inequality in morbidity and mortality and the mismatched distribution of medical resources in relation to them. If doctors in industrial areas are to reach take-off speed in reorganising their work and giving it more clinical content, they must be free enough from pressure of work to stand back and look at it critically. With expanding lists this will be for the most part impossible; there is a limit to what can be expected of doctors in these circumstances, and the alcoholism that is an evident if unrecorded occupational hazard among those doctors who have spent their professional lives in industrial practice is one result of exceeding that limit. Yet list sizes are going up, and will probably do so most where a reduction is most urgent. Fry[15] and Last[16] have criticised the proposals of the Royal Commission on Medical Education[17] for an average annual increase of 100 doctors in training over the next 25 years, which would raise the number of economically active doctors per million population from 1181 in 1965 to 1801 in 1995. They claim that there are potential increases

[13] Department of Health and Social Security, Annual Report for 1969. London, 1970.

[14] General Practice Today. Office of Health Economics, paper no 28, London, 1968.

[15] Frv. J. J.R. *Coll. Gen. Practnrs,* 1969, 17, 355.

[16] Last, J.M. *Lancet,* 1968, ii, 166.

[17] Report of the Royal Commission on Medical Education, 1965-68; p 139. London, 1968.

in productivity in primary care, by devolution of work to ancillary and paramedical workers and by rationalisation of administrative work, that would permit much larger average list sizes without loss of intimacy in personal care, or decline in clinical quality. Of course, much devolution and rationalisation of this sort is necessary, not to cope with rising numbers, but to make general practice more clinically effective and satisfying, so that people can be seen less often but examined in greater depth. If clinically irrelevant work can be devoluted or abolished, it is possible to expand into new and valuable fields of work such as those opened up by Balint and his school,[18] and the imminent if not actual possibilities of presymptomatic diagnosis and screening, which can best be done at primary-care level and is possible within the present resources of NHS general practice.[19] But within the real political context of 1971 the views of Last, and of Fry from his experience of London suburban practice which is very different from the industrial areas discussed here, are dangerously complacent.

Progressive change in these industrial areas depends first of all on two things, which must go hand in hand: accelerated construction of health centres, and the reduction of list sizes by a significant influx of the type of young doctor described by Barber in 1950[20]:

> "so prepared for general practice, and for the difference between what he is taught to expect and what he actually finds, that he will adopt a fighting attitude against poor medicine – that is to say, against hopeless conditions for the practice of good medicine. The young man must be taught to be sufficiently courageous, so that when he arrives at the converted shop with the drab battered furniture, the couch littered with dusty bottles, and the few rusty antiquated instruments, he will make a firm stand and say 'I will not practise under these conditions; I will have more room, more light, more ancillary help and better equipment.'"

Unfortunately, the medical ethic transmitted by most of our medical schools, at least the majority that do not have serious departments of general practice and community medicine, leads to the present fact that the young man just does not arrive at the converted shop; he has more room, more light, more ancillary help, and better equipment by going where these already exist, and no act of courage is required. The career structure and traditions of our medical schools make it clear that time spent at the periphery in the hospital service, or at the bottom of the heap in industrial general practice, is almost certain disqualification for any further advancement. Our best hope of obtaining the young men and women we need lies in the small but significant extent to which medical students are beginning to reject

[18] Balint, M. The Doctor, his Patient, and the Illness. London, 1964.

[19] Hart, J.T. *Lancet*, 1970, ii, 223.

[20] Barber, G. *ibid.* 1950, i, 781.

this ethic, influenced by the much greater critical awareness of students in other disciplines. Some are beginning to question which is the top and which the bottom of the ladder, or even whether there should be a ladder at all; and in the promise of the Todd report, of teaching oriented to the patient and the community rather than toward the doctor and the disease, there is hope that the mood in a minority of medical students may become incorporated into a new and better teaching tradition. It is possible that we may get a cohort of young men and women with the sort of ambitions Barber described and with a realistic attitude to the battles they will have to fight to get the conditions of work and the buildings and equipment they need, in the places that need them; but we have few of them now. The prospect for primary care in industrial areas for the next ten years is bad; list sizes will probably continue to increase, and the pace of improvement in quality of primary care is likely to fall.

Recruitment to general practice in South Wales

Although the most under-doctored areas are mainly of the older industrial type, the South Wales valleys have relatively good doctor/patient ratios, partly because of the declining populations, and partly because the area produces an unusually high proportion of its own doctors, who often have kinship ties nearby and may be less mobile on that account. (In Williams' survey of general practice in South Wales 72% of the 68 doctors were born in Wales and 43% had qualified at the Welsh National School of Medicine.[21]) On Jan. 1, 1970, of 36 South Wales valley areas listed, only 4 were designated as under-doctored. However, this situation is unstable; as our future becomes more apparently precarious, as pits close without alternative local employment, as unemployment rises, and out-migration that is selective for the young and healthy increases, doctors become subject to the same pressures and uncertainties as their patients. Recruitment of new young doctors is becoming more and more difficult, and dependent on doctors from abroad. Many of the industrial villages are separated from one another by several miles, and public transport is withering while as yet comparatively few have cars, so that centralisation of primary care is difficult, and could accelerate the decay of communities. These communities will not disappear, because most people with kinship ties are more stubborn than the planners, and because they have houses here and cannot get them where the work is; the danger is not the disappearance of these communities, but their persistence below the threshold of viability, with accumulating sickness and a loss of the people to deal with it.

[21] Williams, W.O. A Study of General Practitioners' Workload in South Wales 1965-66. Royal College of General Practitioners, reports from general practice no 12. January, 1970.

What should be done?

Medical services are not the main determinant of mortality or morbidity; these depend most upon standards of nutrition, housing, working environment, and education, and the presence or absence of war. The high mortality and morbidity of the South Wales valleys arise mainly from lower standards in most of these variables now and in the recent past, rather than from lower standards of medical care. But that is no excuse for failure to match the greatest need with the highest standards of care. The bleak future now facing mining communities, and others that may suffer similar social dislocation as technical change blunders on without agreed social objectives, cannot be altered by doctors alone; but we do have a duty to draw attention to the need for global costing when it comes to policy decisions on redevelopment or decay of established industrial communities. Such costing would take into account the full social costs and not only those elements of profit and loss traditionally recognised in industry.

The improved access to medical care for previously deprived sections under the NHS arose chiefly from the decision to remove primary-care services from exposure to market forces. The consequences of distribution of care by the operation of the market were unjust and irrational, despite all sorts of charitable modifications. The improved possibilities for constructive planning and rational distribution of resources because of this decision are immense, and even now are scarcely realised in practice. The losses predicted by opponents of this change have not in fact occurred; consultants who no longer depend on private practice have shown at least as much initiative and responsibility as before, and the standards attained in the best NHS primary care are at least as good as those in private practice. It has been proved that a national health service can run quite well without the profit motive, and that the motivation of the work itself can be more powerful in a decommercialised setting. The gains of the service derive very largely from the simple and clear principles on which it was conceived: a comprehensive national service, available to all, free at the time of use, non-contributory, and financed from taxation. Departures from these principles, both when the service began (the tripartite division and omission of family-planning and chiropody services) and subsequently (dental and prescription charges, rising direct contributions, and relative reductions in financing from taxation), have not strengthened it. The principles themselves seem to me to be worth defending, despite the risk of indulging in unfashionable value-judgments. The accelerating forward movement of general practice today, impressively reviewed in a symposium on group practice held by the Royal College of General Practitioners, is a movement (not always conscious) toward these principles and the ideas that prevailed generally among the minority of doctors who supported them in 1948, including their material corollary, group practice from health centres. The doctor/patient relationship, which was held by opponents of the Act to depend above all on a cash transaction between patient and doctor, has been transformed and improved by abolishing that transaction. A general practitioner[22] can now think in terms of service to a defined community, and plan his work according to rational priorities.

[22] *J.R. Coll. Gen. Practnrs*, 1970, 20, suppl. 2.

Godber[23] has reviewed this question of medical priorities, which he sees as a new feature arising from the much greater real effectiveness of modern medicine, which provides a wider range of real choices, and the great costliness of certain forms of treatment. While these factors are important, there are others of greater importance which he omits. Even when the content of medicine was overwhelmingly palliative or magical — say, up to the 1914-18 war — the public could not face the intolerable facts any more than doctors could, and both had as great a sense of priorities as we have; matters of life and death arouse the same passions when hope is illusory as when it is real, as the palatial Swiss tuberculosis sanatoria testify. The greatest difference, I think, lies in the transformation in social expectations. In 1914 gross inequality and injustice were regarded as natural by the privileged, irresistible by the unprivileged, and inevitable by nearly everyone. This is no longer true; inequality is now politically dangerous once it is recognised, and its inevitability is believed in only by a minority. Diphtheria became preventable in the early 1930s, yet there were 50,000 cases in England and Wales in 1941 and 2400 of them died.[24] I knew one woman who buried four of her children in five weeks during an outbreak of diphtheria in the late 1930s. No systematic national campaign of immunisation was begun until well into the 1939-45 war years, and, if such a situation is unthinkable today, the difference is political rather than technical. Godber rightly points to the planning of hospital services during the war as one starting-point of the change; but he omits the huge social and political fact of 1945: that a majority of people, having experienced the market distribution of human needs before the war, and the revelation that the market could be overridden during the war for an agreed social purpose, resolved never to return to the old system.

[23] Godber, G. *ibid.* 1970, 20, 313.

[24] Morris, J. N. *Uses of Epidemiology*, London, 1967.

Perhaps reasonable economy in the distribution of medical care is imperilled most of all by the old ethical concept of the isolated one-doctor/one-patient relationship, pushed relentlessly to its conclusion regardless of cost — or, to put it differently, of the needs of others. The pursuit of the very best for each patient who needs it remains an important force in the progress of care; a young person in renal failure may need a doctor who will fight for dialysis, or a grossly handicapped child one who will find the way to exactly the right department, and steer past the defeatists in the wrong ones. But this pursuit must pay some regard to humane priorities, as it may not if the patient is a purchaser of medical care as a commodity. The idealised, isolated doctor/patient relationship, that ignores the needs of other people and their claims on the doctor's time and other scarce resources, is incomplete and distorts our view of medicine. During the formative period of modern medicine this ideal situation could be realised only among the wealthy, or, in the special conditions of teaching hospitals, among those of the unprivileged with "interesting" diseases. The ambition to practise this ideal medicine under ideal conditions still makes doctors all over the world leave those who need them most, and go to those who need them least, and it retards the development of national schools of thought and practice in medicine, genuinely based on the local content of medical care. The ideal isolated doctor/patient relation has the same root as the 19th-century preoccupation with Robinson Crusoe as an economic elementary particle; both arise from a view of society that can perceive only a contractual relation between independent individuals. The new and hopeful dimension in general practice is the recognition that the primary-care doctor interacts with individual members of a defined community. Such a community-oriented doctor is not likely to encourage expensive excursions into the 21st century, since his position makes him aware, as few specialists can be, of the scale of demand at its point of origin, and will therefore be receptive to common-sense priorities. It is this primary-care doctor who in our country initiates nearly every train of causation in the use of sophisticated medical care, and has some degree of control over what is done or not done at every point. The commitment is a great deal less open-ended than many believe; we really do not prolong useless, painful, or demented lives on the scale sometimes imagined. We tend to be more interested in the people who have diseases than in the diseases themselves, and that is the first requirement of reasonable economy and a humane scale of priorities.

Return to the market?

The past ten years have seen a spate of papers urging that the NHS be returned wholly or partly to the operation of the market. Jewkes,[25] Lees,[26] Seale,[27] and the advisory planning panel on health services financing of the British Medical Association[28] have all elaborated on this theme. Their arguments consist in a frontal attack on the policy of removing health care from the market, together with criticism of faults in the service that do not necessarily or even probably depend on that policy at all, but on the failure of Governments to devote a sufficient part of the national product to medical care. These faults include the stagnation in hospital building and senior staffing throughout the 1950s, the low wages throughout the service up to consultant level, over-centralised control, and failure to realise the

[25] Jewkes, J., Jewkes, S. The Genesis of the British National Health Service. Oxford. 1961.

[26] Lees, D.S. Health through Choice. An Economic Study of the British National Health Service. Hobart paper no 14, Institute of Economic Affairs, London, 1961.

[27] Seale, J. Br. Med. J. 1962, ii, 598.

[28] Report of the Advisory Panel of the British Medical Association on Health Services Financing. BMA, London, 1970.

objective of social and geographical equality in access to the best medical care. None of these failings is intrinsic to the original principles of the NHS; all have been deplored by its supporters, and with more vigour than by these critics. The critics depend heavily on a climate of television and editorial opinion favouring the view that all but a minority of people are rich enough and willing to pay for all they need in medical care (but not through taxation), and that public services are a historically transient social form, appropriate to indigent populations, to be discarded as soon as may be in favour of distribution of health care as a bought commodity, provided by competing entrepreneurs. They depend also on the almost universal abdication of principled opposition to these views, on the part of its official opponents. The former Secretary of State for Social Services, Mr Richard Crossman, has agreed that the upper limit of direct taxation has been reached, and that "we should not be afraid to look for alternative sources of revenue less dependent on the Chancellor's whims.... I should not rule out obtaining a higher proportion of the cost of the service from the Health Service contribution."[29] This is simply a suggestion that rising health costs should be met by flat-rate contributions unrelated to income – an acceptance of the view that the better-off are taxed to the limit, but also that the poor can afford to pay more in proportion. With such opposition, it is not surprising that more extravagant proposals for substantial payments at the time of illness, for consultations, home visits, and hospital care, are more widely discussed and advocated than ever before.

Seale[27] proposed a dual health service, with a major part of hospital and primary care on a fee-paying basis assisted by private insurance, and a minimum basic service excluding the "great deal of medical care which is of only marginal importance so far as the life or death or health of the individual is concerned. Do those who want the Health Service to provide only the best want the frills of medical care to be only the best, or have they so little understanding of the nature of medical care that they are unaware of the existence of the frills?" Frills listed by Seale are:"time, convenience, freedom of choice, and privacy". He says that "it is precisely these facets of medical care – the 'middle class' standards – which become more important to individuals as they become more prosperous". Do they indeed? Perhaps it is not so much that they (and other frills such as courtesy, and willingness to listen and to explain, that may be guaranteed by payment of a fee) become more important, as that they become accessible. The possession of a new car is an index of prosperity; the lack of one is not evidence that it is not wanted. Real evidence should be provided that it is possible to separate the components of medical care into frills that have no bearing on life, death, or health, and essentials which do. Life and happiness most certainly can hang on a readiness to listen, to dig beneath the presenting symptom, and

[29] Crossman, R.H.S. *Paying for the Social Services.* Fabian Society, London 1969.

[27] Seale, J. *Br. Med. J.* 1962, ii, 598.

to encourage a return when something appears to have been left unsaid. And not only the patient – *all* patients – value these things; to practise medicine without them makes a doctor despise his trade and his patients. Where are the doctors to be found to undertake this veterinary care? It need not be said; those of us who already work in industrial areas are expected to abandon the progress we have made toward universal, truly personal care and return to the bottom half of the traditional double standard. This is justified in anticipation by Seale:

> "some doctors are very much better than others and this will always be so, and the standard of care provided by them will vary within wide limits ... the function of the State is, in general, to do those things which the individual cannot do and to assist him to do things better. It is not to do for the individual what he can well do for himself.... I should like to see reform of the Health Service in the years ahead which is based on the assumption of individual responsibility for personal health, with the State's function limited to the prevention of real hardship and the encouragement of personal responsibility."

[26] Lees, D.S. Health through Choice. An Economic Study of the British National Health Service. Hobart paper no. 14, Institute of Economic Affairs, London, 1961.

Lees'[26] central thesis is that medical care is a commodity that should be bought and sold as any other, and would be optimally distributed in a free market. A free market in houses or shoes does not distribute them optimally; rich people get too much and the poor too little, and the same is true of medical care. He claims that the NHS violates "natural" economic law, and will fail if a free market is not restored, in some degree at least, and that in a free market "we would spend more on medical care than the government does on our behalf". If the "we" in question is really all of us, no problem exists; we agree to pay higher income-tax and/or give up some million-pound bombers or whatever, and have the expanding service we want. But if the "we" merely means "us" as opposed to "them", it means only that the higher social classes will pay more for their own care, but not for the community as a whole. They will then want value for their money, a visible differential between commodity-care and the utility brand; is it really possible, let alone desirable, to run any part of the health service in this way? Raymond Williams[30] put his finger on the real point here:

[30] Williams, R. The Long Revolution, London 1961.

> "we think of our individual patterns of use in the favourable terms of spending and satisfaction, but of our social patterns of use in the unfavourable terms of deprivation and taxation. It seems a fundamental defect of our society that social purposes are largely financed out of individual incomes, by

a method of rates and taxes which makes it very easy for us to feel that society is a thing that continually deprives and limits us – without this we could all be profitably spending.... We think of 'my money'... in these naive terms, because parts of our very idea of society are withered at root. We can hardly have any conception, in our present system, of the financing of social purposes from the social product...."

Seale[31] thinks the return to the market would help to provide the continuous audit that is certainly necessary to intelligent planning in the health service:

> "In a health service provided free of charge efficient management is particularly difficult because neither the purpose nor the product of the organisation can be clearly defined, and because there are few automatic checks to managerial incompetence.... In any large organisation management requires quantitative information if it is to be able to analyse a situation, make a decision, and know whether its actions have achieved the desired result. In commerce this quantitative information is supplied primarily in monetary terms. By using the simple, convenient, and measurable criterion of profit as both objective and product, management has a yardstick for assessing the quality of the organisation and the effectiveness of its own decisions."

The purposes and desired product of medical care are complex, but Seale has given no evidence to support his opinion that they cannot be clearly measured or defined; numerous measures of mortality, morbidity, and cost and labour effectiveness in terms of them are available and are (insufficiently) used. They can be developed much more easily in a comprehensive service outside the market than in a fragmented one within it. We already know that we can study and measure the working of the National Health Service more cheaply and easily than the diverse and often irrational medical services of areas of the United States of comparable population, though paradoxically there are certain techniques of quality control that are much more necessary in America than they are here. Tissue committees monitor the work of surgeons by identifying excised normal organs, and specialist registration protects the public from spurious claims by medical entrepreneurs. The motivation for fraud has almost disappeared from the NHS, and with it the need for certain forms of audit. A market economy in medical care leads to a number of wasteful trends that are acknowledged problems in the United States. Hospital admission rates are inflated to make patients eligible for insurance benefit; and, according to Fry[32]:

[31] Seale, J. *Lancet*, 1961, ii, 476.

[32] Fry, J. Medicine in Three Societies, Aylesbury, 1969.

"In some areas, particularly the more prosperous, competition for patients exists between local hospitals, since lack of regional planning has led to an excess of hospital facilities in some localities. In such circumstances hospital administrators are encouraged to use public relations officers and other means of self-advertisement.... This competition also leads to certain hospital 'status symbols', where features such as the possession of a computer; the possession of a 'cobalt bomb' unit; the ability to perform open-heart surgery albeit infrequently; and the listing of a neurosurgeon on the staff are all current symbols of status in the eyes of certain groups of the public. Even small hospitals of 150-200 beds may consider such features as necessities."

And though these are the more obvious defects of substituting profit for the normal and direct objectives of medical care, the audit by profit has another and much more serious fault; it concentrates all our attention on tactical efficiency, while ignoring the need for strategic social decisions. A large advertising agency may be highly efficient and profitable, but is this a measure of its socially useful work? It was the operation of the self-regulating market that resulted in a total expenditure on all forms of advertising of £455 million in 1960, compared with about £500 million on the whole of the hospital service in the same year.[33] The wonderfully self-regulating market does sometimes show a smaller intelligence than the most ignorant human voter.

[33] *Observer*, March 19, 1961.

All these trends of argument are gathered together in the report of the BMA advisory planning panel on health services financing,[28] which recommends another dual service, one for quality and the other for minimum necessity. It states its view with a boldness that may account for its rather guarded reception by the General Medical Services Committee of the BMA:

[28] Report of the Advisory Panel of the British Medical Association on Health Services Financing. BMA, London, 1970.

"The only sacrifice that would have to be made would be the concept of equality within the National Health Service ... any claim that the NHS has achieved its aim of providing equality in medical care is an illusion. In fact, absolute equality could never be achieved under any system of medical care, education or other essential service to the community. The motives for suggesting otherwise are political and ignore human factors."

The panel overlooks the fact that absolute correctness of diagnosis or absolute relief of suffering are also unattainable under any system of medical care; perhaps the only absolute that can be truly attained is the blindness of those who do not wish to see, and the human factor we should cease to ignore is the opposition of every privileged group to the loss of its privilege.

The inverse care law

In areas with most sickness and death, general practitioners have more work, larger lists, less hospital support, and inherit more clinically ineffective traditions of consultation, than in the healthiest areas; and hospital doctors shoulder heavier case-loads with less staff and equipment, more obsolete buildings, and suffer recurrent crises in the availability of beds and replacement staff. These trends can be summed up as the inverse care law: that the availability of good medical care tends to vary inversely with the need of the population served.

If the NHS had continued to adhere to its original principles, with construction of health centres a first priority in industrial areas, all financed from taxation rather than direct flat-rate contribution, free at the time of use, and fully inclusive of all personal health services, including family planning, the operation of the inverse care law would have been modified much more than it has been; but even the service as it is has been effective in redistributing care, considering the powerful social forces operating against this. If our health service had evolved as a free market, or even on a fee-for-item-of-service basis prepaid by private insurance, the law would have operated much more completely than it does; our situation might approximate to that in the United States,[34] with the added disadvantage of smaller national wealth. The force that creates and maintains the inverse care law is the operation of the market, and its cultural and ideological superstructure which has permeated the thought and directed the ambitions of our profession during all of its modern history. The more health services are removed from the force of the market, the more successful we can be in redistributing care away from its "natural" distribution in a market economy; but this will be a redistribution, an intervention to correct a fault natural to our form of society, and therefore incompletely successful and politically unstable, in the absence of more fundamental social change....

[34] Battistella, R.M., Southby, R.M.F. *Lancet*, 1968, i, 581.

Inequalities in health: Report of a   **27**
Research Working Group chaired by
Sir Douglas Black (The Black Report) 1980

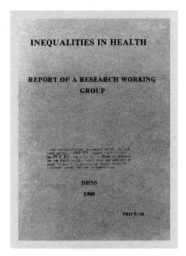

A t the end of the 1970s the departing Labour government appointed Sir Douglas Black to chair a working group to review the evidence on inequalities in health and to suggest policy recommendations that should follow. The report was published (DHSS, 1980), although with no press release and only 260 copies initially printed. Under the incoming Conservative government in 1980 the report received a cold reception. A subsequent edition published by Penguin, however, made the findings widely available, and it was later published in conjunction with The Health Divide, which updated the findings (Townsend and Davidson, 1988 with Whitehead, 1988). The major finding of the Black Report was that there were large differentials in mortality and morbidity that favoured the higher social classes, and that these were not being adequately addressed by health or social services. The report presented a number of costed policy suggestions and proposed the abolition of child poverty as a national policy goal for the 1980s.

Sir Douglas Black is a doctor who hails from Scotland and has been president of the Royal College of Physicians and of the British Medical Association. The legacy of the report of the working group which he chaired has been not only to provide an empirical and analytical starting point for much subsequent research on health inequalities, but it has also ensured continued concern for remedying the social injustice of the continuing connection between poverty and health.

The Black Committee also included J.N. Morris (see also Chapter 21), Cyril Smith and Peter Townsend (see also Chapter 24). Here we present the Summary and Recommendations from the report.

Inequalities in health: Report of a Research Working Group chaired by Sir Douglas Black (The Black report) (1980)

Summary and recommendations

1. Most recent data show marked differences in mortality rates between the occupational classes, for both sexes and at all ages. At birth and in the first month of life, twice as many babies of 'unskilled manual' parents (class V) die as do babies of professional class parents (class I) and in the next eleven months nearly three times as many boys and more than three times as many girls. In later childhood the ratio of deaths in class V to deaths in class I falls to 1.5-2.0, but increases again in early adult life, before falling again in middle and old age. A class gradient can be observed for most causes of death, being particularly steep in the case of diseases of the respiratory system. Available data on chronic sickness tend to parallel those on mortality. Thus self-reported rates of long-standing illness (as defined in the General Household Survey) are twice as high among unskilled manual males and 2½ times as high among their wives as among the professional classes. In the case of acute sickness (short-term ill-health, also as defined in the General Household Survey) the gradients are less clear.

2. The lack of improvement, and in some respects deterioration, of the health experience of the unskilled and semi-skilled manual classes (class V and IV), relative to class I, throughout the 1960s and early 1970s is striking. Despite the decline in the rate of infant mortality (death within the first year of life) in each class, the difference in rate between the lowest classes (IV and V combined) and the highest (I and II combined) actually increased between 1959-63 and 1970-72.

3. Inequalities exist also in the utilization of health services, particularly and most worryingly of the preventive services. Here, severe under-utilization by the working classes is a complex result of under-

provision in working-class areas and of costs (financial and psychological) of attendance which are not, in this case, outweighed by disruption of normal activities by sickness. In the case of GP, and hospital in-patient and out-patient attendance, the situation is less clear. Moreover it becomes more difficult to interpret such data as exist, notably because of the (as yet unresolved) problem of relating utilization to need. Broadly speaking, the evidence suggests that working-class people make more use of GP services for themselves (though not for their children) than do middle-class people, but that they may receive less good care. Moreover, it is possible that this extra usage does not fully reflect the true differences in need for care, as shown by mortality and morbidity figures. Similar increases in the use of hospital services, both in-patient and out-patient, with declining occupational class are found, though data are scanty, and possible explanations complex.

4. Comparison of the British experience with that of other industrial countries, on the basis of overall mortality rates, shows that British perinatal and infant mortality rates have been distinctly higher and are still somewhat higher than those of the four Nordic countries and of the Netherlands, and comparable with those of the Federal Republic of Germany. Adult mortality patterns, especially for men in the younger age groups, compare reasonably with other Western industrialized countries: the comparison for women is less satisfactory. The rate of improvement in perinatal mortality experienced by Britain over the period since 1960 has been comparable to that of most other countries. In the case of infant mortality (which is generally held to reflect social conditions more than does perinatal mortality) all comparable countries – especially France – have shown a greater improvement than has Britain. France, like Britain and most other countries considered (though apparently not Sweden), shows significant class and regional inequalities in health experience. It is noteworthy that through the 1960s the ratio of the post-neonatal death rate (between four weeks and one year) in the least favoured social group to that in the most favoured fell substantially in France. Also important probably has been a major French effort to improve both attendance rates for ante-natal care and the quality of such care. Very high rates of early attendance are also characteristic of the Nordic countries; so too are high rates of attendance at child welfare clinics, combined with extensive 'outreach' capacity. In Finland, for example, whenever an appointment at a health centre is missed, a health visitor makes a domiciliary call. We regard it as significant also that in Finland health authorities report not on the volume of services provided, but on the proportion of all pregnant women and of all children of appropriate ages who register with Health Centres.

5. We do not believe there to be any single and *simple explanation* of the complex data we have assembled. While there are a number of quite distinct theoretical approaches to explanation we wish to stress the importance of differences in material conditions of life. *In our view much of the evidence on social inequalities in health can be adequately understood in terms of specific features of the socio-economic environment:* features (such as work accidents, overcrowding, cigarette-smoking) which are strongly class-related in Britain and also have clear causal significance. Other aspects of the evidence indicate the importance of the health services and particularly preventive services. Ante-natal care is probably important in preventing perinatal death, and the international evidence suggests that much can be done to improve ante-natal care and its uptake. But beyond this there is undoubtedly much which cannot be understood in terms of the impact of so specific factors, but only in terms of the more diffuse consequences of the class structure; poverty, working conditions, and deprivation in its various forms. It is this acknowledgement of the *multicausal* nature of health inequalities, within which inequalities in the material conditions of living loom large, which informs and structures our policy recommendations. These draw also upon another aspect of our interpretation of the evidence. We have concluded that early childhood is the period of life at which intervention could most hopefully weaken the continuing association between health and class. There is, for example, abundant evidence that inadequately treated bouts of childhood illness 'cast long shadows forward', as the Court Committee put it.

6. We have been able to draw upon national statistics relating to health and mortality of exceptional quality and scope, as well as upon a broad range of research studies. We have, however, been conscious of certain inadequacies in the statistics and of major lacunae in the research. For example it is extremely difficulty to examine health experience and health service utilization, in relation to income and wealth.

7. Moreover, we consider that the *form* of administrative statistics may both reflect and determine (as the Finnish example quoted above suggests) the way in which the adequacy and the performance of a service is understood: hence it acquires considerable importance. We also consider systematic knowledge of the use made of the various health services by different social groups to be inadequate: though this is less the case in Scotland than in England and Wales. While conscious of the difficulties in collecting and reporting of occupational characteristics within the context of administrative returns, we feel that further thought must be given to how such difficulties might be overcome. We argue that the monitoring of *ill-health* (itself so

imperfect) should evolve into a system also of monitoring *health* in relation to social and environmental conditions. One area in which progress could be made is in relation to the development of children, and we propose certain modifications to community health statistics.

(1) *We recommend that school health statistics should routinely provide, in relation to occupational class, the results of tests of hearing, vision, and measures of height and weight. As a first step we recommend that local health authorities, in consultation with educational authorities, select a representative sample of schools in which assessments on a routine basis be initiated.*

8. *Accidents* are not only responsible for fully one-third of child deaths, but show (with respiratory disease) the steepest of class gradients.

9. We should like to see progress towards routine collection and reporting of accidents to children indicating the circumstances, the age and the occupational class of the parents. In relation to traffic accidents there should be better liaison between the NHS and the police, both centrally and locally.

(2) *We therefore recommend that representatives of appropriate government departments (Health and Social Security, Education and Science, Home Office, Environment, Trade, Transport), as well as of the NHS and of the police, should consider how progress might rapidly be made in improving the information on accidents to children.*

10. The Child Accident Prevention Committee, if suitably constituted and supported, might provide a suitable forum for such discussions, to be followed by appropriate action by government departments. Further,

(3) *We recommend that the Health Education Council should be provided with sufficient funds to mount child accident prevention programmes in conjunction with the Royal Society for the Prevention of Accidents. These programmes should be particularly directed at local authority planners, engineers and architects.*

11. While drawing attention to the importance of the National Food Survey as the major source of information on the food purchase (and hence diet) of the population, we are conscious of the scope for its improvement.

(4) *We recommend that consideration be given to the development of the National Food Survey into a more effective instrument of*

> *nutritional surveillance in relation to health, through which various 'at risk' groups could also be identified and studied.*

12. We have already referred to the difficulties in examining health experience in relation to income and wealth. In principle this can be done through the General Household Survey in which the measure of income now (since 1979) corresponds to the more satisfactory measure employed in the Family Expenditure Survey. However,

> (5) *We recommend that in the General Household Survey steps should be taken (not necessarily in every year) to develop a more comprehensive measure of income, or command over resources, through either (a) means of modifying such a measure with estimates of total wealth or at least some of the more prevalent forms of wealth, such as housing and savings, or (b) the integration of income and wealth, employing a method of, for example, annuitization.*

13. Beyond this, we feel that a comprehensive research strategy is needed. This is best regarded as implying the need for careful studies of a wide range of variables implicated in ill-health, in their *interaction over time,* and *conducted in a small number of places.* Such variables will necessarily include social conditions (and the interactions of a variety of social policies) as well as individual and behavioural factors. Any major advance in our understanding of the nature of health inequalities, and of the reason for their perpetuation, will require complex research of a multi-disciplinary kind.

> (6) *The importance of the problem of social inequalities in health, and their causes, as an area for further research needs to be emphasized. We recommend that it be adopted as a research priority by the DHSS and that steps be taken to enlist the expertise of the Medical Research Council (MRC), as well as the Social Science Research Council (SSRC), in the initiation of a programme of research. Such research represents a particularly appropriate area for departmental commissioning of research from the MRC.*

14. We turn now to our recommendations for policy, which we have divided into those relating to the health and personal social services, and those relating to a range of other social policies. Three objectives underpin our recommendations, and we recommend their adoption by the Secretary of State:

> – To give children a better start in life.

– To encourage good health among a larger proportion of the population by preventive and educational action.

– For disabled people, to reduce the risks of early death, to improve the quality of life whether in the community or in institutions, and as far as possible to reduce the need for the latter.

Thirty years of the Welfare State and of the National Health Service have achieved little in reducing social inequalities in health. But we believe that if these three objectives are pursued vigorously inequalities in health can now be reduced.

15. We believe that *allocation of resources* should be based on need. We recognize that there are difficulties in assessing need, but we agree that standardized mortality ratios (SMRs) are a useful basis for broad allocation at regional level. At district level, further indicators of health care and social needs are called for. These should be developed as a matter of urgency, and used appropriately to reinforce, supplement or modify allocation according to SMRs. *However, a shift of resources is not enough: it must be combined with an imaginative (and in part necessarily experimental) approach to health care and its delivery.*

(7) *Resources within the National Health Service and the personal social services should be shifted more sharply than so far accomplished towards community care, particularly towards ante-natal, post-natal and child health services, and home-help and nursing services for disabled people. We see this as an important part of a strategy to break the links between social class or poverty and health.*

(8) *The professional associations as well as the Secretary of State and the health authorities should accept responsibility for making improvements in the quality and geographical coverage of general practice, especially in areas of high prevalence of ill-health and poor social conditions. Where the number or scope of work of general practitioners is inadequate in such areas we recommend health authorities to deploy or redeploy an above-average number of community nurses attached where possible to family practice. The distribution of general practitioners should be related not only to population but to medical need, as indicated by SMRs, supplemented by other indicators, and the per capita basis of remuneration should be modified accordingly.*

16. Moreover, we consider that greater integration between the planning process (and the establishment of priorities) and resources

allocation is needed. In particular the establishment of revenue targets should be based not upon the current distribution of expenditure between services, but that distribution which it is sought to bring about through planning guidelines: including a greater share for community health.

(9)   *We recommend that the resources to be allocated should be based upon the future planned share for different services, including a higher share for community health.*

17.   Our further health service-related recommendations, designed to implement the objectives set out above, fall into two groups.

18.   We first outline the elements of what we have called a District Action Programme. By this we mean a general programme for the health and personal social services to be adopted nationwide, and involving necessary modifications to the structure of care.

19.   Second, we recommend an experimental programme, involving provision of certain services on an experimental basis in ten areas of particularly high mortality and adverse social conditions, and for which special funds are sought.

District action programme

Health and welfare of mothers and pre-school and school children

(10)   *A non-means-tested scheme for free milk should now be introduced beginning with couples with their first infant child and infant children in large families.*

(11)   *Areas and districts should review the accessibility and facilities of all ante-natal and child-health clinics in their areas and take steps to increase utilization by mothers, particularly in the early months of pregnancy.*

(12)   *Savings from the current decline in the school population should be used to finance new services for children under 5. A statutory obligation should be placed on local authorities to ensure adequate day care in their area for children under 5, and that a minimum number of places (the number being raised after regular intervals) should be laid down centrally. Further steps should be taken to reorganize day nurseries and nursery schools so that both meet the needs of children for education and care.*

(13) *Every opportunity should be taken to link revitalized school health care with general practice, and intensify surveillance and follow-up both in areas of special need and for certain types of family.*

20. Some necessary developments apply to other groups as well as children and mothers.

(14) *An assessment which determines severity of disablement should be adopted as a guide to health and personal social service priorities of the individual, and this should be related to the limitation of activities rather than loss of faculty or type of handicap.*

21. Though we attach priority to the implementation of this recommendation in the care of disabled children, we believe that it must ultimately apply to all disabled people. We recognize that such assessments are now an acknowledged part of 'good practice' in providing for the disabled – we are anxious that they should become standard practice.

The care of elderly and disabled people in their own homes

22. The meaning of community care should be clarified and much greater emphasis given to tendencies favoured (but insufficiently specified) in recent government planning documents. (See Recommendation 7.)

(15) *A Working Group should be set up to consider:*

(i) the present functions and structure of hospital, residential and domiciliary care for the disabled elderly in relation to their needs, in order to determine the best and most economical balance of future services;

(ii) *whether sheltered housing should be a responsibility of social service or of housing departments, and to make recommendations.*

(16) *Joint funding should be developed and further funding of a more specific kind should be introduced, if necessary within the existing NHS budget to encourage joint care programmes. A further sum should be reserved for payment to authorities putting forward joint programmes to give continuing care to disabled people – for example, post-hospital follow-up schemes, pre-hospital support programmes for families, and support programmes for the severely incapacitated and terminally ill.*

(17) *Criteria for admission to, and for continuing residence in, residential care should be agreed between the DHSS and the local authority associations, and steps taken to encourage rehabilitation, and in particular to prevent homeless elderly people from being offered accommodation only in residential homes. Priority should be given to expansion of domiciliary care for those who are severely disabled in their own homes.*

(18) *The functions of home helps should be extended to permit a lot more work on behalf of disabled people; short courses of training, specialization of functions and the availability of mini-bus transport, especially to day centres, should be encouraged.*

Prevention: the role of government

23. Effective prevention requires not only individual initiative but a real commitment by the DHSS and other government departments. Our analysis has shown the many ways in which people's behaviour is constrained by structural and environmental factors over which they have no control. Physical recreation, for example, is hardly possible in inner city areas unless steps are taken to ensure that facilities are provided. Similarly, government initiatives are required in relation to diet and to the consumption of alcohol. Legislation and fiscal and other financial measures may be required and a wide range of social and economic policies involved. We see the time as now opportune for a major step forwards in the field of health and prevention.

(19) *National health goals should be established and stated by government after wide consultation and debate. Measures that might encourage the desirable changes in people's diet, exercise and smoking and drinking behaviour should be agreed among relevant agencies.*

(20) *An enlarged programme of health education should be sponsored by the government, and necessary arrangements made for optimal use of the mass media, especially television. Health education in schools should become the joint responsibility of LEAs and health authorities.*

24. The following recommendation should be seen not only as a priority in itself but as illustrative of the determined action by government necessary in relation to many elements of a strategy for prevention:

(21)   *Stronger measures should be adopted to reduce cigarette-smoking. These would include:*

a.   *Legislation should be rapidly implemented to phase out all advertising and sales promotion of tobacco products (except at place of purchase);*

b.   *Sponsorship of sporting and artistic activities by tobacco companies should be banned over a period of a few years, and meanwhile there should be stricter control of advertisement through sponsorship;*

c.   *Regular annual increases in duty on cigarettes in line with rises in income should be imposed, to ensure lower consumption;*

d.   *Tobacco companies should be required, in consultation with trades unions, to submit plans for the diversification of their products over a period of ten years with a view to the eventual phasing out of sales of harmful tobacco products at home and abroad;*

e.   *The provision of non-smoking areas in public places should steadily be extended;*

f.   *A counselling service should be made available in all health districts, and experiment encouraged in methods to help people reduce cigarette-smoking;*

g.   *A stronger well-presented health warning should appear on all cigarette packets and such advertisements as remain, together with information on the harmful constituents of cigarettes.*

We have already recommended that steps be taken to increase utilization of antenatal clinics, particularly in the early months of pregnancy (Recommendation 11). Given early attendance there are practical programmes for screening for Down's Syndrome and for neural tube defects in the foetus. In relation to adult disease, screening for severe hypertension is practicable, and effective treatment is available.

(22)   *In the light of the present stage of knowledge we recommend that screening for neural tube defects (especially in high risk areas) and Down's Syndrome on the one hand, and for severe hypertension in adults on the other, should be made generally available.*

Additional funding for ten special areas

(23)   *We recommend that the government should finance a special health and social development programme in a small number of selected areas, costing about £30m in 1981-2.*

25. At least £2m of this sum should be reserved for evaluation research and statistical and information units. The object would be both to provide special help to redress the undeniable disadvantages of people living in those areas but also to permit special experiments to reduce ill-health and mortality, and provide better support for disabled people. Some elements of such a programme are illustrated, particularly in connection with the development of more effective ante-natal services.

Measures to be taken outside the health services

26. In discussing actions outside the Health Care system which need to be taken to diminish inequalities of health we have been necessarily selective. We have attempted to pay heed to those factors which are correlated with the *degree* of inequalities. Secondly, we have tried to confine ourselves to matters which are practicable now, in political, economic and administrative terms, and which will none the less, properly maintained, exert a long-term structural effect. Third, we have continued to feel it right to give priority to young children and mothers, disabled people, and measures concerned with prevention.

27. Above all, we consider that the *abolition of child-poverty* should be adopted as a national goal for the 1980s. We recognize that this requires a redistribution of financial resources far beyond anything achieved by past programmes, and is likely to be very costly. Recommendations 24-27 are presented as a modest first step which might be taken towards this objective.

> (24) *As an immediate goal the level of child benefit should be increased to 5½ per cent of average gross male industrial earnings, or £5.70 at November 1979 prices.*

> (25) *Larger child benefits should be progressively introduced for older children, after further examination of the needs of children and consideration of the practice in some other countries.*

> (26) *The maternity grant should be increased to £100.*

> (27) *An infant care allowance should be introduced over a five-year period, beginning with all babies born in the year following a date to be chosen by the government.*

28. Beyond these initial elements of an anti-poverty strategy, a number of other steps need to be taken. These include steps to reduce accidents to children, to which we have referred above (Recommendation 3). Further.

(28) *Provision of meals at school should be regarded as a right. Representatives of local authorities and community dieticians should be invited to meet representatives of parents and teachers of particular schools at regular intervals during the year to seek agreement to the provision and quality of meals. Meals in schools should be provided without charge.*

(29) *A comprehensive disablement allowance for people of all ages should be introduced by stages at the earliest possible date, beginning with people with 100 per cent disablement.*

(30) *Representatives of the DHSS and DE, HSE, together with representatives of trade unions and CBI, should draw up minimally acceptable and desirable conditions of work.*

(31) *Government departments, employers and unions should devote more attention to preventive health through work organization, conditions and amenities, and in other ways. There should be a similar shift of emphasis in the work and function of the Health and Safety Commission and Executive, and the Employment Medical Advisory Service.*

(32) *Local authority spending on housing improvements under the 1974 Housing Act should be substantially increased.*

(33) *Local authorities should increasingly be encouraged to widen their responsibilities to provide for all types of housing need which arise in their localities.*

(34) *Policies directed towards the public and private housing sectors need to be better co-ordinated.*

(35) *Special funding, on the lines of joint funding, for health and local authorities should be developed by the government to encourage better planning and management of housing, including adaptations and provision of necessary facilities and services for disabled people of all ages by social services and housing departments.*

29. Our recommendations reflect the fact that reduction in health inequalities depends upon contributions from within many policy areas, and necessarily involves a number of government departments. Our objectives will be achieved *only* if each department makes its appropriate contribution. This in turn requires a greater degree of co-ordination than exists at present.

(36) *Greater co-ordination between government departments in the administration of health-related policies is required, by establishing inter-departmental machinery in the Cabinet Office under a Cabinet sub-committee along the lines of that established under the Joint Approach to Social Policy (JASP), with the Central Policy Review Staff also involved. Local counterparts of national co-ordinating bodies also need to be established.*

(37) *A Health Development Council should be established with an independent membership to play a key advisory and planning role in relation to a collaborative national policy to reduce inequalities in health.*

30. Within such co-ordinating machinery major initiatory responsibility will be vested in the Department of Health and Social Security, and we recommend that the Cabinet Committees we have proposed be chaired by a Minister, and by a senior DHSS official respectively, having major responsibility for health and prevention. Similarly it will be an important obligation upon the DHSS to ensure the effective operation of the Health Development Council.

Independent Inquiry into Inequalities in Health (The Acheson Report) 1998   28

The Independent Inquiry into Inequalities in Health was commissioned by the Secretary of State for Health of the incoming Labour government in July 1997 amid concern for widening socio-economic and health inequalities. Sir Donald Acheson, who earlier in his career had worked as a clinician, in epidemiology and has been the Chief Medical Officer to the Department of Health, chaired the inquiry. The investigation was overseen by a Scientific Advisory Group whose members were: David Barker, Jacky Chambers, Hilary Graham, Michael Marmot and Margaret Whitehead. The remit for the inquiry was to review the latest evidence on inequalities in health and in the light of that evidence to identify priority areas for future policy development. These recommendations were to be within the government's overall financial strategy as well as "beneficial, cost effective and affordable interventions to reduce inequalities in health". Together with the consultation document *Our healthier nation* (DoH, 1998) this report shows the continued existence of, and renewed concerns for, inequalities in health. Thus the 20th century came to a close with a government which recognised this social injustice and aimed "to improve the health of the worst off in society and to narrow the health gap".

Independent Inquiry into Inequalities in Health (The Acheson Report) (1998)

Inequalities in health: the current position

[The footnote numbering system has been altered from the original report, Eds]

Socioeconomic inequalities in health and expectation of life have been found in many contemporary and past societies. In England although information based on an occupational definition of social class has only been available since 1921, other data identifying differences in longevity by position in society have been available for at least two hundred years. These differences have persisted despite the dramatic fall in mortality rates over the last century[1].

Inequalities in health exist, whether measured in terms of mortality, life expectancy or health status; whether categorised by socioeconomic measures or by ethnic group or gender. Recent efforts to compare the level and nature of health inequalities in international terms indicate that Britain is generally around the middle of comparable western countries, depending on the socioeconomic and inequality indicators used. Although in general disadvantage is associated with worse health, the patterns of inequalities vary by place, gender, age, year of birth and other factors, and differ according to which measure of health is used[2].

General trends in health

Death rates in England have been falling over the last century, from a crude death rate of 18 per thousand people in 1896 to 11 per thousand in 1996[3,4]. Over the last 25 years, there have been falls in death rates from a number of important causes of death, for example lung cancer (for men only), coronary heart disease and stroke[4].

Life expectancy has risen over the last century[5], but not all life is lived in good health. Healthy life expectancy – the measure of average length of life free from ill health and disability – has not been rising; the added years of life have been years with a chronic illness or disability[6].

The proportion of people reporting a limiting long standing illness has risen from 15 per cent to 22 per cent since 1975. The proportion reporting illness in the two weeks previous to interview has nearly

[1] Whitehead. M. Life and death over the millennium. In: Drever. F, Whitehead. M, eds. Health inequalities: decennial supplement: DS Series no 15. London: The Stationery Office, 1997.

[2] Whitehead M, Diderichsen F. International evidence on social inequalities in health. In: Drever F, Whitehead M, eds. Health inequalities: decennial supplement: DS Series no 15. London: The Stationery Office, 1997.

[3] General Register Office. 59th Annual Report of the Registrar General. Births, deaths and marriages in England – 1896. London: HMSO, 1898.

[4] Office for National Statistics. Mortality statistics: cause 1996, series DH2, no 23. London: The Stationery Office, 1998.

[5] Office for National statistics. English life tables no 15. London: The Stationery Office, 1997.

[6] Bebbington A, Carton R. Healthy life expectancy in England and Wales: recent evidence. Canterbury: Personal Social Services Research Unit, 1996.

doubled from 9 per cent to 16 per cent. There is a slight increase in the proportion of people consulting the NHS[7].

Measuring socioeconomic position

[7] Office for National Statistics. *Living in Britain: results from the general household survey '96.* London: The Stationery Office, 1998.

A number of different measures can be used to indicate socioeconomic position. These include occupation, amount and type of education, access to or ownership of various assets, and indices based on residential area characteristics. There has been much debate as to what each indicator actually measures, and how choice of indicator influences the pattern of inequalities observed. For example, measures based on occupation may reflect different facets of life for men compared to women, and for people of working age compared to older people or children.

Choice of measure is often dictated by what is available. In Britain occupational social class is frequently used, especially for data collected nationally. Table 1 shows examples of the occupations in each social class group.

Table 1: Occupations within social class groupings

Social class		Occupation
I	Professional	accountants, engineers, doctors
II	Managerial & Technical/Intermediate	marketing & sales managers, teachers, journalists, nurses
IIIN	Non-manual Skilled	clerks, shop assistants, cashiers
IIIM	Manual Skilled	carpenters, goods van drivers, joiners, cooks
IV	Partly Skilled	security guards, machine tool operators, farm workers
V	Unskilled	building and civil engineering labourers, other labourers, cleaners

Source: Drever, F. and Whitehead, M. (eds) (1997) *Health inequalities: Decennial supplement: DS Series no 15,* London: The Stationery Office

Mortality

Over the last twenty years, death rates have fallen among both men and women and across all social groups[5,8]. However, the difference in rates between those at the top and bottom of the social scale has widened.

For example, in the early 1970s, the mortality rate among men of working age was almost twice as high for those in class V (unskilled) as for those in class I (professional). By the early 1990s, it was almost

[8] Drever F, Bunting J. Patterns and trends in male mortality. In: Drever F, Whitehead M, eds. *Health inequalities: decennial supplement: DS Series no 15.* London: The Stationery Office, 1997.

three times higher (Table 2). This increasing differential is because, although rates fell overall, they fell more among the high social classes than the low social classes. Between the early 1970s and the early 1990s, rates fell by about 40 per cent for classes I and II, about 30 per cent for classes IIIN, IIIM and IV, but by only 10 per cent for class V. So not only did the differential between the top and the bottom increase, the increase happened across the whole spectrum of social classes[8].

Both class I and class V cover only a small proportion of the population at the extremes of the social scale. Combining class I with class IV with class V allows comparisons of larger sections of the population. Among both men and women aged 35 to 64, overall death rates fell for each group between 1976–81 and 1986–92 (table 3). At the same time, the gap between classes I and II and classes IV and V increased in the late 1970s, death rates were 53 per cent higher among men in classes IV and V compared with those in classes I and II. In the late 1980s, they were 68 per cent higher. Among women, the differential increased from 50 per cent to 55 per cent[9].

These growing differences across the social spectrum were apparent for many of the major causes of death, including coronary heart

[9] Harding S, Bethune A, Maxwell R, Brown J. Mortality trends using the longitudinal study. In: Drever F, Whitehead M, eds. *Health inequalities: decennial supplement: DS Series no 15.* London: The Stationery Office, 1997.

Table 2: European standardised mortality rates, by social class, selected causes, men aged 20-64
England and Wales, selected years

All causes (rates per 100,000)

Social class		1970-72	Year 1979-83	1991-93
I	Professional	500	373	280
II	Managerial & Technical	526	425	300
III(N)	Skilled (non-manual)	637	522	426
III(M)	Skilled (manual)	683	580	493
IV	Partly skilled	721	639	492
V	Unskilled	897	910	806
England and Wales		624	549	419

Lung cancer (rates per 100,000)

Social class		1970-72	Year 1979-83	1991-93
I	Professional	41	26	17
II	Managerial & Technical	52	39	24
III(N)	Skilled (non-manual)	63	47	34
III(M)	Skilled (manual)	90	72	54
IV	Partly skilled	93	76	52
V	Unskilled	109	108	82
England and Wales		73	60	39

Coronary heart disesase (rates per 100,000)

Social class		Year		
		1970-72	1979-83	1991-93
I	Professional	195	144	81
II	Managerial & Technical	197	168	92
III(N)	Skilled (non-manual)	245	208	136
III(M)	Skilled (manual)	232	218	159
IV	Partly skilled	232	227	156
V	Unskilled	243	287	235
England and Wales		209	201	127

Stroke (rates per 100,000)

Social class		Year		
		1970-72	1979-83	1991-93
I	Professional	35	20	14
II	Managerial & Technical	37	23	13
III(N)	Skilled (non-manual)	41	28	19
III(M)	Skilled (manual)	45	34	24
IV	Partly skilled	46	37	25
V	Unskilled	59	55	45
England and Wales		40	30	20

Accidents, poisioning, violence (rates per 100,000)

Social class		Year		
		1970-72	1979-83	1991-93
I	Professional	23	17	13
II	Managerial & Technical	25	20	13
III(N)	Skilled (non-manual)	25	21	17
III(M)	Skilled (manual)	34	27	24
IV	Partly skilled	39	35	24
V	Unskilled	67	63	52
England and Wales		34	28	22

Suicide and undetermined injury (rates per 100,000)

Social class		Year		
		1970-72	1979-83	1991-93
I	Professional	16	16	13
II	Managerial & Technical	13	15	14
III(N)	Skilled (non-manual)	17	18	20
III(M)	Skilled (manual)	12	16	21
IV	Partly skilled	18	23	23
V	Unskilled	32	44	47
England and Wales		15	20	22

Source: Drever, F. and Bunting, J. (1997)[8]

Table 3: Age-standardised mortality rates per 100,000 people, by social class, selected causes, men and women aged 35-64, England and Wales, 1976-92

	Women (35-64)			Men (35-64)		
	1976-81	1981-85	1986-92	1976-81	1981-85	1986-92
All causes						
I/II	338	344	270	621	539	455
IIIN	371	387	305	860	658	484
IIIM	467	396	356	802	691	624
IV/V	508	445	418	951	824	764
Ratio IV/V: I/II	1.50	1.29	1.55	1.53	1.53	1.68
Coronary heart disease						
I/II	39	45	29	246	185	160
IIIN	56	57	39	382	267	162
IIIM	85	67	59	309	269	231
IV/V	105	76	78	363	293	266
Ratio IV/V: I/II	2.69	1.69	2.69	1.48	1.58	1.66
Breast cancer						
I/II	52	74	52			
IIIN	75	71	49			
IIIM	61	57	46			
IV/V	47	50	54			
Ratio IV/V: I/II	0.90	0.68	1.04			

Source: Harding, S., Bethune, A., Maxwell, R. and Brown, J. (1997)[9]

disease, stroke, lung cancer and suicides among men, and respiratory disease and lung cancer among women[8,9].

Death rates can be summarised into average life expectancy at birth. For men in classes I and II combined, life expectancy increased by 2 years between the late 1970s and the late 1980s. For those in classes IV and V combined, the increase was smaller, 1.4 years. The difference between those at the top and bottom of the social class scale in the late 1980s was 5 years, 75 years compared with 70 years. For women, the differential was smaller, 80 years compared with 77 years. Improvements in life expectancy have been greater over the period from the late 1970s to the late 1980s for women in classes I and II than for those in classes IV and V, two years compared to one year[10].

A good measure of inequality among older people is life expectancy at age 65. Again, in the late 1980s, this was considerably higher among those in higher social classes, and the differential increased over the period from the late 1970s to the late 1980s, particularly for women[10].

In adulthood, being overweight is a measure of possible ill health, with obesity a risk factor for many chronic diseases. There is a marked social class gradient in obesity which is greater among women than

[10] Hattersly L. Expectation of life by social class. In: Drever F, Whitehead M, eds *Health inequalities: decennial supplement.* London: The Stationery Office, 1997.

among men[11-13]. In 1996, 25 per cent of women in class V were classified as obese compared to 14 per cent of women in class I. For men, there was no clear difference in the proportions reported as obese except that men in class I had lower rates of obesity, 11 per cent, compared to about 18 per cent in other groups. Overall, rates of obesity are rising. For men, 13 per cent were classified as obese in 1993 compared to 16 per cent in 1996. For women, the rise was from 16 per cent to 18 per cent[13].

Another indicator of poor health is raised blood pressure. There is a clear social class differential among women, with those in higher classes being less likely than those in the manual classes to have hypertension. In 1996, 17 per cent of women in class I and 24 per cent in class V had hypertension. There was no such difference for men where the comparable proportions were 20 per cent and 21 per cent respectively[13].

Among men, major accidents are more common in the manual classes for those aged under 55. Between 55 and 64, the non-manual classes have higher major accident rates (figure 3). For women, there are no differences in accident rates until after the age of 75 when those women in the non-manual group have higher rates of major accidents[13].

[11] Colhoun H, Prescott-Clarke P. *Health Survey for England 1994.* London: HMSO, 1996.

[12] Prescott-Clarke P, Primatesta P. *Health Survey for England 1995.* London: The Stationery Office, 1997.

[13] Prescott-Clarke P, Primatesta P. *Health Survey for England '96.* London: The Stationery Office, 1998.

Figure 3: Annual major accident rates, by age and social class, England 1996

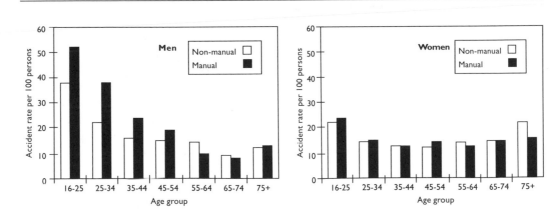

Source: Prescott-Clarke, P., Primatesta, P. (1998)[13]

Figure 4: Prevalence of mental health problems, by social class, men and women aged 16-64, Great Britain

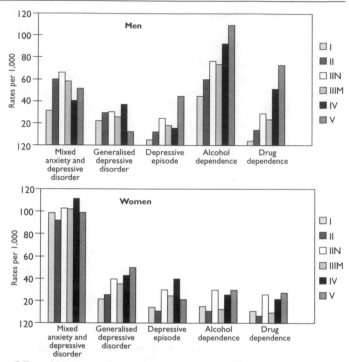

Source: Office of Population Censuses and Surveys (1995)[14]

Mental health also varies markedly by social class. In 1993/4, all neurotic disorders, such as anxiety, depression and phobias, were more common among women in class IV and V than those in classes I and II – 24 per cent and 15 per cent respectively[14]. This difference was not seen among men. However, there were striking gradients for alcohol and drug dependence among men, but not women. For example, 10 per cent of men in classes IV and V were dependent on alcohol compared to 5 per cent in classes I and II, (figure 4)[14].

[14] Meltzer H, Gill B, Petticrew M, Hinds K. *The prevalence of psychiatric morbidity among adults living in private households.* London: Office of Population Censuses and Surveys/HMSO, 1995.

Trends in socioeconomic determinants of health

Income distribution

[15] Church J, Whyman S. A review of recent social and economic trends. In: Drever F, Whitehead M, eds. *Health inequalities: decennial supplement: DS Series no. 15.* London: The Stationery Office, 1997.

Over the last twenty years, household disposable income per head of population has grown both in actual and in real terms. Between 1961 and 1994, average household disposable income (in real terms) rose by 72 per cent[15]. However, this was not experienced to the same extent across the whole of the income distribution. The median real household disposable income, before housing costs, rose over the period 1961 to 1994 from £136 per week, to £234 per week (figure 5). The top decile point more than doubled, from £233 per week to £473 per week. The bottom decile point rose by 62 per cent from £74 per week to £119 per week.

Figure 5: Real household disposable income, before housing costs, United Kingdom, 1961-94

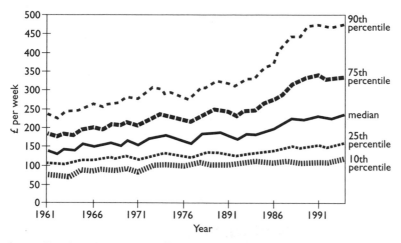

Source: Church J, Whyman S (1997)[15]

Households below average income

The proportion of people whose income is below average has been at about 60 per cent for the last 35 years (figure 6). However, the proportion of people below half of the average income (the European Union definition of poverty) has grown over this period from 10 per cent in 1961 to 20 per cent in 1991. It has decreased since then and was at 17 per cent in 1995[16].

[16] Office for National Statistics. *Social Trends 28, 1998 edition.* London: The Stationery Office, 1998.

Figure 6: Proportion of people whose income is below various fractions of average income, United Kingdom, 1961-95

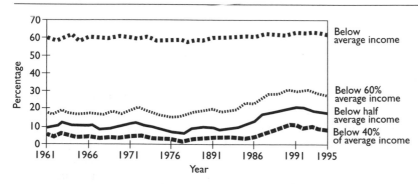

Source: Office for National Statistics (1998)[16]

Education

Since the early 1970s, the proportion of children aged 3 or 4 who attend school has trebled from 20 per cent to nearly 60 per cent[16]. The proportion who attend school (as opposed to playgroups) varies from 84 per cent in the North East to 43 per cent in the South West[17].

Educational attainment – as measured by the proportion of children gaining 5 or more GCSEs at grades A star to C – has risen from less than 25 per cent in 1975/76 to about 45 per cent in 1995/96[16,18]. This measure of attainment varies not only by gender, but also by geographical area and by measures of deprivation.

As well as looking at the future workforce and their qualifications, it is useful to look at the educational attainment of those presently of working age[16]. In 1997, 16 per cent of men and 21 per cent of women of working age had no qualifications. There were also large differences between ethnic groups (figure 7).

[17] Office for National Statistics. *Regional trends, no. 32.* London: The Stationery Office, 1997.

[18] Office for National Statistics. *Social Trends 27, 1997 edition.* London: The Stationery Office, 1997.

Figure 7: Proportion of the working age population without qualifications, by gender and ethnic group, Great Britain

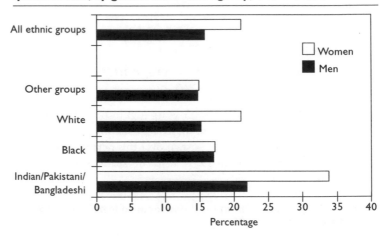

Source: Office for National Statistics (1998)[16]

Employment

The seasonally adjusted unemployment rate for those aged 16 and over stood at 6.2 per cent in summer 1998, almost three times the level of 30 years ago[19]. Although rates have been falling since 1993, there have been changes in the patterns of unemployment over the last thirty years, well beyond what might have been expected from seasonal and cyclical variations (figure 8). Youth unemployment is still at higher rates now than it was in 1991 and unemployment rates

[19] Office for National Statistics. *Labour market statistics release.* London: Office for National Statistics, 1998.

are four times higher among unskilled workers than among professional groups[20].

Across different ethnic groups, there are very different rates of unemployment (table 5). Those from minority ethnic groups have higher rates than the white population. Black men have particularly high unemployment rates as do Pakistani and Bangladeshi women[21].

[20] Philpott J. Unemployment, inequality and inefficiency. The incidence and costs of unemployment. In: Glynn T, Miliband D, eds. *Paying for inequality: the economic costs of social injustice.* London: Rivers Oram Press, 1994.

Figure 7: Unemployment rates, population aged 16 years and over, England and Wales, 1961-1995

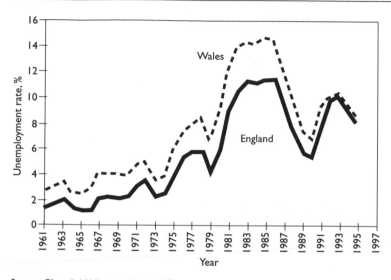

Source: Church J, Whyman S (1997)[15]

[21] Office for National Statistics. *Economic Trends no 533.* London: The Stationery Office, 1998.

Table 5: Unemployment rates, by ethnic group, Great Britain, winter 1997/98 (%)

	Men	Women
White	6.5	5.0
All minority ethnic groups	14.1	13.1
Black	20.5	14.8
Indian	7.4	8.4
Pakistani/Bangladeshi	15.9	22.1
Other	15	14

Note: Sample size is too small to make accurate estimates of unemployment rates among Chinese people.

Source: Office for National Statistics (1998)[21]

[22] Department of the Environment. *Housing policy: technical volume part 1.* London: HMSO, 1977.

[23] Department of the Environment, Transport and the Regions. *Housing and construction statistics, Great Britain, March quarter 1998: part 2 no 73.* London: The Stationery Office, 1998.

Housing

Over the last sixty years, the number of dwellings has doubled from 10.6 million in 1938 to 20.7 million in 1997[22,23]. Housing tenure has also changed dramatically over this period with a doubling of the

24 Office for National Statistics. *Housing in England 1995/96. A report of the 1995/96 survey of English housing carried out by the Social Survey division of Office for National Statistics on behalf of the Department of the Environment.* London: The Stationery Office, 1997.

proportion of owner-occupied dwellings[22,23] and a dramatic fall in the proportion of privately rented dwellings (table 6).

There has also been a growth in the number of one-person households over the last ten years from 4.4 million in 1984 to 5.5 million in 1995/96[24]. The proportion of all households which had only one person rose from 25 per cent to 28 per cent over this period. In 1984, 46 per cent of one-person households were owner occupied. By 1995/96, this had grown to 54 per cent (table 7).

Table 6: Proportion of dwellings by household tenure, England, 1938 and 1997 (Percentage)

	1938	1997
Owner occupied	32	68
Local authority or New Town rented	11	17
Housing association rented	n/a	5
Privately rented	57	10
Number of dwellings	10.6 million	20.7 million

Source: Department of the Environment, Transport and the Regions (1998)[23]

Table 7: Household tenure, one person households, England, 1984 and 1995/6 (Thousands)

	1984	1995/96
Owner occupiers	2,008	2,923
Social rented sector	1,657	1,771
Private rented sector	746	760
All tenures	4,410	5,453

Source: Office for National Statistics (1997)[24]

25 Department of the Environment. *Projection of households in England to 2016.* London: HMSO, 1995.

Between 1991 and 2016, the number of households is expected to rise from 19.2 million to 23.6 million – a rise of 4.4 million households[25].

Conditions of the housing stock vary considerably. In 1996 about 14 per cent of all households were living in poor conditions. About 8 per cent of dwellings in England were unfit, and about 7 per cent of households were living in unfit dwellings. The proportions of households in unfit dwellings varied with the type of tenure, from 4 per cent in the Registered Social Landlord sector to 18 per cent of households who rented from private landlords. In urban areas, 8 per cent of dwellings were deemed unfit whereas in rural areas, 5 per cent were deemed unfit[26].

26 Department of the Environment, Transport and the Regions. *English house condition survey 1996.* London: The Stationery Office, 1998.

Homelessness

Between 1982 and 1992, there was a steep increase in the number of households accepted by Local Authorities as homeless. Since then, there has been a decrease of about a quarter. Of the 166,000 households classified as homeless in 1997, over 103,000 were accepted by local authorities to be unintentionally homeless and in priority need. Over half of households accepted by local authorities as homeless had dependent children and a further tenth had a pregnant household member[27].

Public safety

The crime rate has nearly trebled since 1971. In 1996, the crime rate in England was nearly one crime for every ten people[16]. Crime rates were highest in areas with large conurbations – the North East, Yorkshire/Humberside and London[17]. There were also different crime rates in different types of areas – lowest in affluent suburban and rural areas and highest in council estates and low income areas (table 8).

Different areas of the country have very different rates of particular types of crime. London has the highest rate of fraud and forgery, robbery and sexual offences. The North East has the highest rate of criminal damage and the lowest rate of sexual offences. Yorkshire and the Humber has the highest burglary rate. The East has the lowest overall crime rate[17].

[27] Department of the Environment, Transport and the Regions. *Local authority activities under the homelessness legislation, England: fourth quarter 1997.* London: Department of the Environment, Transport and the Regions, 1998.

Table 8: Risk of being a victim of crime, by type of area, England and Wales, 1995 (%)

	Council estates and low income	Affluent family	Affluent urban	New home-owning	Mature home-owning	Affluent suburban and rural
Thefts of vehicles	25	21	21	21	18	16
Vandalism of vehicles	11	7	12	10	8	6
Bicycle thefts	10	3	8	8	5	3
Burglary	10	4	8	6	6	4
Home vandalism	5	5	5	5	4	3
Other household theft	9	7	8	8	7	5
Any household offence	36	35	35	33	31	27

Source: Office for National Statistics (1998)[16]

Transport

Access to private means of transport has increased in recent years. In 1996, 70 per cent of households had access to a car or a van. This compared with just over half of households in 1972. About a quarter of households had access to two or more cars and vans compared to only 9 per cent in 1972 (figure 9)[7,28,29].

Those with access to two or more cars or vans were not only more likely to be economically active, but also tended to be in the higher socioeconomic groups. Only seven per cent of households had access to two or more vehicles when the head of household was economically inactive compared to 36 per cent of households with an economically active head[7]. In 1991, those who lived in the social rented sector had the highest proportion with no access to a car, 68 per cent, while those in the owner occupied sector had the smallest proportion with no access, 19 per cent[28].

[28] Office of Population Censuses and Surveys. 1991 *Census: housing and availability of cars.* London: HMSO, 1993.

[29] Office for National Statistics. *Living in Britain: results from the general household survey 1995.* London: The Stationery Office, 1997.

Figure 9: Households with access to a car or van, Great Britain, 1971-1996

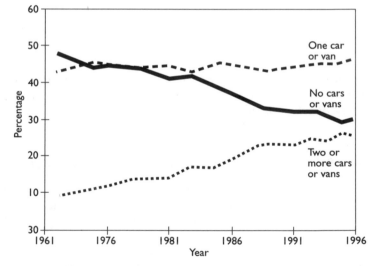

Source: Office for National Statistics (1998)[16]

[30] Office for National Statistics. *1991 Census: key statistics for urban and rural areas, Great Britain.* London: The Stationery Office, 1997.

How people travel to work differs depending on whether the areas in which they live are urban or rural[30]. In England in 1991, 60 per cent of people travelled to work by car in urban areas and 69 per cent in rural areas. Rail and bus accounted for 17 per cent of journeys to work for those in urban areas but only for five per cent for rural areas. A higher proportion of people work at home in rural areas, 12 per cent compared to four per cent in urban areas (table 9).

Table 9: Mode of travel to work, England, 1991 (%)

	Urban	Rural
Car	60	69
Rail or bus	17	5
On foot	12	7
By pedal cycle	3	2
Work at home	4	12

Source: Office for National Statistics[30]

Health related behaviour

Over the last twenty years, the proportion of people who report that they smoke cigarettes has fallen. In 1974, roughly a half of men and two fifths of women smoked cigarettes, compared with less than 30 per cent of men and women in 1996. The trends in drinking alcohol are broadly unchanged over this period. However, the proportion of women who drank more than 14 units of alcohol a week rose from 9 per cent in 1984 to 14 per cent in 1996[7].

There is a clear social class gradient for both men and women in the proportion who smoke. In 1996, this ranged from 12 per cent of professional men to 41 per cent of men in unskilled manual occupations and from 11 per cent to 36 per cent for women[7]. In spite of the major class differences in dependence on alcohol in men[14], there are very small differences in the reported quantities consumed. This is not the case among women where higher consumption is related to higher social class[7].

Among women, there are no differences in levels of physical activity across the social classes. Among men, higher proportions in the manual classes have a high level of physical activity than in the non-manual classes. However, some of this difference is due to work related physical activity. Men in non-manual occupations have higher rates of leisure time physical activity[11].

People in lower socioeconomic groups tend to eat less fruit and vegetables, and less food which is rich in dietary fibre. As a consequence, they have lower intakes of anti-oxidant and other vitamins, and some minerals, than those in higher socioeconomic groups[11,31-34].

One aspect of dietary behaviour that affects the health of infants is the incidence of breastfeeding. Six weeks after birth, almost three quarters of babies in class I households are still breastfed. This declines with class to less than one quarter of babies in class V. The differences between classes in rates of breastfeeding at six weeks has narrowed slightly between 1985 and 1995[35].

[31] Ministry of Agriculture, Fisheries and Food. *National Food survey 1980-1996.* London: HMSO, various years.

[32] Department of Health. *The diets of British schoolchildren.* London: HMSO, 1989.

[33] Gregory J, Foster K, Tyler H, Wiseman M. *The dietary and nutritional survey of British adults.* London: HMSO, 1990.

[34] Gregory J, Collins D, Davies P, Hughes J, Clarke P. *National diet and nutrition survey: children aged 1½ to 4½ years.* London: HMSO, 1995.

[35] Foster K, Lader D, Cheesbrough S. *Infant feeding 1995.* London: The Stationery Office, 1997.

Trends in health differences between minority ethnic groups

[36] Charlton J, Wallace M, White M. Long-term illness: results from the 1991 Census. *Population Trends* 1994; 75:18-25.

There are many indications of poorer health among the minority ethnic groups in England. For example, people in Black (Caribbean, African and other) groups and Indians have higher rates of limiting long standing illness than white people. Those of Pakistani or Bangladeshi origin have the highest rates. In contrast, the Chinese and "other Asians" have rates lower than the white population[36].

[37] Wild S, McKeigue P. Cross-sectional analysis of mortality by country of birth in England and Wales, 1970-92. *British Medical Journal* 1997; 314:705-710.

Although in analysing mortality rates we have to use country of birth as a proxy for ethnicity, a similar pattern emerges[37]. There is excess mortality among men and women born in Africa and men born on the Indian sub-continent and men and women born in Scotland or Ireland (table 10).

Table 10: Standardised mortality ratios, by country of birth, selected causes, men and women aged 20-69, England and Wales, 1989-92

	All causes		Coronary heart disease		Stroke		Lung cancer		Breast cancer
	Men	Women	Men	Women	Men	Women	Men	Women	Women
All countries	100	100	100	100	100	100	100	100	100
Scotland	132	136	120	130	125	125	149	169	114
Ireland	139	120	124	120	138	123	151	147	92
East Africa	110	103	131	105	114	122	42	17	84
West Africa	113	126	56	62	271	181	62	51	125
Caribbean	77	91	46	71	168	157	49	31	75
South Asia	106	100	146	151	155	141	45	33	59

This table was first published in the British Medical Journal, and is reproduced by kind permission of the journal. *Source:* Wild, S. and McKeigue, P. (1997)[37]

Many women from minority ethnic groups giving birth in the 1990s were born in the United Kingdom. Because country of birth of the mother, and not ethnicity, is recorded at birth registration, it is not possible to estimate infant mortality rates by minority ethnic group. However, among mothers who were born in countries outside the UK, those from the Caribbean and Pakistan have infant mortality rates about double the national average. Perinatal mortality rates have also been consistently higher for babies of mothers born outside the UK. The differences between groups have not decreased over the last twenty years[38].

[38] Office for National Statistics. *Series DH3 mortality statistics: perinatal and infant: social and biological factors.* London: The Stationery Office, 1997.

Figure 10: Standardised mortality rates, by gender, all ages, England and Wales, 1971-96

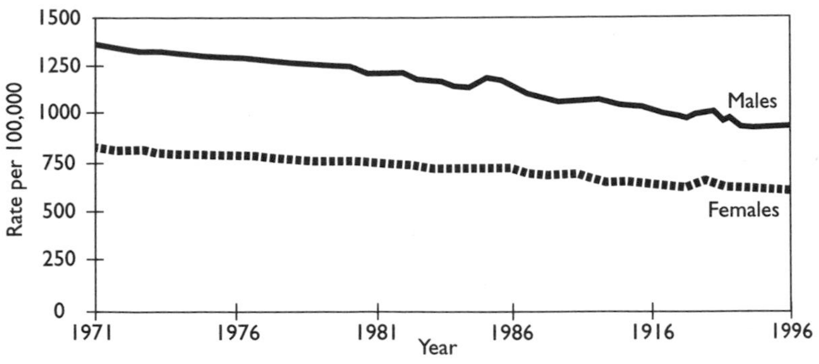

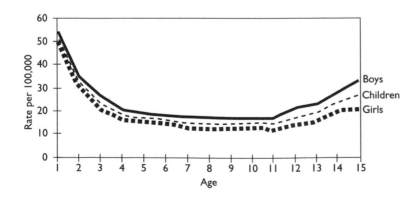

Source: Office for National Statistics (1998)[4]

Trends in health differences between the sexes

Death rates have been falling for both males and for females (figure 10). Since 1971, these have decreased by 29 per cent for males and by 25 per cent for females, narrowing the differential in death rates very slightly. Cancers and coronary heart disease account for 55 per cent of the deaths of men and 42 per cent of the deaths of women[4].

At each age in childhood, and on into adulthood, the age-specific mortality rates for boys is higher than for girls (figure 11)[39]. For the under 5s, nearly half of the difference is due to external causes, in particular accidental drowning and submersion. For children aged 5 to 14, external causes, chiefly motor vehicle traffic accidents, account for nearly 70 per cent of the difference[4].

[39] Botting B. Mortality in childhood. In: Drever F, Whitehead M, eds. *Health inequalities: decennial supplement: DS Series no 15*. London: The Stationery Office, 1997.

Figure 11: Age-specific mortality rates, children, England and Wales, 1991-1995

Source: Botting, B. (1997)[39]

Figure 12: Prevalence of major accidents, by gender and age, England, 1996

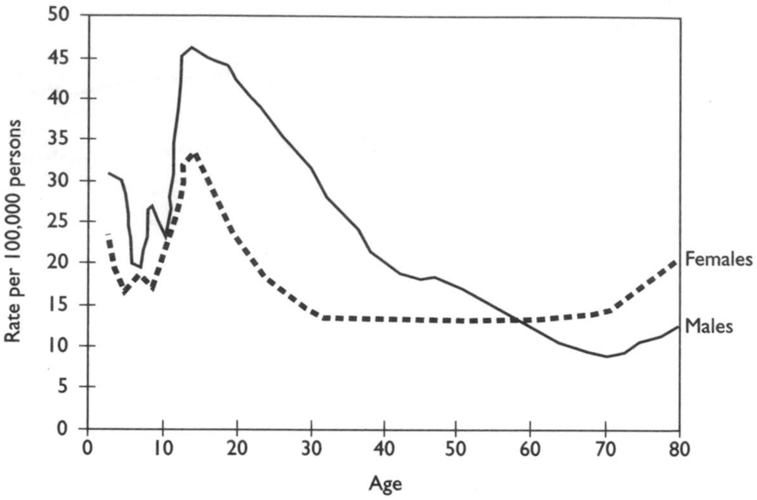

Source: **Prescott-Clarke, P., Primatesta, P. (1987)**[13]

Although the life expectancy gap between males and females is decreasing[5], this is not the case for healthy life expectancy. Healthy life expectancy of females is only two to three years more than that of males[6]. Overall, there is little difference in the proportions of males and females reporting a limiting long standing illness[29]. Women report more illness of many different types than men during the reproductive years[29].

For both children and adults of working ages, males have higher major accident rates than females (figure 12). At older ages, women have higher major accident rates than men[13].

The proportion of smokers is higher among girls than boys[40]. By adulthood, the proportions of men and women smoking are about the same (29 and 28 per cent), compared with 51 per cent of men and 41 per cent of women in 1974[29]. For both children and adults, males are more likely to drink alcohol heavily than females[29].

[40] Office for National Statistics. Smoking in *secondary school children.* London: HMSO/The Stationery Office, various years.

Conclusion

Inequalities by socioeconomic group, ethnic group and gender can be demonstrated across a wide range of measures of health and the determinants of health. Analysis of these patterns and trends in inequalities has informed the development of areas for future policy development, which are considered below.

Reducing inequalities in health

Introduction: assessing the evidence

We have sought to ensure that our recommendations are based on scientific and expert evidence. To this end, we have consulted with a wide range of experts and incorporated a process of peer review. In summary, we commissioned a series of input papers from experts broadly to match the sections of the report. Most of these experts consulted widely amongst other researchers in their field. For each of these commissioned papers, we obtained an independent scientific commentary. We also sought and received a considerable volume of material from institutions and individuals with expertise or experience relevant to inequalities in health, including scientific reviews and papers. A separate Evaluation Group was convened to consider the commissioned papers with associated commentaries and asked to report on the quality of the evidence on which the recommendations in the papers were based, and to identify gaps[41]. A more detailed description of the process is given in annex B [not reproduced here, Eds].

All this material was considered and discussed within the Scientific Advisory Group. The material reflected a wealth of descriptive data documenting inequalities in health and a growing quantity of research exploring mechanisms. However, controlled intervention studies are rare. Indeed, the more a potential intervention relates to the wider determinants of inequalities in health (ie "upstream" policies), the less the possibility of using the methodology of a controlled trial to evaluate it. We have, therefore evaluated many different types of evidence in forming our judgement. The following sections incorporate our assessment of the full spectrum of evidence which we reviewed.

[41] Evaluation Group. Report to the Independent Inquiry into Inequalities in Health. 1998.

Cross-government issues

If future inequalities in health are to be reduced, it will be essential to carry out a wide range of policies to achieve both a general improvement in health and a greater impact on the less well off. By this we mean those who in terms of socioeconomic status, gender or ethnicity are less well off than average in terms of health or its principal determinants – such as income, education, employment or the material environment.

The impact of policies designed to improve health may have different consequences for different groups of people which are not always appreciated. Some policies will both improve health and reduce health inequalities. The introduction of the NHS benefited the health of all sections of the population, particularly women and children, many of whom were excluded from previous arrangements under the National Insurance Act.

A well intended policy which improves average health may have no effect on inequalities. It may even widen them by having a greater impact on the better off. Classic examples include policies aimed at preventing illness, if they resulted in uptake favouring the better off. This has happened in some initiatives concerned with immunisation and cervical screening, as well as in some campaigns to discourage smoking to promote breastfeeding. More recently, the Government's welcome decision to provide a pre-school place for every child aged four in the country is likely to benefit health on average but could have the unintended effect of increasing inequalities. This would happen if the children of the better off made more effective use of the service.

These examples highlight the need for extra attention to the needs of the less well off. This could be accommodated both by policies directed at the least well off and by an approach which would require the need for inequalities to be addressed wherever universal services are provided, such as publicly funded education and the National Health Service, and where other policies are likely to have an impact on health.

A broader approach of this kind which explicitly addresses inequalities could provide a new direction for public policy. It is our view that, in general, reductions in inequalities are most likely to be achieved if policies are formulated with the reduction of inequalities in mind.

1. We RECOMMEND that as part of health impact assessment, all policies likely to have a direct or indirect effect on health should be evaluated in terms of their impact on health inequalities, and should be formulated in such a way that by favouring the less well off they will, wherever possible, reduce such inequalities.

This proposal for a systematic impact assessment of policy on health inequalities is a significant extension to the steps already taken by Government to apply impact assessments to its policies, and to ensure better coordination across Whitehall.

We suggest that this proposal needs to be supported by a small and effective unit with a pan-Government view. Such a lead by Government would allow action on inequalities to be both reviewed and promoted. It would also serve to further encourage the steps being taken to strengthen coordination at both central and local level.

1.1 We recommend establishing mechanisms to monitor inequalities in health and to evaluate the effectiveness of measures taken to reduce them.

The effects of future policies will need to be monitored at regular intervals. For this purpose, the Government will require authoritative statistics on inequalities in health and the factors influencing them at national and local level. These will also be needed in order to set targets for reduction of health inequalities. A number of concerns about the presently available data have been raised with us. These include the scope for monitoring inequalities among older people, when many data sources have an effective cut-off point of age 64. There are continuing inconsistencies in the treatment of males and females in the census and at death registration, where married women are still mainly classified by the social class of their husband. There is also a need for greater consistency between data from the census, from vital registration and from other sources.

1.2. We recommend a review of data needs to improve the capacity to monitor inequalities in health and their determinants at a national and local level.

We have emphasised the priority we will be giving to parents and children in the report as the best way of reducing future inequalities in physical and mental health. This issue is relevant across Government.

2. We RECOMMEND a high priority is given to policies aimed at improving health and reducing health inequalities in women of childbearing age, expectant mothers and young children.

Index